Urban Tourism in the Developing World

Urban Tourism in the Developing World

The South African Experience

Christian M. Rogerson
and Gustav Visser, editors

Transaction Publishers
New Brunswick (U.S.A.) and London (U.K.)

Copyright © 2007 by Transaction Publishers, New Brunswick, New Jersey.

All rights reserved under International and Pan-American Copyright Conventions. No part of this book may be reproduced or transmitted in any form or by any means, electronic or mechanical, including photocopy, recording, or any information storage and retrieval system, without prior permission in writing from the publisher. All inquiries should be addressed to Transaction Publishers, Rutgers—The State University, 35 Berrue Circle, Piscataway, New Jersey 08854-8042. www.transactionpub.com

This book is printed on acid-free paper that meets the American National Standard for Permanence of Paper for Printed Library Materials.

Library of Congress Catalog Number: 2006053026
ISBN: 978-0-7658-0358-0
Printed in the United States of America

Library of Congress Cataloging-in-Publication Data

Urban tourism in the developing world : the South African experience /
   Christian M. Rogerson and Gustav Visser, editor.
      p. cm.
  Includes bibliographical references and index.
  ISBN-10: 0-7658-0358-5 (alk. paper)
  ISBN-13: 978-0-7658-0358-0 (alk. paper)
      1. Tourism—South Africa.   2. Cities and towns—South Africa.
  I. Rogerson, C. M. (Christian Myles). II. Visser, Gustav.

G155.S57U73 2007
916.8'09732—dc22

2006053026

Contents

Acknowledgements

This book is the outcome of several years of research concerning urban tourism in post-apartheid South Africa. The book builds upon an earlier special collection of papers on urban tourism in South Africa that was published as *Urban Forum* Vol. 16 (2-3) April-September 2005. In encouraging the development, expansion and updating of this collection of material into the present volume our thanks are extended, in particular, to the support offered by Irving Louis Horowitz at Transaction Press. Thanks are also extended to the production team at Transaction in moving forward speedily the publication of this book; in particular, acknowledgement is due to the assistance offered by Andrew McIntosh and Cheryl Orson.

For additional support in the research and production of this volume, thanks are extended to the contributions made by a number of individuals and organizations. The efforts made by all contributing authors in meeting a set of tight deadlines, is gratefully recorded. Both editors also acknowledge the enormous contribution made by Mrs. Wendy Job of the Cartographic Unit, University of the Witwatersrand, Johannesburg. Mrs. Job was responsible for the production of nearly all the maps and diagrams that appear in this book. For funding support of several of research outputs contained in this collection Chris Rogerson acknowledges the major funding support from the National Research Foundation, Pretoria under Gun Award 2054064 and additional financial support secured from both the South Africa-Netherlands Research Programme on Alternatives in Development and the University of the Witwatersrand. Equally important for Chris Rogerson has been the very special inputs made into the research process on a daily basis by Jayne, Jonathan and Arabella Rogerson.

Gustav Visser would like to thank the University of the Free State Research Committee for financial assistance during the research process leading to the finalization of this collection. Moreover, thanks are due to his colleagues in the Department of Geography, especially Peter Holmes and Nico Kotze, for providing time and support to complete the research reported here. Special thanks and appreciation are extended to Andreas Viljoen and Anzelle Visser, for their love and understanding.

1

Tourism in Urban Africa: Setting the Scene

Christian M. Rogerson and Gustav Visser

As recently as the early-1980s, Vandermey (1984: 123) noted that "urban tourism has not received extensive recognition in tourism research, policy and planning yet its current and potential market is great." Oddly, nevertheless, the city and its artifacts have long been a source of attraction to tourists (Law, 1992; 1993); but as several tourism scholars have noted, the urban dimension of tourism was given a disproportionately small amount of research attention in international tourism scholarship until very recently (Law, 1992, 1993; Page and Hall, 2003; Suh and Gartner, 2004, Hall and Page, 2006). However, since the 1990s, this relative neglect of tourism in cities, towns and villages, along with the phenomenon of urban tourism, has been addressed as a range of issues relating to tourists in cities attracted a progressive stream of contributions. Furthermore, the field of urban tourism has been consolidated with the appearance of several books that focus mainly upon the Western European and North American experience (Law, 1993; Van den Berg et al., 1995; Law, 1996; Murphy, 1997; Page and Hall, 2003; Tyler et al., 1998; Wober, 2002). Overall, the tempo of urban tourism research has been linked to "two real-world phenomena: escalating demand by tourists for urban historic sights and heritage cities, and concerted efforts by policy makers to focus on the role of tourism in revitalizing urban areas and economies" (Chang and Huang, 2004: 223-224).

The scope and range of urban research has thus widened considerably, as can be seen, for example, in the welcome appearance of studies that examine the tourism phenomenon in cities outside the Euro-American heartland. The frontier of research on urban tourism was extended geographically to encompass studies on Australia, New Zealand, Hong Kong, and Singapore. More recently, Brazil, China, Cuba, and Taiwan have also started to appear on the investigatory radar (Jaguaribe and Hetherington, 2004; Colantonio and Potter, 2006). The increasing prominence of Asian cities stresses the critical importance of cultural and heritage management for urban tourism promotion, especially in Singapore (Chang, 1999, 2000) and Hong Kong (McKercher et al., 2004, 2005). In Singapore a central planning focus is the development of thematic zones and the conservation of ethnic districts in order to promote the city's ambitions of becoming a tourism capital (Yeoh and Huang, 1996; Yeoh and Teo, 1996; Chang et al., 1996; Chang, 1997; 1999; Chang and Yeoh, 1999; Savage et al., 2004). Other significant Asian themes are the promotion of night markets for shopping tourism (Hsieh and Chang, 2006); environmental issues associated with mass urban tourism (Jim, 2000); and the immense potential of major Asian cities for convention or business tourism (Go and Govers, 1999; Lew and Chang, 1999; Hailin et al., 2000).

In addition to increases in the volume, geographical gaze and analytical depth of empirical monitoring studies, a range of parallel theoretical and conceptual advances have also occurred (Tyler, 2000). Importantly, Pearce (2001: 926) offers an "integrative framework" as a means to provide a more systematic and coherent perspective on urban tourism and as a step toward integrating a steadily growing "but as yet largely fragmented body of research." Moreover, in a recent volume, regulation theory is applied in order to bring a theoretical focus to research on urban tourism (Hoffman et al., 2003). Also of note is that Judd and Fainstein (1999) propose a conceptual distinction between three major categories of "tourist city," namely "the resort city" (including casino resorts, spas, and seaside towns); the "tourist-historic city"; and the "converted city," which refers to localities where traditional manufacturing or capital cities change their function to incorporate tourism. Other writers have sought to broaden this classification; for example, in order to include tourism world cities (Tyler, 2000).

In the context of this growing international body of debate and scholarship on tourism and cities, it is evident that the most underdeveloped literature is that which relates to the developing world as a whole and to Africa in particular. In terms of league tables of tourism receipts, the leading destinations for African tourism are shown to be Egypt and South Africa. Despite the growing recognition of tourism's development potential for Africa, especially in terms of the New Economic Partnership for African Development, tourism research as a whole remains limited and is mostly centered upon issues of nature-based tourism, conservation and rural development (Visser and Rogerson, 2004). Moreover, many African governments and development agencies either do not take tourism seriously, or fail to make the link between, for example, tourism and poverty reduction—or both (Mitchell and Ashley, 2006). Nevertheless, the potential agenda for research on tourism in urban Africa, is considerable; and moreover, it is significant from a policy perspective, in view of its potential developmental impacts (Mitchell and Ashley, 2006).

To adopt the categories of Judd and Fainstein (1999), several coastal centers in South Africa (Van Huyssteen and Neethling, 1996; Visser, 2002; 2003a) and

Kenya (de Beer et al., 1997; Kareithi, 2003) provide opportunities for examining the development and restructuring of resort tourism. In addition, the Zambian city of Livingstone, next to Victoria Falls, is a newly emergent resort based upon leisure attractions and, increasingly, also on adventure tourism (Rogerson, 2004a; 2005). In terms of issues that confront the tourist-historic city, many African examples of note can be cited, including Cape Town and Stellenbosch in South Africa (Worden, 1997); Mombasa and Lamu in Kenya (Hoyle, 2001); and Stone Town in Zanzibar, Tanzania (Marks, 1996). Finally, the questions surrounding the promotion and impacts of urban tourism development in "converted cities" are as pertinent in the context of the contemporary research issues of Johannesburg, Nairobi or Lusaka as they are in the case of Baltimore, Boston or Manchester (see, for example, Rogerson, 2002; 2003; 2004b).

Overall, the collection of essays in this volume comprises a response to the recent challenge posed by King (2004) in respect of the need to consolidate the progress made in urban tourism during the past fifteen years by grasping new research opportunities in order to broaden the existing research agendas. In particular, King (2004: 291) highlights the critical, unresearched question of how "cities in less developed countries perform as urban tourism destinations relative to their equivalents in the developed world." It is clear from the small body of existing published research that aspects of tourism development in South African cities are relevant to, and serve to illustrate, several major policy themes and currents of the international literature on urban tourism, especially those related to "converted cities" (Rogerson, 2002; 2003; 2004b) and leisure tourism (Visser, 2002; 2003b; 2004a; 2004b). Nevertheless, in the context of tourism developments taking place in black townships, at localities such as Soweto or Inanda, as well as at heritage sites associated with the anti-apartheid struggle, the South African experience goes further by introducing scholars to fresh research aspects of urban tourism, variously concerning "dark tourism," "justice tourism," and "pro-poor tourism" through the maximization of opportunities for small enterprise development (Hughes and Vaughan, 2000; Strange and Kempa, 2003; Ramchander, 2004; Rogerson, 2004c; 2004d; 2006).

The task of this collection of essays is to augment the current international scholarship concerning urban tourism in the developing world. More especially, it is our aim to provide some starting points to address the uneven scholarly coverage that urban tourism in the African context has received to date. Our attempt to enhance the heretofore limited writings on urban tourism in Africa draws on a range of case studies from South Africa. In pursuing the above-mentioned objectives it is our intention to open a window on research and policy issues concerning tourism in urban Africa.

This volume is structured around three sections of material. Part One provides an analysis of the tourism research issues, as well as tourist visitor trends in the urban areas of South Africa. This review provides a background for the treatises that follow. It is argued that in the South African context, urban tourism, though vast in its actual proportion, has in large part remained invisible to the scholarly gaze (chapter 2). However, it is suggested that despite the initial neglect in this regard, the past decade has witnessed the maturation of the local tourism industry and a drive toward the diversification of the national tourism product offering beyond South Africa's considerable range of nature-based tourism products (Cornelissen, 2005). Urban tourism now forms part of the local and regional development strategies of all major South African cities, as well as those of an increasing number of smaller towns and villages, and comprises a significant aspect of travel agencies' advertised tourism products (Nel and Rogerson, 2005). In the wake of such developments, urban tourism has started to draw increased research attention.

Following this review, two overviews of current visitor trends to South African cities are presented. Firstly, an analysis is made of international tourist movements in South Africa (chapter 3). It is noted that while there are very distinct international tourist segments visiting South Africa, especially in terms of the distinction between tourists from the African continent and those from overseas, these segments have one thing in common: the tourists visit cities. While the motivation for such visitation varies markedly among the different segments, South African cities and towns form a key component of nearly all international tourists' visits to the country. The second investigation into the tourist base that underpins urban tourism in South Africa relates to domestic tourism (chapter 4). Although domestic tourism is generally the backbone of most tourism systems, irrespective of whether or not they are urban-based, domestic tourism has, nevertheless, remained largely under-researched, especially in the South. To address this paucity in our understanding of domestic tourism in the developing world urban context, an attempt is made to document the expansion of domestic tourism in South Africa. This investigation shows that post-apartheid South Africa is emerging as a leader and innovator in terms of the strategic planning and promotion of domestic tourism to cities and towns, and that South Africa may have some useful lessons to offer to other developing world countries, especially those in sub-Saharan Africa. Moreover, it is shown that domestic tourism is primarily focused on urban areas.

In Part Two the emphasis of the analysis falls on the national level, with the presentation of a series of thematic issues concerning the South African urban tourism system. First, the theme of business tourism in urban Africa is explored through an analysis of the evolution and growth of conference and exhibition tourism (chapter 5). The investigation reveals a range of parallels between the South African and the international experiences of this niche tourism sector, with key themes relating to the significant economic impacts that this type of tourism holds. However, it is also pointed out that the intensely competitive nature of conference and exhibition tourism presents many risks for businesses that engage this tourism niche. The focus then turns to grounding the international proliferation of festival tourism in the African context (chapter 6). The chapter furnishes a comprehensive overview of the nature and prevalence of festival tourism in South Africa. A key conclusion relates to the extremely limited understanding that we have of this tourism sector, not least in respect of the question of how best to develop festival tourism in Africa so as to include all sections of society and contribute toward pro-poor tourism growth. Thereafter, further parallels are drawn between international urban tourism trends and the African context, by means of an investigation focusing on second home tourism in South African cities and towns (chapter 7). Here it is suggested that clear similarities are found between the development trends and impacts of second homes on host regions in South Africa, and those experienced in the North.

The focus then shifts to an investigation exploring the various linkages between creative industries and urban tourism (chapter 8). Internationally, the cultural tourism market has become flooded with new "identikit" cultural attractions and heritage centers. In addressing this dilemma of the serial reproduction of culture and of the need for developing new urban tourism products, one of the most fashionable approaches entails the encouragement and nurturing of "creativity," "creative industries," and "creative tourism" in cities. As Smith (2005: 23) reflects, creative industries are increasingly being used "as tools for the regeneration and transfiguration of urban space for consumption." However, the relevant debates have rarely been investigated in the developing world context. Against this background, the aim of this chapter is to profile the emerging relationship between urban tourism and creative industries in Africa through an analysis of the experience of Johannesburg.

Globally, Africa is not portrayed as a destination for tourists who identify as gay. However, in stark contrast to other African countries, South Africa is developing an enviable reputation as a gay tourist destination (chapter 9). As observed in Western European and North American countries, gay tourism is closely linked to the urban leisure tourism resource base. Similarly, the South African gay tourism sector is focused on urban tourism products, with Cape Town comprising the principal gay destination in Africa. Part Two concludes with a contribution that investigates one of those quintessentially African urban phenomena—the township (chapter 10). More specifically, this investigation provides a probing analysis of how township tourism is contributing to small-firm development in South Africa's economic heartland—Johannesburg.

In Part Three, the investigatory gaze shifts to the collective impact of different types of urban tourism experiences on cities and towns across the South African urban hierarchy. The focus first falls on Cape Town (chapter 11), Africa's premier international leisure tourism destination. Thereafter, the city of Durban (chapter 12), South Africa's main domestic leisure tourism destination, comes into view. Historically, Cape Town and Durban have been the centerpieces of South Africa's urban leisure tourism system, with Johannesburg, until recently, not being regarded as a tourism destination. Nevertheless, in the light of the decentralization of a range of economic activities from the Central Business

District, the metropolitan government has embarked upon a tourism development strategy to serve as one of its central sectoral drivers for the economic
regeneration of its decaying inner-city areas. Two investigations (chapters 13
and 14) present in-depth analyses of the evolution and subsequent impacts of
tourism promotion in central Johannesburg. In the final contribution to this
collection, it is argued that South African urban tourism development is not
limited to the large metropolitan areas, but has increasingly become part of
smaller towns' and villages' economic base (chapter 15). In a critical review
of urban tourism in small-town South Africa, the imprint of urban tourism
development is analyzed.

Taken together, this collection of new research material seeks to contribute toward raising the South African, and indeed, the African profile within a growing
international scholarship concerning issues of urban tourism and development.
It has been claimed that South African tourism scholarship is starting to develop
an independent "voice" concerning the tourism and development nexus. However, the critical observation has also been made that in the process, this body
of research appears to have developed in a theoretical vacuum that is divorced
from broader international tourism research discourses. With this collection of
essays, it is our aim not only to further develop an independent South African
tourism "voice," but to present research that is closely linked to international
urban tourism research debates. In addition, however, it is also our hope that
an analysis of urban tourism in the South African context will enrich the rather
Western-centric theorization of urban tourism discourse through recognition
of how urban tourism is evolving in urban Africa.

References

Chang, T.C., 1997: From "Instant Asia" to "multi-faceted jewel": urban imaging
    strategies and tourism development in Singapore, *Urban Geography,* 18, 542-562.
Chang, T.C., 1999: Local uniqueness in the global village: heritage tourism in Singa-
    pore, *Professional Geographer*, 51, 91-103.
Chang, T.C., 2000: Singapore's little India: a tourist attraction as a contested landscape,
    Urban Studies, 37, 343-366.
Chang, T.C. and Huang, S., 2004: Urban tourism: between the global and the local, in
    A.A. Lew, C.M. Hall, and A.M. Williams (Eds.), *A Companion to Tourism*, Black-
    well, Oxford, 223-234.
Chang, T.C. and Yeoh, B.S.A., 1999: "New Asia-Singapore": communicating local
    cultures through global tourism, *Geoforum*, 30, 101-116.
Chang, T.C., Milne, S., Fallon, D. and Pohlmann, C., 1996: Urban heritage tourism: the
    global-local nexus, *Annals of Tourism Research*, 23, 284-305.
Colantonio, H. and Potter, R., 2006: *Urban Tourism and Development in the Socialist
    State: Havana during the Special Period*, Ashgate, Aldershot.
Cornelissen, S., 2005: Producing and imaging "place" and "people": the political
    economy of South African international tourist representation, *Review of International
    Political Economy*, 12, 674-699.
De Beer, G.R.M., Elliffe, S.P., Spangenberg, P.P. and Wheeler, B.A., 1997: *The Socio-
    Economic Benefits of Tourism-Led Development - The Case of the Kenyan Coastline*

from Malindi to Mombasa, Spatial Development Initiatives Programme, Development Bank of Southern Africa, Midrand.

Go, F.M. and Govers, R., 1999: The Asian perspective: which international conference destinations in Asia are the most competitive?, *Journal of Convention and Exhibition Management,* 1(4), 37-50.

Hailin, Q., Lan, L. and Gilder, K.T.C., 2000: The comparative analysis of Hong Kong as an international conference destination in South East Asia, *Tourism Management,* 21, 643-648.

Hall, C.M. and Page, S.J., 2006: *The Geography of Tourism and Recreation: Environment, Place and Space,* Routledge, London.

Hoffman, L., Fainstein, S.S. and Judd, D.R., 2003: *Cities and Visitors: Regulation, People, Markets, and City Space,* Blackwell, Oxford.

Hoyle, B., 2001: Lamu: waterfront revitalization in an East African port city, *Cities,* 18, 297-313.

Hsieh, A.T. and Chang, J., 2006: Shopping and tourist night markets in Taiwan, *Tourism Management,* 27, 138-145.

Hughes, H. and Vaughan, A., 2000: The incorporation of historically disadvantaged communities into tourism initiatives in the new South Africa: case studies from KwaZulu-Natal, in M. Robinson, N. Evans, P. Long, R. Sharpley, and J. Swarbrooke (Eds.), *Management, Marketing and Political Economy of Travel and Tourism,* Center for Travel and Tourism and Business Education, Sunderland, 241-254.

Jaguaribe, B. and Hetherington, K., 2004: Favela tours: indistinct and maples representations of the real in Rio de Janeiro, in M. Sheller, M. and J. Urry. (Eds.), *Tourism Mobilities: Places to Play, Places in Play,* Routledge, London, 155-166.

Jim, C.Y., 2000: Environmental changes associated with mass urban tourism and nature tourism development in Hong Kong, *Environmentalist,* 20, 233-247.

Judd, D.R. and Fainstein, S.S., 1999: *The Tourist City,* Yale University Press, New Haven.

Kareithi, S., 2003: *Coping with Declining Tourism: Examples From Communities in Kenya,* Pro-Poor Tourism Working Paper No. 13, Overseas Development Institute, London.

King, B., 2004: Book Review on "Managing Urban Tourism," *Tourism Management,* 25, 290-291.

Law, C.M., 1992: Urban tourism and its contribution to economics, *Urban Studies,* 29, 599-618.

Law, C.M., 1993: *Urban Tourism: Attracting Visitors to Large Cities,* Mansell, London.

Law, C.M., 1996: *Tourism in Major Cities,* International Thomson Business Press, London.

Lew, A.A. and Chang, T.C., 1999: Where the world meets: regionalism and globalization in Singapore's convention industry, *Journal of Convention and Exhibition Marketing,* 1(4), 17-36.

Marks, R., 1996: Conservation and community: the contradictions and ambiguities of tourism in the Stone Town of Zanzibar, *Habitat International,* 20, 265-278.

McKercher, B., Ho, P.S.Y. and Du Cros, H., 2004: Attributes of popular cultural attractions in Hong Kong, *Annals of Tourism Research,* 31, 393-407.

McKercher, B., Ho, P.S.Y. and Du Cros, H., 2005: Relationship between tourism and cultural heritage management, *Tourism Management,* 26, 539-548.

Mitchell, J. and Ashley, C., 2006: *Can Tourism help Reduce Poverty in Africa?* ODI Briefing Paper March 2006, Overseas Development Institute, London.

Murphy, P.E. (Ed.), 1997: *Quality Management of Urban Tourism,* John Wiley, Chichester.

Nel, E. and Rogerson, C.M. (Eds.), 2005: *Local Economic Development in the Development World: The Experience of Southern Africa*, Transaction Publishers, New Brunswick, NJ.

Page, S.J. and Hall, C.M. 2003: *Managing Urban Tourism*, Pearson, Harlow.

Pearce, D.G., 2001: An integrative framework for urban tourism research, *Annals of Tourism Research*, 28, 926-946.

Ramchander, P., 2004: Soweto set to lure tourists, in A. Bennett, and R. George, (Eds.), *South African Travel and Tourism Cases*, Van Schaik, Pretoria, 200-210.

Rogerson, C.M., 2002: Urban tourism in the developing world: the case of Johannesburg, *Development Southern Africa*, 19, 169-190.

Rogerson, C.M. 2003: Tourism planning and the economic revitalization of Johannesburg, *Africa Insight*, 33(1/2), 130-135.

Rogerson, C.M., 2004a: Adventure tourism in Africa: the case of Livingstone, Zambia, *Geography*, 89, 183-188.

Rogerson, C.M., 2004b; Urban tourism and economic regeneration: the example of Johannesburg, in C. M. Rogerson and G. Visser, (Eds.), *Tourism and Development Issues in Contemporary South Africa*, Africa Institute of South Africa, Pretoria, 466-487.

Rogerson, C.M., 2004c: Urban tourism and small tourism enterprise development in Johannesburg: the case of township tourism, *GeoJournal*, 60, 247-257.

Rogerson, C.M., 2004d: Transforming the South African tourism industry: the emerging black-owned bed and breakfast economy, *GeoJournal*, 60, 273-281.

Rogerson, C.M., 2005: The emergence of tourism-led local development: the example of Livingstone, Zambia, *Africa Insight*, 34(4), 112-120.

Rogerson, C.M., 2006: Pro-poor local economic development in South Africa: the role of pro-poor tourism, *Local Environment*, 11, 37-60.

Savage, V.R., Huang, S. and Chang, T.C., 2004: The Singapore River thematic zone: sustainable tourism in an urban context, *Geographical Journal*, 170, 212-225.

Smith, M., 2005: Tourism, culture and regeneration: differentiation through creativity, in J. Swarbrooke, M. Smith, and L. Onderwater, (Eds.), *Tourism, Creativity and Development: ATLAS Reflections 2005*, Association for Tourism and Leisure Education, Arnhem, 23-38.

Strange, C. and Kempa, M., 2003: Shades of dark tourism: Alcatraz and Robben Island, *Annals of Tourism Research*, 30(2), 386-405.

Suh, Y.K. and Gartner, W.C., 2004: Perceptions in international urban tourism: an analysis of travellers to Seoul, Korea, *Journal of Travel Research*, 43(1), 39-48.

Tyler, D., 2000: A framework from analysing urban tourism, in M. Robinson, R. Sharpley, N. Evans, P. Long, and J. Swarbrooke. (Eds.), *Developments in Urban and Rural Tourism*, Center for Travel and Tourism, University of Northumbria, Newcastle, 287-299.

Tyler, D., Guerrier, Y. and Robertson, M. (Eds.), 1998: *Managing Tourism in Cities: Policy, Process and Practice*, John Wiley, Chichester.

Van den Berg, L., van der Borg, J. and Van der Meer, J., 1995: *Urban Tourism: Performance and Strategies in Eight European Cities*, Avebury, Aldershot.

Vandermey, A., 1984: Assessing the importance of urban tourism: conceptual and measurement issues, *Tourism Management*, 5(2), 123-155.

Van Huyssteen, M.K.R. and Neethling, J.P.N., 1996: Resort development in the False Bay recreational fringe of Metropolitan Cape Town, in R. J. Davies. (Ed.), *Contemporary City Restructuring*, International Geographical Union Commission on Urban Development and Urban Life and Society for Geographers, Cape Town, 501-519.

Visser, G., 2002: Gay tourism in South Africa: issues from the Cape Town experience, *Urban Forum*, 13(1), 85-94.

Visser, G., 2003a: Gay men, tourism and urban space: reflections on Africa's gay capital, *Tourism Geographies*, 5 168-189.

Visser, G., 2003b: Gay men, leisure space and South African cities: the case of Cape Town, *Geoforum*, 34(1), 123-137.

Visser, G., 2004a: Second homes and local development: issues arising form Cape Town's De Waterkant, *GeoJournal*, 60(2), 259-271.

Visser, G., 2004b: Second homes: reflections on an unexplored phenomenon in South Africa, in C.M. Hall and D.K. Müller (Eds.), *Tourism, Mobility and Second Homes: Between Elite Landscape and Common Ground*, Channel View, Clevedon, 196-214.

Visser, G. and Rogerson, C.M., 2004: Researching the South African tourism and development nexus, *GeoJournal*, 60, 201-215.

Wober, K.W. (Ed.), 2002: *City Tourism 2002*, Springer Verlag, Vienna.

Worden, N., 1997: Contesting heritage in a South African city: Cape Town, in B. J. Shaw, and R. Jones. (Eds.), *Contested Urban Heritage: Voices from the Periphery*, Ashgate, Aldershot, 213-223.

Yeoh, B.S. and Huang, S., 1996: The conservation-redevelopment dilemma in Singapore: the case of the Kampong Glam historic district, *Cities*, 13, 411-422.

Yeoh, B.S. and Teo, P., 1996: From Tiger Balm Gardens to Dragon World: philanthropy and profit in the making of Singapore's first cultural theme park, *Geografiska Annaler*, 78B, 27-42.

Part 1

Urban Tourism in Africa: Current Research and Current Trends

2

Tourism Research and Urban Africa:
The South African Experience

Christian M. Rogerson and Gustav Visser

Despite growing international debate and scholarship focused on tourism in urban places in the North, the most undeveloped literature relates to that of the developing world as a whole and to Africa in particular (Rogerson and Visser, 2003). As compared to the vast flow of publications on urban tourism relating to Europe, North America, Australasia, and increasingly East Asia, Africa is on the margins of international tourism scholarship (Rogerson, 2005a). Despite growing recognition of tourism's developmental potential for Africa on a number of fronts, as a whole tourism scholarship remains limited and mostly is centered upon issues of nature-based tourism products, the role of tourism in conservation, and of the potential rural development possibilities tourism can unleash (Visser and Rogerson, 2004). The majority of this research is coarse-grained in scale, focused on the continental, sub-regional or national levels of analysis (Rogerson, 2005a). In this light, the potential agenda for scholarship on tourism in urban Africa, and local level analysis in particular, is both considerable and of policy significance for its potential developmental impact.

The task in this chapter is to furnish an overview of the small, but growing body of research that investigates a range of unfolding dimensions of urban tourism in South Africa. As a background to investigating urban tourism in South Africa, the first section provides a brief synopsis of the main Africa-wide tourism research themes. The emphasis is placed on core research issues at various scales of analysis, in particular highlighting the limited body of locality-based studies. This review demonstrates that a key omission in current scholarship relates to tourism in urban Africa. Against this backdrop, the focus turns toward the South African urban tourism system. The second section demonstrates that while urban tourism has not received much research attention in Africa generally, it has been a feature of the South African tourism landscape for a considerable time. Indeed, from as early as the 1930s, a number of South African coastal cities have attempted to develop a range of leisure-based tourism products. The third section provides an overview of an array of urban tourism niches, and of associated research literature, that have developed over the past decade. Here it is argued that while historically urban tourism has largely been invisible to the scholarly gaze, sets of urban tourism products have developed since the early 1990s, many of these tourism offerings echoing urban tourism products found in the post-industrial North. The final section concludes that in light of the current body of knowledge and the emergence of a range of urban tourism products, urban tourism in South Africa represents fertile ground for future academic and policy research.

Contemporary African Tourism Research

In Africa there are a number of significant investigations that deliberate the potential, feasibility and developmental role of tourism in the region for the promotion of economic growth, employment opportunities, sustainable development and poverty alleviation (Devereux and Chen, 1999; Gartner, 2001; Dieke, 2000, 2003; Gauci et al., 2005 Mitchell and Ashley, 2006a). Furthermore, a number of investigations have as a focal point those factors that constrain tourism expansion. In this respect research has examined air transport networks (Oxford Economic Forecasting, 2003; Richman and Lyle, 2005); skilled labour resources (Ankomah, 1991; Dieke, 2000; 2001; Doswell, 2000; Kaplan, 2004a; 2004b); weak institutional frameworks (Vrahimis and Visser, 2006); and, the impact of political instability (Ankomah and Crompton, 1990). In these investigations tourism is portrayed as having considerable unrealised potential across many parts of Africa, albeit the sector has developed unevenly across the continent with some countries and regions benefiting much more than others (Rogerson, 2005a; 2006).

The important debates introduced through the work of the World Bank, particularly in terms of its general view of tourism in Africa as a whole, highlight the role of national governments as central to tourism development, not least in terms of designing policy frameworks and formulating incentives and regulatory frameworks to ensure economic and environmental sustainability, as well as poverty reduction (Christie and Crompton, 2001a; 2001b). These World Bank studies illuminate several key policy issues that include human resource deficiencies, standards of tourism services, infrastructure, linkages, demand fluctuations and financing. While the linkage of tourism and poverty alleviation in Africa is mentioned in the World Bank studies, it is strongly profiled in works that come out from the Economic Commission for Africa (Gerosa, 2003) and the British Overseas Development Institute (Ashley and Mitchell, 2005; Mitchell and Ashley, 2006a, 2006b). Such works provide a detailed analysis of the potential of tourism to contribute to pro-poor growth and of the extent to which tourism presently is a key theme in African Poverty Reduction Strategy Papers.

The role of tourism in the context of the New Economic Partnerships for African Development (NEPAD) has come under scrutiny (Ndiaye, 2003; Rukato, 2003). In the view of some commentators, the publication of the NEPAD Action Plan for Tourism (2004a; 2004b) represents a "critical landmark policy paper" (Rogerson, 2005a: 114). The Action Plan interprets tourism as a sector in Africa's transformation, as well as future development and highlights the fact that by global measures, tourism across Africa is performing below international standards. Key objectives are to create an enabling regulatory environment; strengthen institutional capacity of tourism planning; improve tourism marketing, especially on a regional basis; enhance research and development, including improved data; upgrade tourism infrastructure and products; improve skills in tourism; and, address the cross-cutting issues of gender, community involvement and AIDS. Of particular significance is that the NEPAD action plan asserts the imperative for improved marketing links between, and among, other African sub-regions and markets, as well as identifies the urgent need for common regional or sub-regional marketing strategies (NEPAD, 2004a: 11).

At the sub-regional scale of analysis, among the leading foci for African tourism scholarship so far, has been the evaluation of the activities of existing regional marketing organisations such as the Regional Tourism Association of Southern Africa (RETOSA), cross-border planning initiatives for tourism, and the emergence of regional flows of tourism within the continent (Dieke, 1998; Rogerson, 2003a; 2004a; Ramutsindela, 2004). The significance of the "African" regional tourist is beginning to be acknowledged in tourism development planning and reaches its strongest expression in the South African experience (Rogerson and Visser, 2004).

A considerable volume of material exists at the national level of analysis. Butler's notion of the "tourism resort cycle" has been applied to interpret African tourism development with case studies undertaken on the evolution of tourism in Kenya and Swaziland (Butler, 1980; Harrison, 1995; Akama, 1999). Not surprisingly, the largest body of research and debate concerns policy development at the national scale for tourism (Dieke, 1991; Dieke, 1992; Thompson et al., 1995; Mashinini, 2003; Rogerson, 2003b; Kiambo, 2005). The importance of national planning for domestic tourism is also a theme that is highlighted by several African researchers (Sindiga, 2000; Koch and Massyn, 2001; Kiambo, 2005; Rogerson and Lisa, 2005).

Other significant works focus on the contribution of tourism to national economic growth (Youngstedt, 2003); the impact of structural adjustment (Koandu-Agyemang, 2001); employment issues (Farver, 1984); factors affecting small firm development in tourism (Gartner, 1999; Gartner, 2004; Rogerson, 2003c; 2004b; 2004c; 2004d; 2005b); and, the wider role of tourism in national economic planning within particular countries (Durbarry, 2004; Mansfield and

Winckler, 2004). The role and impact of eco-tourism, nature-based tourism or wildlife tourism has garnered considerable attention in several parts of the continent (Sindiga, 1995; 1996; 1999; Parslar, 1997; Weaver, 1999; Fennell, 2003; Massyn and Koch, 2004; Nzengy'a, 2004). Other themes of concern have included human resource development (Doswell, 2000; Kaplan, 2004); community-based tourism (Baker, 1997; Victurine, 2000; Mearns, 2003); adventure tourism (Rogerson, 2004e); sex tourism (Harrison, 1994); and, the role of the informal sector (Bah and Goodwin, 2003). In terms of thematic research at the national level of analysis, the South African tourism literature currently exhibits the most diverse set of debates (Rogerson and Visser, 2004; Visser and Rogerson, 2004; Rogerson and Visser, 2005).

In reviewing African tourism research scholarship, it is apparent that, relative to other regions of the world, the pursuit of local-level studies and of locality-focused research is undeveloped. Such local-level studies seek to document the impact of tourism and tourism development at particular localities across the continent. The importance of such research investigations is underlined by the fact that tourism development has been spatially uneven within countries such that its impact is concentrated, according to NEPAD, at "important tourist zones and localities" (NEPAD, 2004a: 11). While limited even in terms of rural Africa, a number of local impact studies have been conducted in some of the leading rural tourist zones of the continent (Gossling, 2001; Adams and Infield, 2003; Diagne, 2004). Currently, the richest local level research in rural Africa is, perhaps, the recent contributions made by Mbaiwa, who has undertaken several investigations concerning the socio-economic impact of "enclave tourism" in the Okavango Delta region of Botswana (Mbaiwa, 2003; 2005). Of note also is a wave of South African rural studies conducted through the lens of local-level investigations using the framework of pro-poor tourism with its focus on the maximisation of linkages with local small business entrepreneurs (Mahony and Van Zyl, 2001; Spenceley and Seif, 2003; Ashley and Ntshona, 2002; Ashley, 2005).

Lately, urban Africa is increasingly emerging as a locus of investigation. A number of recent local-level analyses of the developmental impact of tourism in the urban context have emerged. Kenya's coastal region from Mombasa to Malindi has been researched in several studies which have examined, *inter alia*, the local socio-economic impact of tourism developments, the sex trade, and of waterfront re-vitalization initiatives (De Beer et al., 1997; Hoyle, 2001; Kibicho, 2003a; 2003b). In Ghana, local resident support for urban tourism has been an interesting research focus (Sirakaya et al., 2001; 2003). The interaction of tourists with marginalised groups has been highlighted in Antananarivo, Madagascar (Gossling et al., 2004) and the theme of prostitution emerges in work conducted in urban areas of Swaziland (Harrison, 1994). In Zambia, the local development experience of the tourism resort town of Livingstone represents a good example of the emergence of tourism as a key sectoral driver for local urban development

(Rogerson, 2005). In South African research, a central concern is tourism's role and potential as a vehicle for urban economic regeneration, small enterprise development and local economic development (Binns and Nel, 2002; Nel and Binns, 2002; Rogerson, 2002; 2003c; 2003d; 2004c; 2004f; 2005b; Rogerson and Kaplan, 2005; Rogerson and Nemasetoni, 2005).

Notwithstanding that which represents the starting point of an urban tourism discourse, it must be concluded from this review of current tourism scholarship in Africa that few scholars focus on issues of tourism in urban Africa. Indeed, it can be observed that a range of debates seen in both the established urban tourism research literature of the developed North, and the emerging scholarship in terms of the developing South, are not currently being explored in urban Africa as a whole. Nevertheless, while somewhat limited, some research work concerning the tourism and urban development nexus is emerging in South Africa.

The Discovery and Growth of Urban Tourism

In South Africa, urban tourism, while vast in its actual proportion, has largely remained invisible to the scholarly gaze. The lack of research into urban tourism is somewhat perplexing for unlike many developing countries, the contours of its development can be traced through an extensive urban geography. Indeed, the development of many neighbourhoods in cities such as Cape Town, Durban or Port Elizabeth, as well as a host of smaller coastal and increasingly interior rural towns and villages is inextricably linked to urban tourism growth (figure 2.1). Several reasons account for this neglect. First, tourism as an industry, while established some decades ago, was not taken seriously as a developmental focus until quite recently (Visser and Rogerson, 2004). Both private and public sector planners alike were largely blind to the extraordinary reach of tourism across a range of economic sectors. Second, the impact of urban tourism was relatively small, mainly because it was constrained under apartheid by the limitation of the free movement of people in and to cities. Third, tourism and leisure seeking in South Africa had a distinctive nature-based tourism bias (Visser and Rogerson, 2004). Fourth, and related, while tourism as a vehicle for development has received considerable recognition since the advent of multi-racial democracy, the urgency with which the grinding poverty in many rural areas needs to be addressed has led to a national policy focus that has aimed to harness tourism opportunities in those areas.

While researchers and most policy makers alike did not "see" urban tourism development as important until comparatively recently, urban tourism has been pursued since at least the early-1930s. Indeed, during the early twentieth century urban leisure tourism formed the base for considerable employment growth in several coastal centers of South Africa. By 1930 the East London Publicity Association (1930) was already promoting the town as "the home of the surfboard—where Sea and Sunshine call." The most important tourism focus was Durban, which established itself as a major tourist destination from

Figure 2.1
South Africa: Location of Tourism Centres

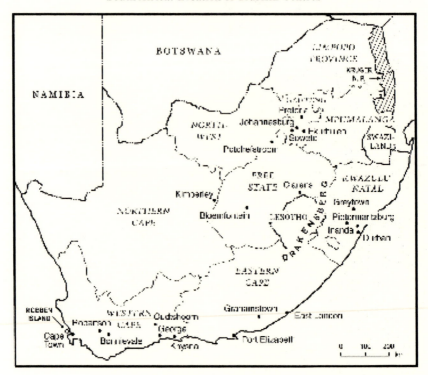

as early as the 1920s (Grant and Butler-Adam, 1992). In 1937, local publicity brochures waxed eloquently on the virtues of holiday making in the city:

> The magic of Durban's lure is in the rich, warm kiss of the sun with health in every ray, in the mellow climate, brisk and bracing in the winter, in her vivid colours, in the glorious sweep of her sea front, in her variedness. She is, as Dryden says, "A town so various that she seemed to be. No one, but all the world's epitome." That is her charm (Durban Publicity Association, 1937: 3).

Although the domestic visitor was the early focus of tourism planning, advertising for the city did not miss an opportunity to draw parallels for the potential international visitor:

> Durban's greatest asset, as is that of all the coastal communities, is, of course, her beach. The city has followed a vigorous policy of developing its sea front, where, in splendidly spectacular line, dignified hotels have risen which blend well with the general atmosphere of Durban. There in the season, on the crowded beaches, may be seen fashions as colourful and gay as on the Lido or at Deauville (Durban Publicity Association, 1937: 15).

While Durban developed its tourist appeal, other cities and indeed towns were also aiming to harness their tourism potential. The first South African academic studies into the deployment of tourism as an urban development strategy appeared from the 1970s. Muller's (1971) pioneering study of tourism as an alternative development strategy in George and Knysna, Steyn's (1972) doctoral study on the impact of domestic tourism on the development of a number of southern Cape coastal towns, as well as Taylor's (1974) investigation into the tourism patterns of East London's tourism system, and likewise Urwin's (1980) in the Cape Town context, all hinted at the significant linkages between tourism and urban development, and more importantly that tourism could be built around the attractions of an urban environment, albeit in these investigations closely tied to beach recreation.

A new chapter in tourism planning in South Africa's cities began to open from the mid-1980s. In common with the international experience of urban economic restructuring, the promotion of tourism grew markedly in significance on the South African urban policy agenda. This interest was reflected in an upsurge of research into urban tourism. Indeed, in a series of studies the impact of urban tourism on business formation and development (Olivier, 1990), urban conservation (Van As, 1990), and small town development and restructuring (Roos, 1991; Prinsloo, 1991; Gilfellan, 1992) were conducted. Recreation and tourism became a key influence on metropolitan planning, with research focusing especially on Cape Town (Oliver, 1990; Van Huyssteen and Neethling, 1996), Durban (Kohler, 1993) and Port Elizabeth (Grant and Kohler, 1996). In terms of a more pronounced research agenda for local economic development (LED) planning, tourism has been a significant item since at least 1995 (Rogerson, 1995).

Currently, tourism promotion is an element of economic development planning in all South Africa's major cities (see City of Cape Town, 2001; Buffalo City, 2005), including even the unlikely case of Ekurhuleni (Ekurhuleni Municipality, 2003). The most dramatic manifestations of tourism promotion are perhaps in the waterfront redevelopments that have transformed areas of inner-city Cape Town and Durban (Grant and Scott, 1996; Kilian et al., 1996). Indeed, it is perhaps not surprising that the traditional leisure destinations of Cape Town and Durban were pioneers in the use of tourism in local development planning (Gretton, 1995; MacMenamin, 1995). Currently, the deployment of tourism in a broader drive for economic development remains noticeable in terms of a wave of exploratory policy reports and situation analyses for these two cities in particular (Bob and Moodley, 2001a; City of Cape Town, 2001; Turco et al., 2003; Wesgro, 2003). None the less, the most significant newcomer to the urban tourism scene is Johannesburg where significant amounts of capital have been invested in a range of urban-based tourism products including casinos, museums, theatres and entertainment complexes (Rogerson, 2002; 2003d; 2004f).

The Promotion of Tourism in Urban South Africa

It is clear from the above that South Africa's urban managers and policy makers recognise tourism development as a means by which to stimulate their local economies. Currently, there are a number of strategies being deployed to further enhance and develop the tourism potential of South African cities. The following provides a broad review.

New leisure markets are being sought, for example in Cape Town where the significance of gay tourism has recently been profiled (Visser, 2002, 2003a, 2003b; Bennett, 2004a). Internationally one of the most "urban" of tourism product offerings relate to gay tourism. Even the most casual glance at the gay "travel-bible" *Spartacus*, or popular gay press in the form of *Boyz, Pink Paper* and *Exit*, will confirm that urban tourism forms a key component of gay travel, not only internationally but in South Africa too. In this respect international gay tourism to South Africa clearly underlines that trend (Visser, 2003a 2003b). Since the demise of apartheid, Cape Town, in particular, has become a very popular destination for gay and lesbian travellers (Visser, 2002). Indeed, based on British Airways research, it is billed as the second largest "gay capital" in the world, voted as being one of the "Top 3 travel destinations" and "number 1 in terms of value for money" gay destinations. This has led to the development of a gay neighbourhood—De Waterkant—boasting tourist accommodation, bars, interior shops, up-market clothing outlets, nightclubs, restaurants, saunas and escort agencies (Visser, 2003a, 2003b). Cape Town also lays claim to hosting one of *the* internationally recognized gay festivals—the Mother City Queer Project (Visser, 2002).

As can be discerned from the above, these activities are primarily focused on the urban leisure infrastructure of Cape Town. The impact of gay tourism has only recently started to attract critical analysis. Exploratory research has demonstrated that owing to gay-based urban tourism a range of linkages between gay tourism and leisure activity has physically transformed part of Cape Town (Visser, 2003a). The impact of urban tourism linked to gay identity is, however, not confined to metropolitan areas such as Cape Town but has also been noted in small towns, particularly in the Western Cape. Indeed, in pursuit of gay tourist spending, a number of small rural towns along "Route 62" now market themselves as the Pink Route. While the development of the gay tourism market has been impressive, our understanding of gay tourism in South Africa is poorly developed with a range of impacts, both positive and negative, remaining unexplored.

With the changes in gaming legislation since 1994, large casino investments in South Africa's cities have made them major national foci for casino tourism (Rogerson, 2003e). The total number of casinos has risen from seventeen during the apartheid era to the current total of thirty-three casinos. Whereas casino development prior to 1994 was exclusively based in rural or peri-urban areas of apartheid "homelands," its subsequent development has seen the urbanisation of casino gambling. These mega-developments, ranging investments of hundreds of millions and often billions of Rands, has led to the significant expansion of leisure tourism product offerings in several casinos in different South African cities and towns (Rogerson, 2003e; Rousseau, 2004; Strydom, 2004). While these developments are significant both in terms of their size and location, in-depth academic understanding of these new entertainment centers has been limited. Perhaps one of the most important questions that must be asked relates to the "pro-poor" tourism development credentials of casinos, as well as their contribution to reworking the urban fabric in the areas they are located.

The development of urban casino-resorts has not taken place in isolation but has typically formed part of a larger tourism expansion strategy linked to local economic development initiatives. Ancillary to casino development, a range of new tourism initiatives is occurring in all the coastal cities, as well as Johannesburg and other cities and towns in the interior. Not least is the case of Port Elizabeth where a re-branding and repositioning of the city has been occurring (Heath, 2004). Alongside new theme park developments, the most imaginative initiative is the planned construction of Africa's "Statue of Liberty," a sixty-five meter tall statue of former President Nelson Mandela, which is to be erected in Port Elizabeth Harbour (Heath, 2004; van Zyl, 2004). Overall, the growing significance of tourism as a vehicle for local economic development (LED) in urban South Africa was highlighted by findings from a national survey of municipalities during 2001-2002 that disclosed that tourism was one of the most popular LED strategies (Nel and Binns, 2003).

Despite its growth, the politics of integrating tourism in LED planning in South African cities has been little examined. In Durban's tourism development record, a range of flagship property development projects including a new convention center and tourism developments (Lootvoet and Freund, 2004), have been interpreted as the beginning of creating a new alliance between old and new business elites in the city (Moffett and Freund, 2004). For Lootvoet and Freund (2004) the new commitment to projects such as the Shaka Island Development involves the creation of substantial business opportunities for the city's new elites through tendering opportunities of affirmative procurement. Nevertheless, it is argued that "their impact on the mass of poor people is at best ambiguous" (Lootvoet and Freund, 2004: 7).

The unfolding promotion of South African cities as centers for consumption has taken various forms and approaches that clearly reflect international patterns (Rogerson, 2002). Business tourism has been promoted through the building of new international convention centers and linked hotel developments in Durban, Johannesburg and most recently in Cape Town (Nel and Binns, 2003; Nel et al., 2003; Ingram 2004; Gibb, 2006). The development of business tourism has been identified as a vital base for urban economic development in these three cities. The critical and lucrative activity of MICE (meetings, incentives, conferences and exhibitions) tourism has been augmented by the attraction of "mega-events" to South Africa such as the World AIDS Congress and the World Summit on Sustainable Development (Rogerson, 2002). Although a large international literature has mapped out the significant impact that MICE tourism holds for the post-industrial North (Cope, 2001; Alford, 2002; Bradley et al., 2002; Ladkin, 2002; Weber and Ladkin, 2003) as well as the emerging South (Dwyer and Mistillis, 1999; Wei and Go, 1999), until recently, South African scholarship was confined to general research of the economic impact of this industry (Black Business Quarterly, 2000a; 2000b) and of the reported undesirable rise in sex work in the popular MICE locations of Cape Town and Johannesburg.

The traditional market of leisure tourism has been boosted through new waterfront redevelopment programs (such as in Cape Town or Durban) or flagship projects such as the Shaka Island development in Durban (Lootvoet and Freund, 2004). In Port Elizabeth, the linking of the conference market, through the development of a conference center and the redevelopment of parts of the harbour as a waterfront, is only the latest in a number of similar developments (The Bay Bulletin, 2003). Indeed, even the small city of Bloemfontein now boasts such a waterfront to entertain its regional visitors (Nel and Strydom, 2003). Moreover, other developments linked to the creation of spaces for leisure and tourism consumption include Kimberley, where its urban re-development and renewal projects place tourism at the center of these initiatives (Sol Plaatjes Municipality, 2004). Despite the extraordinary range and sheer number of urban redevelopment programs underpinned by urban tourism expansion, there is very little critical reflection on how successful these projects are in providing quality employment opportunities, their sustainability, or whether they will lead to social and economic exclusion and marginalization, and a host of related issues highlighted in the international literature (Gotham, 2001; Clark, 2004).

Cruise tourism is a further growing element of leisure tourism in coastal cities, in particular for Cape Town and Durban (Vos, 2004). In South Africa, this type of tourism is currently driven by the international market, with the United Kingdom being the key source market (Kohler, 2003). Recently, British newspapers such as *The Mail on Sunday* (2005: 106-107) for example, ran travel features advertising holidays that are exclusively focused on South Africa's main coastal cities including Cape Town, Durban, East London and Port Elizabeth. Perhaps most interesting is the fact that the nature and wildlife components of the South African tourism system are wholly ignored in these promotions. Indeed, South African cities are emerging as cruise tourist attractions in their own right. Nevertheless, little research attention has been given to the manner in which the cruise tourism sector is developing and ways in which it might be improved to maximise developmental potential. In exploratory research by Kohler (2003: 1), it is argued that the cruise tourism sector "is a highly lucrative one ... [however] largely ignored and left simply to continue with no support or even understanding on the part of the tourism role players." The neglect is regrettable for cruise tourism has been identified as one of the fastest growing sectors in two of South Africa's largest markets, *viz.* North America and the United Kingdom (Kohler, 2003). In the case of Durban, Kohler's (2003) investigation found that 12 000 cruise passengers were recorded in 2003, spending R11 million. Income derived from re-provisioning (food, drink, fuel, water and the like) equated to R44 million. It is argued that even if a conservative estimate of crew on shore is included, the economic impact of one season of the cruise tourism sector brings over R60 million to the province of KwaZulu-Natal (Kohler, 2003).

Shopping tourism has been the target of "mega-mall" developments such as Century City in Cape Town (Marks and Bezzoli, 2001) as well as Johannesburg's effort to attract revenue from regional tourist flows from countries in sub-Saharan Africa. Currently there are no detailed investigations that aim directly to analyse the dimensions and impact of shopping tourism. None the less, existing research into the dimensions of regional tourism in South Africa indirectly hints at the important role that shopping plays in drawing African tourists from neighbouring states (Rogerson, 2004a). The cross-border retail economy is of particular significance to the city of Johannesburg and more widely to Gauteng province. Recent estimates suggest that Johannesburg attracts one million visitors a year by both air and land transportation for purposes of shopping in the city (Com-Mark Trust, 2006). Currently, this potentially crucial urban tourism market in South Africa remains desperately under-explored and requires more intensive research in order to develop this tourism niche in an appropriate manner.

Hallmark events have become significant for cities and their future development. Hallmark tourism encompasses a range of sporting events, fairs, festivals and expositions, and plays a distinctive role in shaping contemporary urban tourism (Shaw and Williams, 2004: 267). Weiler and Hall (1992: 1) argue that collectively, hallmark events are the image builders of modern tourism although it is a form of tourism that we know relatively little about. In the South African context, the claim holds true in terms of research, though it is evident that cities and towns across South Africa certainly recognise the importance of hallmark events for the expansion of urban development (City of Cape Town, 2001; Turco et al., 2003).

For example, the City of Cape Town has included hallmark events hosting and promotion as one of the key aspects of their local tourism development strategy (Hiller, 2000; City of Cape Town, 2001; Gibb, 2006). The city is now being marketed internationally as "The Cape of Great Events." It is argued that "events are the shop window of the city or region and as such the number of people looking in and the quality of the window dressing plays a big role in building national and international impressions of the place" (City of Cape Town, 2001: 19). Hallmark events can be classified in a number of ways including scale, ranging from major international events through to national, regional and local activities, as well as focusing on a number of sport and entertainment events. In this respect two major foci have developed in urban tourism in South Africa: sports tourism and cultural festivals.

Sports tourism has been an important element for growing the tourism economy in cities (Van der Heever, 1996) with the hosting of the Rugby and Cricket World Cups and the forthcoming 2010 FIFA World Soccer Cup. Much of the success in terms of hosting these events is linked to the government-launched sports tourism campaign, South Africa Sports Tourism (SAST), as part of a theme-based initiative (Turco et al., 2003). SAST has been conceived to act as an umbrella enterprise under which existing events may receive unified promotional support. Additional sporting events and recreational activities can be developed to the greater benefit of the tourism sector, and the country's recreational resources can be publicised to potential international and domestic tourists (Saayman, 1997).

In order to operationalize the objectives of SAST and promote event tourism more generally, cities such as Durban launched the Durban Events Corporation (Turco et al., 2003). Through this body a number of mainly consultancy and local government driven investigations have been undertaken for the coastal regions of KwaZulu-Natal (Bob and Moodley, 2000; Durban Metro, 2000; Durban Africa, 2001). The research conducted by Grant Thornton Kessel Feinstein (2001) for example, considered the various linkages that could be forged between Durban's traditional sun and beach tourism, with other activities such as sport, nature and culture. Moreover, several investigations have been conducted into the social-economic impact of sport tourism events held in Durban (Bob and Moodley, 2000; 2001a; 2001b; 2001c; 2001d; 2001e; 2001f; Bob et al., 2006). This research, for example, demonstrated that the Comrades Marathon which is run annually between Durban and Pietermaritzburg, generated revenue of R20 million through 58,000 tourists, while the Vodacom Beach Africa Festival drew an estimated 960,000 visitors along with tourist spending for Durban in excess of R76 million.

Internationally, numerous types of festivals are increasingly being used as instruments for promoting tourism and boosting the regional economy (Chabra et al., 2003; Felsentein and Fleischer, 2003). Similarly, many South African towns and cities have introduced festivals as a way by which to generate income and promote tourism development. Nearly every city and town in South Africa has an arts/cultural/heritage festival specifically designed to draw tourists to their area (Visser and Kotze, 2004). Although the festival market is not well understood in the South African context, a number of recent studies have been completed (see Snowball and Antrobus, 2001, 2002; Van Zyl and Botha, 2003).

Several investigations into the monetary significance of festival tourism have been undertaken. Among many interesting findings it was, for example, shown that the Klein-Karoo Nasionale Kunstefees (KKNK) in Oudtshoorn drew 100,000 visitors, generating a total of R100 million in local expenditure. In addition, this research pointed out that the Grahamstown, Aardklop and KKNK festival together generated more than R200 million annually (see Snowball and Antrobus, 2001). A further finding was that economic leakages out of the local economies of Grahamstown and Oudtshoorn were far larger than for Potchefstroom (Saayman and Saayman, 2003; Aardklop, 2004). The reason for this was that the latter location was a larger urban economy and that many of the services the festival uses were from local services providers. This situation leads to the retention of income generated by the festival in the local economy. By contrast, in the smaller centers of Grahamstown and Oudtshoorn, many of the services have to be contracted in from service providers outside the respective regions (Aardklop, 2004).

Related to the "festivals market," heritage and cultural tourism has been supported through the building of new museum complexes such as Constitution Hill, the Apartheid Museum and the Newtown cultural precinct in Johannesburg (Rogerson, 2002, 2003d, 2004f). As has been documented elsewhere, the Constitution Hill and Newtown cultural precinct projects are joint initiatives between the Johannesburg council and Blue IQ, the Gauteng provincial economic development agency (Rogerson, 2004f). The significance of these projects is heightened for the regeneration and re-imaging of Johannesburg's inner-city and for generating day visitors (Rogerson and Kaplan, 2005).

The market attractions of political tourism, or justice tourism linked to the struggle against apartheid, are reflected in developments at Robben Island or the promotion of township tourism in localities such as Soweto, Alexandra or Inanda among others and present another site for urban tourism expansion (Hughes and Vaughan, 2000; Shackley, 2001; Strange and Kempa, 2003; Bennett, 2004b; Kaplan, 2004a; Rogerson, 2004c; 2004d). In South Africa the current body of research into this form of urban tourism is rather limited. However, a recent investigation into the potential of "justice tourism," focusing on apartheid's "atrocity heritage sites" has revealed some difficulties in developing this type of urban tourism. Ashworth's (2004) investigation, for example, indicates that the management of "atrocity heritage" sites is riddled with difficulties because of the multiple use of the sites, of which tourism is only one, as well as of the problem of the emotions evoked by such sites, which impose constraints and responsibilities on their management for tourism. Nevertheless, it would appear that this type of tourism holds potential to enrich the urban travel experience, as well as having potential for broader-based community participation (Boqo, 2001).

Second homes tourism has emerged over the past decade as a key driver for urban (re)development (Hall and Müller, 2004). Internationally it has been demonstrated that second homes are an important part of the tourism and leisure lifestyle of many people in the developed world (Hall and Müller, 2004). In particular, second homes are an integral component of tourism experiences in rural and peripheral areas. Although these complex and varied relationships receive detailed research attention internationally (see Hall and Müller, 2004 for a comprehensive review), these concerns have only recently emerged as an area of investigation within the South African context (Hoogendoorn and Visser, 2004). Nevertheless, research into this phenomenon has started to emerge as one that requires academic attention, with some exploratory work recently coming to press. In the first academic investigation to address squarely the development of second homes in South Africa, Visser (2004a) set out to provide a general geography of this phenomenon in the local context. A key conclusion was that significantly more empirical investigation was required to elucidate the nature and impact of second homes on host communities, not only in the predictable second home hot-spots of the coastal provinces, but also the county's interior and metropolitan areas where growing numbers of second homes are to be found (Hoogendoorn and Visser, 2004; Visser, 2004a; 2004b).

On the other end of the scale, budget tourism is a particular form of tourism that also strongly involves South Africa's urban places. Research focusing on backpacker tourists as generally representative of budget tourists, has demonstrated that urban places form an important focus of these tourists' travels in South Africa (Visser, 2004c; Visser and Barker, 2004a, 2004b). In particular the cities of Cape Town and Johannesburg are shown to act as international gateways through which overseas tourists enter South Africa. Moreover, cities such as Cape Town, Durban, Port Elizabeth and Johannesburg not only contain the highest number of established accommodation focused on the budget tourist market segment, but also form the key nodal structure for budget tourist travels throughout South Africa (Visser, 2004c; Visser and Barker, 2004b).

South Africa's cities are major focal points for domestic health tourism, as well as key nodes in the lucrative international industry of medical tourism (George, 2004; Bass, 2005; Tourism Research and Marketing, 2006). In view of the expanded international recruitment of South African health professionals and of growing shortages of several types of medical personnel in the public health sector, considerable sensitivity surrounds the promotion of health tourism to South Africa which is in competition with Austria, Hungary, India or South East Asian destinations such as Malaysia, Singapore, and Thailand (cf. Henderson,. 2003; Connell, 2006; Tourism Research and Marketing, 2006). The most important and pioneering South African company is Surgeon & Safari, which has been organising medical tourism packages since 1999 with a special focus on cosmetic surgery undertaken in Cape Town or Johannesburg and combined with a luxury visit to the country's game reserves (George, 2004). The therapeutic menu "currently includes dental prosthetics, elective orthopaedic surgery, ophthalmology, and a host of complementary and alternative therapies" (Bass, 2005: 42). More sinister recent additions have appeared with the offerings of elective medical treatment that is available in South Africa, including organ transplants (Bass, 2005).

In terms of the development of all forms of urban tourism, issues of crime and the safety of tourists presents a matter of concern. Not surprisingly then, a further avenue of investigation has been the impact of crime on the South African tourism system. However, given the proportions of crime locally, particularly in South African cities, it is in fact somewhat surprising that only Ferreira (1999) and George (2003) have considered crime as an important impediment to tourism development in South Africa. In both investigations empirical field research was compared with several studies conducted at other international tourist destinations, while incorporating South African Tourism data on foreign visitor's perceptions of tourism facilities in the country. The findings recommended that the tourism industry and law enforcement agencies should co-ordinate efforts to improve crime prevention measures in South African cities, not least its key urban tourist destination—Cape Town. On the whole, the investigations suggested that crime has not as yet affected tourism levels in South Africa in a substantial manner. However, as both the authors point out, it is not whether those tourists that visit South Africa are overly concerned with crime, but rather how many international tourists have avoided South Africa as a destination owing to its reputation for crime, that should be the focus of policy development and research attention.

The Future Development of Urban Tourism in South Africa

It is evident from the foregoing analysis that historically, research into the urban African tourism system has been sparse. However, within South African tourism scholarship the starting point of a potential urban tourism discourse can be discerned, albeit still at an early stage. In part, this neglect reflects the historically limited importance traditionally accorded to the tourism system within the broader South African urban economy, and more generally it is the consequence of the youthfulness of urban tourism studies, both locally and internationally.

In light of the political transition since 1994 South Africa experienced a phase of dramatic tourism growth (Rogerson and Visser, 2004). It is significant that the initial tourism products on offer to both domestic and international tourists were mainly centered on South Africa's well-established game park and reserve systems. These nature-based products were the key tourist offerings in the eyes of both international and domestic tourists' imagination of South Africa. Over the past decade however, the local tourism industry has matured and one aspect of this drive toward greater maturity is diversification of the tourism products on offer (Cornelissen, 2005). Moreover, echoing experiences in the post-industrial North (Law, 1996), South African cities have added tourism development as part of their local and regional economic development strategies. Urban tourism now forms a significant aspect of travel agencies' advertised offerings in all South Africa's metropolitan areas. Nevertheless, it is not only the large urban centers that are benefiting from the expansion in urban tourism. The tourism-led development of a number of small towns such as Bonnievale, Clarens, Greyton and Robertson, in the face of a general decline in the agricultural sector, stands testament to the rise of small town tourism in South Africa.

It must be concluded that urban tourism in South Africa is now an established aspect of the larger national tourism economy. None the less, it is our contention that this emergence is only the starting point of the significant future potential of urban tourism in South Africa. Several recent trends suggest that urban tourism will become of far greater scope, size and importance in future South Africa. For example, one of the most important trends in global tourism has been the rise in short-break trips as evidenced in the reduction in the average length of tourist trips to most destinations worldwide. Owing to the changing nature of leisure time-management, along with more affordable travel options, people are taking several shorter breaks instead of a long holiday. These developments have benefited short-haul, accessible destinations and have contributed to the growth in short breaks. While these short breaks certainly provide opportunities for nature-based, sun and sea holidays, and a range of other leisure types, there is a widespread global trend toward "city-breaks" (Law, 1996).

Of particular importance to the local tourism industry is the emergence of South African cities, especially Cape Town, as a "short-break," city-based tourism destination. Over the past decade, while South Africa has become a popular long haul destination and feature travel programs that include mainly nature and culture-based products, it is significant to observe that Cape Town is increasingly marketed in Europe as an ideal five-day "city-break." For example, the British newspaper *The Mail on Sunday* (2005:106-107), recently ran a two page travel feature showcasing a holiday specifically focused on Cape Town as destination, while totally ignoring South Africa's traditional nature-based tourism products such as the Kruger National Park and KwaZulu-Natal Drakensberg.

In terms of the more traditional long-haul (longer stay) tourist destination markets, the emergence of South African cities as destinations in themselves rather than add-ons to a primarily nature-based travel program, is also being echoed in the international travel press. Illustratively, the London-based African Safari Club currently promote holidays that are exclusively focused on South Africa's main coastal cities, including Cape Town, Durban, East London and Port Elizabeth. The particular prominence of Cape Town as a city destination should perhaps not come as a surprise, as during 2003-2004 the city was voted among the top ten destinations in the BBC's national poll of "places to see before I die."

Looking forward to the 2010 FIFA World Cup, South Africa's hosting of this "mega-event" will offer enormous opportunities for the further development of urban tourism across the country. During March 2006 the location of the ten stadiums that will host matches for the 2010 soccer world cup was announced. These ten stadiums provide the focal points for the group stage of matches that will open the tournament. Of the ten selected venues, as shown on figure 2.2, six of these venues are situated in the country's major metropolitan areas; the remaining four venues (Bloemfontein, Nelspruit, Polokwane, and Rustenburg) represent important secondary cities. The major "showcase" games of the tournament, such as the opening and closing matches, will be scheduled at venues either in Cape Town or Johannesburg. South Africa's major city, Johannesburg, is the only city with two stadium venues selected for the hosting of matches. It is not surprising therefore that the municipal economic development department for Johannesburg recently targeted "sports tourism" as one of its core "priority economic sectors" for municipal support in terms of local economic development programs. International tourism flows linked to sporting attractions, such as the FIFA World Cup, provide considerable potential for Johannesburg, as well as other South African cities, to boost the volume and spend of urban tourists.

With the potential future boost in the importance of urban places in the South African tourism economy, a critical agenda for tourism researchers relates to the impact of tourism on poverty in cities. Over the last five years, one of the most vibrant themes in South African tourism research relates to what has been termed "pro-poor tourism" which is anchored in maximising the potential and increasing the net benefits of tourism development for the poor (Visser and Rogerson, 2004). Currently, South Africa is both a leader and laboratory for the

Figure 2.2
The Location of Stadiums for the Hosting of the FIFA 2010 Soccer World Cup

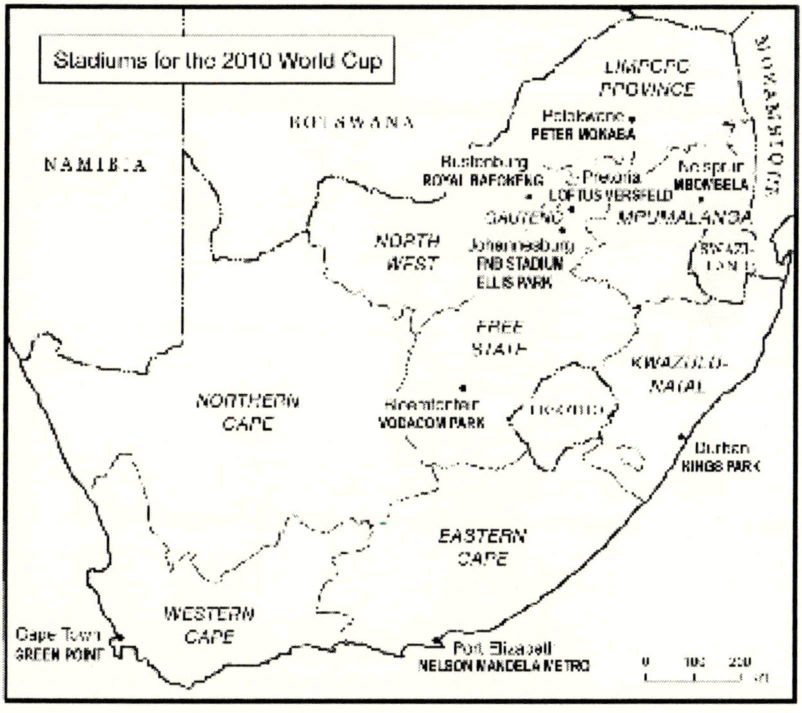

Source: Saturday Star, 18 March, 2006

development of pro-poor tourism and of strengthening local linkages between well-established businesses and local micro-entrepreneurs and small business enterprise (Ashley and Ntshona, 2002; Ashley and Roe, 2002; Mahony and van Zyl, 2002; Spenceley and Seif, 2003; Roe et al., 2004; Ashley and Mitchell, 2005; Mitchell and Ashley, 2006b).

It is significant, however, that the prime focus of existing pro-poor tourism scholarship has been in rural areas and upon maximising local linkages to opportunities related to South Africa's traditional nature-based attractions (Rogerson, 2006). We argue that a shift is needed to embrace more widely the challenges of developing pro-poor tourism in South Africa's urban areas. South African research concerning the urban dimensions of pro-poor tourism and local linkages would represent a potentially important and innovative contribution, out of Africa, toward international scholarship on urban tourism.

Acknowledgements

For financial support in this research project, Chris Rogerson acknowledges assistance from the National Research Foundation, Pretoria Gun 2054064. Thanks are due to Mrs Wendy Job of the Cartographic Unit, University of the Witwatersrand for preparation of the diagrams.

References

Aardklop, 2004: Impakstudie, available at http://www.aardklop.co.za.

Adams, W.M. and Infield, M., 2003: 'Who is on the gorilla's payroll', claims on tourist revenue from a Uganda National Park, *World Development*, 31, 321-343.

Akama, J.S., 1999: The evolution of tourism in Kenya, *The Journal of Sustainable Tourism*, 7, 6-25.

Alford, P., 2002: The European meetings and incentives industry, *Travel and Tourism Analyst*, 4, 1-26.

Ankomah, P.K., 1991: Tourism skilled labour: the case of sub-Saharan Africa, *Annals of Tourism Research*, 18, 433-442.

Ankomah, P.K. and Crompton, D.E., 1990: Unrealised tourism potential: the case of sub-Saharan Africa, *Tourism Management*, 11, 11-28.

Ashley, C., 2005: *Facilitating Pro-poor Tourism with the Private Sector: Lessons Learned from Pro-poor Tourism Pilots in Southern Africa*, ODI Working Paper 257, Overseas Development Institute, London.

Ashley, C. and Mitchell, J., 2005: *Can Tourism Accelerate Pro-Poor Growth in Africa*, Overseas Development Institute, London.

Ashley, C. and Ntshona, Z., 2002: *Transforming Roles but not Reality?: Private Sector and Community Involvement in Tourism and Forestry Development on the Wild Coast*, Overseas Development Institute, London.

Ashley, C. and Roe, D., 2002: Making tourism work for the poor: strategies and challenges in Southern Africa, *Development Southern Africa* 19 (1): 61-82

Ashworth, G.J., 2004: Tourism and the heritage of atrocity: managing the heritage of South African apartheid for entertainment, in T.V. Singh (Ed.), *New Horizons in Tourism: Strange Experiences and Stranger Practices*, CABI Publishing, Wallingford, 95-108.

Bah, A. and Goodwin, H., 2003: *Improving Access for the Informal Sector to Tourism in The Gambia*, Overseas Development Institute, London.

Baker, J.E., 1997: Trophy hunting as a sustainable use of wildlife resources in Southern and Eastern Africa, *Journal of Sustainable Tourism*, 5, 306-321.

Bass, D., 2005: Kidneys for cash and egg safaris—can we allow "transplant tourism" to flourish in South Africa, *South African Medical Journal*, 95 (1), 42-44.

BBQ, 2000a: Meetings, incentives, conferences, exhibitions: MICE, *Black Business Quarterly,* 2(3), 117-122.

BBQ, 2000b: The meetings/initiative/conventions/exhibitions business starts at home: MICE. *Black Business Quarterly*, 2(4), 96-99.

Bennett, A., 2004a: The Cape of Storms, in A. Bennett and R. George (Eds.), *South African Travel and Tourism Cases,* Van Schaik, Pretoria, 39-49.

Bennett, A., 2004b: Robben Island: the conscience of a nation, in A. Bennett and R. George (Eds.), *South African Travel and Tourism Cases*, Van Schaik, Pretoria, 158-167.

Binns, T. and Nel, E., 2002: Tourism as a local development strategy in South Africa, *Geographical Journal*, 168, 235-247.

Bob, U. and Moodley, V., 2000: Socio-economic impact of the sevens rugby event. Unpublished Report commissioned by the Durban Event Corporation.

Bob, U. and Moodley, V., 2001a: Socio-economic impact of the Flying Fifteen event, Unpublished Report commissioned by the Durban Event Corporation.

Bob, U. and Moodley, V., 2001b: Socio-economic impact of the Investec Cycling Tour event, Unpublished Report commissioned by the Durban Event Corporation.

Bob, U. and Moodley, V., 2001c: Socio-economic impact of the Trinations Lifesaving event, Unpublished Report commissioned by the Durban Event Corporation.

Bob, U. and Moodley, V., 2001d: Socio-economic impact of the Comrades Marathon event, Unpublished Report commissioned by the Durban Event Corporation.

Bob, U. and Moodley, V., 2001e: Socio-economic impact of the Bafana Bafana vs Congo match, Unpublished Report commissioned by the Durban Event Corporation.

Bob, U. and Moodley, V., 2001f: Socio-economic impact of the Vodacom Beach Africa festival, Unpublished Report commissioned by the Durban Event Corporation.

Bob, U., Moodley, V. and Pillay, S., 2006: Sustaining marine ecosystems and beach tourism events: case studies from Durban, South Africa, *Western Indian Ocean Journal of Marine Science*, (in press).

Boqo, S.G., 2001: Sustainable tourism in South African townships: a case study of Sobantu township in Pietermaritzburg, Unpublished MA thesis, University ofNatal, Pietermaritzburg.

Bradley, A., Hall, T. and Harrison, M., 2002: Selling cities: promoting new images for meetings tourism, *Cities*, 19, 61-70.

Buffalo City, 2005: Revitalising Buffalo City 2006 Plan, available at http://www.buffalocity.gov.za/municipality/ecdev.stm.

Butler, R.W., 1980: The concept of a tourist area cycle of evolution, *Canadian Geographer*, 24, 5-21.

Chabra, D., Sills, E. and Cubbage, F.W., 2003: The significance of festivals to rural economics: estimating the economic impact of Scottish Highland Games in North Carolina, *Journal of Travel Research,* 41 (May), 421-427.

Christie, I.T. and Crompton, D.E., 2001a: *Tourism in Africa,* World Bank Africa Region Working Paper Series No. 12, Washington, DC.

Christie, I.T. and Crompton, D.E., 2001b: *Tourism in Africa,* World Bank Environmental, Rural and Social Development Findings No 179, Washington, DC.

City of Cape Town, 2001: Economic Development, Tourism and Property Management Achievements 2000/2001, Unpublished Report, City of Cape Town.

Clark, T.N. (Ed.) 2004: *The City as an Entertainment Machine*, Elsevier, Oxford.

ComMark Trust, 2006: Tourism overview, available at www.commark.org

Connell, J., 2006: Medical tourism: sea, sun, sand and surgery, *Tourism Management*, 27, 1093-1100.

Cope, R., 2001: The European MICE market, *Travel and Tourism Analyst*, 3, 81-106.

Cornelissen, S., 2005: Producing and imaging "place" and "people": the political economy of South African international tourist representation, *Review of International Political Economy,* 12, 674-699.

De Beer, G.R.M., Elliffe, S.P., Spangenberg, P.P and Wheeler, B.A., 1997: *The Socio-Economic Benefits of Tourism-Led Development—The Case of the Kenyan Coastline from Malindi to Mombasa,* Spatial Development Initiatives Programme, Development Bank of Southern Africa, Midrand.

Devereux, J. and Chen, L., 1999: Tourism and welfare in sub-Saharan Africa: a theoretical analysis, *Journal of African Economics*, 8, 209-227.

Diagne, A., 2004: Tourism development and its impacts in the Senegalese Petite Cote: a geographical case study in center-periphery relations, *Tourism Geographies*, 6, 472-492.

Dieke, P.U.C., 1991: Policies for tourism development in Kenya, *Annals of Tourism Research*, 18, 269-294.

Dieke, P.U.C., 1992: Cross-national comparison of tourism development: lessons from Kenya and the Gambia, *Journal of Tourism Studies*, 4 (1), 558-561.

Dieke, P.U.C., 1998: Regional tourism in Africa: scope and critical issues, in E. Laws, B. Faulkner and G. Moscardo (Eds.), *Embracing and Managing Change in Tourism: International Case Studies*, Routledge, London, 29-48.

Dieke, P.U.C. (Ed.), 2000: *The Political Economy of Tourism Development in Africa*, Cognizant Communication, New York.

Dieke, P.U.C., 2001: Human resources in tourism development: African perspectives, in D. Harrison (Ed.), *Tourism and The Less Developed World: Issues and Case Studies*, CABI, Wallingford, 61-75.

Dieke, P.U.C., 2003: Tourism in Africa's economic development: policy implications, *Management Decision*, 41 (3), 287-295.

Doswell, R., 2000: African tourism training and education: hits and misses, in P.U.C. Dieke (Ed.), *The Political Economy of Tourism Development in Africa*, Cognizant Communication, New York, 263-287.

Durban Africa, 2001: Corporate Plan 2000-2003: Executive summary, Unpublished Report.

Durban Metro, 2000: Durban beachfront '2010': Project Proposal, Unpublished report, Development and Planning Unit.

Durban Publicity Association, 1937: *Durban: A Sunlit City by the Sea*, South African Railways and Harbours Department, Johannesburg.

Durbarry, R. 2004: Tourism and economic growth: the case of Mauritius, *Tourism Economics*, 10, 389-401.

Dwyer, L. and Mistillis, N., 1999: Development of MICE tourism in Australia: opportunities and challenges, *Journal of Convention and Exhibition Management*, 1(4), 85-99.

East London Publicity Association, 1930: *East London, Where Sea and Sunshine Call – The Home of the Surfboard*, South African Railways and Harbours Department, Johannesburg.

Ekurhuleni Municipality, 2003: *LED policy and strategy implementation framework*, Department of Local Economic Development, Ekurhuleni Metropolitan Municipality.

Farver, J., 1984: Tourism and employment in The Gambia, *Annals of Tourism Research*, 11, 249-265.

Felsentein, D. and Fleischer, A., 2003: Local festivals and tourism promotion: the role of public assistance and visitor expenditure, *Journal of Travel Research*, 41(May), 85-392.

Fennell, D., 2003: Ecotourism in the South African context, *Africa Insight*, 33(1/2), 3-8.

Ferreira, S.L.A., 1999: Crime: a threat to tourism in South Africa, *Tourism Geographies*, 1 (2), 325-342.

Gartner, W.C., 1999: Small scale enterprises in the tourism industry in Ghana's Central region, in D.G. Pearce and R.W. Butler (Eds.), *Contemporary Issues in Tourism Development*, Routledge, London, 158-175.

Gartner, W.C., 2001: Issues of sustainable development in a developing countries context, in S. Wahab and C. Cooper, (Eds.), *Tourism in the Age of Globalisation*, Routledge, London, 306-318.

Gartner, W.C., 2004: Factors affecting small firms in tourism: a Ghanaian perspective, in R. Thomas (Ed.), *Small Firms in Tourism: International Perspectives*, Elsevier, Amsterdam, 35-52.

Gauci, A., Gerosa, V. and Mwalwanda, C., 2005: *Tourism in Africa and the multilateral trading system: challenges and opportunities*, Draft paper for the Economic Commission for Africa, Addis Ababa.

George, R., 2003: Tourist's perceptions of safety and security while visiting Cape Town, *Tourism Management*, 24, 575-587.

George, R., 2004: Medical tourism: Surgeon & Safari, in A. Bennett and R. George (Eds.), *South African Travel and Tourism Cases*, Van Schaik, Pretoria, 238-249.

Gerosa, V., 2003: Pro-poor growth strategies in Africa–Tourism: a viable option for pro poor growth in Africa?, Paper prepared for the Economic Commission for Africa Expert Group Meeting, Kampala, Uganda, 23-24 June.

Gibb, M.W., 2006: The "global" and the "local": a comparative study of development practices in three South African municipalities, Unpublished Ph.D. thesis, Rhodes University, Grahamstown.

Gilfellan, C.T., 1992: The impact of tourism development on the socio-economic, cultural and morphological structures of historical mission stations in the Western Cape: Genadendal, Elim and Wupperthal, Unpublished MA thesis, University of the Western Cape.

Gossling, S., 2001: Tourism, economic transition and ecosystem degradation: interacting processes in a Tanzanian coastal community, *Tourism Geographies*, 3, 430-453.

Gossling, S., Schumacher, K., Morelle, M., Berger, R. and Heck, N., 2004: Tourism and street children in Antananarivo, Madagascar, *Tourism and Hospitality Research*, 5 (2), 131-149.

Gotham, K.F. (Ed.), 2001: *Critical Perspectives on Urban Redevelopment*, Elsevier, Oxford.

Grant, L. and Butler-Adam, J., 1992: Tourism and development needs in the Durban region, in D.M. Smith (Ed.), *The Apartheid City and Beyond*, Routledge, London, 205-215.

Grant, L. and Kohler, K., 1996: Evaluating tourism as a policy tool for urban reconstruction in South Africa: focus on the Point Waterfront Development, Durban, KwaZulu-Natal, in R.J. Davies (Ed.), *Contemporary City Restructuring*, International Geographical Union Commission on Urban Development and Urban Life and Society for Geographers, Cape Town, 531-541.

Grant, L. and Scott, D., 1996: Waterfront development as tools for urban reconstruction and regeneration in South Africa: the planned Point Waterfront Development in Durban, *Urban Forum*, 7 (2), 125-138.

Grant Thornton Kessel Feinstein, 2001: Beach tourism internationally and on South Africa's eastern seaboard. Unpublished Report, Durban.

Gretton, D., 1995: Local economic development in Cape Town, in E. Nel (Ed.), *Local Economic Development in South Africa: A Review of Current Policy and Applied Case Studies*, Friedrich Ebert Stiftung and South African National Civics Organisation, Johannesburg, 14-20.

Hall, C.M. and Muller, D. (Eds.), 2004: *Tourism, Mobility and Second Homes: Between Elite Landscape and Common Ground.* Channelview Publication, London.

Harrison, D., 1994: Tourism and prostitution: sleeping with the enemy, *Tourism Management*, 15, 435-443.

Harrison, D., 1995: Development of tourism in Swaziland, *Annals of Tourism Research*, 11, 135-156.

Heath, E., 2004: Branding and positioning of the Nelson Mandela metro, in A. Bennett and R. George (Eds.), *South African Travel and Tourism Cases*, Van Schaik, Pretoria, 143-157.

Henderson, J.C., 2003: Healthcare tourism in Southeast Asia, *Tourism Review International*, 7 (3/4), 111-121.

Hiller, H.H., 2000: Mega-events, urban boosterism and growth strategies: an analysis of the objectives and legitimations of the Cape Town 2004 Olympic Bid, *International Journal of Urban and Regional Research*, 24, 439-458.

Hoogendoorn, G. and Visser, G. 2004: Second homes and small town (re)development the case of Clarens. *Journal of Family Ecology and Consumer Science*, 32, 105-115.

Hoyle, B.S., 2001: Lamu: waterfront revitalization in an East African port-city, *Cities*, 18, 297-313.

Hughes, H. and Vaughan, A., 2000: The incorporation of historically disadvantaged communities into tourism initiatives in the new South Africa: case studies from KwaZulu-Natal, in M. Robinson, N. Evans, N. Long, R. Sharpley and J. Swarbrooke (Eds.), *Management, Marketing and Political Economy of Travel and Tourism.* Center for Travel and Tourism and Business Education, Sunderland, 241-254.

Ingram, Z., 2004: Cape Town International Convention Center, in A. Bennett and R. George (Eds.), *South African Travel and Tourism Cases*, Van Schaik, Pretoria, 50-58.

Kaplan, L., 2004a: Skills development in tourism: South Africa's tourism-led development strategy. *GeoJournal* 60 (3), 217-227.

Kaplan, L., 2004b: Skills development for tourism: Alexandra township, Johannesburg, *Urban Forum*, 15, 380-398.

Kiambo, W., 2005: The emerging role of tourism in Mozambique's post war reconstruction, *Africa Insight*, 35 (4), 142-148.

Kibicho, W., 2003a: Tourism and the sex trade: roles male sex workers play in Malindi, Kenya, *Tourism Review International*, 7 (3/4), 129-141.

Kibicho, W., 2003b: Community tourism: a lesson from Kenya's coastal region, *Journal of Vacation Marketing*, 10, 33-42.

Kilian, D., Goudie, S. and Dodson, B., 1996: Postmodern f[r]ictions: history, text and identity at the Victoria and Alfred Waterfront, Cape Town, in R.J. Davies (Ed.), *Contemporary City Restructuring*, International Geographical Union Commission on Urban Development and Urban Life and Society for Geographers, Cape Town, 520-530.

Koandu-Agyemang, K., 2001: Structural adjustment programs and the international tourism trade in Ghana, 1983-99: some socio-spatial implications, *Tourism Geographies*, 3, 187-206.

Koch, E. and Massyn, P., 2001: South Africa's domestic tourism sector: promises and problems, in K. Ghimire (Ed.), *The Native Tourist: Mass Tourism within Developing Countries*, Earthscan, London, 142-171.

Kohler, K., 1993: The development and socio-spatial meaning of the "Two-Day" phenomenon: low-income weekend tourism in Durban. Unpublished MA-thesis University of Durban-Westville, Durban.

Kohler, K., 2003: *KwaZulu-Natal's Cruise Tourism Industry*, Tourism KwaZulu-Natal Occasional Paper No. 8, KwaZulu-Natal Provincial Government, Pietermaritzburg.

Ladkin, A., 2002: Research issues and challenges for the convention industry, in K. Weber and K.S. Chon (Eds.), *Convention Tourism: International Research and Industry Perspectives*, Haworth Hospitality Press, Binghamton, 101-118.

Law, C.M., 1996: *Tourism in Major Cities*, International Thomson Business Press, London, 1-22.

Lootvoet, B. and Freund, B., 2004: Local economic development: utopia and reality in South Africa; the example of Durban, KwaZulu-Natal, Paper presented at the Conference on the First Decade of Democracy and Development in South Africa, Durban, 20-22, October.

MacMenamin, V., 1995: Local economic development in the city of Durban, in E.Nel (Ed.), *Local Economic Development in South Africa: A Review of Current Policy and Applied Case Studies*, Friedrich Ebert, Stiftung and South African National Civics Organisation, Johannesburg, 21-23.

Mahony, K. and Van Zyl, J., 2001: *Practical Strategies for Pro-Poor Tourism: Case Studies of Makuleke and Manyeleti Tourism Initiatives*, Overseas Development Institute, London.

Mahony, K. and Van Zyl, J., 2002: The impacts of tourism investment on rural communities: three case studies in South Africa, *Development Southern Africa* 19, 83-104.

Mail on Sunday, 2005: The rise of the exotic short break, 6 February, 106-107.

Mansfield, Y. and Winckler, O., 2004: Options for viable economic development through tourism among the non-oil Arab countries: the Egyptian case, *Tourism Economics*, 10, 365-388.

Marks, R., 1996: Conservation and community: the contradictions and ambiguities of tourism in the Stone Town of Zanzibar, *Habitat International*, 20, 265-278.

Marks, R. and Bezzoli, M., 2001: Palaces of desire: Century City, Cape Town and the ambiguities of development, *Urban Forum*, 12, 27-47.

Mashinini, V., 2003: Tourism policies and strategies in Lesotho: a critical appraisal, *Africa Insight*, 33 (1/2), 87-92.

Massyn, P. and Koch, E., 2004: African game lodges and rural benefit in two Southern African countries, in C.M. Rogerson and G. Visser (Eds.), *Tourism and Development Issues in Contemporary South Africa*, Africa Institute of South Africa, Pretoria, 102-138.

Mbaiwa, J.E., 2003: The socio-economic and environmental impacts of tourism development in the Okavango Delta, north-western Botswana, *Journal of Arid Environments*, 31, 447-467.

Mbaiwa, J.E., 2005: Enclave tourism and its socio-economic impacts in the Okavango Delta, Botswana, *Tourism Management*, 25, 157-172.

Mearns, K., 2003: Community-based tourism: the key to empowering the Sankuyo community in Botswana, *Africa Insight*, 33 (1/2), 29-32.

Mitchell, J. and Ashley, C., 2006a: *Can Tourism Help Reduce Poverty in Africa?*, Briefing Paper, Overseas Development Institute, London.

Mitchell, J. and Ashley, C., 2006b: *Tourism Business and the Local Economy: Increasing Impact through a Linkages Approach,* Briefing Paper, Overseas Development Institute, London.

Moffett, S. and Freund, B., 2004: Elite formation and elite bonding: social structure and development in Durban, *Urban Forum,* 15, 134-161.

Muller, E.E.C., 1971: Tourism versus ground use: a geographical study of the lagoon region George-Knysna, Unpublished M.A. Thesis, Rand Afrikaans University, Johannesburg.

Ndiaye, O.M., 2003: NEPAD and tourism, in World Tourism Organisation, *Tourism, Peace and Sustainable Development*, WTO, Madrid, 55-65.

Nel, E. and Binns, T. 2003: Putting 'developmental local government' into practice: the experience of South Africa's towns and cities, *Urban Forum*, 14, 165-184.

Nel, E. and Binns, T., 2002: Place marketing, tourism promotion and community-based local economic development in post-apartheid South Africa: the case of Still Bay–the "Bay of Sleeping Beauty," *Urban Affairs Review*, 32, 184-208.

Nel, E., Hill, T. and Maharaj, B., 2003: Durban's pursuit of economic development in the post-apartheid era, *Urban Forum*, 14, 223-243.

Nel, R.G. and Strydom, A.J., 2003: The role of image/perception in urban tourism development: a case study of Bloemfontein, *Interim*, 3 (2), 166-185.

NEPAD, 2004a: *AU/NEPAD Tourism Action Plan*, NEPAD Secretariat, Midrand.

NEPAD, 2004b: *NEPAD Tourism action plan*, Discussion document prepared for the 41st meeting of the World Tourism Organisation Commission for Africa, Mahe, Seychelles, 10-13 May 2004.

Nzengy'a D.M., 2004: Temporal trends in ecotourism in the Eastern Highlands of Zimbabwe, *Journal of Ecotourism*, 3 (2), 129-146.

Olivier, J., 1990: The impact of increasing tourism for a tourism destination with specific reference to the business economical implications for the Cape Metropole: a preliminary study, Unpublished M.Com. Thesis, University of Stellenbosch.

Oxford Economic Forecasting, 2003: *The Contribution of Air Transport to Sustainable Development in Africa*, Unpublished Final Report for the Air Transport Action Group, available at www.atag.org.

Parsler, J., 1997: Tourism and the environment in Madagascar, in M. Stabler (Ed.) *Tourism and Sustainability: Principles to Practice*, CAB International, Wallingford, 213-231.

Prinsloo, E., 1991: The segmentation of the tourism market with specific reference to the Cape Peninsula, Unpublished M. Econ. Thesis, University of Stellenbosch.

Ramchander, P., 2004: Soweto set to lure tourists, in A. Bennett and R. George (Eds.), *South African Travel and Tourism Cases*, Van Schaik, Pretoria, 200-210.

Ramutsindela, M., 2004: Glocalisation and nature conservation strategies in 21st century southern Africa, *Tijdschrift voor Economische en Sociale Geografie*, 95, 61-72.

Richman, A. and Lyle, C., 2005: The economic benefits of liberalising regional air transport–a review of global experience, Unpublished Report Prepared for the Com-Mark Trust, Johannesburg.

Roe, D., Goodwin, H. and Ashley, C., 2004: Pro-poor tourism: benefiting the poor, in T.V. Singh (Ed.) *New Horizons in Tourism: Strange Experiences and Stranger Practices*, CABI Publishing, Wallingford, 147-161.

Rogerson, C.M., 1995: International issues, strategies and models, in E. Nel (Ed.), *Local Economic Development in South Africa: A Review of Current Policy and Applied case Studies*, Friedrich Ebert Stiftung and South African National Civics Organisation, Johannesburg, 57-60.

Rogerson, C.M., 2002: Urban tourism in the developing world: the case of Johannesburg, *Development Southern Africa*, 19, 169-190.

Rogerson, C.M., 2003a: The OUZIT Initiative: re-positioning Southern Africa in global tourism, *Africa Insight*, 33 (1/2), 33-35.

Rogerson, C.M., 2003b: Developing Zambia's tourism economy: planning for "the real Africa," *Africa Insight*, 33 (1/2), 48-55.

Rogerson, C.M., 2003c: Tourism and transformation: small enterprise development in South Africa, *Africa Insight*, 33 (1/2), 108-115.

Rogerson, C.M., 2003d: Tourism planning and the economic revitalisation of Johannesburg, *Africa Insight*, 33 (1/2), 130-135.

Rogerson, C.M., 2003e: Changing casino tourism in South Africa, *Africa Insight*, 33 (1/2), 142-149.

Rogerson, C.M., 2004a: Regional tourism in South Africa: a case of "mass tourism of the South," *GeoJournal*, 60, 229-237.

Rogerson, C.M., 2004b: Tourism, small firm development and empowerment in post-apartheid South Africa, in R. Thomas (Ed.), *Small Firms in Tourism: International Perspectives*, Elsevier, Amsterdam, 13-34.

Rogerson, C.M., 2004c: Urban tourism and small tourism enterprise development in Johannesburg: the case of township tourism, *GeoJournal*, 60, 247-257.

Rogerson, C.M., 2004d: Transforming the South African tourism industry: the emerging black-owned bed and breakfast economy, *GeoJournal*, 60, 273-281.

Rogerson, C.M., 2004e: Adventure tourism in Africa: the case of Livingstone, Zambia, *Geography*, 89, 183-188.

Rogerson, C.M., 2004f: Urban tourism and economic regeneration: the example of Johannesburg, in C.M. Rogerson and G. Visser (Eds.), *Tourism and Development Issues in Contemporary South Africa*, Africa Institute of South Africa, Pretoria, 466-487.

Rogerson, C.M., 2005a: The emergence of tourism-led local development: the example of Livingstone, Zambia, *Africa Insight*, 34 (4), 112-120.

Rogerson, C.M., 2005b: Unpacking tourism SMMEs in South Africa: structure, support needs and policy response, *Development Southern Africa*, 22, 623-642.

Rogerson, C.M., 2006: Pro-poor local economic development in South Africa: the role of pro-poor tourism, *Local Environment*, 11, 37-60.

Rogerson, C.M. and Kaplan, L., 2005: Tourism promotion in difficult areas: the experience of Johannesburg inner-city, *Urban Forum*, 16, 214-243.

Rogerson, C.M. and Lisa, Z., 2005: "Sho't left": promoting domestic tourism in South Africa, *Urban Forum*, 16 , 88-111.

Rogerson, C.M. and Nemasetoni, I., 2005: Developing small firms in township tourism: the South African experience, *Urban Forum*, 16, 196-213.

Rogerson, C.M. and Visser, G., 2003: Tourism and development in Africa, *Africa Insight*, 33 (1/2), 2.

Rogerson, C.M. and Visser, G. (Eds.), 2004: *Tourism and Development Issues in Contemporary South Africa*, Africa Institute of South Africa, Pretoria.

Rogerson, C.M. and Visser, G. 2005: Tourism in urban Africa: the South African experience, *Urban Forum*, 16 (2/3), 63-87.

Roos, G.J., 1991: Tourism and economic base for a local government, Unpublished Masters Report in Town and Region Planning, University of Stellenbosch.

Rousseau, G.G., 2004: The Boardwalk Casino and Entertainment World, in A. Bennett and R. George (Eds.), *South African Travel and Tourism Cases*, Van Schaik, Pretoria, 21-27.

Rukato, H., 2003: The high road for development in Africa: NEPAD and tourism, in World Tourism Organisation, *Tourism, Peace and Sustainable Development*, WTO, Madrid, 45-53.

Saayman, M., 1997: South Africa sports tourism, Unpublished SAST Campaign Overview and Status Report, Cape Town.

Saayman, M. and Saayman, A., 2003: Impakstudie, accessible at http://www.aardklop. co.za/Index1.htm.

Shackley, M., 2001: Potential futures for Robben Island: shrine, museum or theme park?, *International Journal of Heritage Studies*, 7, 355-363.

Shaw, G. and Williams, A.M. 2004: *Tourism and Tourism Spaces*, Sage, London.

Sindiga, I., 1995: Wildlife-based tourism in Kenya: land use conflicts and government compensation policies over protected areas, *Journal of Tourism Studies*, 6(2), 15-55.

Sindiga, I., 1996: Domestic tourism in Kenya, *Annals of Tourism Research*, 23, 19-31.

Sindiga, I., 1999: Alternative tourism and sustainable development in Kenya, *Journal of Sustainable Tourism*, 7(2), 108-127.

Sindiga, I., 2000: Tourism development in Kenya, in P.U.C. Dieke (Ed.), *The Political Economy of Tourism Development in Africa*, Cognizant Communication, New York, 129-153.

Sirakaya, E., Teye, V. and Sonmez, S.F., 2001: Examining the sources of differential support for tourism industry in two Ghanaian cities, *Tourism Analysis*, 6 (1), 29-40.

Sirakaya, E., Tye, V. and Sonmez, S.F., 2003: Understanding residents' support for tourism development in the Central Region of Ghana, *Journal of Travel Research and Analysis*, 41, 57-67.

Snowball, J.D. and Antrobus, G.G., 2001: Measuring the value of the arts to society: the importance of the value of externalities for lower income and education groups in South Africa, *South African Journal of Economics*, 69, 752-766.

Snowball, J.D. and Antrobus, G.G., 2002: Valuing the arts: pitfall in economic impact studies of arts festivals, *South African Journal of Economics*, 70, 1297-1319.

Sol Plaatje Municipality, 2004: Galeshewe Urban Renewal Programme, available at http:www.solplaatje.org.za/gurp/main.htm.

Spenceley, A. and Seif, J., 2003: *Strategies, Impacts and Costs of Pro-poor Tourism Approaches in South Africa*. Pro-Poor Tourism Working Paper No. 11, Department For International Development, London.

Steyn, J.N., 1972: The South African tourism industry, geographical patterns and influences on regional development. Unpublished D.Phil. Thesis, University of Stellenbosch.

Strange, C. and Kempa, M., 2003: Shades of dark tourism: Alcatraz and Robben Island, *Annals of Tourism Research*, 30, 386-405.

Strydom, L., 2004: Hail Caesars, in A. Bennett and R. George (Eds.), *South African Travel and Tourism Cases*, Van Schaik, Pretoria, 28-38.

Taylor, V., 1974: Spatial patterns of tourism in the East London area, Unpublished M.A. Thesis, University of Stellenbosch.

The Bay Bulletin, 2003: *The Bay Bulletin*, Nelson Mandela Metropolitan Council, Port Elizabeth.

Thompson, C., O'Hare, G. and Evans, K., 1995: Tourism in the Gambia: problems and proposals, *Tourism Management*, 16, 571-581.

Tourism Research and Marketing, 2006: *Medical Tourism: A Global Analysis*, Association of Tourism and Leisure Education, Arnhem.

Turco, D.M., Swart, K., Bob, U. and Moodley, V., 2003: Socio-economic impacts of sport tourism in the Durban Unicity, South Africa, *Journal of Sport Tourism*, 8 (4), 223-239.

Tyler, D., Guerrier, Y. and Robertson, M. (Eds.), 1998: *Managing Tourism in Cities: Policy, Process and Practice*, John Wiley, Chichester.

Urwin, F.M.J., 1980: The tourism potential of Cape Town and the South Western Cape, Unpublished MBA Research Report, University of Cape Town.

Van As, M., 1990: Urban conservation: a profit for tourism, Unpublished Masters Report of Town and Regional Planning, University of Stellenbosch.

Van der Heever, I.C., 1996: Sport marketing in the Western Cape with specific reference to the implications for tourism. Unpublished M.Com. Thesis, University of Stellenbosch.

Van Huyssteen, M.K.R. and Neethling, J.P.N., 1996: Resort development in the False Bay recreational fringe of Metropolitan Cape Town, in R.J. Davies (Ed.), *Contemporary City Restructuring*, International Geographical Union Commission on Urban Development and Urban Life and Society for Geographers, Cape Town, 501-519.

Van Zyl, C and Botha, C., 2003: Motivational factors of local residents to attend the Aardklop national arts festival, *Events Management*, 8, 213-222.

Van Zyl, I., 2004: Municipality kick-start major tourism developments, *Imiesa* (March), 24-25.

Victurine, R., 2000: Building tourism excellence at the community level: capacity building for community-based entrepreneurs in Uganda, *Journal of Travel Research*, 38, 221-229.

Visser, G., 2002: Gay tourism in South Africa: issues from the Cape Town experience, *Urban Forum*, 13 (1), 85-94.

Visser, G., 2003a: Gay men, tourism and urban space: reflections on Africa's gay capital, *Tourism Geographies*, 5, 168-189.

Visser, G., 2003b: Gay men, leisure space and South African cities: the case of Cape Town, *Geoforum*, 34, 123-137.

Visser, G., 2004a: Second homes and local development: issues arising form Cape Town's De Waterkant, *GeoJournal*, 60, 259-271.

Visser, G., 2004b: Second homes: reflections on an unexplored phenomenon in South Africa, in C.M. Hall and D.K. Müller (Eds.), *Tourism, Mobility and Second Homes: Between Elite Landscape and Common Ground*, Channel View, Clevedon, 196-214.

Visser, G., 2004c: The development impacts of backpacker tourism in South Africa, *GeoJournal*, 60, 283-299.

Visser, G. and Barker, C., 2004a: A geography of British backpacker tourists in South Africa, *Geography*, 89, 226-239.

Visser, G. and Barker, C., 2004b: Backpacker tourism in South Africa: its role in an uneven tourism space economy, *Acta Academica*, 36, 97-143.

Visser, G. and Kotze, N., 2004: Toward a tourism development strategy for the Free State Province, Unpublished Report for the Premier's Economic Advisory Council, Free State Provincial Government, Bloemfontein.

Visser, G. and Rogerson, C.M., 2004: Researching the South African tourism and development nexus, *GeoJournal*, 60, 201-215.

Vos, K. 2004: Starlight Cruises, in A. Bennett and R. George (Eds.), *South African Travel and Tourism Cases*, Van Schaik, Pretoria, 211-220.

Vrahimis, S. and Visser, G., 2006: Institutional impediments to the implementation of the Maloti Drakensberg Transfrontier Conservation Project: the case of the Free State Government. *South African Geographical Journal*, 88, 102-110.

Weaver, D.B., 1999: Magnitude of eco-tourism in Costa Rica and Kenya, *Annals of Tourism Research*, 28, 926-946.

Weber, K. and Ladkin, A., 2003: The convention industry in Australia and the United Kingdom: key issues and competitive forces, *Journal of Travel Research*, 42, 125-132.

Wei, Z. and Go, F., 1999: The meetings, conventions and expositions industry in Beijing: problems and strategies, *Journal of Travel and Tourism Marketing*, 8 (1), 101-110.

Weiler, B. and Hall, C.M. (Eds.), 1992: *Special Interest Tourism*, Belhaven Press, London.
Wesgro, 2003: *Western Cape Tourism Report Card*, Wesgro, Cape Town.
Youngstedt, S., 2003: Tourism in Morocco: opportunities, challenges, threats, *Africa Insight*, 33 (1/2), 61-68.

3

International Tourist Flows and Urban Tourism in South Africa

Christian M. Rogerson and Gustav Visser

Since the demise of apartheid, tourism development has been viewed as a priority in South Africa's broader development frameworks (Rogerson and Visser, 2004). The past decade has witnessed the introduction of significant national government support for tourism development. This has taken the form of a constant stream of new and enabling policy frameworks and strategy documents, as well as institutional support mechanisms, all aiming to expand the tourism system in such a manner so as to be both robust and cognizant of pro-poor developmental outcomes (see RSA, 1996; Department of Environmental Affairs and Tourism [DEAT], 2003, 2004, 2005). During 2006 the important role accorded to tourism in the national economy was re-iterated once again in the release of the *Accelerated and Shared Growth—South Africa* (Asgi-SA) development strategy document (RSA, 2006). Within this new macro-policy framework for South Africa, tourism is profiled, alongside business process outsourcing and bio-fuels development, as an economic sector that requires immediate and unqualified support for expansion from both the public and private sectors (RSA, 2006: 7). Accordingly, from a tourism product supply-side perspective, for a period of at least the next two decades, the South African tourism system can expect to see further rounds of support initiatives and interventions that will assist in the expansion of the tourism system.

The analysis presented in this chapter is based upon new data on international tourism arrivals as released by the Strategic Research Unit of South African Tourism (2005). Until recently, reliable data on international tourism arrivals into South Africa, especially from other parts of Africa, was unavailable. But, in light of the increased policy significance of tourism in the national economy, significant improvements have been made in the quality of data that is regularly collected on the South African tourism system (Rogerson and Visser, 2004).

Conventionally, in a national tourism system, tourism flows are presented in two main categories, viz., international and domestic tourists. In this discussion the international tourist cohort itself is differentiated into the sub-components of "overseas" and "regional" tourists. It is argued that in South Africa the category of "international tourist" flows, as statistical denotation, has to be unpacked with considerable care. As will be demonstrated, the types of impacts that "international tourists" hold for the South African tourism system are closely linked to whether these tourists are sourced from other continents (i.e. overseas), or are regional tourists from Africa. This distinction between different types of international tourists is made here in the context of increased research interest and growth of "intra-regional" tourism in the developing world (Ghimire, 1997, 2001a, 2001b; Rogerson, 2004). For Africa the significance of regional tourism is confirmed by a recent report produced by the Economic Commission for Africa that highlights "the greatest numbers of international tourists are intraregional" (Gerosa, 2003: 49). The stimulation of regional tourism as well as regional cooperation for tourism was one of the recommendations to be "vigorously explored" during the conference on tourism, peace and sustainable development in Africa held in Luanda, Angola during May 2003 in the framework of the thirty-ninth meeting of the World Tourism Organisation's Commission for Africa (World Tourism Organization, 2003a).

In reflecting upon both the current state of international tourist flows to South Africa, as well as future increases in tourist numbers, it is necessary to consider that tourist flows and associated tourist development have particular geographies. These geographies, we argue, illustrate the central role of urban places in the local tourism system. Against this backdrop, the aim in this chapter is to unpack and make visible the current contours of international tourist flows to South Africa and more particularly to consider the spatial distribution of tourists while visiting the country. Two key and distinctive sub-streams of international tourist arrivals are discussed; the overseas or long-haul international traveler and the regional or African tourist.

The African Context

Within the international league tables of international tourist flows, the continent of Africa ranks poorly relative to the mature tourism destinations of North America, Europe, as well as East Asia and the Pacific Rim (Sharpley, 2002: 17). Overall, Europe is the world's number one tourist destination region, with the European Union countries hosting 414 million tourists in 2002; that is, 54.6 percent of the global market, and earning 52 percent of global tourism receipts. Africa, with only 29 million international tourist arrivals in 2003 (World Tourism Organization, 2003b) accounts for no more than four percent of global foreign tourist receipts, albeit high rates of growth have been recorded over the past decade, admittedly from a low base (Mitchell and Ashley, 2006).

The WTO (2003b) reports that international tourist arrivals are concentrated in a relatively small number of destinations in the north-west and south-east of the African continent. North Africa, with 35 percent of the regional total and southern Africa, with 30 percent, attracted two-thirds of the total tourist arrivals, while East Africa received 23 percent, leaving only ten percent for West Africa and three percent for Central Africa. In terms of league tables of tourism receipts, the leading destinations for African tourism are shown to be Egypt and South Africa (Mitchell and Ashley, 2006) (figure 3.1). Between the four main African regions, the industry was worth an estimated $73.6 billion in 2005, and supported approximately 10.6 million employment opportunities (WTTO, 2005). According to the WTTO, Africa will see the sector grow fourfold between 1995 and 2020. Of that growth in tourist arrivals, southern Africa, and South Africa in particular, is expected to take the lion's share of the increase in visitor numbers. According to WTTO (2005) forecasts, the southern African region by 2020 may well experience over 300 percent growth in tourist arrivals.

In South Africa since the early-1990s there has been already an explosive growth in tourism that was boosted both by the peaceful democratic transition and, in the immediate post-apartheid years, by the "Mandela factor." In 2004 South Africa received the largest number of foreign visitors in its history of recording tourist arrivals. The nearly seven million international tourist arrivals, of which more than two million came from other continents, ranked South Africa thirty-second in terms of international tourist receipts (South African Tourism, 2005). Between 1990-2004, South Africa's share of world tourism arrivals quadrupled, a phenomenon that has fundamentally changed the face of the country's tourism industry. The recent numbers of foreign tourist arrivals is a far cry from the 50,000 overseas visitors South Africa received in the mid-1980s, at the height of apartheid and of international sanctions against the country (Rogerson and Visser, 2004). The objective in the following section is to provide a comparative analysis of the importance of urban centers for the two distinctive segments of South Africa's international tourism economy, *viz.*, the long-haul or "overseas" tourist on the one hand and of 'regional tourists' or visitors from Africa on the other.

Overseas and Regional Tourist Flows to South Africa

Figure 3.2 shows the sources of foreign visitor arrivals to South Africa for 2004. It is revealed that the African market generates the largest volume of international tourist arrivals for South Africa (Saayman and Saayman, 2003; Rogerson, 2004). Of a total of 6.67 million international tourist arrivals during 2004, 70 percent were intra-regional tourists from the African continent (South African Tourism, 2005). Moreover, by far the largest category of arrivals from Africa, originated from neighboring states of South Africa with most visitors

Figure 3.1
Africa: International Tourism Receipts, 2003

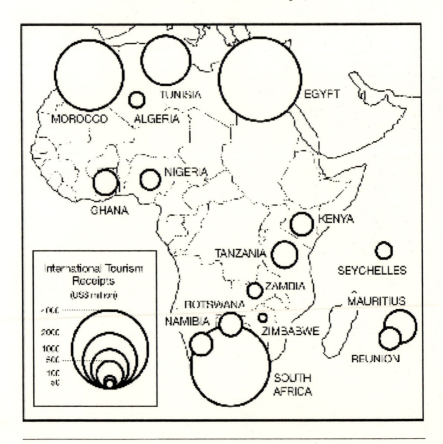

Source: WTO, 2005

traveling to the country by land as opposed to air transportation. Indeed, of the 4.5 million arrivals from the countries of the Southern African Development Community (SADC), only approximately 204,000 or less than 4.5 percent were air travelers.

Figure 3.3 highlights the leading twenty country sources of foreign arrivals in South Africa for 2004. It is immediately evident that the leading four source markets, and six of the leading eight source markets, are South Africa's neighboring states. The largest single tourist generating countries are Lesotho (1.47 million visitors) followed by Swaziland (849 179) and Botswana (802 715). The key overseas source markets are the United Kingdom (456 368), Germany (245 452) and the U.S. (208 159). The importance of land travel as a means of access for regional tourists to South Africa once again is underlined. Collectively the

Figure 3.2

The geography of international visitor arrivals in South Africa, 2004

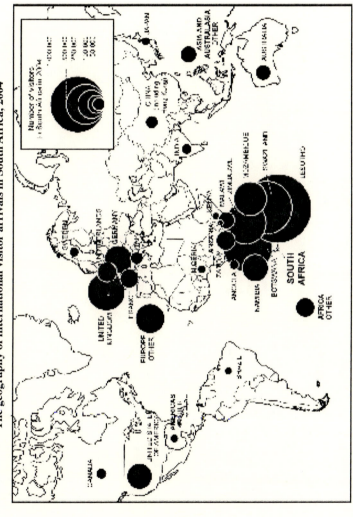

Source: South African Tourism, 2005

Figure 3.3
Leading country sources of foreign arrivals in South Africa

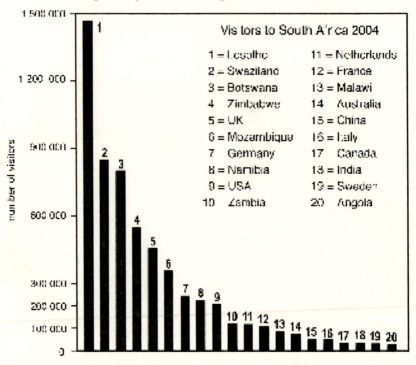

Source: South African Tourism 2005

number of SADC regional air travelers to South Africa from Africa (approx. 200,000) is considerably less than the total for arrivals from the United Kingdom (approx. 450,000), which ranks as fifth overall in terms of its significance as a source market as indexed by numbers of visitor arrivals.

It is evident from table 3.1 that South Africa's two groups of "international" tourists visit the country for very different reasons. In terms of the overseas market it is clear that North American and European tourists visit South Africa mainly for holiday or leisure purposes. By contrast, most regional African tourists are visiting South Africa for purposes of business as opposed to leisure. In terms of individual African source markets, the highest share of business tourists occurs in the cases of Mozambique (71.5 percent), Tanzania (63.9 percent), and Botswana (60 percent) (South African Tourism, 2005). The highest shares of travelers from African sources for purposes of leisure are recorded respectively for Angola (38.5 percent) and Zimbabwe (38.2). Not surprisingly, in the category of VFR (Visiting Friends, and Relatives) tourism the highest shares were recorded in the case of the surrounding countries of Namibia (47

Table 3.1
Purpose of Visit to South Africa, by Geographical Origin (by Percent)

	Holiday	Business	VFR	Other
Angola	38.5	31.4	16.1	14.1
Australia	50.0	18.7	25.6	5.6
Botswana	11.5	60.0	19.8	8.7
Canada	55.9	21.1	16.9	6.2
China	43.7	41.4	11.0	4.0
France	73.7	17.3	6.5	2.5
Germany	76.7	13.0	6.8	2.5
India	22.7	59.3	15.1	2.9
Italy	72.7	19.8	5.7	1.8
Lesotho	9.7	35.1	40.8	14.4
Malawi	27.8	47.2	16.5	8.4
Mozambique	17.7	71.5	7.6	3.1
Namibia	25.9	20.1	47.0	7.1
Netherlands	78.1	10.3	8.1	3.5
Swaziland	22.7	42.1	25.5	9.6
Sweden	63.1	25.4	7.4	4.1
United Kingdom	70.1	10.8	16.7	2.4
U.S.	61.0	21.9	10.3	6.9
Zambia	25.9	41.9	20.7	11.4
Zimbabwe	38.2	26.9	28.4	6.6

Source: South African Tourism 2005

percent), Lesotho (40.8 percent), Zimbabwe (28.4 percent), and Swaziland (25.5 percent).

Table 3.2 provides some insight into the manner in which international tourists organize their visits to South Africa. On the whole, travelers to South Africa prefer independent travel options. By far the majority of African tourists to South Africa fall into the category of independent travelers rather than tourists visiting the country on some form of inclusive tourism (where airfare, accommodation, internal travel, and food are included) or package (airfare and accommodation)

Table 3.2
Organization of Visit to South Africa, by Geographical Origin (by percent)

	Fully Inclusive Package	Full Package	Package	Independent
Angola	9.8	1.0	1.3	87.8
Australia	17.8	3.8	2.2	70.9
Botswana	23.4	1.8	5.6	69.2
Canada	27.1	2.7	2.6	71.4
China	38.2	9.1	5.4	48.8
France	44.9	4.4	3.0	44.5
Germany	27.9	4.9	3.3	62.3
India	23.0	4.8	1.3	60.9
Italy	39.0	6.3	7.5	50.1
Lesotho	25.6	5.3	1.7	67.4
Malawi	13.4	4.9	1.7	79.9
Mozambique	7.1	5.2	3.2	84.5
Namibia	13.2	5.6	1.5	79.7
Netherlands	28.3	3.4	5.2	58.5
Swaziland	27.8	2.5	1.7	67.9
Sweden	23.5	3.4	5.5	62.3
United Kingdom	22.1	3.8	2.6	72.2
U.S.	28.9	4.2	2.5	65.9
Zambia	10.8	3.2	3.4	82.6
Zimbabwe	12.8	5.4	1.6	80.1

Source: South African Tourism 2005

arrangement. Typically, in the case of visitors from South Africa's neighboring states, at least three-quarters of the visitors are independent travelers. Overall, the market segment that makes the greatest use of all-inclusive packages is comprised of tourists from France, China and Japan, probably reflecting the fact that these markets are still not that highly familiar with South Africa. Moreover, the English-language barrier is a factor that prevents many of these tourists from engaging in independent travel, particularly when considering the far higher levels of independent travel among tourists from English-speaking countries such as Australia, the U.K. and the U.S.

During 2004 the total direct spend in South Africa by foreign tourists was R 47.8 billion. The total spend by African visitors was estimated at R 25 billion which represents roughly a 53 percent share. This figure should be compared to the nearly R13 billion contributed to the tourist economy from visitors sourced from Europe and R 2.5 billion from the Americas. In terms of individual source markets the ten most significant in ranked order were Mozambique (R 7548 million), the United Kingdom (R 5819 million), Zimbabwe (R 4516 million), Lesotho (R 3967 million), Swaziland (R 3304 million), Germany (R 2338 mil-

Table 3.3
**Average Spend (Rand) in South Africa, by Geographical Origin
and Purpose of Visit**

	All Categories of Tourist	Holiday	Business	VFR	Other
Angola	10 860	11 909	10 743	7 788	11 982
Australia	8 955	7 573	15 914	7 434	4 085
Botswana	4 103	3 822	5 118	1 773	2 436
Canada	8 479	8 738	9 982	7 239	......
China	10 993	10 993	8 582	5 049	......
France	6 811	6 888	6 398	6 873	7 626
Germany	9 626	9 787	8 104	7 222	14 903
India	12 185	6 783	16 423	5 205	......
Italy	7 601	7 636	8 127	7 340	......
Lesotho	2 697	3 745	3 766	1 346	2 320
Malawi	8 126	7 775	8 781	5 731	9 854
Mozambique	21 213	12 435	25 949	14 076	8 413
Namibia	8 425	8 383	15 653	4 464	8 986
Netherlands	8 999	8 356	12 405	7 706	12 466
Swaziland	3 891	5 255	3 936	2 791	3 166
Sweden	9 197	10 775	6 617	8 079	......
United Kingdom	12 751	9 242	33 376	10 625	16 033
U.S.	8 687	9 124	8 403	7 345	7 943
Zambia	7 606	8 380	8 313	3 093	10 666
Zimbabwe	8 196	9 118	7 977	6 615	10 313

Source: South African Tourism 2005

lion), Namibia (R 1903 million), U.S. (R 1808 million) and the Netherlands (R 1087 million).

Despite the higher average spend patterns of overseas, as opposed to, African travelers, African countries still represent five of the most significant source markets as measured by direct spend (table 3.3). Significant variations are observed in terms of average direct spend with the average tourist arrival from Europe or North America spending between R 9,000–R 13,000 per visit as compared to between R 2,000 (Lesotho) and more than R 21,000 (Mozambique) for certain source markets of African travelers. Of note is that some of the highest average spend figures within South Africa are recorded by travelers coming from African destinations. Indeed, according to the latest available South African Tourism data, the average tourist arrival in South Africa from Angola, Kenya, and Mozambique was spending more in the country than even visitors from the U.S. or Europe. Overall, however, of the African visitors as a whole there was relatively little difference in the average spend of business as opposed to holiday visitors, for example from Lesotho the average business visitor spent R 3,766 as opposed to R 3,745 for leisure travelers. Major differences emerge, however, on data concerning average spend per day with the average per day by business travelers considerably more than for leisure travelers. Again, taking the case of Lesotho visitors, those in South Africa as holiday tourists are recorded as spending R 801 per day as compared to R 1,682 per day for those on business travel (figure 3.6). A consistent finding is that the lowest expenditure both in total and on a per diem basis are recorded by VFR tourists. For example, a Lesotho VFR tourist spends only R 376 a day.

Table 3.4 provides important insight into the geographic distribution of international tourism in South Africa. It is shown that the spatial distribution of the overseas and regional visitor cohorts differ significantly. Indeed, it is apparent that two distinctive geographies can be recognized. The mass of overseas tourists, who are mainly leisure seekers, demonstrate a high level of visitation to the Western Cape and secondarily to Gauteng, a finding which is mostly explained by Johannesburg's function as international gateway for the country. In an exhaustive study of overseas tourists travel itineraries Cornelissen (2005), unpacked the travel geography of this tourist cohort. It was shown that the typical tour for overseas tourist of South Africa ran from Johannesburg in the north of the country to Cape Town in the south. An example of such a tour was presented as follows (Cornelissen, 2005):

> Tourists typically arrive at Johannesburg airport where they visit Gauteng's urban attractions such the Apartheid Museum, Gold Reef City, Sandton City, and the Union Buildings in Pretoria. The tour than goes on to Mpumalanga (private game reserves) and the Kruger National Park, Swaziland, to Zululand and then Durban. In the city of Durban the beach and a cultural village are visited. From there tourists go on to the city of Port Elizabeth, which is the gateway to the Garden Route where the resort towns of Knysna and Plettenberg Bay are the main focal points. From there the town of Oudtshoorn is visited with the tour moving on to Cape Town. In Cape

Table 3.4

Geographic Visitation by Province of Tourists by Country of Origin

	Gauteng	Western Cape	Eastern Cape	KwaZulu-Natal	Mpumalanga	Limpopo	North West	Northern Cape	Free State
Angola	87.7	14.8	0.4	6.5	2.1	2.5	7.5	0.5	2.1
Australia	62.0	55.7	16.7	28.3	26.2	7.7	12.7	3.6	5.5
Botswana	45.6	2.0	0.6	9.7	1.2	2.2	42.7	1.6	1.5
Canada	57.6	50.5	20.4	35.4	29.7	7.6	9.1	1.0	9.1
China	79.2	58.8	7.5	13.5	6.1	0.9	30.2	2.5	3.4
France	57.3	61.1	21.4	43.5	46.2	5.2	8.4	4.6	7.1
Germany	41.8	69.2	33.3	34.4	36.0	4.5	7.1	6.4	7.5
India	73.3	34.4	7.1	34.3	8.6	0.8	20.0	0.0	2.6
Italy	49.3	67.3	32.4	36.0	41.6	3.3	9.0	2.8	2.2
Lesotho	42.1	5.6	2.6	13.5	1.8	2.1	2.5	0.9	34.1
Malawi	79.0	10.0	4.7	21.4	16.0	5.5	7.5	3.6	9.2
Mozambique	53.0	3.2	0.4	7.8	53.1	1.5	0.4	0.0	0.4
Namibia	14.4	68.7	2.9	2.7	0.6	0.1	0.3	28.1	1.2
Netherlands	52.1	59.0	28.0	32.6	45.9	9.8	10.3	6.0	12.2
Swaziland	53.3	1.6	0.9	35.0	16.9	2.9	1.2	0.5	2.1
Sweden	40.4	67.4	34.8	25.3	27.6	3.5	5.5	2.5	6.7
United Kingdom	39.8	66.4	22.6	28.2	25.1	2.9	8.8	2.2	2.6
USA	54.5	53.9	15.0	23.6	27.9	6.6	10.4	3.1	5.0
Zambia	76.6	4.2	4.2	21.9	8.9	6.2	6.2	4.7	10.7
Zimbabwe	74.1	6.0	6.0	20.6	5.8	34.8	1.4	0.4	2.4

Source: South African Tourism 2005

Town key attractions include the V&A Waterfront, Cape Town Central Business District which comprise visits to the Castle of Good Hope, the Company Gardens, St Georges Mall and the Cathedral, the Cape Town Parliamentary Buildings, and more generally different examples of Cape Dutch architecture (based on Cornelissen, 2005: 687-688).

From this typical itinerary what is of critical importance is that while the South African tourism system is portrayed as consisting largely of nature-based tourism products, urban places, and hence urban tourism, play a very important role in the visits of overseas tourists to South Africa.

Table 3.4 shows also the distribution of visitors from African sources in terms of provinces that were visited. The picture emerges that Gauteng, South Africa's economic heartland, which includes the cities of Johannesburg and Pretoria, is the most significant focus for regional tourism, followed by Western Cape and KwaZulu-Natal provinces. In terms of the dominance of business travel, the core focus on Gauteng and in particular Africa's economic hub Johannesburg, is not surprising. In addition, because of their geographical proximity for land travelers, respectively Mpumalanga emerges as a significant focus for visitors from Swaziland and Mozambique, Free State for visitors from Lesotho, Northern Cape for visitors from Namibia, and North West for visitors from Botswana.

Overall, it is evident that Gauteng province secures the greatest benefit from international tourist flows in South Africa, with the regional tourist component particularly strongly represented. The importance of regional tourists for the retail economy of Gauteng has been recognized by economic development planners. It has been estimated that African shopping tourists spend annually R 10 billion in the province, across accommodation, transport, food, and other services (Sebelebele, 2005). The land cross-border trade accounts for approximately 750,000 tourists spending more than R 6 billion each year (ComMark Trust, 2006). A major element in Johannesburg's retail tourism economy is comprised of small-scale and informal cross-border traders drawn from surrounding countries, most importantly from Mozambique and Zimbabwe (Peberdy, 2000a, 2000b; Peberdy and Crush, 2001; Peberdy and Rogerson, 2003). It is estimated that the retail tourism sector has experienced a consistent annual growth of about 3 percent and stands out as having significant further potential for expansion (ComMark Trust, 2006).

Finally, table 3.5 gives a breakdown of international tourists' use of different types of accommodation during their visit to South Africa. Several major trends can be highlighted from these statistics. First, it is important to note that family and relatives (VFR) represent the single largest source of accommodation provision for international visitors to South Africa. The majority of tourists coming from countries in Africa use this form of accommodation. As more than 70 percent of South Africa's population reside in urban places, this means that these VFR tourists would be based in cities and towns, at least for part of their visit to South Africa. Secondly, in the "overseas" category, the use of this form of tourist accommodation is also prevalent. The high levels of VFR tourism among Australian and British tourists can be linked to the South African diaspora concentrated in those countries, visiting family and relatives in South Africa. Again the geographic spread of the country's population suggests that these tourists also would find their way to the country's major urban concentrations, particularly Johannesburg, Cape Town, Durban, and Port Elizabeth. Third, it is noticeable that hotel accommodation is frequently used as tourist accommodation across all sectors of the international market. Nevertheless, it is clear that tourists from China and Japan prefer hotel accommodation to all other forms of accommodation. With regard to the rest of the international market, hotel accommodation is primarily preferred by Continental European visitors. Hotel accommodation is also the secondary preference amongst tourists from African countries. What is significant here is that hotel accommodation in South Africa is primarily located in the urban context, and not resort enclaves in rural areas. Perhaps most surprising is the relatively low usage of guesthouses and bed-and-breakfast accommodation. However, the support patterns of these

Table 3.5
Accommodation Usage of Tourists by Country of Origin (by percent)

	Hotels	Guest Houses	B & Bs	Game Lodges	Self-Catering	VFR	Backpacker Hostels	Camping & Caravans
Angola	28.6	16.3	0.2	1.1	12.0	38.9	1.0	0.0
Australia	17.0	3.7	2.9	7.4	4.5	43.6	11.6	1.9
Botswana	23.8	12.4	7.4	5.1	5.7	37.9	0.1	1.4
Canada	22.6	6.6	5.5	7.0	8.6	38.5	5.0	0.4
China	24.8	4.7	1.0	3.3	8.6	27.4	3.4	0.1
France	32.9	5.8	6.3	10.5	9.6	16.4	6.6	2.1
Germany	21.8	8.7	10.2	7.2	12.3	15.8	9.9	3.2
India	26.8	5.5	0.8	1.6	19.8	27.5	4.8	0.4
Italy	34.3	6.7	9.3	11.4	4.1	22.2	4.0	3.5
Lesotho	18.9	5.9	2.7	0.2	1.3	62.8	1.0	0.5
Malawi	49.6	7.8	3.0	2.3	2.4	28.8	0.4	2.8
Mozambique	62.5	3.0	2.9	2.2	0.4	27.3	0.7	0.1
Namibia	8.5	5.7	4.9	0.9	2.0	61.3	6.4	0.4
Netherlands	20.9	14.5	8.6	7.2	3.5	21.5	9.8	6.0
Swaziland	22.7	7.8	6.3	3.4	2.4	51.8	0.9	1.7
Sweden	25.1	9.0	10.0	5.6	11.4	20.3	8.8	2.8
United Kingdom	22.9	6.4	4.8	6.1	7.8	32.4	10.0	1.8
U.S.	27.3	4.3	5.8	11.6	7.4	25.2	6.6	4.5
Zambia	32.0	9.6	4.0	2.9	2.5	43.6	1.3	2.0
Zimbabwe	9.2	3.7	5.2	2.8	11.4	60.5	1.3	2.1

Source: South African Tourism 2005

accommodation types are probably more a reflection of the share of such establishments in the accommodation supply, than of a demand on the part of these tourists. Finally, it is also clear that holiday resorts, camping sites and backpacker hostels do not feature prominently in terms of current international visitors' accommodation demands.

In terms of the length of stay of international tourists in South Africa, a significant difference is disclosed between regional and overseas tourist markets (South African Tourism, 2005). The most common length of stay in South Africa by regional, African tourists was between two to four days with the highest figure recorded by travelers coming from Nigeria and Tanzania (six days), followed by Kenya, Namibia, Zambia (four days), and Zimbabwe (three days). The short stay and more frequent visits to South Africa by regional tourists should be compared to the much longer length of stay of overseas visitors from Europe (fourteen days) or the U.S. (seven days). One factor that underpins this pattern is the existence of differential entry conditions for nationals from different countries (Cassim and Jackson, 2003). Under present conditions citizens of most of the industrialized North are typically issued visitor permits on arrival in South Africa for stays of up to ninety days according to return/onward flight dates. By contrast, nationals of the neighboring Southern African Development Community countries do not enjoy the same treatment and are granted visas not exceeding thirty days. In addition, the nature of the visit also plays a significant role, with the regional visitors conducing business (often shopping) visits, while the overseas visitor is mainly pursuing leisure activities. The common denominator for both the overseas and regional tourist is visits to South Africa's urban places.

Conclusion—Implications for Urban Tourism

South Africa is emerging as a tourist destination in which urban places have become a focal point in the country's overall tourism product portfolio. Although a range of nature-based tourist products play a vital role in the destination choices of overseas tourists to South Africa, it has been demonstrated that the country's urban centers are also central places for these tourists' experiences of South Africa. For the regional tourists to South Africa—visiting for purposes of business with the largest number for cross-border retail tourism—urban areas are the core foci with Johannesburg the shopping Mecca. The different profiles, characteristics and geographies of these two segments of international tourism arrivals in South Africa have been revealed.

An understanding of the differences between overseas and regional tourists is of special significance in terms of policy and planning for urban tourism. The role played by urban places in terms of the tourism experience of overseas and regional African visitors must be appreciated as somewhat different. For the overseas tourist, cities comprise an important element within their general experience of South Africa, which includes the country's rural-focused nature-based tourism products. The urban focus provides a number of opportunities where overseas tourists can make a valuable contribution to broadening the visitor-base of various urban attractions that might, if only dependent upon domestic or regional tourists, not otherwise be viable. In this respect a range of urban tourism-led local economic development initiatives seen in the North, can be explored in the South African urban context, not least in cities such as Cape Town, Durban, Johannesburg, and Pretoria. Importantly, the further development of a host of cultural, heritage and creative tourism industry segments can significantly enhance the urban experience for the overseas tourist market as well as maximizing opportunities for urban tourism.

For regional tourists, the cities are the major attractions, for purposes of business, shopping and increasingly also for health tourism. The policy issues around regional tourism are of particular significance for the major cities of Gauteng and in particular for Johannesburg. With national policy recognition of the importance of African tourists for the country, South African Tourism has launched a number of aggressive marketing campaigns, particularly in Kenya and Nigeria, designed to increase the flow of high spending African visitors. In addition, the City of Johannesburg has acknowledged the need to further maximize the developmental opportunities offered by the city's attractions for cross-border shoppers. It has been shown that inefficiencies in long distance transportation, visa access difficulties, and issues around safety and security are constraints that are costing Johannesburg tourism millions of Rand annually in lost revenue from regional tourists (Com-Mark Trust, 2006). Addressing these issues through targeted policy interventions would lead to an increase in arrivals as well as an increased spend through longer stays of visitors. In addition, they would open up opportunities for the marketing and development of tourism products outside of Gauteng in order to achieve a greater geographical spread of the impact of regional tourists.

Acknowledgements

For financial support in this research project, Chris Rogerson acknowledges assistance from the National Research Foundation, Pretoria Gun 2054064. Thanks are due to Mrs. Wendy Job of the Cartographic Unit, University of the Witwatersrand for preparation of the diagrams.

References

Cassim R. and Jackson W. (Eds.), 2003: International trade in services and sustainable development: the case of energy and tourism in South Africa. Unpublished report Trade Knowledge Network.

ComMark Trust, 2006: Tourism overview, available at www.commark.org

Cornelissen, S., 2005: Producing and imaging 'place' and 'people': the political economy of South African international tourist representation, *Review of International Political Economy,* 12, 674-699.

DEAT, 2003: *Tourism: 10 Year Review*, DEAT, Pretoria

DEAT 2004: *10 Year Review*, DEAT, Pretoria.

DEAT, 2005: *Tourism BEE Charter and Scorecard*, DEAT, Pretoria.

Gerosa, V., 2003: Pro-poor growth strategies in Africa—Tourism: a viable option for pro poor growth in Africa?, Paper prepared for the Economic Commission for Africa Expert Group Meeting, Kampala, Uganda, 23-24 June.

Ghimire, K.B., 1997: *Emerging Mass Tourism in the South: Reflections on the Social Opportunities and Costs of National and Regional Tourism in Developing Countries,* Discussion Paper No. 85, United Nations Research Institute for Social Development, Geneva.

Ghimire, K.B., 2001a: Regional tourism and South-South economic cooperation. *Geographical Journal,* 167, 99-110.

Ghimire, K.B., 2001b: The growth of national and regional tourism in developing countries: an overview, in K.Ghimire (Ed.), *The Native Tourist: Mass Tourism Within Developing Countries,* Earthscan, London, 1-29.

Mitchell, J. and Ashley, C., 2006: *Can Tourism Help Reduce Poverty in Africa?*, Briefing Paper, Overseas Development Institute, London.

Peberdy, S., 2000a: Mobile entrepreneurship: informal cross-border trade and street trade in South Africa, *Development Southern Africa,* 17, 201-219.

Peberdy, S., 2000b: Border crossings: small entrepreneurs and informal sector cross-border trade between South Africa and Mozambique, *Tijdschrift voor Economische en Sociale Geografie*, 91,361-378.

Peberdy, S. and Crush, J., 2001: Invisible trade, invisible travelers: the Maputo Corridor Spatial Development Initiative and cross-border trading. *South African Geographical Journal* 83, 115-123.

Peberdy, S. and Rogerson, C.M., 2003: South Africa: creating new spaces?, in R. Kloosterman and J. Rath (Eds.), *Immigrant Entrepreneurs: Venturing Abroad in the Age of Globalization,* Berg, Oxford, 79-99.

Republic of South Africa, 1996: *White Paper on the Development and Promotion of Tourism in South Africa*, Department of Environmental Affairs and Tourism, Pretoria.

Republic of South Africa, 2006: Media briefing by Deputy-President Phumzile Mlambo-Ngcuka, Background document, A catalyst for accelerated and shared growth—South Aifrca (ASGISA), available at http://www.info.gov.za/speeches/briefings/asgiback-ground.pdf

Rogerson, C.M., 2004: Regional tourism in South Africa: a case of "mass tourism of the South," *GeoJournal*, 60, 229-237.

Rogerson, C.M. and Visser, G. (Eds.), 2004: *Tourism and Development Issues in Contemporary South Africa*, Africa Institute of South Africa, Pretoria.

Saaayman, M. and Saayman, A., 2003: International and African tourism markets for South Africa: an economic analysis, *Africa Insight*, 33 (1/2), 93-98.

Sebelebele, M., 2005: SA opens doors to African tourists, available at www.eprop.co.za

Sharpley, R., 2002: Tourism: a vehicle for development?, in R. Sharpley, and D. J. Telfer (Eds.), *Tourism and Development: Concepts and Issues*, Channel View, Clevedon, 11-34.

South African Tourism, 2005: *2004 Annual Tourism Report*, South African Tourism Strategic Research Unit, South African Tourism, Johannesburg.

World Tourism Organization, 2003a: Introduction, in WTO (Ed.), *Tourism, Peace and Sustainable Development for Africa*, WTO, Madrid, 1-2.

World Tourism Organisation, 2003b: *WTO in Africa, 1996-2003*, World Tourism Organization, Madrid.

WTTO, 2005: *South Africa Travel and Tourism: Sowing the Seeds of Growth*, World Travel and Tourism Council, London.

4

"Sho't Left": Changing Domestic Tourism in South Africa

Christian M. Rogerson and Zoleka Lisa

Domestic tourism has been a largely under-researched aspect of tourism economies in the developing world (Ghimire, 1997). At present, the bulk of international tourism scholarship relates to the socio-economic impacts of tourism in the North or concerns the patterns, preferences and impacts of Northern tourists in the South. As Ghimire (2001: 2) observes, we have "little knowledge" of Southern tourists. This neglect of domestic tourism is partly a result of the emphasis accorded by national governments and policy makers to the foreign exchange earnings derived from international tourism flows (Scheyvens, 2002). In addition, the lack of research is linked also to the fact that domestic tourism is more difficult to track than international tourism as it occurs within the country of residence and thus does not involve the crossing of international borders at entry points into a country where visitors are counted (Keyser, 2002). The weakness of knowledge concerning domestic tourism explains why "existing policies in developing countries tend to concentrate overwhelmingly on expanding international tourist arrivals from the North" and to ignore the potential benefits from the emergence of domestic tourism (Ghimire, 2001: 1). Reinforcing the policy bias towards promoting international tourism is the higher expenditures of such tourists as compared to local domestic tourists, which sometimes are categorized as "budget tourists" (Scheyvens, 2002). Until recently, therefore, the unglamorous phenomenon of mass domestic tourism has "been virtually ignored" by government planners and policy makers alike in developing countries (Scheyvens, 2002: 143).

During the past decade, tourism researchers and policy makers belatedly have begun to address this research lacuna and to discover the phenomenon of domestic tourism (Ghimire, 2001). Behind this recent upturn of research interest in domestic tourism are factors that underpin a well-established stream of research in developed countries, namely the demonstrated sheer size, rapid growth and economic value of domestic tourism, its ability to provide a base load to counter the seasonality of international tourist arrivals, and its developmental role especially for peripheral or marginal regions (see Archer, 1978; Jaakson, 1986; Becker, 1987; Seaton and Palmer, 1987; Hall and Kearsley, 2001; Turner and Reisinger, 2001; Carr, 2002; Seckelman, 2002; Williams and Hall, 2002). Across Africa domestic tourism remains a "neglected" research theme (Thomas, 2005: 38). Post-apartheid South Africa offers a case study of particular interest for tourism researchers as the country represents one of the few examples in the developing world, where national government explicitly has acknowledged the importance of domestic tourism, undertaken regular domestic tourism surveys and introduced a growth strategy targeted to expand the domestic tourism economy (South African Tourism, 2003; DEAT, 2004).

This chapter seeks to contribute to the limited body of recent research on domestic tourism in South Africa (Futter and Wood, 1997; Koch and Massyn, 2001; Saayman et al., 2001; Rule et al., 2004; Visser, 2004a, 2004b) and more widely to the international scholarship on "Southern tourists" or domestic tourism in the developing world. The specific focus of attention is upon documenting a set of recently launched initiatives to catalyse the expansion of domestic tourism. Current South African government efforts at promotion are targeted particularly at the country's black population, who under apartheid legislation were largely excluded from "mainstream hotels, beaches, and other tourist facilities" (Rwigema, 1996: 647). As black South Africans were not permitted to be accommodated in the same hotels as whites or even visit the same beaches as whites, domestic tourism under apartheid geared itself to serve the interests of the privileged white minority population (Mkhize, 1994). From the mid-1980s, however, the racially discriminatory restrictions placed on black participation in the tourism economy as well as on freedom of movement were eased gradually, posing a suite of new challenges for the South African domestic tourism industry (Ferrario, 1986; Mkhize, 1994; Koch and Massyn, 2001). Since the 1994 democratic transition a progressive trend has been for national government policy initiatives in South Africa to incorporate the formerly excluded black communities as part of wider strategies for promoting the domestic tourism economy as a whole. At the heart of current marketing for domestic tourism is the "Sho't Left" campaign. This term derives from everyday taxi language and refers to a situation when a passenger wants to jump off the taxi immediately or just around the corner, that is, "Sho't Left driva."

Organizationally, the chapter falls into three uneven sections of discussion and analysis. First, the international debates and scholarship on domestic tourism in the developing world are reviewed as background or context. Second, attention turns to examine the features of the domestic tourism industry in South Africa. In section three, the focus narrows to explore the range of new initiatives that seek to counter the former exclusion of black South Africans from the domestic tourism economy and instead to encourage their participation via promotional campaigns under the umbrella of "Opening the doors of travel to all" South Africans (Atos KPMG Consulting, 2004; South African Tourism, 2004a).

Domestic Tourism in the Developing World

It is significant that the World Tourism Organisation (WTO) predicts that during the next twenty years the expansion of domestic tourism will be especially strong in several developing countries, most notably in China, India, Thailand, Brazil, and Mexico. These countries illustrate that domestic mass tourism constitutes already a large and growing industry in several parts of the developing world (Ghimire, 2001: 11). Moreover, based upon projections of the WTO, the number of domestic tourists could soon be "as much as ten times greater than current international tourist arrivals" (Ghimire, 2001: 2). This observation serves to underline the imperative for "policy makers to look at what benefits such forms of tourism could bring to their countries" (Scheyvens, 2002: 6) and for conducting more serious research and analysis of domestic tourism across the developing world.

Overall, the motivations and patterns of domestic tourism represent the major theme of scholarship. The existing research on domestic tourism in the South discloses certain parallels to the European experience in terms of factors that underpin the growth of this form of leisure tourism, viz., an increased capacity and desire to travel among the urban population, improvements in national economies and living standards, rapid developments in transport, increased workers' benefits, and expansion in the supply of tourist facilities as well as marketing for domestic tourism (Ghimire, 1997, 2001). Scheyvens (2002: 144) argues that the contemporary enormous growth of domestic tourism across the South is linked to the emergence of "an exalted middle-class with reasonable affluence and disposable income and a strong desire for travel." The rise of domestic leisure travel by affluent urban strata that can afford traveling for leisure is well-exemplified by the tourism experiences sought out by the well-off, educated members of the new upper- and middle-classes in urban Thailand (Peleggi, 1996). The expansion of second home development as holiday accommodation is a new influence on flows of domestic tourism in several countries, including Thailand and South Africa (Peleggi, 1996; Kaosa-ard et al., 2001; Visser, 2004a, 2004b). Leisure tourism involving visits to national parks and areas of scenic beauty has been examined also in Saudi Arabia (Paul and Rimmawi, 1992; Bogari et al., 2003), Sri Lanka (Buultjens et al., 2005) and India (Rao and Suresh, 2001).

In particular, the greatest expansion of touristic consumerism has occurred in urban China (Wang, 2004). Here, the accompanying rapid growth of domestic leisure markets, has been "clearly sizeable" (Ghimire and Li, 2001: 104). The post-1990s forces that have galvanized the enormous expansion of domestic tourism in China, the patterns and current tends of tourism flows, local impacts and national government policy initiatives towards the domestic tourism industry are several of the key threads in an expanding corpus of research and writings concerning the country's burgeoning domestic tourism economy (Wen, 1997; Xu, 1998, 1999; Wu et al., 2000; Cai et al., 2001; Ghimire and Li, 2001; Aramberri and Xie, 2003; Gu and Liu, 2004; Xie and Xu, 2004; Walsh and Swain, 2004; Wang, 2004; Wang and Qu, 2004).

Across many countries of the South—Brazil, India, Mexico, or Thailand as well as China—leisure travel is no longer, however, the exclusive prerogative of the upper classes as it extends beyond the growing middle-class to include the participation in leisure travel of the lower middle-classes. In Kenya, domestic tourism is encouraged through offering reduced accommodation rates for local people (Sindiga, 1996). Within socialist economies the special role of the state in encouraging a form of "socially driven" domestic tourism has been documented for Cuba (Hinch, 1990). In developing market economies the usual motivations for domestic travel encompass pilgrimages, visiting friends and relatives, business travel, health tourism, as well as leisure travel (see Wen, 1997; Bleasdale and Kwarko, 2000; Barkin, 2001; Diegues, 2001; Kaosa-ard et al., 2001; Rao and Suresh 2001; Rule et al., 2004). In several research case studies, the significance of religious pilgrimages and festivals as an early force for driving the growth of domestic tourism industries is highlighted variously for India (Rao and Suresh, 2001; Singh, 2004), Mexico (Barkin, 2001), Brazil (Diegues, 2001), Cambodia (Winter, 2004), Thailand (Peleggi, 1996; Kaosa-ard et al., 2001), Sri Lanka (Buultjens et al., 2005) and Saudi Arabia (Bogari et al., 2003), Visiting friends and relatives (VFR) is shown to constitute an important base load for the domestic tourism economies of several other developing countries including Mexico (Barkin, 2001), Ghana (Bleasdale and Kwarko, 2000), Indonesia (Gunawan, 1996), Nigeria (Mustapha, 2001) and South Africa (Koch and Massyn, 2001; Rule et al., 2004). The segments of business travel and health tourism as an element of domestic tourism are, perhaps, the least well-documented, with the exception of some findings concerning business tourism in Korea (Pyo and Koo, 2002) and health tourism in India (Dhall, 2004).

In addition to researching the factors and motivations for escalating domestic tourism in the South, a significant body of work defines the differences between the preferred destinations of domestic and international travelers. Spatial differences in the travel patterns of domestic and international tourists have been recorded in a number of studies including research on Thailand (Kaosa-ard et al., 2001) and Nigeria (Awaritefe, 2004a, 2004b). In South Africa, different preferences have also been recorded between local and international visitors (Kepe, 2001). Such observed differences have important ramifications for destination planning, marketing, and human resource planning as well as critical implications for local economic development impacts (Gunawan, 1996; Singh, 1997; Xu, 1998, 1999; Buultjens et al., 2005). Indeed, one policy benefit of promoting domestic tourism for national governments is that of contributing to redressing spatial inequalities because domestic tourism often can be encouraged in geographical regions that are not favored by international tourists (Kaosa-ard et al., 2001; Saayman et al., 2001).

Lastly, the role of public policies on domestic tourism has come under scrutiny. Of the experience of the South, Scheyvens (2002: 155) writes: "countries searching for an alternative, less exploitative form of tourism development than that dominated by the interests of multinational capital, should encourage domestic tourism as this results in greater community ownership of tourism enterprises." Nevertheless, the general trend across the developing world has been to affirm a situation of systematic bias in national tourism development planning towards international as opposed to regional or domestic tourism (Ghimire, 1997). For example, tourism policy in Nigeria and Rwanda (Mazimhaka, 2006), as is true of so much of Africa, gives priority to planning for international tourism (Mustapha, 2001). Indeed, even though Kenya has introduced measures to support domestic tourism (Sindiga, 1996) and Zambia has acknowledged its potential role in tourism planning (Rogerson, 2003), government resources in both countries are still channelled primarily towards the promotion of international tourism.

Ghimire (2001: 24) asserts that "most developing countries are just beginning to develop measures" concerning the phenomenon of domestic tourism. Among the first policy initiatives are those that have been introduced by national governments and agencies in Brazil (Diegues, 2001) and Kenya (Sindiga, 1996; Kassilly, 2003) in order to foster the expansion of local domestic tourism. In several other countries, the focus is on support for an improved infrastructure for developing domestic tourism (Ghimire and Li, 2001; Kaosa-ard et al., 2001; Rao and Suresh, 2001). In certain regions of the world, such as Southeast Asia, greater policy attention to domestic tourism has been precipitated by falling numbers of international arrivals (Mena et al., 2004).

It is against the backcloth of an emergent policy interest in the South around issues of domestic tourism that an examination of the South African experience is of considerable relevance. South Africa offers an advanced example of the implementation of new policy initiatives that are designed to support an expanded domestic travel market within overall national tourism development planning.

Domestic Tourism in South Africa

The rise of domestic tourism in South Africa occurred during the early years of the twentieth century. The important segment of leisure tourism was promoted most strongly by marketing initiatives that were launched by South African Railways in order to encourage travel from the interior to coastal destinations. The emergent tourism economy witnessed the development of several seaside resorts along the coast, the most important around Durban, the Natal

South Coast, East London, and the Garden Route from Port Elizabeth to Cape Town (Ferrario, 1978). The establishment of Kruger National Park in 1926 and improved access through a national road-building program further extended the focus of leisure tourism to include visits to South Africa's wildlife attractions. By the time of the 1948 general elections, which ushered in the apartheid era, the domestic tourism industry of South Africa already was established and at localities such as Durban or East London, domestic tourism assumed a significant role within the local economy.

The Developing Market for Domestic Tourism

Throughout the apartheid period (1948-1994) South Africa experienced the further growth and consolidation of the domestic tourism economy. Traditionally, as Koch and Massyn (2001: 144) argue, the domestic tourism market was dominated by the white population that enjoyed the highest levels of wealth, mobility and access to amenities. Indeed, from 1948-1970 there was virtually no black tourism market as a direct consequence of apartheid legislation which meant that South Africa's black population was "not welcome" at tourist facilities (Silva and Butler-Adam, 1988; Mkhize, 1994). Nevertheless, based upon the largely white market, as compared to other developing world countries, by the 1980s South Africa exhibited one of the strongest and most well-developed domestic tourism economies (Ghimire, 2001; Koch and Massyn, 2001). Indeed, given the collapse of international tourism arrivals in apartheid South Africa at the height of the country's pariah status, during the 1980s domestic tourism became the foundation of the South African national tourism economy (Rogerson and Visser, 2004).

Since the ending of apartheid and with the democratic transition in 1994, South Africa has recorded a further burst of growth in domestic tourism flows. By the late 1990s, however, scholars were observing "the rapidly changing nature of the domestic holiday market" in South Africa (Futter and Wood, 1997: 58). The dismantling of apartheid restrictions (beginning in the 1980s) and of access to tourist attractions and amenities as well as growing prosperity among some sections of the black (African), colored and Indian communities precipitated an expansion of black domestic tourism from the 1980s (Ferrario, 1986, 1988). As an outcome of government initiatives taken in the post-apartheid period, including strategies of black economic empowerment, affirmative action, employment equity and preferential procurement, the 1990s has seen the growth of a substantial black middle-class as well as increased levels of mobility amongst the black population as a whole (Southall, 2004a, 2004b). A recent analysis of the share of "affluent households" by racial group disclosed major shifts in the composition of the affluent in South Africa (Burger et al., 2003). It was shown that by 1995 of the national proportion of households that would be classed as affluent, blacks constituted 22 percent and whites 71 percent. By 2000 the black share of affluent households had advanced to 36 percent and the white share of affluence had shrunk to 53 percent (Burger et al., 2003).

One indicator of the rising market for domestic travel among the growing black middle-class is the increased attention given to tourism in the leading newspapers that have a predominantly black readership. An analysis was conducted of *The Sowetan* newspaper, which is published in Johannesburg, of recent content about tourism and travel advertisements. The findings disclosed for the period 1994-2000 that whilst the actual number of tourism advertisements was low, a definite increase was evident by the end of the decade (Lisa, 2004). Moreover, post-2000 it can be observed that the size of advertising increases considerably from small blocks to market an individual beachfront hotel in Durban to entire pages that are taken out by major tourism companies including South African Airways, Southern Sun and Sun International. Most advertising was seasonal and occurred at the peak Easter and Christmas/New Year holidays and, in terms of destinations, Durban was the major focus. Marketing offered family get-aways, self-catering options and affordable hotels in areas with close access to the beach. Another important advertising focus was upon the promotion of musical events and especially jazz festivals around the country, the most significant being the North Sea Jazz Festival that has been held annually in Cape Town since 2000 (Lisa, 2004).

In addition to tourism advertisements *The Sowetan* also carried a number of features that broadly were aimed at increasing knowledge of its readers about travel and tourism. During school terms, the "Let's go traveling" segment explored different places in the country and engaged young learners on a range of issues on tourism. A regular feature running in the newspaper for several years is "Holiday Destinations" which contains promotional material, specials on travel rates, information and articles of interest to readers. Indicative of the different emphases of marketing to black tourists is that articles on traveling to Limpopo province typically profiled "the Rain Queen" Modjadji, the local history and culture, offered advice for disabled travelers as well as giving tips on keeping homes safe whilst away on holiday (Lisa, 2004).

Current Profile of Domestic Tourism

Over the last fifteen years, several domestic national tourism surveys have been undertaken in South Africa. The first survey was undertaken in 1992 and thereafter in 1994, 1997, 2001 (Rule et al., 2001) and, most recently, in 2003. Although the initial surveys were based on small sample populations, they served importantly to highlight the lack of government focus upon domestic tourism and that promotional advertising by SATOUR was primarily targeted at the international traveler. Taken together, the three domestic tourism surveys conducted during the 1990s showed that South Africa's domestic tourism economy evidenced a surge in levels of activity and a change in its composition and nature "which is attributable to the ending of apartheid and an increase in prosperity among 'previously disadvantaged' social groups" (Koch and Massyn, 2001: 144).

A profile of the current status of domestic tourism in South Africa, its structure and key features can be drawn from the findings of the two most recent, and largest national surveys which were undertaken during 2001 (Rule et al., 2001) and 2003 (South African Tourism, 2004b). The most recent data for 2003 suggests that the domestic tourism market is currently valued at R 23.4 billion as compared to the R 53 billion earned from international tourism (Atos KPMG Consulting, 2006). The total number of domestic trips, 49.3 million far exceeds the numbers of international arrivals in South Africa, a total of 6.5 million for 2003 (South African Tourism, 2004b). Figure 4.1 provides a breakdown of the domestic market in terms of five major categories of travel. It discloses that visits to friends and relatives (VFR tourism) is the largest element, as indexed by numbers of trips (Rule et al., 2001, 2004). Although nearly two-thirds of all trips are for VFR purposes, figure 4.1 shows that holiday travel, which accounts for 16 percent of trips, accounts for 44 percent of expenditure. Business travel is the third most important segment of domestic tourism as indexed by share of value. Travel for religious or medical reasons represent the smallest

Figure 4.1
Key Segments of Domestic Tourism in South Africa

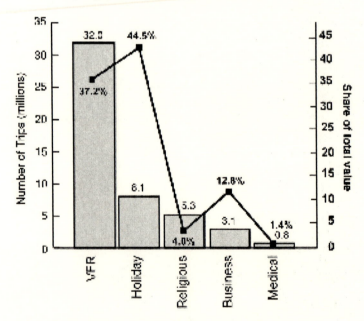

Source: DEAT, 2004

segments of the South African domestic tourism industry. Surveys of the activities undertaken by domestic tourists reveal the significance of social activities (in terms of visits to friends and relatives) followed by shopping for personal use, nightlife (theater, restaurants) and water-based activities (South African Tourism, 2004b).

Figure 4.2 and 4.3 show that there exists considerable spatial unevenness in the flows of domestic tourism. Overall, it is recorded that 60 percent of all domestic travel occurs intra-provincially and only 40 percent of domestic tourism involves inter-provincial travel. The most significant inter-provincial flow occurs from Gauteng to the coastal areas of KwaZulu-Natal and to the game parks of Mpumulanga. Three key provinces—KwaZulu-Natal, Gauteng, and the Eastern Cape—account for 64 percent of total trips in terms of source of travel and correspondingly receive 60 percent of the domestic tourism trade. It is evident that the seasonality, length of visit, and geography of domestic tourism flows in South Africa exhibit marked differences to that of international tourism. In terms of seasonality, domestic travel exhibits a more pronounced seasonal pattern than international tourism, albeit both markets peak in the months of December and April, which correspond to school holiday periods (figure 4.4). In terms of length of visit, the most common length of domestic trip is between

Figure 4.2
Volume of Domestic Tourism Trips by Province

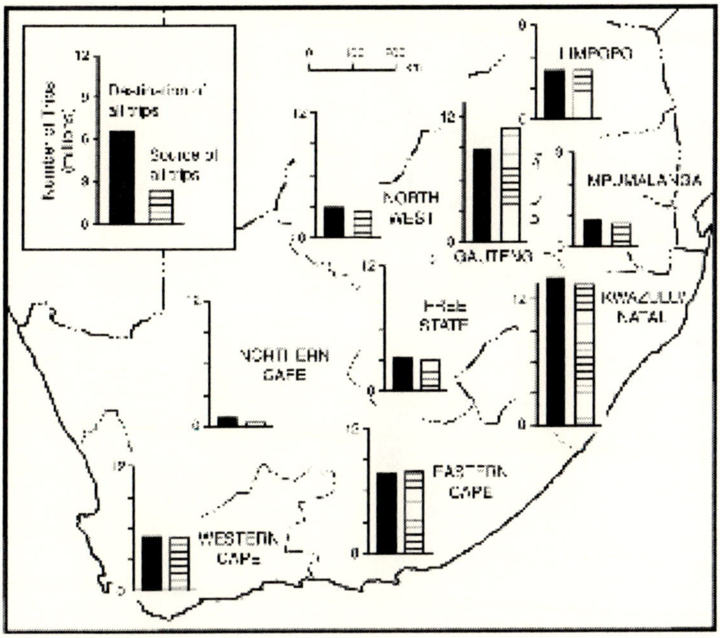

Source: South African Tourism, 2004b

Figure 4.3
Domestic Tourism Direct Spend by Province

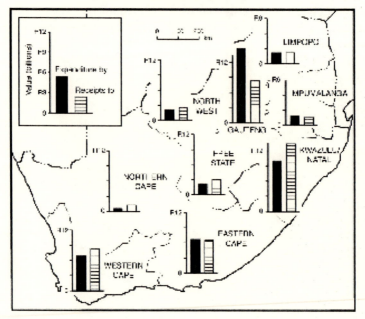

Source: South African Tourism, 2004b

Figure 4.4
Seasonality of Domestic Tourism in South Africa

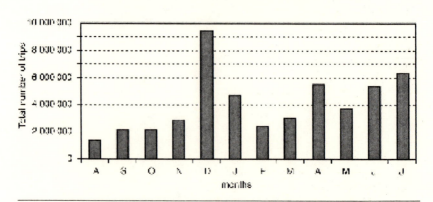

Source: South African Tourism, 2004b

two to three days as compared to the seventeen-day average for international travelers. Finally, in terms of spatial flows, it is significant that the Western Cape province, which includes most of the top ten ranked attractions for international tourists, is placed only fourth among South Africa's nine provinces in the league of domestic tourism. One factor behind the poor domestic tourism performance of Western Cape is a strong perception of the region, or more especially of Cape Town, as "unfriendly to blacks" (Viljoen, 2003).

Based upon the spatial information provided in the 2001 national domestic tourism survey (Rule et al., 2001), a more detailed profile of the geography of domestic tourism can be constructed. On figure 4.5 is shown the volume of estimated trips and leading destinations for different segments of domestic tourism, namely VFR tourism, leisure tourism, business tourism, religious tourism, and health tourism. Figure 4.5 shows that geographical variations clearly exist in the patterns of domestic tourism and local impacts of the different segments of domestic tourism. The VFR market is spread approximately in proportion to patterns of the national population and is dominated by flows to the major inland urban centers of Johannesburg, Pretoria and Ekurhuleni as well as to Cape Town and Durban. The Wild Coast, Transkei and Ciskei areas, which are major foci of out-migration, also emerge as leading destinations for VFR travel. The coastal areas of KwaZulu-Natal, the Western Cape and Garden Route, are dominant in terms of leisure travel; of note, however, is that Johannesburg ranks as the third most important individual node for leisure travel. Business travel is heavily concentrated upon South Africa's major commercial centers, with the dominance of Johannesburg strongly evident. Domestic health tourism focuses also mainly upon the major urban centers where the quality and availability of health care is greatest; once again Johannesburg is the leading node. Finally, the spatial flows of religious tourism in South Africa are the most distinctive of all the five segments of domestic tourism. Figure 4.5 discloses the overwhelming dominance of the Polokwane region, where Moria is the national focus of the annual gathering of members of the Zionist Christian Church. Above all, what is most striking about figure 4.5 is the massive dominance of South Africa's urban areas—and especially of the country's major cities—in terms of capturing the benefits of domestic tourism flows.

On Table 4.1 is disclosed the estimated racial profile of the five segments of domestic tourism which is based upon numbers of trips rather than value of spending. This table highlights the dramatically changing complexion of the domestic tourism economy in post-apartheid South Africa. It is evident that black tourists are numerically the most important element in all segments of domestic tourism, with the exception of business travel in which whites are estimated to be of equal significance.

Overall, table 4.1 reveals the widened base for South Africa's domestic tourism economy, as since the democratic transition the traditional dominance of whites has been reduced in importance, albeit with the exceptions of business

Figure 4.5
The Geography of Domestic Tourism in South Africa: Most Important
Destinations for Key Segments

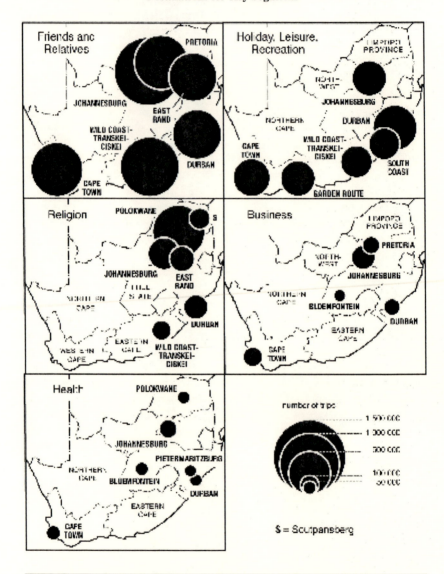

Source: Data from Rule et al.., 2001

and leisure travel. Nevertheless, as compared to their proportionate share of national population in 2000, whites (11.5 percent) are over-represented in all segments of domestic tourism, except religious travel, and blacks (77.4 percent) are over-represented only in religious travel and marginally so in the category of VFR tourism. Of significance in terms of future growth is that, relative to their share of the national population, blacks are considerably under-represented in terms of their participation in the domestic leisure and business tourism economy. Historically, a key factor in the underdevelopment of black tourism was the lack of knowledge amongst new travelers about tourism, the lack of marketing of tourism products to black consumers, and absence of information about how to travel. The results of domestic tourism surveys showed that advertising primarily targeted at international travelers or the sophisticated white consumer market provided a clear rationale for a radical change in direction and focus concerning tourism marketing in South Africa (Lisa, 2004).

New Initiatives for Promoting Domestic Tourism

In 2004 the national Department of Environmental Affairs and Tourism together with South African Tourism launched the country's first national domestic tourism growth strategy (DEAT, 2004). The strategy is anchored upon a recognition of the untapped value and potential for growth of the country's domestic tourism economy and of potential wider benefits for international tourism of growing the domestic tourism economy. It is acknowledged that in addition to reducing the exposure of tourism to the vagaries of international tourism, support of the tourist industry by local residents "can realise improved quality in product and services, maintenance of occupancy levels and ultimately the confidence of international visitors" (Atos KPMG Consulting, 2004: 2). Thus, the competitiveness of the industry to attract foreign arrivals could be enhanced by ensuring that the domestic market has a wide experience of the South African tourism product, not least because of the critical finding that lo-

Table 4.1
Racial Composition of Different Segments of
Domestic Tourism in South Africa, 2001

	Whites	Blacks	Colored	Indian
VFR	12	78	7	3
Leisure	34	50	11	5
Business	42	42	10	6
Religion	2	93	4	1
Health	13	74	8	5

Source: Based upon data extracted from Rule et al., 2001

cal "word of mouth" is a vital source of information for most foreign tourists visiting South Africa (Monitor, 2004). Among the critical perceived advantages of promoting domestic tourism in South Africa are "to combat issues of seasonality, geographic spread and limited trip expenditure" (DEAT, 2004: 3). The three core objectives of enhanced GDP growth, job creation and transformation of the tourism industry were to be addressed by a set of strategies designed to increase expenditure (more trips, length of stay, average trip expenditure), reduce seasonality (encourage year round travel), improve the spatial spread of tourism (more destinations and activities) and increase volumes of domestic tourism flows (DEAT, 2004: 4).

National government initiatives are committed to grow the South African domestic tourism market as a whole. Ministerial pronouncements are made that "Tourism belongs to all South Africans, black, white, colored and Indian, men and women. Let's all take a journey of discovery in our own country. We are declaring the doors of travel and tourism open to all" (Van Schalkwyk, 2004). Nevertheless, in the new marketing campaigns for domestic tourism and statements of government ministers, the priority is for expanding black domestic tourism. As indicated earlier, black South Africans are currently under-represented in certain key segments of domestic tourism, most importantly in leisure travel.

The special focus accorded to promoting tourism among black communities was evident in the keynote speech of the Minister of Environment and Tourism at the launch of South Africa's domestic marketing campaign on 11 June 2004. The speech represented the beginning of the Sho't Left campaign that was described as "the sustainable future of tourism in South Africa" (Van Schalkwyk, 2004). It is highly symbolic that the venue for the speech and campaign launch was at a cultural center in Langa, one of Cape Town's black townships. The opening statement made by the Minister provides the clearest indication of the changing directions of marketing and the stress to be given to supporting the growth of black leisure tourism:

> For too long tourism in South Africa has been something that most South African communities have heard about, but had little first-hand experience of. We must open up tourism to all. We want South Africans to travel more in our own country.

> For too long our people have seen streams of visitors from Europe, America, Asia and other African countries flocking to our shores and experiencing, in a few days, more of our incredible country than most South Africans see in a lifetime. International tourists are important but local tourists are just as important.

> We want the people of communities like Langa to know the beauty of a Kruger Park sunset. We want the people of Chatsworth to experience the waters of our Atlantic coast. We want families from Alexandra to walk the paths of ancient elephants in the Knysna forests. We want the children of Klerksdorp, Bonteheuvel and Prieska to join our Dutch, German and English visitors exploring the mysteries of the Cango Caves, the Drakensberg, and the Great Karoo. We want South Africans to travel more in our own country (Van Schalkwyk, 2004).

Figure 4.6
Promotional Material for the Sho't Left Marketing Campaign

Overall, the Sho't Left campaign is an integral part of South African Tourism's domestic marketing and geared to stimulate a travel culture amongst communities which, as a result of apartheid, had been previously marginalised, if not excluded entirely, from participation in tourism (figure 4.6). Essentially, the campaign promotes the message that there are so many affordable places just "around the corner" in South Africa to take a holiday for a day, or weekend or longer. A major emphasis in the campaign is to improve information access and of consumer knowledge of how to travel. The campaign was widely advertised on television, billboards and local radio stations. A key element of Sho't Left was the broadcasting for thirteen weeks (June-September 2004) on a national channel (SABC2) of the South African Broadcasting Corporation of a short feature just before the Sesotho News, which profiled the attractions of a variety of places across South Africa's nine provinces. Television competitions offering contestants the opportunity to win a holiday getaway attracted over 150,000 entrants. Likewise, similar promotions continue to be held on popular radio stations, for example by encouraging listeners to call in with their Sho't Left story.

An interesting innovation was the establishment by South African Tourism of a dedicated website in order to provide information and travel tips to assist first time travelers (South African Tourism, 2005). Under the section on FAQs (Frequently Asked Questions), the first time holiday-maker is given simple and clear information to answer the following questions:

- How much does it cost to take a holiday?
- Do I need a passport or ID book to travel to other provinces?
- How long in advance do I need to book a holiday?
- Can I take my own food and drink to the accommodation I book?
- If I am staying at the hotel—do I have to eat all my meals there as well?
- Do children have to pay full price?
- When do I have to pay for my holiday?
- What clothes do I need to take on holiday?
- How do I book a holiday?

Under travel tips, five key steps are set forth to taking a holiday:

1. Decide on the destination
2. Know your holiday budget
3. Make the Booking
4. Paying for your holiday
5. Take a Sho't Left

Several tips and step-by-step guides also are offered to new travelers. For example, it is cautioned that, in terms of budgeting: "Hotel breakfasts are fantastic, but can be expensive. To save—either eat a great breakfast and skip lunch or head to a coffee shop or take-away restaurant in town for a smaller affordable breakfast" (South African Tourism, 2005).

In support of the Sho't Left campaign South African Tourism in partnership with several large tour operators has put together information and packages on a range of different "affordable" holiday options, including city breaks, bush retreats, coastal getaways, and so on. The most prominent product innovation was the special Sho't Left package tour running from Johannesburg to Durban on the "Fun Bus." This reasonably priced package, which included bus travel, two nights accommodation at a beachfront Holiday Inn hotel and vouchers for entry into casinos and cinemas in Durban, was targeted at making travel affordable and focussed on those people who previously were not able to participate as tourists. The success of this venture has contributed to a growing number of other marketing initiatives led by leading private sector tour operators (Holiday Tours, Thompsons Tours, South African Airways, Avis) to promote other special holiday breaks and packages designed to be affordable to new travelers. In interviews conducted with leading South African tour operators it was disclosed that rather than develop and market specific products for the "black domestic market" per se, the emphasis was upon lowering price margins in order to offer competitive and affordable leisure packages to local consumers (Lisa, 2004).

Further assisting the opening of domestic markets to novice travelers is the introduction of the "Hotel Voucher" scheme that is linked to the countrywide network of the South African Post Office (South African Post Office, 2004).

Potential holiday-makers are offered the flexibility to purchase and accumulate Hotel Vouchers in small cash denominations with each voucher valid for a period of three years and accepted for "your dream holiday" at a network of 140 hotels, lodges and game reserves across South Africa. Finally, based upon similar principles to the hotel voucher, South African Tourism is in negotiation with provincial tourism organizations for the introduction of a card system that offers local visitors cheaper admission and access to popular local attractions, such as Robben Island in Cape Town. The card is a parallel to a similar existing scheme of South African National Parks that is designed to afford cheaper access for local visitors to national parks.

One potential impact of the promotion of black domestic tourism is an expansion of opportunities for informal and small-scale enterprise development. Over the past decade the major beneficiaries of the growth of the South African tourism economy have been large tourism enterprises and a vibrant segment of white-owned accommodation establishments and tour operators (Rogerson and Visser, 2004). Low budget domestic tourism affords potential niches for the progress and development of tourism businesses operated by black entrepreneurs. Based upon the experience of the Western Cape, recent work by Thomas (2005) identifies an array of core and specialized tourism activities in which opportunities exist for advancing the role of informal and small-scale entrepreneurship. Among the core activities are those in accommodation, food preparation and catering, beverage supply, transport services, visitor-guide services and the production of crafts. Specialized services include brokering contacts for/to local business, provision of contacts to local leisure and recreation facilities and the facilitation of linkages with conventional tour facilities.

Conclusion

Policy development and planning for the growth of domestic tourism are issues of growing significance for many developing world countries (Ghimire, 2001; Scheyvens, 2002; Mazimhaka, 2006). Overall, there is increasing evidence of the several potential benefits of promoting domestic tourism. The promotion of domestic tourism will necessarily require some reversal of the established policy bias towards the attraction of international tourism, which is evident in national tourism planning as pursued by many African countries.

Unlike many developing world countries, South Africa has clearly acknowledged the critical role played by domestic tourism. Within the national Tourism Investment Framework, which was released in January 2005, domestic tourism is described "as particularly important as the engine room for a national tourism economy" (DTI, 2005: 27). Post-apartheid South Africa is emerging as a leader and innovator in terms of strategic planning and promotion for domestic tourism. Indeed, the degree to which different levels of government have grasped the importance of policy development towards domestic tourism is underlined by the fact that the Johannesburg Economic Development department is seeking to prepare in 2005 a local tourism strategy that is specifically dedicated to maximising the local opportunities for domestic tourism in the city (Naidoo, 2005).

During 2004 the Chief Operating Officer for South African Tourism, Moeketsi Mosala, responded to a question on areas where there might exist value in the local tourism industry:

> There is a massive black middle-class that has emerged in the last decade in our country. That actually now has the money to travel, but they have no history of travel. And all that you need is somebody with really brilliant ideas to tap into this market, and start to move volumes in terms of domestic marketing (Lisa, 2004: 12).

The Sho't Left campaign is the current flagship of the new marketing initiatives launched by South African Tourism and designed to address the untapped potential of black domestic tourism. As yet it is too early to evaluate the full impacts of the range of new initiatives that have been part of the Sho't Left campaign. None the less, the early results are certainly promising in terms of potential expansion of the domestic tourism economy (South African Tourism 2004c, 2004d, 2004e). Regular monitoring of the changing landscape of domestic tourism in South Africa may offer potential lessons to other developing world countries, and especially those in sub-Saharan Africa, of useful practices and policy interventions to maximise the developmental potential of this group of "Southern" tourists.

Acknowledgements

Thanks are due to Mrs Wendy Job, Cartographic Unit, University of the Witwatersrand for preparation of all the diagrams. Research funding from the South Africa-Netherlands Research Programme on Alternatives in Development is gratefully acknowledged.

References

Aramberri, J. and Xie, Y-J., 2003: Off the beaten track: domestic tourism in China, *Tourism Recreation Research*, 28, 87-92.

Archer, B., 1978: Domestic tourism as a development factor, *Annals of Tourism Research*, 5, 126-141.

Atos KPMG Consulting, 2004: Opening the doors of travel to all – It's possible, Unpublished report for the Department of Trade and Industry and South African Tourism.

Atos, KPMG Consulting, 2006: *South Africa: Domestic Tourism Growth Strategy Final Report—Revised Value*, Report for South African Tourism, Johannesburg.

Awaritefe, O.D., 2004a: Motivation and other considerations in tourist destination choice: a case study of Nigeria, *Tourism Geographies*, 6, 303-330.

Awaritefe, O.D., 2004b: Image difference between destination visitors in Nigeria, *Tourism*, 52, 235-254.

Barkin D., 2001: Strengthening domestic tourism in Mexico: challenges and opportunities, in K. Ghimire (Ed.), *The Native Tourist: Mass Tourism Within Developing Countries*. Earthscan, London, 30-54.

Becker, C., 1987: Domestic tourism in FRG: trends and problems, *Annals of Tourism Research*, 14, 516-530.

Bleasdale S. and Kwarko P., 2000: Is there a role for visiting friends and relatives in Ghana's tourism development strategy? in M.Robinson, N. Evans, P.Long R. Sharpley and J. Swarbrooke (Eds.), *Management, Marketing and the Political Economy of Travel and Tourism,* Centre for Travel and Tourism, University of Northumbria, Newcastle, 13-22.

Bogari, N.B., Crowther, G. and Marr, N., 2003: Motivation for domestic tourism: a case study of the Kingdom of Saudi Arabia, *Tourism Analysis*, 8, 137-141.

Buultjens, J., Ratnayake, I., Gnanapala, A. and Aslam, M., 2005: Tourism and its implications for management in Ruhuna National Park (Yala), Sri Lanka, *Tourism Management*, 26, 733-742.

Burger, R., Burger, R. and van der Berg, S., 2003: Emergent black affluence and social mobility, Unpublished paper, University of Stellenbosch.

Cai, L.A., Hu, B. and Feng, R.M., 2001: Domestic tourism demand in China's urban centers: empirical analyses and marketing implications, *Journal of Vacation Marketing*, 8, 64-74.

Carr, N., 2002: A comparative analysis of the behaviour of domestic and international young tourists, *Tourism Management*, 23, 321-325.

DEAT (Department of Environmental Affairs and Tourism), 2004: *Domestic Tourism Growth Strategy 2004 to 2007*, DEAT and South African Tourism, available at www.southafrica.net

Dhall, S.S.C., 2004: Indian tourism—the silver lining, *State Bank of India Monthly Review*, 43, 100-108.

Dieges A.C., 2001: Regional and domestic mass tourism in Brazil: an overview, in K. Ghimire (Ed.), *The Native Tourist: Mass Tourism Within Developing Countries,* Earthscan, London, 55-85.

DTI (Department of Trade and Industry), 2005: *Tourism Investment Framework*, DTI, Pretoria.

Ferrario, F., 1978: *An Evaluation of the Tourism Resources of South Africa*, Publication 1, Department of Geography, University of Cape Town.

Ferrario, F.F., 1986: black and white holidays: the future of the local tourist industry in South Africa, *Annals of Tourism Research*, 13, 331-348.

Ferrario, F.F., 1988: Emerging leisure market among the South African black population, *Tourism Management*, 9, 23-38.

Futter, M. and Wood, L., 1997: Domestic tourism in South Africa: (un) limited options?, *Indicator South Africa*, 14 (2), 58-63.

Ghimire, K.B., 1997: *Emerging Mass Tourism in the South*, Discussion Paper No. 85, United Nations Research Institute for Social Development, Geneva.

Ghimire K.B., 2001: The growth of national and regional tourism in developing countries: an overview, in K.Ghimire (Ed.), *The Native Tourist: Mass Tourism Within Developing Countries,* Earthscan, London, 1-29.

Ghimire K.B. and Li Z., 2001: The economic role of national tourism in China, in K. Ghimire (Ed.), *The Native Tourist: Mass Tourism Within Developing Countries.* Earthscan, London, 86-108.

Gu, H-M and Liu, D., 2004: The relationship between resident income and domestic tourism in China, *Tourism Recreation Research* 29 (2), 25-33.

Gunawan, M.P., 1996: Domestic tourism in Indonesia, *Tourism Recreation Research,* 21 (1), 65-69.

Hall, C.M. and Kearsley, G., 2001: *Tourism in New Zealand: An Introduction*, Oxford University Press, Melbourne.

Hinch, T.D., 1990: Cuban tourism industry – its re-emergence and future, *Tourism Management*, 11, 214-226.

Jaakson, R., 1986: Second home domestic tourism, *Annals of Tourism Research*, 13, 367-391.

Kaosa-ard M., Bezic D. and White S., 2001: Domestic tourism in Thailand: supply and demand, in K. Ghimire (Ed.), *The Native Tourist: Mass Tourism Within Developing Countries*. Earthscan, London, 109-141.

Kassilly, F.N., 2003: Towards promotion of local tourism: the case of Lake Nakuru National Park in Kenya, *African Journal of Ecology*, 41, 187-189.

Kepe, T., 2001: Tourism, protected areas and development in South Africa: views of visitors to Mkambati Nature Reserve, *South African Journal of Wildlife Research*, 31, 155-159.

Keyser, H., 2002: *Tourism Development*, Oxford University Press, Cape Town.

Koch E. and Massyn P., 2001: South Africa's domestic tourism sector: promises and problems, in K. Ghimire (Ed.), *The Native Tourist: Mass Tourism Within Developing Countries*. Earthscan, London, 142-171.

Lisa, Z., 2004: The nature, organization and trends in the black domestic tourism market in post-apartheid South Africa, Unpublished BA Hons dissertation, University of the Witwatersrand, Johannesburg.

Mazimhaka, J., 2006: The Potential Impact of Domestic Tourism on Rwanda's Tourism Economy, Unpublished MA Research Report, University of Witwatersrand, Johannesburg.

Mena, M.M., Chon, K. and Alampay, R.B.A., 2004: Discovering the potentials of domestic tourism in Southeast Asia from the perspective of regional demography, *Tourism Recreation Research*, 29, 13-24.

Mkhize, I.B., 1994: South African domestic tourism beyond apartheid, *Development Southern Africa*, 11, 249-252.

Monitor, 2004: *Global Competitiveness Project: Summary of Key Findings of Phase 1*, South African Tourism Johannesburg.

Mustapha A.R. 2001: The survival ethic and the development of tourism in Nigeria, in K. Ghimire (Ed.), *The Native Tourist: Mass Tourism Within Developing Countries*. Earthscan, London, 172-197.

Naidoo, K., 2005: Development of domestic tourism strategy and implementation plan for the city of Johannesburg, Request for Quotation/Proposal by the City of Johannesburg Economic Development Department, Johannesburg, 15 February.

Paul, B.K. and Rimmawi, H.S., 1992: Tourism in Saudi Arabia: Asir National Park, *Annals of Tourism Research*, 19, 501-515.

Peleggi, M., 1996: National heritage and global tourism in Thailand, *Annals of Tourism Research*, 23, 432-448.

Pyo, S. and Koo, Y-S., 2002: The convention industry in South Korea, in K. Weber and K.S. Chon (Eds.), *Convention Tourism: International Research and Industry Perspectives*, Haworth Hospitality Press, Binghamton, 171-184.

Rao N. and Suresh K.T., 2001: Domestic tourism in India, in K.Ghimire (Ed.), *The Native Tourist: Mass Tourism Within Developing Countries*, Earthscan, London, 198-228.

Rogerson, C.M., 2003: Developing Zambia's tourism economy: planning for "the real Africa," *Africa Insight*, 33 (1/2), 48-54.

Rogerson, C.M. and Visser, G., 2004: Tourism and development in post-apartheid South Africa: a ten year review, in C.M. Rogerson and G. Visser (Eds.), *Tourism and Development Issues in Contemporary South Africa*, Africa Institute of South Africa, Pretoria, 2-25.

Rule, S., Struwig, J., Langa, Z., Viljoen, J. and Bouare, O., 2001: South African domestic tourism survey: marketing the provinces, Unpublished report for South African Tourism and DEAT, Pretoria.

Rule, S., Viljoen, J., Zama, S., Struwig, J., Langa, Z. and Bouare, O., 2004: Visiting friends and relatives: South Africa's most popular form of domestic tourism, in C.M. Rogerson and G. Visser (Eds.), *Tourism and Development Issues in Contemporary South Africa*, Africa Institute of South Africa, Pretoria, 78-101.

Rwigema, H., 1996: Tourist habits among residents of the Transkei subregion: a case study, *Development Southern Africa*, 13, 647-657.

Saayman, M., Saayman, A. and Rhodes, J.A., 2001: Domestic tourist spending and economic development: the case of North West Province, *Development Southern Africa*, 18, 443-455.

Scheyvens R., 2002: *Tourism for Development: Empowering Communities,* Pearson, Harlow.

Seaton, A.V. and Palmer, C., 1997: Understanding VFR tourism behaviour: the first five years of the United Kingdom tourism survey, *Tourism Management*, 18, 345-355.

Seckelman, A., 2002: Domestic tourism—a chance for regional development in Turkey, *Tourism Management*, 23, 85-92.

Silva, P. and Butler-Adam, J., 1988: *Terrae Incognitae: A Journey into the Unknown Lands of Domestic Tourism in South Africa*, Institute of Social and Economic Research, University of Durban-Westville, Durban.

Sindiga, I., 1996: Domestic tourism in Kenya, *Annals of Tourism Research*, 23, 19-31.

Singh, S., 1997: Developing human resources for the tourism industry with reference to India, *Tourism Management*, 18, 299-306.

South African Post Office, 2004: *The Hotel Voucher*, The South African Post Office (pamphlet).

South African Tourism 2003: *2002 Annual Tourism Report.* South African Tourism, Johannesburg.

South African Tourism, 2004a: News Release- Opening the doors of travel to all, available at www.southafrica.net (11 June).

South African Tourism, 2004b: *2003 Domestic Tourism Report*, South African Tourism Strategic Research Unit, Johannesburg.

South African Tourism, 2004c: News Release—Rousing send off given to first funbus departure, available at www.southafrica.net (30 July)

South African Tourism, 2004d: News Release—Overwhelming response to domestic Fun bus promotion, available at www.southafrica.net (26 July)

South African Tourism, 2004e: News Release—Public support for sho't left exceeds expectations, available at www.southafrica.net (15 July)

South African Tourism, 2005: Welcome South African travelers!, available at www.southafrica.net/sho't_left/

Southall, R., 2004a: The ANC and the black middle-class in democratic South Africa, Unpublished paper, Human Sciences Research Council, Pretoria.

Southall, R., 2004b: South Africa's emerging black middle-class, *HSRC Review*, 2 (3), 12-13.

Thomas, W.H., 2005: *"Second Economy" Paths into South African Tourism Business*, Research Report No. 1, Centre for Tourism Research in Africa, Cape Peninsula University of Technology, Cape Town.

Turner, L.W. and Reisinger, Y., 2001: Shopping satisfaction of domestic tourists, *Journal of Retailing and Customer Services*, 8, 15-27.

Van Schalkwyk, M., 2004: Keynote speech by Minister of Environmental Affairs and Tourism at Gugu S'Thebe Art and Cultural Centre, Langa, Cape Town, 11 June, available at www.southafrica.net (11 June)

Viljoen, T., 2003: Cape Town's racist blot—even locals admit Mother City is unfriendly to blacks, *Sowetan Sunday World*, 12 January.

Visser, G. 2004a: Second homes and local development: issues arising from Cape Town's De Waterkant, *GeoJournal*, 60, 259-271.

Visser, G., 2004b: Second homes: reflections on an unexplored phenomenon in South Africa, in C.M. Hall and D.K. Muller (Eds.), *Tourism, Mobility and Second Homes: Between Elite Landscape and Common Ground,* Channel View, Clevedon, 196-214.

Walsh, E.R. and Swain, M.B., 2004: Creating modernity by tourism paradise: domestic ethnic tourism in Yunnan, China, *Tourism Recreation Research*, 29 (2), 59-68.

Wang, N. 2004: The rise of touristic consumerism in urban China, *Tourism Recreation Research*, 29 (2), 47-58.

Wang, S.S. and Qu, H.L., 2004: A comparison study of Chinese domestic tourism: China vs. the U.S., *International Journal of Contemporary Hospitality Management*, 16 (2), 108-115.

Wen, Z., 1997: China's domestic tourism: impetus, development and trends, *Tourism Management*, 18, 565-571.

Williams A.M. and Hall C.M., 2002: Tourism, migration, circulation and mobility: the contingencies of time and place, in C.M. Hall and A.M. Williams (Eds.), *Tourism and Migration: New Relationships Between Migration and Consumption.* Kluwer, Dordrecht, 1-52.

Winter, T., 2004: Landscape, memory and heritage: New Year celebrations at Angkor, Cambodia, *Current Issues in Tourism*, 7, 330-345.

Wu, B-H., Zhu, H. and Xu, X-H., 2000: Trends in China's domestic tourism development at the turn of the century, *International Journal of Contemporary Hospitality Management*, 12, 296-299.

Xie, Y-J. and Xu, J-F., 2004: Cultural tourism vs. tourist culture: case of domestic tourism in modern Beijing, *Tourism Recreation Research*, 29 (2), 81-88.

Xu, G., 1998: Domestic tourism and its economic effect in Beidaihe, the largest seaside resort in China, *Pacific Tourism Review*, 2 (1), 43-52.

Xu, G., 1999: Socio-economic impacts of domestic tourism in China: case studies in Guilin, Suzhou and Beidaihe, *Tourism Geographies*, 1, 204-218.

Part 2

Urban Tourism Types in Africa

5

Conference and Exhibition Tourism in South African

Christian M. Rogerson

Over the past quarter-century strong growth was recorded in flows of business tourism, both domestically and internationally, and tourism scholars have accorded the phenomenon increased research significance (Cooper, 1979; Lawson, 1982; Hughes, 1988; Owen, 1992; Davidson, 1993; Bradley et al., 2002; Kulendran and Witt, 2002). Nevertheless, business travel and tourism is one of most diverse and fragmented themes in tourism scholarship. Indeed, the topic of "business tourism" has been divided into at least fifteen different categories of travel, including individual general business trips, training courses, product launches, and corporate hospitality and incentive travel (Swarbrooke and Horner, 2001). The most important elements of business tourism are acknowledged to be the hosting of meetings, conferences or exhibitions (Law, 1987, 1993; Oppermann and Chon, 1997). Often these are combined with incentive travel into discussions of the category of MICE (Meetings, Incentives, Conferences and Exhibitions) tourism.

For destination planners, the benefits of attracting business tourism are several. At international level, these include, inter alia, contributions to employment and income, increased foreign exchange earnings, the generation of investment in tourism infrastructure, the facilitation of opportunities for access to new technology and ideas, and the establishment of business contacts (Dwyer and Mistilis, 1997). At local level, the attractions of business tourism involve the sheer size and expansion of this market, the relatively higher daily expenditures recorded by business travellers as opposed to leisure or VFR tourists, the tendency of business travel to occur outside peak periods for leisure travel, and the multiple local spin-offs for an array of local small businesses, including photographers, printers and florists (Braun and Rungeling, 1992; Oppermann,

1997; Wootton and Stevens, 1995; Bradley et al., 2002; Solberg et al., 2002; Suh and McAvoy, 2005). On the whole, the market for meetings tourism has grown substantially and seems destined to continue at a rate of growth above that recorded even for most European national economies (Bradley et al., 2002).

Despite its global expansion and acknowledged importance, a recent introductory text on business tourism by Swarbrooke and Horner (2001: xiii) could bemoan the fact that "there is relatively little literature on any aspect of the subject." In common with most areas of tourism scholarship, the available fragmented literature concerning business tourism is dominated by research on the developed world. A number of studies have appeared which document various dimensions of international or domestic business tourism in Europe (Law, 1987; Wootton and Stevens, 1995; Bradley et al., 2002; Dorfler, 2002; Weber and Chon, 2002; World Tourism Organisation, 2003; Jansen-Verbeke et al., 2005) and North America (Zelinsky, 1994; Hiller, 1995; Weber and Chon, 2002; Weber and Ladkin, 2003), which are the two leading international foci for business travel and business tourism. Increased research interest is evident also in the expanding markets of Australia and Pacific Rim Asia (see Cooper, 1979; Dwyer and Mistilis, 1997; Oppermann, 1997; Go and Govers, 1999; Lew and Chang, 1999; Qu et al., 2000; Pyo and Koo, 2002; Kim et al., 2003; Suh and McAvoy, 2005). By contrast, the developing world as a whole has been a limited focus for research on business tourism, not least the continent of Africa that has received no scholarly attention. Notwithstanding academic neglect, Dieke (1998: 39) observes that "one of the most important aspects of travel in Africa is related to 'business purposes.'" Indeed, business travel represents a core driver of the growing phenomenon of "regional tourism" flows within sub-Saharan Africa as observed during the last decade (Dieke, 1998; Ghimire, 2001; Mustapha, 2001; Rogerson, 2004a).

The objective in this chapter is to furnish an introduction to the theme of business tourism in urban Africa by examining key issues in the evolution and growth of conference and exhibition tourism within South Africa. As Law (1987: 85) points out: "Conference and exhibition tourism is usually considered part of business tourism." The discussion is organized into two sets of material. The first section provides a review of key themes in the existing body of international writings on business tourism in general and on conference and exhibition tourism in particular. The second section turns attention to analyse business tourism in South Africa, the growing local supply of conference and exhibition facilities, and to highlight the increasing competition that is emerging between South Africa's leading cities for dominance of the lucrative market of conference and exhibition tourism.

Research on Conference and Exhibition Tourism

Conferences and exhibitions are usually treated together rather than as two separate activities because "there is an increasing convergence between them"

(Law, 1987: 86). Traditionally, many conferences include exhibitions and exhibitions often give rise to conferences. None the less, as Law (1987: 87) observes the "apogee" of convergence between conferences and exhibitions is the emergence of the multi-purpose "convention center" which consists of several large venues which can be used flexibly either for conference or exhibition purposes. Hiller (1995: 375) argues that conferences and exhibitions are a "special kind of tourism" as theoretically they represent the propelling factor for attendance rather than the characteristics of the destination itself. The meeting, convention, or exhibition serves as the primary purpose for travel and the focus is a multi-faceted event of a fixed time duration that involves speakers, seminars, workshops, exhibitions, banquets, association meetings, and social events. Accordingly, the conference or exhibition event is, therefore, interpreted as markedly different from other forms of business travel in which the primary purpose is individual or small-group encounters (Hiller, 1995).

In practical terms a commitment to the purpose of the conference or exhibition is not a guarantee of attendance. Issues relating to accessibility, marketing, investment, infrastructure, human resources and service quality are among a range of variables that can be influential (Weber and Ladkin, 2003). The markets for conference and exhibition tourism at both the international and domestic scale of analysis have been shown to be "extremely competitive" (Dwyer and Mistilis, 1997: 230) with more and more countries building conference centers "in order to capitalize on this newly emerging tourism sector" (Oppermann, 1997: 245). Considerable care is taken by meetings or conference organizers in terms of the selection of locations for the hosting of conferences or exhibitions. Accordingly, a critical research focus in business tourism scholarship is understanding the decision-making processes and destination images as held both by association meeting planners and potential attendees (Zelinsky, 1994; Oppermann, 1996a, 1996b; Oppermann and Chon, 1997; Crouch and Ritchie, 1998; Getz et al., 1998; Oppermann, 1998; Weber, 2001). The results of such research, including the application of choice modelling exercises, are used to improve the competitive positioning and branding of individual destinations for the attraction of business tourism (Var et al., 1985; Oppermann, 1996a; Crouch and Louviere, 2003; Weber and Ladkin, 2003; Hankinson, 2005). Illustratively, much recent attention has been given to the primacy of Singapore over the competition offered from Hong Kong for international conferences in Southeast Asia and more broadly, the Pacific Rim region. The significance of factors such as capacity of facilities, quality of service, accessibility as well as cost considerations have been put forward to explain the regional competitive dominance of Singapore and correspondingly to suggest areas for improvement for enhancing the position of Hong Kong (Go and Govers, 1999; Lew and Chang, 1999; Qu et al., 2000).

At national level, the importance of this segment of business tourism is underscored by the fact that certain countries have prepared national policies or strategies that are designed specifically to ensure long-term growth and to maximise the local economic and social impacts of conference and exhibition tourism. In terms of policy development, one of the most pro-active countries is Australia. During the 1990s the national government encouraged the development of a marketing strategy which is geared, inter alia, to enhance international awareness of the country as a premier conference and exhibition destination; to promote coordinated and cooperative marketing of the industry; to encourage national associations to attract overseas delegates to meetings and exhibitions in Australia, particularly from the Asia-Pacific region; and, to boost the number of delegates attending conferences in Australia at local, national and international level (Dwyer and Mistilis, 1997).

For destinations, the economic impacts of capturing the market of business tourism are potentially considerable. Figure 5.1 shows the economic impacts of business tourism on localities. It discloses that whilst there are both potential positive and negative impacts, "it is generally accepted that the economic benefits of business tourism are positive in most places" (Swarbrooke and Horner, 2001: 77). In the U.S. the hosting of conventions and meetings is viewed as highly beneficial in that they can complement the seasonal fluctuations experienced in leisure tourism activities (Braun and Rungeling, 1992). Success in business

Figure 5.1
The Economic Impacts of Business Tourism at Local Level
(Adapted after Swarbrooke and Horner, 2002: 76).

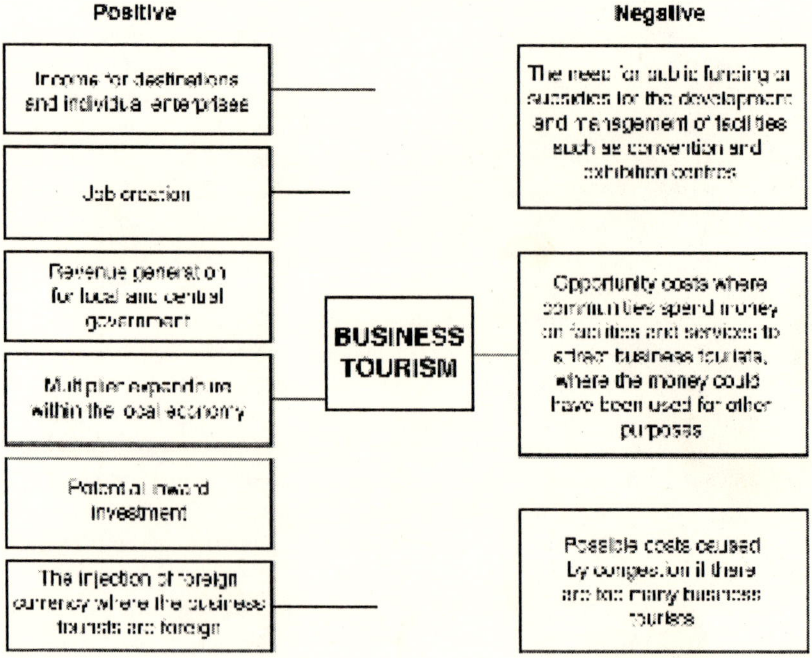

tourism has been shown to bring also an array of non-financial rewards to localities, the most significant associated with image and profile enhancement, the
physical upgrading and regeneration of decaying areas, and the generation of
civic pride among residents (Law, 1987; Zelinsky, 1994; Bradley et al., 2002).
Taken together, given the several potential economic and non-economic impacts
of business tourism, it is not surprising that many different kinds of localities
have been encouraged to seek a slice of this lucrative market by attracting
conferences and exhibitions.

Historically, in Western Europe, resort towns recognised earliest the potential
benefits of conference and exhibition tourism and started to develop specialist
conference facilities during the inter-war period (1919-1939). Indeed, a long-
established feature of seaside resorts in the United Kingdom, such as Blackpool,
Brighton or Scarborough, is the hosting of the annual conferences of political
parties, trade unions and associations in order to attract visitors and extend the
length of the tourism season (Douglas, 1979). The market for meetings tourism
became more competitive from the early 1980s with the entry of several provincial centers, such as Birmingham, Cardiff, Glasgow, Harrogate, Manchester,
Nottingham and Newcastle. In the majority of these centers, multi-purpose
facilities were developed (Law, 1987; Bradley et al., 2002). The major exception was Birmingham, which followed the United States model, developing a
planned large downtown convention center to complement its National Exhibition Centre. The meetings tourism market has been aggressively sought after by
a large number of former industrial cities in the U.K., continental Europe, the
U.S., and Australia, within their strategies of post-industrial regeneration (Law,
1987, 1992, 1993; Bradley et al., 2002). The capital city function also offers
opportunities for the development of business tourism as a whole, including
for meetings and conferences (Hall, 2002). As the administrative "capital" for
the European Union, the city of Brussels offers considerable potential for the
development of business tourism, not least with the enlargement of the European
Union (Jansen-Verbeke et al., 2005)

The factors affecting the competitiveness of individual localities in the U.S. or
Western Europe offer parallels with the Asian experience. The general consensus
is that meetings organizers take account of four key attributes when selecting
meetings venues (Bradley et al., 2002). In order of importance these relate to the
quality of meetings facilities, cost, accessibility and image of potential locations
(Law, 1993). The relative importance of these four factors will vary, however, according to the nature of particular conferences or exhibitions. Considerable debate
surrounds the role of "image" in meetings tourism with Zelinsky (1994) arguing
that in the experience of U.S., image is a prime pull-factor. In more recent work
the role of image has been re-evaluated; image is viewed as important for meetings organizers, albeit not as important as other factors (Bradley et al., 2002).
Overall, Law (1987: 93) asserts that for international conferences, meetings
organizers "are attracted to places with good air links, a high standard of facili-

ties and an attractive image" whereas the role of image and the attractiveness of locations is of lesser significance for exhibition venues.

Conference and Exhibition Tourism: Evidence from South Africa

South Africa offers a case study from the developing world to explore the dynamics of conference and exhibition tourism. Within the existing inventory of academic research on tourism in South Africa, no detailed studies presently are available on the theme of conference and exhibition tourism. The only relevant research material is contained as part of broader investigations of local economic development planning in which reference is made to the development and potential local impacts of new convention centers (e.g., Maharaj and Ramballi, 1998; Rogerson, 2004b; Nel and Rogerson, 2005; Gibb, 2006; Lootvoet and Freund, 2006). At present, most South African writings on conferences and exhibitions are special reports prepared by tourism consultants evaluating the potential of a series of proposed new conference venues. One common issue raised in several of these reports is that "little research has been conducted on the South African MICE industry" in general and on the segment of conferences and exhibition tourism in particular (Grant Thornton Kessel Feinstein, 1999: 12).

In this section the available fragmentary primary and secondary source material on conference and exhibition tourism in South Africa is synthesized in order to provide a foundation for more detailed future research investigations. The specific focus is conference and exhibition tourism as part of the broader categorization of MICE tourism. In terms of primary source material, the most significant information base is that provided by the annual yearbook that is produced by the Southern African Association for the Conference Industry (SAACI). This organisation mainly serves the conference industry and recently "introduced an accreditation scheme for professional conference organizers to ensure credible performance and standards in the industry" (Ingram, 2004: 53). The SAACI yearbooks generally are regarded as the most detailed comprehensive listing and database of conference and exhibition facilities in South Africa; information from this source was supplemented by listings of such facilities available through the Internet.

Two sub-sections are presented below. The first discusses the development and characteristics of conference and exhibition tourism in apartheid South Africa. The second section reviews the growth and changing features of conference and exhibition tourism in the post-apartheid period highlighting the expanded levels of competition for the attraction of conferences and exhibitions especially between South Africa's three largest cities.

Initial Developments in Apartheid South Africa

Conference and exhibition tourism is a relatively recent phenomenon in South Africa. During the apartheid period, the country's pariah status and economic sanctions combined to ensure that the domestic, rather than the international, market was the anchor for MICE tourism. On the whole, most conferences and venues were relatively small and geared to accommodate a maximum of 300 persons in one facility.

Traditionally, South Africa's large city hotels—such as the Carlton in Johannesburg or Elangeni in Durban—represented the major suppliers of conference facilities (Kessel Feinstein Consulting, 1991). The importance of hotels for conference development was promoted and assisted by generous tax incentives made available for hotel projects by national government. In addition to hotels, there were many civic halls, theatres and other multi-purpose buildings that also served the local conference market. Further, as in the United Kingdom, many educational institutions, particularly universities, began to offer their venues for occasional use for the hosting of conferences. Nevertheless, one unique aspect of the supply of conference facilities in apartheid South Africa was the establishment during the 1970s and 1980s of several meeting venues which were linked to the casino project developments taking place in the so-termed "independent" black homelands of Transkei, Venda, Ciskei, and Bophuthatswana. In these projects the gaming revenues derived from casinos largely provided the finance or, at least made possible, the development of large conference facilities. The most important of these hotel-casino developments that incorporated a large multi-purpose facility used for conferences was at Sun City in former Bophuthatswana (Rogerson, 1990).

During the late-1980s and early-1990s several important developments began to re-shape the country's conference and exhibition tourism economy. First, was the withdrawal in 1988 of the tax incentives that had supported the development of new hotel projects. This action by national government "put paid to significant new hotel development, let alone that with expensive and extensive conference facilities particularly in the context of the poor trading conditions in the hotel industry" (Kessel Feinstein Consulting, 1991: 28). Second, was the appearance of a number of specialised conference facilities, some of which (for example, the Indaba Hotel and Conference Centre in Johannesburg) were linked with accommodation but others (such as the Volkswagen center in Midrand or the CSIR Conference Centre in Pretoria) without accommodation facilities. The 1991 yearbook of SAACI drew attention to the increasing growth in numbers of these non-hotel conference venues and even suggested that 1991 be recognised as the year of the independent venue (SAACI, 1991). Whilst the meeting facilities at most of these independent venues were of good quality, as a whole they were generally limited in seating capacity with a maximum capacity mainly of 200-250 persons. Moreover, it was observed that the majority of "the emerging non-hotel conference centers are merely adjuncts to some other primary core business or activity of the owners" with their owners letting out "conference suites to the public to help defray operating costs and, in a sense, to partly justify the large amounts invested in these expensive facilities" (Kessel Feinstein Consulting, 1991: 29).

Finally, notwithstanding the imminent demise of the "independent" Home-lands, in 1991 a major purpose-built conference venue financed by the "Govern-ment of Bophuthatswana" was opened at Mmabatho, the "capital city" of the Homeland. This conference center with a seating capacity for 3,000 in the main auditorium, was a major purpose-built facility which was managed by the large Sun International hotel group, albeit financially and physically independent of any hotel. The Mmabatho Convention Centre was to be the forerunner of later developments in South Africa's major cities and represented "the first major purpose-designed public-funded conference center to be built in South Africa" (Kessel Feinstein Consulting, 1991: 29).

Towards the close of apartheid era, in 1991 the SAACI yearbook recorded a total of 137 venues that offered conference facilities with a capacity of 200 or more seats (SAACI, 1991). Of these venues, approximately one-half of the listed venues offered accommodation. As South Africa's major center for business and location of headquarter offices, the Johannesburg-Pretoria area represented the prime spatial focus with nearly half of all listed venues situated there. Domestic business tourism remained at the heart of the growing South African MICE economy. Typically, as was observed in the Western Cape, the supply of facilities was predominantly for venues that could accommodate up to 300 delegates. A core infrastructural supply-gap in order for the region to emerge as "a major national and international conference destination" was sophisticated venues of international standard (City of Cape Town, 1990: 8). Indeed, it was significant that nationally there existed only twelve venues across South Africa that could potentially accommodate more than 1,000 delegates, ten of these were halls and exhibition centers and the others were the multi-purpose Sun City Superbowl and the Mmabatho Convention Centre (Kessel Feinstein Consulting, 1991: 30).

Post-Apartheid Growth and Change

New opportunities were offered for the expansion of conference and exhibi-tion tourism in South Africa with the democratic transition of 1994. Since 1994 the most important developments have surrounded the growth of conference and exhibition tourism economy as a whole driven by the rise of international MICE tourism, the establishment of international convention centers offering world-class facilities for conferences and exhibitions, and increased levels of competition amongst South Africa's major cities to attract the conference and exhibition market. It is evident that both national and local governments in South Africa's major cities recognise the potential development opportunities associ-ated with MICE tourism (South African Tourism, 2004; Van Wyk, 2005a).

The rapid expansion of the conference and exhibition tourism economy since the democratic transition is evidenced by the fact that nationally the MICE sec-tor was estimated to be worth approximately R2.6 billion in 1995 and R 17.4 billion by 2004 (South African Tourism, 2005). The growth of the MICE sector was boosted especially by the emergence of a vibrant sector of international conference and exhibition tourism. In 1993 before the democratic transition, the numbers of such visitors to South Africa was estimated as only 14,000 per annum (City of Johannesburg, 2003: 4). In 2004 it was estimated that at least 110,000 foreign MICE participants visit South Africa annually, which ranks the country as twenty-second in a global listing of world conference destinations. Within Africa, South Africa is the leading conference/meeting destination and obtains 61 percent of the total conference market for the continent (South African Tourism, 2005).

The most high profile international conferences have been large congresses such as the World AIDS Congress hosted by Durban and the World Summit for Sustainable Development held in Johannesburg. The city of Cape Town, with its range of natural attractions, remains, however, the most popular South African venue for international conferences. The average international conference delegate stays in South Africa for six days spending an average of 4.2 days at the conference event and a further 1.8 days at the conference destination. The total of six days is considerably less than the average international leisure traveller's stay of seventeen days in South Africa (Ingram, 2004). Nevertheless, the high per capita levels of expenditure of conference travellers as well as the fact that nearly 20 percent of delegates bring an accompanying person (spouse, partner, or family member) ensure that the MICE industry and international conferences, in particular, represents "an important component of the tourism industry and makes a significant impact on the economy" (Ingram, 2004: 52-53).

Notwithstanding the rise of international MICE tourism, the domestic South African MICE market remains substantial with Gauteng province and Johannesburg in particular the leading focus of activity, with an estimated 64 percent market share. Likewise, Johannesburg is dominant in terms of the national market for exhibitions, capturing a 51 percent share that is far ahead of Cape Town (15 percent) and Durban (11 percent) (Davie, 2003). Given the dominance exerted by Johannesburg it is not surprising that one recent investigation disclosed that almost 90 percent of the leading national professional conference organizers were based in the city (Grant Thornton Kessel Feinstein, 1999: 20). Overall, the domestic market comprises of a mix of corporate training; association meetings; launch events; academic, NGO and business conferences; and, an increasing segment of government meetings and training courses. Taken together, it is estimated that the MICE industry in South Africa—both international and domestic—is estimated at 101,000 events, including 1,900 exhibitions, which are attended by 11 million participants and generating more than 200,000 employment opportunities (Davie, 2003; Ingram, 2004). Significantly, there is a geographical divide between the international and domestic market demands with Cape Town traditionally the prime focus for international meetings whereas Johannesburg is pre-eminent in domestic conference markets and for exhibitions.

Important changes have been evident in the supply of conference and exhibition venues since 1994. According to the listings provided in the SAACI yearbooks for 1996 and 2004 considerable growth has taken place during the post-apartheid period in the number of conference and exhibition facilities. Between 1996 and 2004 there is recorded a doubling in the numbers of conference and exhibition facilities available in South Africa (Gelling, 2004). Although hotels remain numerically the most dominant type of venue, it is shown that there has been a marked expansion in multi-purpose and specialised conference and exhibition facilities. Another observed trend is for the growth in country hotels and bush venues as newer foci for the offering of conference facilities (Gelling, 2004). In terms of location, figure 5.2 discloses that whilst the largest concentration of conference venues is in the Western Cape, most of these venues are small in scale. The greatest capacity for conferences, in terms of maximum delegate capacity, exists in Gauteng. In Johannesburg, the major center of Gauteng, several large conference facilities have been initiated since the early 1990s (Davie, 2004). Amongst the most important is Gallagher Estate that in 1994 served as the nerve center of South Africa's first democratic elections and in 1995 as the venue for a banquet in honor of Queen Elizabeth II (Rogerson, 2002; City of Johannesburg, 2003). During 2004 Gallagher Estate was selected also as the venue for the inaugural meeting of the Pan-African Parliament, a decision that is seen as enhancing Johannesburg's position in terms of business tourism in Africa (Johannesburg Tourism Company, 2004).

On figure 5.3 the national pattern in terms of supply of exhibition venues is mapped. In common with the situation concerning conference centers, the greatest number of potential facilities once again is in the Western Cape albeit the largest available exhibition space occurs in Gauteng. The most significant development is the 42,000 square metres of exhibition space made available at the Nasrec Expo Centre located in the south of Johannesburg (City of Johannesburg 2003: 20).

Over the past decade, the most critical shift in the supply of conference and exhibition venues in South Africa is the establishment of a series of major convention centers of international standards with the objective of competing aggressively in the global MICE market. It must be acknowledged that planning for this market and for the development of new conference and exhibition centers was undertaken even prior to the democratic transition in all of South Africa's largest three cities—Johannesburg, Cape Town and Durban. By 1990 the Cape Town municipal authorities already had identified tourism as a sector with considerable growth potential and envisioned the city as a national and international conference destination. Assessments were commissioned for the potential development of a new conference center in the city (City of Cape Town, 1990). At the same time the city of Johannesburg was examining the potential development of a convention center as one off its proposed "Top Ten" projects for inner-city re-development, part of wider economic planning

Figure 5.2
Location of Conference Venues and Maximum Delegate Capacity

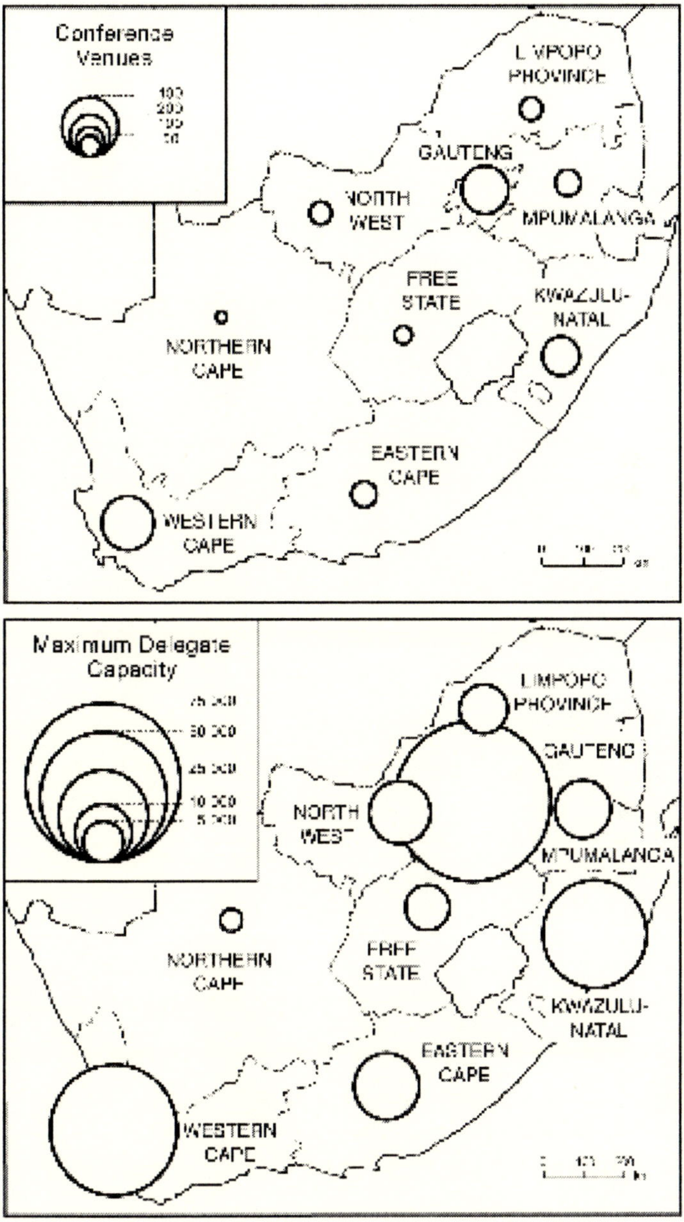

Source: SAACI 1996 and 2004; Gelling 2004, Table 8

Figure 5.3
Location of Exhibition Venues and Available Exhibition Space

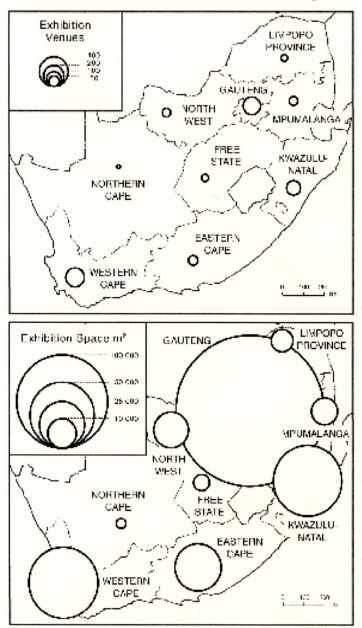

Source: SAACI 1996 and 2004; Gelling 2004, Table 8

for attaining world city status (Rogerson, 1996). It should be acknowledged, however, that both of these early planned convention centers in Johannesburg and Cape Town were never realized.

By contrast, in Durban the decision was finalised in 1991 to build an International Convention Centre (ICC) with funding of R280 million drawn from the local metropolitan council. Lootvoet and Freund (2006) maintain that the planned ICC development in Durban was one of the Council's flagship projects and represents an aggressive response to initiatives from other South African cities to attract the anticipated flow of wealth from international tourism and conferences. In Johannesburg, the competing R 400 million Sandton Convention Centre (SCC) was constructed as part of the bid commitment for the lucrative Montecasino hotel and gaming project, opening during 2000 (Keyser, 2000). Nevertheless, this major convention center for Johannesburg was built not as part of the initial proposals for inner-city redevelopment but instead at one of the city's new upmarket decentralized commercial and office zones which have emerged also as new tourism spaces in the city (Rogerson, 2002). Custom-built to accommodate the largest and most technologically driven events, the SCC was designed to compete with the finest convention facilities in the world and was the focal point for the activities of the 2002 World Summit on Sustainable Development (WSSD), the largest international conference ever held in South Africa.

The most recent addition to the list of international standard conference facilities in South Africa is the R320 million mega-project for the Cape Town International Convention Centre (CTICC). This multi-purpose convention and exhibition center is situated on the Foreshore area of Cape Town CBD (Gibb, 2006). The CTICC is operated and managed by Amsterdam RAI, an operator and manager of other comparable convention facilities elsewhere in the world (van Wyk, 2005b). The convention center forms part of a more holistic development project for linking the existing working harbour and port with the city center and the waterfront redevelopment in order to catalyse a cluster of commercial, retail and tourism-linked activities (Haase, 2002; Keyser, 2002). With the coming on stream in June-2003 of the CTICC, South Africa now has three cities competing for the MICE market with international standard facilities (Dlamini, 2004). This heightened level of inter-urban competition is based upon the positive perceived spin-offs for image enhancement and economic development from the hosting of major international conferences such as the WSSD (City of Johannesburg, 2002).

The list of South African cities that are seeking to attract conferences and exhibitions is not confined merely to Johannesburg, Cape Town and Durban. Other cities that have established conference centers and seek to compete for the conference and exhibition tourism market include Bloemfontein, Port Elizabeth and Pretoria. Linked to the rise of local economic development (LED) planning in post-apartheid South Africa, all these cities have incorporated the promotion of conferences and exhibitions as part of urban growth initiatives (Rogerson, 2006).

The critical importance attached by LED planners in South African cities to the attraction of conferences and exhibitions can be illustrated by recent developments in Johannesburg. In July 2003 the City of Johannesburg established the Johannesburg Tourism Company (JTC) as a special institution of council with the mandate of establishing "tourism as a key sector for Johannesburg and thereby improve job creation and retention" (Johannesburg Tourism Company, 2005a: 2). The operations of the JTC are responsible to the city's Finance and Economic Development Department that seeks to make Johannesburg a world-class African city (Rogerson, 2004b). As part of the project for economic development in Johannesburg "the city intends to ensure that it bids for, and attracts, key international conferences and events" (City of Johannesburg, 2004). The core focus of JTC is clear from the statement that "Business tourism in Johannesburg is what the Johannesburg Tourism Company is about" (Johannesburg Tourism Company, 2005a: 1). The activities of the JTC find a close parallel with the services undertaken elsewhere, for example, in Durban by that city's convention bureau which is committed "to stimulate interest in the Durban Metropolitan Region as a venue for meetings, conferences, conventions, and incentive travel" (Durban Metropolitan Tourism Authority, 2004), and by the Cape Town Convention Bureau which seeks to establish Cape Town "on the same footing as other leading MICE destinations in the world" (Ingram, 2004: 53).

The prime role of JTC is to furnish quality tourism information relevant to business travellers to Johannesburg (Johannesburg Tourism Company, 2005a: 1). Through its public relations and marketing drives the function of the JTC is "to advance Johannesburg as a business tourism destination" (Johannesburg Tourism Company 2005a: 1). In terms of its promotional material Johannesburg is sold as "your ideal conference city" (Johannesburg Tourism Company, 2005b). The JTC advertising proclaims that "Johannesburg dazzles on the African continent as an ideal conference and exhibition location. The city will impress you with its choice of venues and support services, competitive with the best internationally in every respect" (Johannesburg Tourism Company 2005b: 1). The Johannesburg Convention Bureau (JCB) is a dedicated division within the JTC with the mission "to develop Johannesburg city as a dynamic destination to international convention, conference and event organizers" (Johannesburg Tourism Company, 2005c: 1). In search of the international conference and exhibition market, considerable emphasis is given by the JCB to the "value for money" aspect of hosting conferences and exhibitions in the city with business tourists lured by the fact that they "will find their Dollars, Euros and Pounds go a long way in Jozi" (Johannesburg Tourism Company, 2005d: 1). Special attention is paid by the JCB to the attraction of large international conferences to the city. To support this goal the bureau offers familiarisation and inspection trips for professional event organizers, the media and other interest groups.

Further support for conference and exhibition tourism in Johannesburg is provided by the activities of the South African Federation of Conference Cities (SAFCC) which has six member cities: Bloemfontein, Cape Town, Durban, Johannesburg, Port Elizabeth and Pretoria. In a joint marketing initiative the SAFCC seeks to promote South Africa as a whole as a preferred MICE destination by attracting international MICE events to the country and allowing individual cities to bid for them (Rogerson, 2002).

Since 2004 national government has become an aggressive supporter of the development of "business tourism" in South Africa as a vehicle to contribute toward achieving the goals of increasing the volume of visitor flows, length of stay and spend as well as to address challenges of seasonality in the national tourism economy. A dedicated national Convention Bureau was initiated in 2004 to drive the further growth of this segment of the tourism economy (South African Tourism, 2004). By 2005 it was estimated that the business tourism economy of South Africa was sustaining a total of nearly 260,000 jobs and paying an estimated R6 billion annually in salaries as well as contributing R4 billion to the central fiscus in taxes (Van Schalkwyk, 2005). As a platform for generating leisure travel, business tourism has been targeted by South African Tourism and a major new campaign for building business tourism was launched (Van Wyk, 2005a) The economic importance attached to business tourism was highlighted at the 2005 National Tourism Conference in the Opening Speech made by South Africa's Minister of Environmental Affairs and Tourism in which he pledged government support to ensure that South Africa moves ahead into the global Top 20 most popular business tourism destinations (Van Schalkwyk, 2005).

Conclusion

Tourism scholarship concerning conferences and exhibitions is dominated by writings concerned with developed countries. An examination of the South African experience, therefore, provides a useful complement to the existing writings and reveals certain parallel themes, particularly concerning issues of local development.

Historically, in the apartheid period the market for conference and exhibition tourism was based upon domestic demand. After the democratic transition, however, it is evident that new opportunities were opened for the attraction of international conferences and exhibitions to South Africa. Undoubtedly, a watershed event in the development of South African participation in the global market for conferences was the successful hosting in Johannesburg during 2002 of the World Summit on Sustainable Development. The positive local development impacts of the attraction of such conferences have been the essential catalyst for the development and continuous upgrading of three international quality convention centers in the country. These three major convention facilities represent the apex of an estimated 1,700 conference and exhibition centers that currently exist across South Africa and serve both domestic and international

MICE markets. With heightened levels of competition for the conference and exhibition market—both domestic and international—uncertainty surrounds the long-term prospects of many of these facilities. The task of monitoring the progress, dynamics and changing fortunes of conference and exhibition tourism merits a place on the research agenda of urban tourism studies in South Africa over the next decade.

Acknowledgements

The financial support of the National Research Foundation, Pretoria Gun 2054064 is gratefully acknowledged in this research.

References

Bradley, A., Hall, T. and Harrison, M., 2002: Selling cities: promoting new images for meetings tourism, *Cities*, 19, 60-70.

Braun, B.M. and Rungeling, B., 1992: The relative economic impact of convention and tourist visitors on a regional economy: a case study, *International Journal of Hospitality Management*, 11, 65-71.

City of Cape Town, 1990: A Conference Centre and Related Issues Regarding the Civic Centre, TP3630/BA, Town Planning Branch, City of Cape Town.

City of Johannesburg, 2002: *World Summit on Sustainable Development 26 August to 4 September 2002: Project Completion Report*, City of Johannesburg, Johannesburg.

City of Johannesburg, 2003: *Joburg Conference Venues*, City of Johannesburg, Johannesburg.

City of Johannesburg, 2004: Finance & Economic Development, available at www. joburg.org.za/finance/index.stm

Cooper, C., 1979: *The Convention Industry and Sydney: An Analysis of Market Trends and Location Parameters for a Major Convention Centre*, Department of Geography, University of New England, Armidale.

Crouch, G.I. and Louviere, J.J., 2003: Experimental analysis of the choice of convention site, *Tourism Analysis*, 8, 171-176.

Crouch, G.I. and Ritchie, J.R.B., 1998: Convention site selection research: a review, conceptual model and propositional framework, *Journal of Convention and Exhibition Management*, 1 (1), 49-69.

Davidson, R., 1993: European business tourism – changes and prospects, *Tourism Management*, 14, 167-172.

Davie, L., 2003: Joburg country's top exhibitions venue, available at www.joburg.org. za (19 December).

Davie, L., 2004: Joburg an "emerging giant" for business tourism, available at www. joburg.org.za (21 June).

Dieke, P.U.C., 1998: Regional tourism in Africa: scope and critical issues, in E. Laws, B. Faulkner and G. Moscardo (Eds.), *Embracing and Managing Change in Tourism: International Case Studies*, Routledge, London, 29-48.

Dlamini, N., 2004: Sandton Convention Centre targets growth, available at www.joburg. org.za (3 May).

Dorfler, C., 2002: M.I.C.E.—success factors and opportunities, *Tourism and Hospitality Management*, 8, 169-176.

Douglas, I., 1979: Preface, in C. Cooper, *The Convention Industry and Sydney: An Analysis of Market Trends and Location Parameters for a Major Convention Centre*, Department of Geography, University of New England, Armidale, iv-v.

Durban Metropolitan Tourism Authority, 2004: *Durban, South Africa—Convention Directory*, Durban Metropolitan Tourism Authority, Durban.

Dwyer, L. and Mistilis, N., 1997: Challenges to MICE tourism in the Asia-Pacific region, in M. Oppermann (Ed.) *Pacific Rim Tourism*, CAB International, Wallingford, 219-229.

Gelling, J., 2004: The changing dynamics of business tourism in South Africa—structure, geography and transformation, Unpublished BA Hons Dissertation, University of the Witwatersrand, Johannesburg.

Getz, D., Anderson, D. and Sheehan, L., 1998: Roles, issues and strategies for convention and visitors bureaux in destination planning and product development: a survey of Canadian bureaux, *Tourism Management*, 19, 331-340.

Ghimire K.B., 2001: The growth of national and regional tourism in developing countries: an overview, in K.Ghimire (Ed.), *The Native Tourist: Mass Tourism Within Developing Countries,* Earthscan, London, 1-29.

Gibb, M.W., 2006: The "global" and the "local": a comparative study of development practices in three South African municipalities, Unpublished Ph.D. thesis, Rhodes University, Grahamstown.

Go, F.M. and Govers, R., 1999: The Asian perspective: which international conference destinations in Asia are the most competitive?, *Journal of Convention & Exhibition Management*, 1 (4), 37-50.

Grant Thornton Kessel Feinstein, 1999: Re-feasibility study for a proposed conference center development, Unpublished report prepared for the University of the Witwatersrand Income Generation Group, Johannesburg.

Haase, C., 2002: Centre to form core of business tourism in Mother City, *Engineering News*, 13 December 2002- 16 January 2003, 48-54.

Hailan, Q., Lan, L. and Gilder, K.T.C., 2000: The comparative analysis of Hong Kong as an international conference destination in South East Asia, *Tourism Management*, 21, 643-648.

Hall, C.M., 2002: Tourism in capital cities, *Tourism* (Zagreb), 50 (3), 235-248.

Hankinson, G., 2005: Destination brand images: a business tourism perspective, *Journal of Services Marketing*, 19, 24-32.

Hiller, H.H., 1995: Conventions as mega-events: a new model for convention-host city relationships, *Tourism Management,* 16, 375-379.

Hughes, C.G., 1988: Conference tourism—a salesman's dream, *Tourism Management,* 9, 235-238.

Jansen-Verbeke, M., Vandenbroucke, S. and Tielen, S., 2005: Tourism in Brussels, capital of the "new Europe." *International Journal of Tourism Research*, 7 (2), 109-122.

Johannesburg Tourism Company, 2004: A flood of convention bookings for venues in Johannesburg, available at www.joburgtourism.com (10 September).

Johannesburg Tourism Company, 2005a: About JTC, available at www.joburgtourism. com

Johannesburg Tourism Company, 2005b: Your ideal conference city, available at www. joburgtourism.com

Johannesburg Tourism Company, 2005c: International events hosted in Johannesburg, driven by JTC's Convention Bureau, available at www.joburgtourism.com

Johannesburg Tourism Company, 2005d: Johannesburg: much more than you expect, available at www.joburgtourism.com

Keyser, H., 2002: *Tourism Development*, Oxford Southern Africa, Cape Town.

Kim, S.S., Chon, K. and Chung, K.Y., 2003: Convention industry in South Korea: an economic impact analysis, *Tourism Management,* 24, 533-541.

Kulendran, N. and Witt, S.F., 2002: Forecasting the demand for international business tourism, *Journal of Travel Research*, 41, 265-271.

Law, C.M., 1987: Conference and exhibition tourism, *Built Environment*, 13 (2), 85-95.

Law, C.M., 1992: Urban tourism and its contribution to economic regeneration, *Urban Studies*, 29, 599-618.

Law, C.M., 1993: *Urban Tourism: Attracting Visitors to Large Cities*, Mansell, London.

Lawson, F.R., 1982: Trends in business tourism management, *Tourism Management*, 3, 298-302.

Lew, A.A. and Chang, T.C., 1999: Where the world meets; regionalism and globalization in Singapore's convention industry, *Journal of Convention and Exhibition Management*, 1 (4), 17-36.

Lootvoet, B. and Freund, B., 2006: Local economic development: utopia and reality—the example of Durban, KwaZulu-Natal, in V. Padayachee (Ed.), *The Development Decade: Economic and Social Change in South Africa, 1994-2004*, HSRC Press, Cape Town, 254-271.

Maharaj, B. and Ramballi, K., 1998: Local economic development strategies in an emerging democracy: the case of Durban in South Africa, *Urban Studies*, 35, 131-148.

Mustapha, A.R. 2001: The survival ethic and the development of tourism in Nigeria, in K. Ghimire (Ed.), *The Native Tourist: Mass Tourism Within Developing Countries*. Earthscan, London, 172-197.

Nel, E. and Rogerson, C.M. (Eds.), 2005: *Local Economic Development in the Developing World: The Experience of Southern Africa*, Transaction Press, New Brunswick NJ and London.

Oppermann, M., 1996a: Convention destination images: analysis of meeting planners' perceptions, *Tourism Management*, 17, 175-182.

Oppermann, M., 1996b: Convention cities—images and changing fortunes, *Journal of Tourism Studies*, 7 (1), 10-19.

Oppermann, M., 1997: The future of tourism in the Pacific Rim, in M. Oppermann (Ed.), *Pacific Rim Tourism*, CAB International, Wallingford, 240-249.

Oppermann, M., 1998: Perceptions of convention destinations: large-half versus small-half association meeting planners, *Journal of Convention and Exhibition Management*, 1 (1), 35-48.

Oppermann, M. and Chon, K.-S., 1997: Convention participation decision-making process, *Annals of Tourism Research*, 24, 178-191.

Owen, C., 1992: Changing trends in business tourism, *Tourism Management*, 13, 224-226.

Pyo, S. and Koo, Y.-S., 2002: The convention industry in South Korea, in K. Weber and K.S. Chon (eds.), *Convention Tourism: International Research and Industry Perspectives*, Haworth Hospitality Press, Binghamton, 171-184.

Qu, H., Li, L. and Chu, G.K.T., 2000: The comparative analysis of Hong Kong as an international conference destination in Southeast Asia, *Tourism Management*, 21, 643-648.

Rogerson C.M., 1990: Sun International: the making of a South African tourism multinational. *GeoJournal*, 22, 345-354.

Rogerson, C.M., 1996: Image enhancement and local economic development in Johannesburg, *Urban Forum*, 7, 139-156.

Rogerson, C.M., 2002: Urban tourism in the developing world: the case of Johannesburg, *Development Southern Africa*, 19, 169-190.

Rogerson, C.M., 2004a: Regional tourism in South Africa: a case of "mass tourism of the South," *GeoJournal*, 60, 229-237.

Rogerson, C.M., 2004b: Towards the world-class African city: planning local economic development in Johannesburg, *Africa Insight*, 34 (4), 12-21.

Rogerson, C.M., 2006: Local economic development in post-apartheid South Africa: a ten-year research review, in V. Padayachee (Ed.), *The Development Decade: Economic and Social Change in South Africa, 1994-2004*, HSRC Press, Cape Town, 227-253.

SAACI, Annual Yearbooks, *Southern Africa Conference, Exhibition and Incentives Guide* 1990/1991, 1996/7, 2003/4.

Solberg, H.A., Andersson, T.D. and Shibli, S., 2002: An exploration of the direct economic impacts from business travellers at world championships, *Event Management*, 7 (3), 151-164.

South African Tourism, 2004: MICE hits the dust: long live business tourism, available at www.southafrica.net

South African Tourism, 2005: South Africa—conference country, available at www.southafrica.net

Suh, Y.K. and McAvoy, L., 2005: Preferences and trip expenditures—a conjoint analysis of visitors in Seoul, Korea, *Tourism Management*, 26, 325-333.

Swarbrooke, J. and Horner, S., 2001: *Business Travel and Tourism*, Butterworth-Heinemann, Oxford.

Van Schalkwyk, M., 2005: Opening speech by Marthinus van Schalkwyk, Minister of Environmental Affairs and Tourism, addressing the fourth Annual National Tourism Conference, Sun City, 6 October, available at www.info.gov.za/speeches

Van Wyk, S., 2005a: Business tourism: business is booming, *Mail and Guardian*, 15-21 July, 39.

Van Wyk, S., 2005b: South Africa's very own world-class convention venues, *Mail and Guardian*, 15-21 July, 42-43.

Var, T., Cesario, F. and Mauser, G., 1985: Convention tourism modelling, *Tourism Management*, 6, 194-204.

Weber, K., 2001: Meeting planners' use and evaluation of convention and visitor bureaus, *Tourism Management*, 22, 599-606.

Weber, K. and Chon, K. (Eds.), 2002: *Convention Tourism: International Research and Industry Perspectives*, Haworth Hospitality Press, Binghamton.

Weber, K. and Ladkin, A., 2003: The convention industry in Australia and the United Kingdom: key issues and competitive forces, *Journal of Travel Research*, 42, 125-132.

Wootton, G. and Stevens, T., 1995: Business tourism: a study of the market for hotel-based meetings and its contribution to Wales's tourism, *Tourism Management*, 16, 305-313.

World Tourism Organisation, 2003: *MICE Outbound Tourism 2000*, WTO, Madrid.

Zelinsky, W., 1994: Conventionland U.S.: the geography of a latterday phenomenon, *Annals of the Association of American Geographers*, 84, 68-86.

6

Festival Tourism in Urban Africa: The Case of South Africa

Gustav Visser

Internationally, ever-increasing numbers of cities, towns, and villages are eager to share their customs, as well as natural or built environments and local produce with visitors through the staging of festivals (McKercher and Du Cros, 2002). While historically, not all festivals were initiated with income-generation in mind, the overwhelming majority of festivals currently staged are clearly focused on attracting income to a particular urban area or region (Law, 2000). Increasingly, too, festival tourism has become a key feature of many towns' and cities' tourism development strategies and now forms an integral part of their urban redevelopment and/or economic development planning (Van den Berg et al., 1995; Law, 1996).

Within the South African context, festivals and their links to urban tourism development are also starting to emerge as an important aspect of urban development thinking (Turco et al., 2003). Indeed, the growth of festivals in seemingly every village, town or city in South Africa has been immense, and would even appear to have become almost obligatory for any urban development planning framework (cf. Rogerson, 2002). However, despite the vast number and range of festivals currently staged in South Africa, there appears to be very little by way of published research that might assist in understanding their occurrence, both in space and over time, or the purpose for which these festivals have been introduced, or what their impact on host communities might be. Indeed, echoing an international trend, South African festival tourism has not been the subject of much research attention (O'Sullivan and Jackson, 2002).

In the context of the current paucity of research focused on festivals in South Africa, this chapter aims to make a contribution toward bringing about a better understanding of the general contours of the national festival tourism segment.

This objective will be reached through six areas of investigation. The first section provides a brief overview of the international literature focused on festival tourism in urban areas. Here it is argued that despite the magnitude of festival tourism, it remains a neglected area of investigation; and as a consequence, our understanding of its various impacts on the urban form is limited. The second section focuses on festival tourism investigations in the South African context. It is suggested that the available body of research in this regard is extremely limited, and also highly uneven in terms of the number and types of festivals focused upon. Thereafter, in the third section, the methodology employed in the empirical part of this investigation is briefly outlined. The fourth section provides some insights into the spatio-temporal occurrence of festivals in South Africa, while section five reviews the types of festivals that are staged. The sixth section focuses on a case study—namely the Volksblad Kunstefees. The aim is to provide some outline in respect of a key South African arts festival that has not received any research attention to date. In the context of the preceding sections, the final part of the chapter furnishes an indication of those aspects of South African festival tourism that require future research attention.

Festivals and the International Research Arena

More than a decade ago festival tourism was highlighted by Getz and Frisby (1988: 22) as "an emerging giant." However, despite a dramatic increase in the number of festivals staged annually since then, there still appears to be a relatively small and disparate body of literature on the subject (O'Sullivan and Jackson, 2002: 326). Festival tourism in general refers to a phenomenon in terms of which people from outside a festival locale visit during "a festival period" (O'Sullivan and Jackson, 2002: 325). Other definitions include that of Ritchie (1984: 2), who points out that such tourism is linked to "events of limited duration developed primarily to enhance the awareness, appeal and profitability of a tourist destination." Festival tourism encompasses a range of activities (Shaw and Williams, 2002: 266). Indeed, as O'Sullivan and Jackson (2002: 326) point out, it is "most frequently used as a catch-all term to include special events tourism and festivals of any size or organizational persuasion" and, as a consequence, makes festival tourism a complex topic of study. Currently, at least three perspectives inform the manner in which festivals are studied. The perspectives most frequently cited include those of sociological and leisure participation, as well as community development and tourism industry approaches.

On the whole, these perspectives agree that festival tourism—like all types of tourism—is pursued by organizations and institutions in all manner of localities because of the opportunities it provides for community development and environmental enhancement, in addition to the more obvious benefits of income generation (Shaw and Williams, 2002: 265). More specifically, festivals are understood to contribute toward place marketing; extend tourist seasons (or create them); generate revenue for different levels of government;

and generally to have a positive impact on the local economy by generating incomes, supporting existing businesses and encouraging new small, medium, and micro-enterprise development (cf. Thomas, 2004). Urban tourism research has been particularly interested in the large-scale events and festivals viewed through the lens of place marketing as a strategy within a broader entrepreneurial city framework which has become a near-obligatory planning aspect for the post-industrial urban economies of the North. Although it is generally assumed that festival tourism generates income, its true economic, social, and cultural impacts on localities are complex, and surprisingly, not well understood (Shaw and Williams, 2002: 267).

Notwithstanding a general dearth of festival tourism research, some general indications of how festivals impact upon host locations can be identified. As a whole it is now known that both the economic and social impacts are unevenly distributed through urban communities and can sometimes amount to very limited positive input. Snowball and Antrobus (2001), following the pioneering work of Mitchell and Wall (1986), demonstrated that smaller festivals produced the greatest economic benefit, but that as festivals became more established, the economic impact became relatively less significant. However, Snowball and Antrobus' (2001) research also complicates these claims to some extent by finding, for example, that owing to economic leakages out of local economies, festivals in smaller urban centers are more pronounced than in larger towns and small cities. The reason for this is that the latter locations have a larger, more diverse urban economy and that in such areas, many of the services utilized by the festival are provided locally. This situation ensures that the income generated by the festival remains within the local economy. By contrast, in the smaller centers many of the services have to be contracted in from service providers outside the region.

The impacts of festival tourism are, however, not always so self-evident. The influx of tourists can result in a change in the community infrastructure to serve the needs of festival visitors with the result that, as festivals grow and begin to establish stronger links outside the locality, local entrepreneurs may become resentful and the economic benefits of the festival may become less significant (O'Sullivan and Jackson, 2002: 326-327). Moreover, the important question is not only that of whether or not economic benefit accrues from urban festival tourism, but also that of who the beneficiaries are. In the main, economic benefits are most significant for product providers and facility owners, and not for the ordinary citizen. A number of studies suggest that the general population of urban centers hosting festivals seldom derive any sustainable employment opportunities from festival tourism (Janniskee and Drews, 1998). Other criticism relates to the development of tourist enclaves diverting the attention of visitors away from other parts of a city or town (Judd, 1999). Further issues of concern include the spatial concentration of festival-related economic opportunities in particular parts of cities. For example, festivals often occur far away from the residential neighborhoods of those who need employment opportunities most (Judd, 1999). Moreover, questions have been asked concerning the quality of festival tourism-related employment (Shaw and Williams, 2002: 270).

O'Sullivan and Jackson (2002: 327) contend that the benefits of festival tourism in the urban context are not confined to the economic impact alone. Social impacts often also come into play. In their view, festival tourism can contribute to increased organizational activity in a locality, bringing about improved leadership; positive impacts on local accountability; stimulation of better public-private co-operation; and the investment of profits back into the community. In addition, it has been argued that particularly for smaller urban centers, the development of a festival is not solely about income generation; it also entails the celebration of community and the cultivation of place aware-ness, which will hopefully generate future tourist flows (Janniskee and Drews, 1998; Falassi, 1987).

Finally, beyond these social impacts, although still underpinned by a certain economic rationale, festival tourism can also lead to environmental improve-ments in festival locations (Janniskee, 1996). Indeed, the link between tourism in general and environmental preservation and conservation has long been recognized (Mathieson and Wall, 1982). Similarly, the role of festivals in rela-tion to the urban environment has been acknowledged (O'Sullivan and Jackson, 2002: 328). Janniskee (1996: 395), for example, points out that in the run-up to festival time, residents and business owners become involved in activities to make the locality more presentable. Furthermore, it is argued that as a festival becomes more established, there is increased motivation and available funding for community improvement projects such as redeveloping down-town areas, preserving and restoring historic buildings, renovating old theatres, construct-ing parks, and community centers, planting trees, paving streets, and installing holiday decorations (Janniskee, 1996: 395; Gahr, 2004).

Festival Tourism Research in South Africa

Within the South African context academic research into festival tourism is sparse, while investigation into the deployment of festivals as an economic driver for urban tourism in particular, is almost non-existent. Within the very limited body of published and unpublished research focused on festival tour-ism, there is a clear bias in terms of the spatial foci of these investigations, the key research questions concerning the impact of festivals, as well as the types of festivals under investigation. In the first instance, most of the investigations focus on festivals in smaller urban areas (cf. Snowball and Antrobus, 2001; 2002; Witepski, 2002; Tassiopoulos and Haydam, 2003).

This is probably owing to the fact that it has been argued in international investigations that the impact of festival tourism on smaller localities is more significant than in larger urban centers (Snowball and Antrobus, 2001; 2002). Secondly, the research attention in South Africa is possibly biased in favor of smaller urban settlements such as Grahamstown (National Arts Festival), Potchefstroom (Aardklop), and Oudtshoorn (KKNK), because these are university towns (in the first two instances), or close to universities (as in the case of Oudtshoorn), and consequently comprise convenient research themes (Snowball, 2001; Snowball and Antrobus, 2001; 2002; Snowball and Willis, 2006). Thirdly, in nearly all cases, the research question is concerned with the economic impact of these festivals (Nuntsu, Haydam, and Tassiopoulos, 2003; Snowball and Willis, 2006). Fourthly, all these festivals are large-scale arts festivals, covering all artistic disciplines and receiving considerable media exposure. As a consequence they are foremost in investigators' minds when festival tourism impacts are being considered (Snowball and Willis, 2006). Finally, the accurate measurement of the value of the arts to society is becoming increasingly important, in a context where the arts must compete with housing, health, education, and the like for public funds and corporate sponsorships (Snowball and Willis, 2006). Hence, motivation for the public funding of arts events such as the National Arts Festival in Grahamstown, for example, has become critical (Snowball and Antrobus, 2001).

Taken as a whole, and as will be demonstrated below, the available research on South African festival tourism is very limited and deals with only two different types of festivals located in two very different types of settings. In the first instance there are investigations that deal with festivals in the large metropolitan areas. This type of research focuses mainly on existing festivals and their impact within the jurisdictional area of the local authority, or on the impact of festivals that are supported and developed by local authorities. These investigations are largely geared toward monitoring the actual impacts of particular festivals (Department of Economic Development and Tourism, 2003). The second strand of South African festival tourism research relates to festivals that are not linked to local government interventions, as well as those that were not conceived as a vehicle for local economic development, nor as a place-marketing strategy, nor with a view to their inclusion in urban tourism development strategies.

Festival Tourism and Larger Cities

Certainly, one of the greatest ironies concerning festival tourism research in South Africa is the fact that the city with the most advertised festivals—Cape Town—has received the least academic research attention. Indeed, most of what is known about festival tourism in Cape Town is based on exploratory research reports that resulted from local government investigations (Du Plessis, 2002). Notwithstanding academic research neglect, decision-makers of the City of Cape Town are certainly aware of the impact that festivals could have on the economic fortunes of the city, as well as the role of such festivals in stimulating urban tourism (Du Plessis, 2002).

More generally, the local authority of Cape Town is also conscious of the place-marketing possibilities that festivals present, in addition to the festivals' potential to stimulate future development investments (Du Plessis, 2002). In the research conducted by the City of Cape Town's Department of Economic Development and Tourism (2003), it was found that the Cape Town International Jazz Festival (formerly the North Sea Jazz Festival) generated R58.4 million, while the Cape Town Minstrel Carnival had a total economic impact of R21.4 million. One-day events such as the J&B Met Race and the Argus Cycle Tour generated R311.8 million (R221.4 million of which came from outside Cape Town) and R56.2 million, respectively. Indeed, the three one-day events and the three festivals surveyed, collectively generated more than R650 million (Anon, 2004). On the whole, however, this research is at most suggestive, with detailed research still needing to be undertaken.

Research neglect is, however, not limited to Cape Town, but is also seen in respect of other South African metropolitan areas, including Durban, Johannesburg and Pretoria. For instance a key annual arts festival—Arts Alive—staged in Johannesburg, presents an example of a festival that is not only focused on the promotion of culture, but which was also very specifically instituted to reposition Johannesburg as a cultural hub that could revive the inner city. Indeed, this goal is reflected in the key mission statement of the festival (Van Oerle, 2004). While the development of arts and culture is promoted as the primary reason for staging the festival, the underlying outcome that the organizers aim to achieve is the economic development of the city. However, despite the importance accorded to the Arts Alive festival by the city council, no published research has been forthcoming in terms of the actual impact that this festival has on Johannesburg generally and the inner city in particular.

A further example of the development of a festival to attain place-marketing objectives with a view to broader economic development is that of the Mangaung African Cultural Festival (Macufe) in the Free State city of Bloemfontein. In contrast to other arts festivals in South Africa, this festival aims to be "renowned as South Africa's only 'true African festival' and titled the biggest arts and cultural showcase of its kind on the continent. Macufe focuses internationally, rather than locally and offers a home to the vast range of cultural groups represented in Africa" (Macufe, 2004, no page numbers). In developing such a festival, a key "festival mission" is to "promote the Free State . . . as a top-of-the-list tourist destination to arts and culture lovers in Africa and the rest of the world" (Macufe, 2004). Despite being supported by no fewer than 134 000 patrons, Macufe, like for most festivals in South Africa, has received no academic research attention. The only investigation into the impact of this festival was generated by the festival's organizers themselves. This investigation indicated that "an estimated R46 million was injected into the Free State economy ... beneficiaries included hotels, B&B's, guesthouses, lodges, restaurants, car rental firms ... and retail outlets" (Macufe, 2004: no page numbers).

Whereas international literature has developed a clear focus on the various linkages between festivals, urban tourism and urban (re)development strategies, it has to be stressed that not all festivals are necessarily deployed for place promotion, or to serve as an economic stimulus for urban economic growth. The oldest festival in South Africa—the annual Cape Town Minstrel Carnival, established in the mid-nineteenth century—is a case in point. The Minstrel Carnival is an identity-based festival that celebrates the emancipation of the Malay people from slavery in South Africa, and has historically symbolized a challenge to white cultural and political hegemony over the so-called colored community (Martin, 2000; Pollack, 2004). With tourism having become a pillar of the Cape Town urban economy, city officials are planning to turn the Minstrel Carnival into a celebration that will rival festivals in New Orleans and Rio de Janeiro.

However, the minstrels themselves are apprehensive about opening up the festival to a broader audience, particularly international tourists. There is a widespread fear, reports Pollack (2004: 2), "that organizing the Carnival to appeal to foreign tourists and commercial sponsors would mean taking it away from the local communities that have kept it alive for over a hundred years, in effect reserving the best seats for tourists just as they were once reserved for whites at segregated stadiums." Moreover, "there is an enduring ambivalence in Cape Town about colored identity and whether it is something that can or should be embraced and celebrated ... If Capetonians are unsure about how to respond to a parade of blackface[d] minstrels, the feeling goes, how might the rest of the world react?" (Pollack, 2004: 2).

In addition, there are also issues concerning identity and class differences internal to the colored community that are exposed through the staging of this festival. Many of the middle-class and elite groupings within the colored community do not want to identify with the working-class roots of the carnival. Indeed, statements have been made that "it's so local, it's just a bunch of skollies, just a bunch of riff-raff, getting together and jumping up and down" (Pollack, 2004: 1). The transformation of such a festival (which is ultimately a celebration of identity) for the purposes of a more general expansion of Cape Town's urban tourism offering, could ultimately segment and divide a community.

Festival Tourism and Smaller Urban Areas

It is ironic that South African festivals that were developed for reasons other than place-marketing or the need for an urban tourism development strategy, comprise some of the largest of the local annual festivals, as well as the key focus of the limited available academic and consultancy research. While the analysis of South African festivals presented later in the chapter will highlight the types of festivals that are held annually, and indeed show that these festivals cover an extraordinary array of foci, those festivals that have received local research attention are all larger-scale general arts festivals.

The festival that has received the most research attention is the National Arts Festival that has been held annually in Grahamstown since 1974 (Snowball,

2001; Snowball and Antrobus, 2001; 2002). Other festivals that have emerged more recently as themes of research attention are the Klein Karoo National Arts Festival (established 1995) and Aardklop (established 1998).[1] A key unifying feature of these festivals is that they were both developed by private organizations/institutions, with a view to language development through the promotion of all artistic disciplines (Briers, 2005). Neither of these festivals were established with local economic development, urban tourism development, or place-marketing as key objectives. However, while these aspects were not necessarily key issues of consideration at the inception of these festivals, they have certainly subsequently assumed important roles in the urban development planning strategies of their respective local host authorities (Snowball and Willis, 2006).

The National Arts Festival in Grahamstown is the longest running, and it is consequently not surprising that it has received the most research attention. Echoing international experiences, the initial research into this festival has primarily focused on understanding the dynamics of the visitor base and the economic impact associated with the activities of these visitors (Snowball and Antrobus, 2002). The most recent investigations have established that 131 900 people attended the Grahamstown festival (2002), supporting 494 events at 1,829 presentations. Further findings include the fact that 60 percent of the festivalgoers fell within the eighteen to thirty-five year age category, with 21 percent between the ages of thirty-six and forty-five, 15 percent between forty-six and sixty and a mere four percent older than sixty (Snowball and Antrobus, 2002). The most sophisticated investigation into this festival has been the research by Snowball and associates, who set out to measure the value of the arts festival to the host community, beyond the benefits experienced by the owners of local tourism and leisure enterprises in Grahamstown. Snowball argued that economic impact studies generally consider the primary recipients of economic benefit, who often belong to the middle- and upper-income groups. This investigation shows that the festival holds social benefits for the poorer section of Grahamstown, too, and that non-market benefits are worth approximately R3 million a year. These benefits in turn comprise a very important part of the value that accrues to the low-income groups in the area. This research also introduced a number of new techniques aimed at improving the manner in which the impact of festivals is measured (Snowball, 2001).

The first investigations into both Aardklop and the KKNK have not yet produced any highly sophisticated research, and have thus far mainly been concerned with the general demographic features of the festival-goers and the direct economic impact of their activities on the host community. A key finding in this regard is that, although the Grahamstown festival is far more established than the two Afrikaans language festivals, Aardklop and KKNK have grown rapidly in terms of visitor numbers. For example, Aardklop annually draws 180,000 visitors and KKNK 140,000 (Nieman, 2003). The demographic profile of the festival-goers is largely similar to the profile of those visiting Graham-stown, although the language categories are obviously different and, given the festivals' locations, the regions of origin also differ (Snowball and Antrobus, 2002). Moreover, while festival visitors were significantly more representative in terms of race at Grahamstown than in the case of either Aardklop or KKNK, these festivals have generally been supported by the white community.

A further significant theme emerging from current research relates to the rapid growth in the number of visitors to the newer festivals, which could possibly be explained in a number of ways. Key factors include the fact that Afrikaans stage productions feature less often in the mainstream theatre offering of the large cities; that the changed position of Afrikaans as a language of government has generated new strategies through which the Afrikaans community aims to develop and maintain language specific performing arts; and—probably the most important factor—that these productions take place in or close to areas that have relatively large Afrikaans-speaking populations with sufficient disposable income (Nieman, 2003).

As far as the proportions of income generated at these festivals are concerned, considerable variation has been recorded. Currently, the National Arts Festival, Grahamstown and Aardklop earn approximately R33 million each, while the KKNK earns nearly R100 million (Snowball and Antrobus, 2002; Aardklop, 2003; Nieman, 2003; Anon, 2004). In the main, the higher earning of the KKNK can be explained by the fact that the KKNK is staged over a longer period of time and the visitors stay slightly longer.

While the initial establishment of these festivals was mainly aimed at the development of the performing arts, some investigations point out that additional objectives have subsequently been introduced, not the least of which is place promotion (Aardklop, 2003; Nieman, 2003). For example, both the Afrikaans language festivals of Aardklop and the Volksblad-Kunstefees, have seen close co-operation between the local universities and festival organizers in Potchefstroom (University of the North-West) and Bloemfontein (University of the Free State), respectively. In both instances the festivals are increasingly being used as a marketing vehicle for these institutions of higher learning. In both cases the universities claim that they have seen significant increases in student enrolment, and argue that this is partly owing to the exposure that these festivals have given to their campuses and the various facilities they offer students (Nieman, 2003).

Further findings point to the alignment of international discourse that links the size of the urban centers hosting festivals and the magnitude of these festivals' economic impacts (Aardklop, 2003; Volksblad, 2003). In research commissioned by Aardklop (2003), it was demonstrated that, because Potchefstroom has a larger economy, less money leaks from the festival to other towns and cities, as a result of the fact that most of the services associated with the staging of the festival are supplied locally. Similarly, the same suggestion is put forward in respect of Bloemfontein's Volksblad and Macufe festivals (Briers, 2005), as far more formal theatres and associated support staff and services are located in this city than in the towns hosting Aardklop, the Grahamstown Festival, or KKNK. Additional impacts relate to increased investment in physical infrastructure. The Aardklop research, for example, found that the value of building plans submitted for leisure and tourism-related development in Potchefstroom had increased from R100 million in 2000 to R180 million in 2003. The same investigation also found that festival-goers were of the opinion that the arts festivals had made a significant contribution toward changing their perception of festival locations, with towns such as Potchefstroom and Oudsthoorn, as well as smaller cities like Bloemfontein, being less limited in their leisure and recreational offerings than they had previously thought (Aardklop, 2003).

As can be deduced from the above, a small stream of festival tourism research is starting to emerge. The work is highly descriptive, and is in the main concerned with analyzing the economic impact of particular festivals. None of this research has specifically focused on the development of urban tourism, nor on urban tourism as a strategy for urban development and the planned expansion of the urban economic system. However, perhaps the greatest oversight in this small body of literature is the lack of investigations aimed at providing an overview of the general magnitude of festivals in South Africa. It is this omission in research on local festivals that the following part of the chapter aims to address.

Methodology

The key aim of this investigation is to compile a general geography of festivals in South Africa. To achieve this objective a number of sources were searched. Provincial tourism guidebooks, the respective provincial and local authority tourism websites and SA-venue.com (a key events website) were consulted. In addition, the national and regional printed media were searched for references to local festivals. The focus on festivals was the main criteria in making the decision as to whether or not an "event" was included in these references. Thus, it was necessary that the event carried the name of "Festival," or was listed in the directories as being a festival. Moreover, the emphasis was on festivals that were at least two days in duration. Had this criterion not been followed, the listing would literally have comprised thousands of items. As a result, important events categories that were omitted from the dataset included marathons (canoeing, cycling, running, etc.), as well as regularly scheduled sporting events involving cricket, football and rugby. It was decided that since these events were so numerous, they would require dedicated sector-specific research attention (see, for example, Turco et al., 2003). Moreover, the available information on when these events take place and where, was not of sufficient quantity or quality to make such an analysis viable. Finally, the festivals included had to take place in urban areas.

A total of 211 annual festivals were identified across South Africa. Whereas this figure is certainly not representative of all the festivals held in South Africa, the dataset is significantly more comprehensive than the list of seventy-nine festivals identified by Van Zyl and Botha (2004). In the sections to follow, attention will first be focused on the spatio-temporal distribution of festivals in South Africa. Secondly, the thematic focus of these festivals will be considered, after which the final part of the chapter will present an outline of different avenues of investigation that could be explored in order to address the current paucity of research into festival tourism and its potential for urban tourism development in South Africa.

The discussion of the investigation will be augmented with a brief but focused account of an investigation concerning a key arts festival in a smaller city in South Africa—Bloemfontein—in respect of which no published research concerning festival tourism has been undertaken as yet. In the relevant section, a different methodology was followed. It must be kept in mind that the scientific measurement of festival attendance and impacts has been problematic ever since researchers have aimed to come to a better understanding of these events (Ralston and Stewart, 1990; Sylvester and Caldwell, 1991; Breen, Bull and Walo, 2001). Following an established survey method used in many studies investigating festivals (cf. Reid and Boyd, 1991), the findings in this investigation draw on a random sampling technique, conducted over a five-day period (13-17, July 2005) at the festival location. As the 2004 visitor estimates suggested that approximately 40,000 people visited the festival, a point one-percent sample of 400 interviews was set for the survey. This sample size was necessary to ensure some level of statistical significance. In total, 423 questionnaires were completed; and the researcher feels confident that some significant conclusions can be drawn from this sample. First, however, an overview of festivals in South Africa will be provided.

Spatio-Temporal Distribution of Festivals Across the Urban Hierarchy

Currently, at least 211 annual festivals take place in South Africa. Spatially these festivals are distributed very unevenly, with the Western Cape Province hosting 40 percent (n=84) of all annual festivals and Mpumalanga only two percent (n=5). The two most highly populated provinces, namely Gauteng and KwaZulu-Natal, host twenty-five annual festivals each (see figure 6.1). There appears to be no necessary link between the population size of the province and the number of festivals staged. For example, the Free State, a sparsely populated province, hosts nine percent (n=19) of festivals, although it accounts for less than six percent of South Africa's population. Likewise, the Northern Cape hosts four percent of festivals, while the far more densely populated province of Mpumalanga hosts only two percent.

The distribution of festivals internal to the provinces differs significantly. In the Free State, the Northern and Western Cape provinces, as well as the North-

West Province, for example, it was found that most urban centers, irrespective of their size, host annual festivals. However, in Mpumalanga the five annual festivals are hosted in only four urban centers. A key commonality is that generally, larger urban centers host a greater number of festivals. For example, all the main metropolitan regions have a higher incidence of annual festivals than do smaller towns and villages. However, a notable exception in this regard is found in the Eastern Cape Province, where Grahamstown hosts three festivals, including one of South Africa's largest arts festivals, while cities such as East London and Port Elizabeth host only one festival each. Moreover, even small towns in that province, including Jeffrey's Bay, Queenstown and Somerset East, each host two annual festivals. Likewise, the university town of Stellenbosch hosts ten festivals—a significantly higher number than in the case of cities such as Bloemfontein or Pietermaritzburg.

Not only is the geographical distribution of South African festivals diverse; their temporal pattern varies as well. The temporal distribution of festivals is

Figure 6.1
Spatial Distribution of Festivals in South Africa

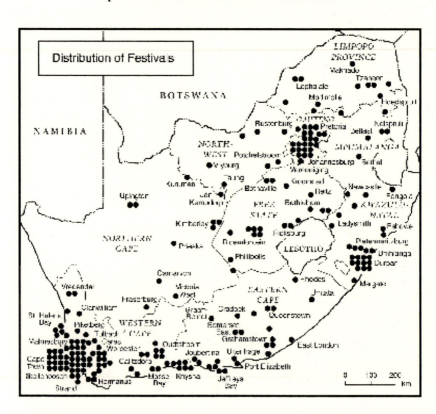

shown in figure 6.2. On the whole, it is clear that festivals generally take place in the second half of the year. However, closer examination of the temporal pattern reveals that there are two main festival periods, one of which in fact falls in the first half of the year. The first temporal concentration occurs from the end of March to the beginning of April during the Easter holiday period.

Figure 6.2
Temporal Distribution of Festivals in South Africa

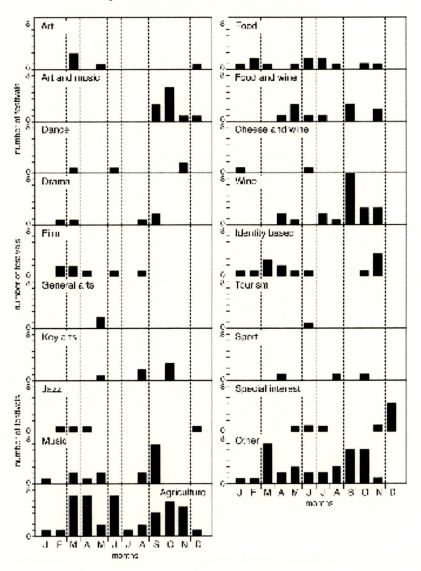

The second temporal concentration of festivals occurs from late September to early October, coinciding with the Michaelmas school holidays. The months of January, June, November, and December are not popular with regard to the staging of festivals. Again, this can be attributed to the temporal distribution of school holidays and the numerous responsibilities and constraints that festival-goers, and indeed, festival organizers are faced with during these periods.

The two main festival seasons largely comprise the agricultural and related produce segments, as well as what can broadly be described as the arts segment. During the March and April season, sixteen arts-related and seventeen agriculture-related festivals (out of a total of forty-eight) are presented. Similarly, during the September/October season, forty-five of the seventy festivals fall within these festival categories. Whereas these temporal clusters coincide with holiday periods, the presentation of festivals at these particular times can also be explained by factors other than school breaks, which are often associated with those times of the year when particular products come onto the market. For example, the high incidence of festivals during September and October can be explained by the fact that agricultural products such as the young wines from the preceding summer, are customarily presented during festivals at that time. Likewise, a range of agricultural festivals in February and March, as well as September and October, are linked to the cycles of harvesting related to certain types of produce, ranging from cherries, maize, and wheat to shellfish.

The distribution of festivals is, however, not always linked to seasonal cycles but can also be explained in relation to the timing of already-existing festivals. Whereas the data used in this survey did not always reveal the reason for choosing particular dates in the year, discussions with festival insiders, such as the organizers of Macufe and the Volksblad Kunstefees, for example, revealed that the timing of festivals that have only recently emerged is directly linked to the scheduling of more established arts festivals. It was pointed out that, in particular, large-scale arts festivals—tagged Key Arts Festivals in the survey—have all developed their scheduling in relation to the most established of the main festivals, namely the National Arts Festival in Grahamstown. Thus, in viewing the dates of the six key arts festivals in the country, one finds that there are never any overlaps in the hosting of the festivals. Nowhere is this more clearly demonstrated than in the timing of the two key arts festivals in the July holiday season—the National Arts Festival (Grahamstown) and the Volksblad Kunstefees (Bloemfontein). These festivals have historically nearly always been separated by four days. Similarly, the three key festivals held during the September/October break, Arts Alive (Johannesburg), Macufe (Bloemfontein) and Aardklop (Potchefstroom), follow directly upon one another.

A further variable that has in recent years started to determine the scheduling of arts festivals in particular, relates to the availability of artists to perform at these festivals. Many artists now very literally travel from one arts festival to another, and organizers have to factor this into their programming arrange-

Figure 6.3
Spatial distribution of festival types in South Africa

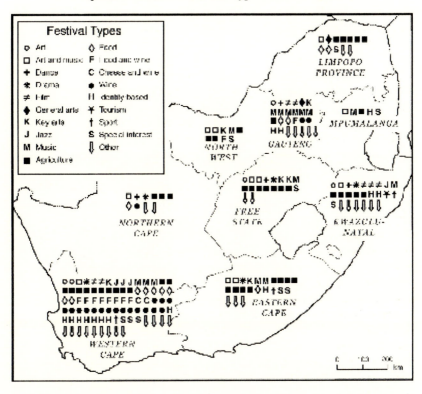

ments. Finally, the need for sponsorship also means that festivals of any great magnitude cannot overlap in terms of their timing, since such overlapping does little to provide brand recognition for the sponsor and, consequently, income for the festival organizers.

South African Festival Types

The festivals currently on offer in South Africa cover a wide range of themes and foci. Nevertheless, two significant clusters emerge (figure 6.3). The first cluster relates to what may broadly be termed as agriculture-related festivals, involving the exhibition of general agricultural produce, wine and specialized foods (accounting for 43 percent of the festivals). The second cluster focuses on the arts, both performing and visual, as well as more general combinations thereof, which together account for 28 percent of festivals. A notable third festival cluster (tagged "other" in this study) focuses on combinations of both arts and agriculture, as well as general trade festivals, combined with entertainment, often targeting family audiences. This category accounts for 16 percent of all festivals in South Africa. A fourth focus relates to those festivals dealing with cultural or ethnic group-identities, such as Zulu history, or the history of early colonial settlers. This focus also includes identity groupings such as the gay community, who have no fewer than four annual festivals to choose from.

The distribution of festival types reveals a particular geography, often linked to the main economic base of the region in which particular festivals are located. The provinces with large agricultural bases, such as the Eastern and Western Cape and the Free State, have a number of agricultural product-specific festivals (oddly, Limpopo, despite the size and range of its agricultural sector hosts very few agricultural festivals). The largest of these festivals is the Nampo agricultural show in Bothaville, which is in fact the largest of its kind in the Southern Hemisphere. The province with the highest number of agriculture-based festivals (twelve out of forty-four) is the Western Cape and includes festivals during which grapes, deciduous fruit, as well as fynbos products, are exhibited. Given the diverse geography and climatic range of the Western Cape, this is not surprising since a very expansive range of products, harvested at various times of the year, is produced in that region. Although many different agricultural product foci are found, the most prominent festival type is that of wine festivals (n=17), organized to promote one of that province's key agricultural products.

The Western Cape is also the location of the highest number of festivals dedicated to the visual and performing arts (n=13), followed by Gauteng (n=10), KwaZulu-Natal (n=9), and surprisingly, considering its small population, the Free State Province (n=8). Internal to this general category, the Western Cape also dominates with three dedicated Jazz festivals. However, there is much variation in this regard. Gauteng, for example, leads in terms of purely music-focused festivals (e.g., Oppikoppi and Woodstock), while Durban takes the lead in presenting film festivals. In terms of both music and film festivals, it is particularly interesting to note that most of these festivals had their origins in the post-1994 era, not least as a result of South Africa's re-entry into the international cultural fold.

One of the most striking findings of this investigation is that although the larger urban centers dominate in terms of the sheer number of festivals, the most important of these events, tagged "key arts festivals," take place in non-metropolitan areas. With the exception of the Arts Alive Festival in Johannesburg, the six festivals are either hosted in the small city of Bloemfontein (Macufe and the Volksblad Kunstefees), or in the even smaller urban centers of Grahamstown (the National Arts Festival), Potchefstroom (Aardklop) and Oudsthoorn (the Klein Karoo Nasionale Kunstefees).

The survey further reveals that particular regions host a greater diversity of festival types. In this respect the Western Cape Province takes the lead, hosting festivals in sixteen out of the nineteen festival categories. Although the types of festivals relate largely to different types of agriculture and agricultural products, the region also organizes festivals that cover a number of arts-related foci, as well as a considerable number of identity-based festivals, including those relating to sexuality, early colonial settler history, and the "colored" community of the Cape. The region showing the least variation in festivals is Mpumalanga, with festivals focusing on only five themes.

As can be seen from the above review, a key arts festival that has not received any research attention to date, is the medium-sized Afrikaans language festival presented in the small city of Bloemfontein. In the section that follows, a small case study outlines some of the key features of a South African arts festival.

The Volksblad Kunstefees: A Case Study

The Volksbald Kunstefees was established in 2001 in the city of Bloemfontein, which is home to some 400,000 inhabitants. Mayfield and Crompton (1995) suggest that there are eight generic reasons for staging festivals, including recreation/socialisation, culture/education, tourism, internal revenue generation, natural resources, agriculture, external revenue generation, and community pride/spirit. The key motivation for establishing the Volksbald festival was related to culture/education—with a view to promoting Afrikaans performing arts among audiences in central South Africa, most notably the Free State province (Briers, 2005). In the main the festival represents a response to the demise of the former (apartheid government-funded) regional performing arts councils during the first half of the 1990s, which led to a substantial decrease in the number of Afrikaans-based productions being staged in places such as Bloemfontein. The festival thus provides an opportunity to view a large number of contemporary Afrikaans language productions that would usually not be staged in the Free State. In the main, this festival is what Dawson (1991) refers to as a mono-ethnic festival, with its key meaning system comprising a "cultural text" of lived ethnicity. As in the case of a large proportion of festivals elsewhere (Getz, 1993), the festival-producing organization is a non-profit concern and is heavily reliant upon sponsorship (cf. Cicora, 1991; Decker, 1991).

The festival developed from very modest beginnings, hosting thirty productions over a three-day period and selling only 6,007 tickets in 2001 (table 6.1). During the early stages of its establishment, visitor numbers could not be estimated. Following renewed support from the University of the Free State, which provides the main performance venues for the festival (free of charge), in addition to sponsorship from private-sector companies such as the Media24 group, the publisher of most Afrikaans-language newspapers and lifestyle magazines, the festival started to gain momentum as from 2003. In that year the festival hosted no fewer than fifty-three productions, and over 22,000 tickets were sold. Currently the festival is presented over a six-day period, staging sixty productions. There is a marked emphasis on Music and Drama productions that appeal to students, as well as young adult audiences (see table 6.1). Ticket sales have escalated beyond the 27,000 mark, and for the first time visitor estimates have been established at around 40,000 festival-goers (Briers,

Table 6.1
Key indicators of the Volksblad Arts Festival (2001-2005)

Year	Number of tickets	Growth (%)	Number of productions
2001	6007	-	30
2002	14 914	129	38
2003	22 607	91	53
2004	24 354	19	57
2005	27 671	23	60

Type of production (2005)	Number of performances
Dance	2
Drama	48
Children's Theatre	14
Music (Classical)	11
Music (Popular)	56
Music Theatre	6
Poetry	3
Talks	13

Source: Briers (2005)

Box 6.1
The remuneration structure of the Volksblad Kunstefees

The income stream of the artists performing at the Festival is structured in three different ways.

a. The selection panel chooses artists or productions that they would like to have at the Festival. These productions are either critically acclaimed, or the artists in the production are known attractions. In this case the Festival committee invites the artists and pays them a pre-agreed sum to the artists.

b. The selection committee goes through the application listings for productions/ artists and selects artists who, although they were not initially considered by the committee, are either critically acclaimed, or who are known attractions in specific productions. In such cases the Festival committee invites the artists and pays them a sum that has been previously agreed on.

c. The selection committee goes through the application listings for productions/ artists and selects candidates. In this case the production is wholly dependent upon earnings arising from ticket-sales. 70% of the proceeds from the door sales go to the artists, and 30% to the Festival funds.

2005). According to the festival organizer the festival is now the fourth-largest arts festival in South Africa, after the KKNK, the Grahamstown Arts Festival and Aardklop (Briers, 2005).

Despite its considerable growth, it is evident that, compared to the other arts festivals in South Africa, the Volksblad Kunstefees is relatively small. However, this event is growing in stature among performing artists. Two important factors have contributed to this. Firstly, unlike the other main arts festivals (Grahamstown, Potchefstroom and Oudtshoorn), the Volksblad festival is the only festival that stages all its productions in venues specifically designed for music and drama performances. This obviously greatly assists performers in presenting their productions. Secondly, performers enter into contracts with the festival organizers that significantly reduce their financial risk exposure (see box 6.1).

Festival-goers at the Volksblad Kunstefees are gender-balanced in terms of their numbers (females 46 percent; males 54 percent), mainly white (66 percent), and generally young (49 percent are under the age of twenty-six years). The age profile correlates with the fact that nearly half the festival-goers are students (43 percent). This in turn explains the relatively low average monthly income of less than R1 000. On the whole the visitor profile strongly correlates with that of the other key arts festivals around the country (table 6.2).

Unlike the visitors to the other "key" Afrikaans language festivals, the overwhelming majority of the festival-goers are from the Free State (73 percent); and in fact, as many as 64 percent are from Bloemfontein itself. Of the 36 percent of the festival-goers who traveled to Bloemfontein to attend the festival, the

Table 6.2
Demographic characteristics of Volksbald Arts Festival festival-goers

Gender	Female 46%	Male 54%					
Age	<19 19%	19-25 30%	26-30 17%	31-40 16%	41-50 13%	51-60 3%	>60 2%
Race	Asian 5%	Black 19%	Coloured 10%	White 66%			
Monthly Income	<R1 000 25%	R1 001- R3 000 22%	R3 001- R6 000 15%	R6 001- R9 000 20%	R9 001- R12 000 8%	>R12 000 10%	
Occupation	Student 43%	Professions 33%	Technical 17%	Service Sector 3%	Other 4%		

majority (44 percent) stayed for the length of the festival, most (56 percent) being accommodated by family or friends, with a small group supporting formal tourist accommodation establishments such as guesthouses (14 percent), hotels (14 percent) and bed-and-breakfast institutions (8 percent). On average these festival "tourists" spent R275 on accommodation during the festival period, and R140 to get to Bloemfontein from their permanent place of residence. Not surprisingly, then, tourist accommodation service providers indicated that the festival only had a marginal impact on occupancy levels. Overwhelmingly, the festival-goers are well acquainted with Bloemfontein, with only six percent of the survey group comprising first-time visitors to the city. In addition, the festival-goers are well acquainted with festivals generally (81 percent) and the Volksblad festival in particular, with no less than 63 percent having attended the festival previously. There is a very high incidence of repeat visitation. The key medium through which festival-goers were made aware of the festival was the printed news media (43 percent), as well as family and friends (37 percent).

Considering that the vast majority of the festival-goers are local residents, or well acquainted with the city, it is not surprising that the staging of the festival had little impact on how the respondents experienced the host city of Bloem-fontein. Of the 40 percent of the respondents who did indicate that the festival had had an impact on their experience of the city, half (49 percent) indicated that the festival made the city "feel more alive, with more to do," or that the festival made them see a different side to Bloemfontein and enhanced the feeling of the city as a place of very friendly people (20 percent).

Crompton and McKay (1997) identified a number of motivation domains for festival attendance. In the Volksblad festival's case, "known group socialization" was of central importance (40 percent). Visiting family/friends and consolidating these bonds (11 percent) also played a role in the motivation for attending the festival. These findings resonate with Formica and Murrmann's (1998) conclusion that family groups attend festivals to consolidate family togetherness, while friendship groups emphasize socialization and group togetherness. This "socialization" function, as opposed to, for example, cultural exploration, is reflected both in the group composition of the festival visitors and in the number of performances that the survey group attended. Most of the survey group attended the festival with friends (40 percent), family (27 percent), or their partners (20 percent), while over the six-day period most festival visitors (78 percent) attended fewer than four productions. In view of this finding, it is not surprising that the festival-goers spent, on average, no more than R127 on tickets.

Interest in (arts) festivals, beyond their intrinsic value as vehicles for cultural engagement, relates to the economic activity that they induce. There are a number of income streams to a festival such as the Volksblad Kunstefees, including inter alia, direct ticket sales, sponsorship; stall owners selling art-and-crafts items; food and beverage providers and entertainers. As there are a host of different service providers who facilitate the staging of the festival, it is not possible to speculate on the total incomes generated from the festival. In addition, neither the organizers, nor the service providers were willing to divulge their financial contributions or incomes. In the main, this "secrecy" has to do with the fact that all costs are open to negotiation, depending on the type of relationship between performers, organizers and support service providers. Services are often provided on a "barter" basis. The only income stream that can be relatively accurately estimated is the income derived from ticket sales. The average ticket price is R60, although prices range from as little as R10 to as much as R140. Given that the largest cohort of the sample spent R127 on tickets and generally did not attend more than two performances, this aggregate seems plausible. Consequently, the total income from ticket sales can be estimated at R 1 660,260.

While the modest income is certainly welcomed by the performing artists, it has to be kept in mind that these funds in fact represent a loss to Bloemfontein and the Free State. With very few exceptions, the performers are not based in the region, but mostly in Gauteng, and to a lesser extent in the Western Cape Province. As the festival (along with the festival trusts) is mainly supported by visitors from Bloemfontein and the Free State Province, this means that there is an outflow of capital from the region. A further income stream may be connected to the various stalls that provide products ranging from arts and crafts (n=285), to food and beverages (n=65). Although the turnover of these enterprises is unknown, we do know that 85 percent of them are based in the Free State (tables 6.3 and 6.4). In this case leakages out of the province are fewer, as only 15 percent of the stall owners come from outside the province. Collectively, when the incomes of stall owners, ticket-sales, tourist accommodation, etc., are considered, the total "income" of the festival is estimated at R27 million (Briers, 2005). However, the impact of the festival relates to the circulation of capital, not the inflow of "new money." Generally, the main economic impact of the festival would appear to be the diversification of the local economic base. A further impact relating to the staging of these performances is connected to the provision of training for staff at the various theatres. It was noted by the festival organizer that this training provides valuable experience for students and recent appointees in theatre management and production (Briers, 2005).

Towards a South African Festivals Tourism Research Agenda

From the preceding analysis, it is clear that a number of festivals are staged annually in South Africa. These festivals vary significantly in terms of their spatial and temporal distribution, while also having a vast number of different thematic foci. Despite the number and scale of festivals, our understanding of these events in the South African context is very limited. Moreover, the way in which these festivals could contribute toward urban tourism, and the manner in which they could be developed to provide maximum benefit to various

Table 6.3
Place of origin of arts and crafts stall exhibitors at the Volksblad Arts Festival (2001-2005)

Bloemfontein and the Free State	Gauteng	Rest of South Africa
85%	5%	10%

Total number of arts and crafts exhibitors = 285

Source: Rall (2005)

Table 6.4
Places of origin of food stall owners at the Volksblad Arts Festival (2001-2005)

Bloemfontein and the Free State	Gauteng	Rest of South Africa
85%	5%	10%

Total number of food stalls = 65

Source: Rall (2005)

components in the host communities, remains largely unexplored. The objective of this final section is to provide a starting point for a more systematic research engagement with the South African festival market, and to outline some avenues for future investigation.

First, whereas it is hoped that the investigation will significantly improve baseline data concerning the spatio-temporal distribution of different types of festivals in South Africa, much more research is required in this respect. It is necessary to develop an even more comprehensive listing of the current festival market in South Africa. In this chapter only festivals taking place over a two-day or longer period were included. As a consequence, a number of festivals were excluded from this investigation. Moreover, given the methodology of this investigation, only festivals that are sufficiently promoted and thus relatively easily traced, were included. Another aspect which relates to the general insight into the magnitude of festival tourism in South Africa, comprising an important area of future investigation, would entail an empirical investigation into the reasons why certain locations present/host far more festivals than others. In addition, the choice of festival types, along with their links, if any, to urban tourism development strategies and place-marketing, requires scrutiny.

Secondly, the only way in which to develop an accurate understanding of the economic impact of festivals in South Africa, is to conduct detailed investigations into the different types of festivals held in different locations across the country. Only by means of a representative sample of all the festival sizes, will it be possible to obtain greater clarity on the economic benefits that festivals might offer, and why such benefits would be likely to accrue. This will require detailed analysis of how these studies are conducted internationally. The standardization of research methodologies will also greatly assist local investigators to conduct internationally comparative studies.

Third, and related to the work of Snowball (2001), research that aims to cast the investigatory net wider, particularly in terms of understanding the economic benefits of festivals beyond those that accrue to individuals who own tourism infrastructure, is required. Currently, there is certainly little insight regarding the question as to who all the beneficiaries of festival tourism are. This, it could be argued, would be an appropriate starting point for local scholarship to address more general issues concerning festival research methodology. However, despite Snowball's 2001 innovative methodological approach, his research nevertheless suggested that it would largely appear that those who gain the most from festivals remain the economically empowered, while the majority of people in festival host communities remain excluded from real participation in the economic gains that festivals yield.

Fourth, questions need to be asked as to whether or not festival tourism can be reworked to improve its pro-poor credentials. If this form of tourism is to have any real impact on the lives of the majority of South Africans, the benefits derived from festivals will need to reach the poor communities in the host locations. Strategies that might assist in attaining such an objective appear to be non-existent; yet, given the national tourism policy environment, such strategies should be regarded as being of the utmost importance for South African tourism researchers and festival organizers alike.

Fifth, it was demonstrated that the limited local research is centrally concerned with the economic impact of festival tourism. However, as Snowball (2001) argues, there are a range of other issues that require research attention. Apart from his investigation, there is very little available information on the social and environmental impact of these festivals on the host communities, as well as the festival locations.

Sixth, internationally speaking, festivals are often developed as a means by which to enhance public perceptions of a particular place. In the local context, there is some evidence to suggest that local authorities are becoming involved in festival planning, for similar reasons. However, we do not have much information concerning which local authorities are becoming involved in this way, or their reasons for choosing such a strategy. Moreover, even in cases where we know that festivals form part of a local government place-marketing strategy, we have little or no evidence to suggest that these festivals are having the desired effect.

Seventh, while it seems obvious that festivals, particularly art festivals, make a valuable contribution to the development of culture in South Africa, there have been virtually no investigations that have aimed to explore the impact of these types of festivals on cultural development and reproduction. For example, has the extraordinary success of the Afrikaans language festivals changed the manner in which the Afrikaans linguistic community understands the current and future development possibilities of their culture/identity? Moreover, does the absence of other cultural festivals linked to linguistic/cultural communities undermine the development of those societal segments and their future advancement?

Eighth, and perhaps at a more mundane level, there are also issues concerning the sustainability of festivals over time—and also, one might argue, issues of market saturation. How many festivals can South Africa ultimately support before they become unviable as a vehicle for urban tourism development and place marketing?

Finally, the most practical aspect relates to the need for research to map out the main stumbling blocks for festival organizers in South Africa, and to investigate ways in which these obstacles might be overcome.

Acknowledgements

Thanks are due to Chris Rogerson for initiating interest in festival tourism and to Wendy Job of the Cartographic Unit at the University of the Witwatersrand for the preparation of the maps; and also to Nthonyana Raputsoe for administering the questionnaire survey.

Note

1. It must be stressed, however, that although these festivals have received most research attention, this research nevertheless constitutes only a few academic investigations.

References

Aardklop, 2003: Impakstudie, available at www.aardklop.co.za.

Anon, 2004: North Sea Jazz Festival Cape Town generated R58.4 million for city coffers, available at http://www.gal/co.za/newsitem.php?id=555.

Breen, H., Bull, A. and Walo, M., 2001: A comparison of survey methods to estimate visitor expenditure at a local event, *Tourism Management*, 22, 473-479.

Cicora, K., 1991: Sponsoring special events, *Parks and Recreation Arlington*, 26(12), 26-29.

Crompton, J.L. and McKay, S.L., 1997: Motives of visitors attending festival events, *Annals of Tourism Research*, 24, 425-439.

Dawson, D., 1991: Nanem et circenses? A critical analysis of ethnic and multicultural festivals, *Journal of Applied Recreation Research*, 16(1), 35-52.

Decker, J., 1991: Seven steps to sponsorship, *Parks and Recreation Arlington*, 26(12), 44-48.

Department of Economic Development and Tourism, 2003: Executive Summary: Tourism and Development Strategy for the City of Cape Town, Atos KPMG Consulting, Cape Town.

Du Plessis, H., 2002: The Cape of good events makes money, *Cape Argus,* 13 June 2004, 12.

Falassi, A. (Ed.), 1987: *Time Out of Time: Essays on the Festival,* University of Mexico Press, Mexico City.

Formica, S. and Murrmann, S., 1998: The effects of group membership on attendance: an international festival case, *Tourism Analysis,* 3(3/4), 197-207.

Gahr, H.S., 2004. Attitudes of residents and tourists toward the use of urban historic sites for festival events, *Event Management,* 8, 231-242.

Getz, D., 1993: Corporate culture in not-for-profit festival organizations: concepts and potential applications, *Festival Management and Event Tourism,* 1(1), 11-17.

Getz, D. and Frisby, W., 1988: Evaluating management effectiveness in community-run festivals, *Journal of Travel Research* (Summer), 22-29.

Janniskee, R., 1996: Historic houses and special events, *Annals of Tourism Research* 23, 395-414.

Janniskee, R. and Drews, P., 1998: Rural festivals and community re-imagining, in R. Butler, C. Hall, I. and Jenkins, (Eds.), *Tourism and Recreation in Rural Areas,* Chichester, Wiley, 135-153.

Judd, D.R., 1999: Constructing the tourist bubble, in D. R. Judd, and S. Fainstein, (Eds.), *The Tourist City,* Yale University Press, New Haven, 35-53.

Law, C.M., 1996: *Tourism in Major Cities,* Thompson International Press, London.

Law, C.M., 2000: Regenerating the city center through leisure and tourism, *Built Environment,* 26, 117-129.

Klein Karoo Nasionale Kunstefees (KKNK), 2004: Key facts, available at http://www.kknk.co.za/mainpages/korporatief.htm.

Macufe, 2004: 2003 Statistics, available at www.macufe.co.za.

Martin, D. C., 2001: The burden of the name: classification and constructions of identity: the case of the "Coloureds" in Cape Town (South Africa), *African Philosophy,* 13(2), 99-124.

Mathieson, A. and Wall, G., 1982: *Tourism: Economic, Physical and Social Impacts,* Longman, London.

Mayfield, T.L. and Crompton, J.L., 1995: Development of an instrument for identifying community reasons for staging a festival, *Journal of Travel Research,* 33(3), 37-44.

McKercher, B. and Du Cros, H., 2002: *Cultural Tourism: The Partnership between Tourism and Cultural Heritage Management,* The Haworth Hospitality Press, New York.

Mitchell, C. and Wall, G., 1986: Impacts of cultural festivals on Ontorio communities, *Recreation Research Review,* 13(1), 28-37.

Nieman, N., 2003: Kunstefees bring geldelike voordeel, available at www.volksblad-fees.co.za/03_feesnuus/46_feesvoordee1.htm.

Nuntsu, N., Haydam, N. and Tassiopoulos, D., 2003: A profile of the 2002 South African National Arts Festival: a pilot study, *Event Management,* 8, 213-222.

O'Sullivan, D. and Jackson, M., 2002: Festival tourism: a contributor to sustainable local economic development? *Journal of Sustainable Tourism,* 10, 325-342.

Pollack, J., 2004: Cape Town Minstrel Carnival, available at http://www.2camels.com/Cape Town Minstrel Carnival.

Ralston, L.S. and Stewart, W.P., 1990: *Annals of Tourism Research,* 17, 289-292.

Reid, L. and Boyd, A., 1991: The social impacts of tourism and their effects on attitudes toward a major cultural attraction, *Tourism: Building Credibility for a Credible Industry,* Proceedings of the Travel and Tourism Research Association 22 Annual Conference, Hyatt Regency Hotel, Long Beach, 9-13 June 1991, 123-133.

Ritchie, J.R., 1984: Assessing the impact of hallmark events: conceptual and research issues, *Journal of Travel Research,* 23(1), 2-11.

Rogerson, C.M., 2002: Urban tourism in the developing world: the case of Johannesburg, *Development Southern Africa,* 19, 169-190.

Shaw, G. and Williams, A.M., 2002: *Critical Issues in Tourism: A Geographical Perspective,* Blackwell Oxford.

Snowball, J.D., 2001: Towards More Accurate Measurement of the Value of the Arts to Society: Economic Impact and Willingness to Pay Studies at the Standard Bank National Arts Festival, MA thesis, Department of Economics and Economic History, Rhodes University.

Snowball, J.D. and Antrobus, G.G., 2001: Measuring the value of the arts to society: the importance of the value of externalities for lower income and education groups in South Africa, *South African Journal of Economics,* 69, 752-766.

Snowball, J.D. and Antrobus, G.G., 2002: Valuing the arts: pitfalls in economic impact studies of arts festivals, *South African Journal of Economics,* 70, 1297-1319.

Snowball, J.D. and Willis, K.G., 2006: Estimating the marginal utility of different sections of an arts festival: the case of visitors to the South African National Arts Festival, *Leisure Studies,* 25(1), 43-56.

Sylvester, C. and Caldwell, L., 1991: Reliable sample gathering at open access festivals and events, *Abstracts of the Proceedings of the 1991 NRPA Leisure Research Symposium,* Baltimore, 17-20 October 1991, 82.

Tassiopoulos, D. and Haydam, N., 2003: Wine tourists in South Africa: a demographic and psychographic study, *Journal of Wine Research,* 15(1), 51-63.

Thomas, R. (Ed.), 2004: *Small Firms in Tourism: International Perspectives,* Elsevier, Amsterdam.

Turco, D.M., Swart, K., Bob, U. and Moodley, V., 2003: Socio-economic impacts of sport tourism in the Durban Unicity, South Africa, *Journal of Sport Tourism,* 8, 223-239.

Van den Berg, L., Van der Borg, J. and Van der Meer, J., 1995: *Urban Tourism: Performance and Strategies in Eight European Cities,* Avebury, Aldershot.

Van Oerle, B., 2004: ArtsAlive, BUZ Publicity, Johannesburg.

Van Zyl, C. and Botha, C., 2004: Motivational factors of local residents to attend the Aardklop National Arts Festival, *Event Management,* 8, 213-222.

Volksblad, 2003: Feesnuus, available at www.volksbladfees.co.za.

Witepski, L., 2002: The show must go on: tourism festivals, *Journal of Southern African Tourism,* 2, 52-53.

Interviews

Mrs. Doks Briers, Organizer of the Volksblad Kunstefees, telephone interview 20 October 2005.

Mrs. Elize Rall, Arts Market and Food Stalls Organizer of the Volksblad Festival, telephone interview 22 November 2005.

7

Second Homes Tourism in Africa: Reflections on the South African Experience

Gijsbert Hoogendoorn, Robyn Mellett and Gustav Visser

Large numbers of towns and villages along the South African coastline, and increasingly in the interior, have grown significantly as a result of consumption led migration. However, South African social science investigations have failed to recognise the role of a particular type of leisure consumption—second home development, investment, and visitation—as a key variable leading to the considerable changes taking place across the South African urban hierarchy, particularly in high natural amenity areas. Internationally, second homes are investigated as an integral part of contemporary tourism and mobility, with the development of various types of urban areas explained owing to second home development and investment (Williams and Hall, 2000; Hall and Müller, 2004). The international body of research demonstrates, among other findings, that second homes are an important part of the urban tourism and leisure lifestyle of many people in the developed North (Hall and Müller, 2004). As a result of the increasing mobility of ever-larger sections of the industrial and post-industrial world, in addition to escalating levels of regional and international leisure migration associated with contemporary globalization, second homes development is currently receiving renewed research attention. In this discourse the advantages for host communities, the factors that contribute to second homes location and the role that second homes play in contemporary society, are re-examined (Hall and Müller, 2004).

Although second homes have received extensive research attention internationally, these concerns have only recently emerged as an area of investigation within the South African context, while analyses for the African continent as a whole, remains to be undertaken (Hoogendoorn and Visser, 2004; Visser, 2003a, 2004a). Currently, there is only a limited body of exploratory research that investigates the significance of the second home phenomenon in South African (e.g., Hoogendoorn and Visser, 2004; Visser, 2003a, 2004a). These first academic investigations have set out to provide a general geography of this phenomenon in the local context (see section 3 for a brief review of these findings). This work was subsequently augmented by a set of papers (Visser, 2003a, 2004b) that started to relay the significance of international second home debates to the South African situation. In addition, these investigations presented some general outlines of the dynamics and ranges of second home development (Visser, 2004a), as well as case studies in the context of some established second home locations (Hoogendoorn and Visser, 2004; Visser, 2004b). A key conclusion drawn from these investigations was that significantly more empirical research was required to elucidate the nature of second homes and their impacts on host communities, not only in the predictable second home hot-spots of the coastal provinces, but also in the county's interior and metropolitan areas where growing numbers of second homes are to be found (Hoogendoorn and Visser, 2004; Visser, 2003a, 2004a, 2004b.) Moreover, it was argued that only through further investigation would it be possible for the South African experience to contribute to the international conceptual debates concerning second homes.

Against this backdrop, the over-arching aim of this investigation is to make a contribution toward addressing the paucity of academic reflection on second home development in South Africa.[1] More specifically, the chapter aims to provide some preliminary insights into the question of what types of second homes there are in South Africa and what impacts second home development holds for different types of urban settlements. The examples drawn upon in this investigation cover diverse urban settings. These case studies include: 1) the coastal towns of the southern part of the Western Cape Province—Overstrand; 2) a small rural town in the eastern Free State province—Clarens; 3) a small coastal village in KwaZulu-Natal—Zinkwasi; and 4) a neighborhood in the Cape Town metropolitan area—De Waterkant. The different settings in which these investigations took place, present a glimpse of the diversity of second home development in South Africa. However, while each case study elucidates unique development characteristics and impacts, the investigations also highlight some commonalities. In particular, it is firstly argued that second home development in South Africa demonstrates similarities to developments found internationally; and secondly, that the near-generic impacts of second homes found elsewhere are echoed in the South African context, too. Here, in particular, the generation of employment and property price appreciation stand out as key similarities. The only particular impact that generally does not feature in the international debates is the fact that limited residential property mobility in the South African context inadvertently leads to the maintenance of apartheid's racially segregated residential areas and divisions of labor.

These aspects are explored through eight sections. First, an outline of the possible meanings of the concept "second homes" is provided and attention is focused on some of the underlying reasons for the development of second homes. In addition, consideration is given to some of the most commonly encountered issues that arise as a result of second home development. In the second section a brief outline of second home development in South Africa is provided. The third section deals with the methodology employed in this investigation. Thereafter, in the fourth, fifth, sixth, and seventh sections, the focus falls on the empirical realities of the case studies, providing detailed analyses of the nature and dynamics of second home-owners and their use of such properties in these respective areas. Moreover, consideration is given to the general economic impacts that second home development holds for each location. The final section draws the investigation to a close, arguing that the type of second home development taking place in these locations holds a number of positive, but also negative, implications for the host communities.

Defining Second Homes and Their Impacts

Since the emergence of second homes as a topic of investigation in the 1970s there has been a great deal of ambiguity concerning the definition of second homes. Indeed, there is considerable variety in respect of terms that refer to second homes: recreational homes, vacation homes, summer homes, cottages, and weekend homes (Gallant et al., 2004; Hall and Müller, 2004: 4-5). This definitional conundrum can be traced back to basic issues concerning these properties' relationship to other fixed-property assets, the types of physical structures concerned, and the location of these properties in relation to other land uses (Marsden, 1977). Moreover, the problems of definition also arise from the fact that second homes do not constitute a discrete type, nor are they sharply distinguishable from other kinds of accommodation, but from a somewhat arbitrarily identified segment within a housing continuum. The dynamic character of the second home, with particular reference to the changing relationship between the first and second homes, also makes identification and measurement difficult. Clearly, the definition adopted will affect the number of second homes identified and, by the inclusion or exclusion of particular classes of accommodation with distinctive spatial distributions, the geography of second homes will also be affected. Indeed, as Coppock (1977) noted decades ago, the distribution might include many properties on the urban fringe, where such properties also include the first homes of commuters; it might include holiday resorts and accommodation used predominantly for holiday purposes; or it might be confined largely to areas of poor land and scattered population.

While acknowledging these many definitional issues, this investigation follows the central tenet of Goodall's (1987) view, namely that a second home is a property owned or rented on a long lease, as the occasional residence of a household that usually lives elsewhere. Moreover, the research draws on Marsden's (1977) typology, or four-part categorisation, of second homes, in which they were defined as immobile and unserviced supplementary accommodation which: 1) comprised a private home often visited at the weekend and on holidays by the family and non-paying guests; 2) intermittently served as commercial holiday homes, which were used as private holiday homes but were let at high season to defray costs; 3) intermittently comprised private holiday homes, often purchased for retirement but meanwhile let out as commercial holiday homes, apart from occasional family use; and 4) served as commercial holiday homes, owned as an investment and usually let and managed by an agent. While certainly open to debate, this broad definition and categorisation provides a useful starting point to the systematic consideration of second homes in the South African context.

Whereas the definition of second homes in complex, the reasons for their development present even greater challenges. In addition, the impacts of second home development have also proved to be highly variable. The earlier literature on second homes demonstrates that this phenomenon was symptomatic of more fundamental changes affecting European and North American societal systems as a whole (Coppock, 1977). The arrival of greater economic prosperity in most industrial economies led to higher disposable incomes, fewer working hours and longer periods of leisure time (Sharpley and Telfer, 2002). These processes, in turn, have been seen to have led to explosive growth not only in the tourism system generally, but also in second home development in particular (Williams and Hall, 2000). On the consumption side, this has led to second home development linked to different types of migration as the properties are employed for holiday use, weekend use, or as holiday or weekend homes that will become retirement homes, or second homes that are acquired mainly for investment return. This, too, leads to labor migration that, in turn, may set off new rounds of consumption-led migration.

As has been demonstrated at length over more than two decades of detailed research, these processes have not developed evenly, nor do they have the same impacts (Sharpley and Telfer, 2002). As some areas experienced the benefits of economic buoyancy, others were being relegated to peripheral regions within and across state boundaries, leading to the formation of so-called, "importing" and "exporting" leisure regions respectively (Gallant and Tewdwr-Jones, 2001:60). This, in turn, resulted in some regions experiencing positive growth in terms of foreign receipts, employment, and infrastructure development, to name a few aspects. Others, however, have experienced this relationship through tourism flows differently, with low-wage employment, dependent economic development through economic leakages and negative social, cultural and environmental impacts (Müller et al., 2004).

Important here is that these negative impacts are seen as near-generic in terms of second home development. Most of the work on second homes has established that their occurrence at elevated levels holds significant implications for the destination communities, not only in terms of employment creation, the infusion of new ideas and capital, but also in terms the distortion of land, house and other prices in local markets, to name a few aspects (Williams and Hall, 2000). Indeed the frequently cited works of Gartner (1987) and Riebsame et al., (1996) demonstrate that the price of agricultural land, and that of rural towns and hamlets, may be inflated by high demand from "lifestylers" migrating from urban centers (with higher urban incomes and wealth). Moreover, rural gentrification may lead to fragmented land ownership and increased human presence and disturbance of local ecosystems. It has furthermore been noted that many of these migrants have idealised perceptions of rurality, and that these may conflict with everyday practices in, and the values of, local communities. This conflict may be limited to personal disputes between neighbors, or may spill over into community-wide political conflicts over such issues as development permissions and landscape management (Phillips, 1993, 1998)

In this context, the aim of the discussion that follows is to demonstrate which processes underpin second home development in the three case study areas and how these homes have impacted upon their host communities. Moreover, the paper seeks to make connections between second home debates at the international level. First, however, brief notes on the general development of second homes in South Africa will provide a backdrop to the case studies presented in this chapter.

Historical Notes on Second Home Development in South Africa

Although South African academic attention has not focused on second home development, the local media have made a significant contribution toward understanding this phenomenon (see Visser, 2004a). In this section, the aim is to provide a brief outline of Visser's (2004a) investigation (using these general media contributions) into the development of second homes in South Africa and the processes that underlay their development. In reviewing this desperate literature, Visser (2004a) aimed to demonstrate that the development of second homes in South Africa can be traced back to the establishment and expansion of a number of coastal towns and villages. The oldest of these are those on Cape Town's pleasure periphery of False Bay, where the small fishing villages of Muizenberg and St. James became the holiday and weekend retreats for the Victorian and Edwardian Capetonian (and Johannesburg) gentry (figure 7.1).

Similarly, along the south and north coasts of KwaZulu-Natal, the landed gentry of the sugar-cane industry, as well as the mining magnates of Johannesburg, built weekend and holiday retreats in seaside hamlets (of which the Zinkwasi case study in this paper is representative). Over the next half-century, second homes were developed further along the KwaZulu-Natal south coast while locations such as Muizenberg and St. James were systematically absorbed into the sprawling urban hinterland of Cape Town and in the process ceded their former exclusivity. A clear pattern concerning the development (and developers) of second homes emerged from the outset—namely that the metropolitan

Figure 7.1
Historical Locations of Second Homes in the Cape Region

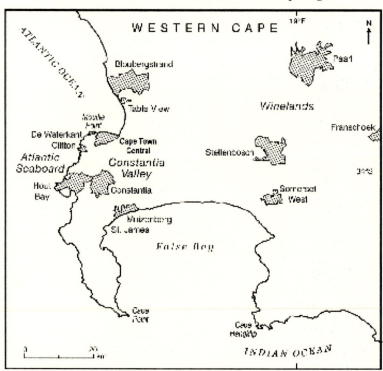

regions, particularly the economic heartland of South Africa, Johannesburg, would dominate second home investment.

The economic boom from the late 1950s to the early 1970s led to significantly higher disposable incomes and discretionary time that in turn would lead to large-scale second home development along South Africa's coastline (figures 7.1 and 7.2). This development was not even, with the KwaZulu-Natal coastline at the time enjoying considerable precedence over that of the Cape. A further important point was that these second homes were developed specifically for use as holiday homes during the main summer and winter vacations. A further trend that emerged was that the middle classes increasingly started to acquire second homes too, although often in the form of holiday flats, or later, timeshare units. However, as the KwaZulu-Natal south coast became more developed, and the lower classes started to frequent these areas, this region, too, ceded its exclusivity to more "exotic" and "pristine" locations elsewhere. This is not to say that second home development did not continue. On the contrary, the region remains a popular second home investment area. It is just that it is no longer regarded by the elite as the most desirable area. The north coast, however,

Figure 7.2
Distribution of Selected Second Home Concentrations in South Africa

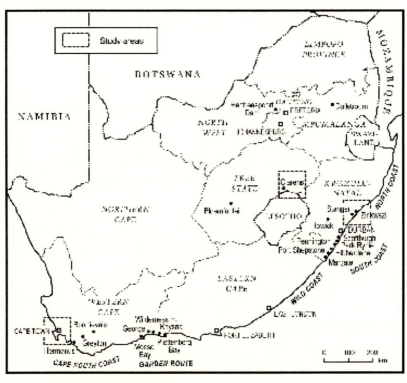

retained its appeal and would, by the late 1990s, regain its popularity among second home investors from Gauteng (hence the Zinkwasi case study in this investigation).

It was in the late 1970s and early 1980s that the archetypal second home locations of present-day South Africa, such as Plettenberg Bay, Knysna, and Hermanus, started to develop along the south coast of the Western Cape Province. Hermanus and Plettenberg Bay are probably the textbook example, developing from whaling-stations to towns of more than 70,000 inhabitants, and the location of some of the most expensive real estate in South Africa (hence the focus on Overstrand Municipality, which is focused on Hermanus, in this study). Systematically, towns further south on the so-called Garden Route (George, Knysna, Mossel Bay, Plettenberg Bay, and Sedgefield) became the focus of the desire of the well-heeled for pristine landscapes for holiday homes.

In the wake of the opening up of South African urban areas to all of the country's citizens, the greatest reworking of the South African property market occurred in the late 1980s and early 1990s. The demise of apartheid underpinned the emergence of a range of popular discourses as to which areas of the country were desirable for both permanent and semi-permanent residence. First, urban areas such as Pretoria and Johannesburg were increasingly perceived as danger-ous and unstable investment locations. Furthering this view was the fact that the emergence of an increasingly post-industrial economy was finding spatial expression in the physical form of industrial cities such as Johannesburg.

In this context, a broader-ranging movement away from central city areas, ever deeper into the suburban sprawl of Johannesburg and Pretoria, began to be apparent. A wave of emigration, which has only recently started to subside, ensued, along with a semi-migration of wealthy individuals to cities and towns perceived as less vulnerable to black urban in-migration, physical transformation and economic restructuring. It was in this context that Cape Town became the main beneficiary of "white and wealthy" southward migration for both perma-nent and holiday purposes (hence the De Waterkant study in the investigation that follows), which in the process caused Johannesburg and Pretoria to experience some of their worst property slumps. A recent, allied occurrence has been the increased participation of international second home investors in Cape Town, not least because of the city's buoyant property market and perceived social stability. Moreover, second homes that are acquired almost exclusively for use as tourist accommodation are also an emerging trend (hence the De Waterkant study in the investigation to follow).

Relative to second homes that serve as holiday homes, often with investment returns in mind, the number of regions that are exclusively or more closely associated with weekend leisure consumption is smaller, and such regions are much more difficult to identify in the South African context. However, over the past decade very clear evidence of second home development for weekend leisure has developed in locations that are relatively close to the main metropoli-tan regions. As in the case of holiday homes, the prime weekender-generating region is undoubtedly that of Johannesburg and Pretoria, which are the loci of nearly 50 percent of the country's Gross Geographical Product, with the secondary regions being Durban and Cape Town. What makes it difficult to identify weekend second homes in the case of the latter two regions is the fact that these zones of development are inevitably located in the same areas as those that are popular amongst holiday second home developers (as the De Waterkant study later will show). For this reason this brief outline considers the impact of weekend leisure consumption on second home development in the immediate hinterland of Gauteng. This hinterland may be defined as those places within a three-hour distance of Johannesburg (cf. Rogerson, 2002).

Within a one-to-two-hour drive from this massive Gauteng concentration of urban and industrial development, an extraordinary array of different natural landscapes are to be found, ranging from subtropical forests and the Drakens-berg escarpment to numerous rivers and large dams. Two established destina-tions and one emerging destination for weekenders have been identified as this metropolitan region's pleasure periphery. Dullstroom, about two hours' drive from Johannesburg in the Mpumalanga Province, as well as Hartbeespoort Dam, located about an hour from Johannesburg in the North-West Province, have both developed rapidly since the mid-1990s. The developments at Dullstroom were highly regulated and were linked to the trout-fishing industry of the region. Thus, Dullstroom was and remains a retreat for those who seek to escape the city. During this time, too, Hartbeespoort Dam became the favored weekend getaway, particularly among the financial-services sector and stock-market millionaires, interested in water sports and gold. However, the perception of over-development had led to this location not being quite as appealing as it was a decade ago. The latest trend for weekend homes is a movement toward the south of the province, to the Vaal River. This is supremely ironical, in that this area was and remains a favorite recreational area for the working classes, with historically little "snob" value.

The most recent developments in terms of second homes relate to properties that are acquired for weekend occupation but with the opportunity for future retirement use, as well as the development of yet another set of locations. Located three hours' drive away from Johannesburg, a new emerging area of weekend second home development is Clarens (hence the case study later in this investigation), in the sandstone mountain ranges of the eastern Free State. Many role-players in the real estate market refer to this town as "the next Dullstroom." Other metropolitan areas that are also located within a three-hour radius are those found in the KwaZulu-Natal midlands, clustered mainly around Howick and Nottingham Road. In the Western Cape province, towns such as Greyton, Montagu, Bonnievale, and McGregor, share a similar popularity as weekend retreats, with potential value as places of retirement (Donaldson, personal communication). As far as second home development for the purpose of retirement use at a later stage is concerned, many of the locations already mentioned have been popular among retirees over the years. Indeed, many retired persons have retreated from their primary residences in the cities to holiday or weekend homes. The demographic shift to an increasingly ageing population, particularly among the wealthier white classes, underlies a natural process of expansion in housing development for this cohort, as the structure of families has changed to one in which parents and their grown-up children live independently. As a result, a number of locations in South Africa have experienced retiree growth in coastal towns such as Hermanus, Wilderness, George, Plettenberg Bay, and Jeffrey's Bay. Another area that has traditionally been popular among retirees from the interior is the KwaZulu-Natal south coast, including towns such as Hibberdene, Margate, Scottburgh, and Ramsgate, to name a few. Moreover, there has for a long time been a trend among the farming communities of the Free State Province, Northern Cape, and North West Province in the interior, for people to retire to the main towns in the region, migrating between the *dorpshuis* (town house) and the farm for varying periods of time. Furthermore, similar trends have been experienced both historically and presently, on a continual basis in the Western and Eastern Cape Provinces. However, the most important, or perhaps the most interesting trend in retirement migration and its reflection of, and impact on, second home development in South Africa has little to do with domestic retirement migration, but rather relates to the migration of international retirees. Currently, it is estimated that up to 10 percent of all property transactions by international investors in the Western Cape, and as many as 15 percent of all property transactions in Cape Town itself, are carried out by this investor category.

This brief review of second home development in South Africa shows that this phenomenon is not new to this country and in fact is prevalent in a large number of locations. Moreover, at least on the surface, it would appear that the same processes drive the development of second homes in South Africa. However, this review is very general, and significantly more detailed investigation would be needed in order to provide clarity on how and why second homes developed in South Africa and what types of impacts they hold. The investigation that follows aims to make a contribution toward achieving this goal. However, attention will first be given to the methodology employed in this investigation

Study Methodology

No official data concerning second homes are collected in South Africa. Therefore, second home investigations in South Africa are totally dependent upon general media statements, the accuracy of which cannot be established, or empirical data gathered by the researcher. This investigation falls into the latter category, comprising data gathered over several months during 2003 and 2004 in four locations that are known to have substantial concentrations of second homes (see previous section). In this regard it is important to note that this research forms part of the first efforts to understand second home development in South Africa and that it is mainly exploratory in nature. Thus, this investigation led to a rethink in respect of the data-gathering methods after every field trip, resulting in subsequent refinement of the data-gathering method in each successive case study. As a result, there is a certain lack of uniformity between the four case studies presented in the investigation.

The second homeowners were identified through the rates base address listings of the relevant municipalities within which the Overstrand area, Clarens, De Waterkant, and Zinkwasi are located. If a homeowner's tax and services accounts were sent out to an area other than the respective municipal area in which the property was located, the owner was identified as a likely second homeowner. The first case study has as focus the estimation of the total number of second homes in a very popular second homes location—the Overstrand Municipality within which towns such as Hermanus, Onrus, Pearly Beach, Pringle Bay, and Rooiels are located. In this case 22,693 municipal property records were searched of which 8,312 (36.6 percent) were identified as second homes. The main aim of this investigation was to see whether or not there were second homes in the area and where owners' primary place of residence was. Given the size of the data set, it was decided that the universum was too large to analyze properly. Hence three other towns were selected that was more manageable in terms of in-depth analysis.

In these case studies a different methodology was employed. The rates base information was augmented with semi-structured interviews that included key informants such as governmental officials, private developers, district-council members, entrepreneurs, property agents, art-gallery managers, and community representatives from both the black and white constituencies. In addition, detailed interviews conducted with second homeowners completed the dataset. As these case study areas were much smaller it was possible to contact second homeowners directly. In Clarens, a total of forty-seven second homeowners, accounting for nearly 20 percent of all formal residential housing units (281 units), were identified. Of these, twenty-two participated in the interviews, providing a 46.8 percent response rate. In the case of Zinkwasi 198 second homeowners were identified among the 394 homeowners. Forty owners were willing to participate in the survey. In this case a 20 percent response rate was achieved. The De Waterkant residents' association refused to provide resident participation in the survey, but did provide an alternative source of information. Thus, the De Waterkant case study developed from a different empirical base, drawing heavily on interview material with *Village and Life*, a key property development and tourism service provider. The area has a total of 175 houses, of which 126 were identified as second homes. In this case, three in-depth interview, representing fifty-two units out of the 126 second home units in the area, were undertaken. Taken as a whole, the paper draws upon information obtained from a relatively small but richly textured sample of informants closely associated with second home development in South Africa. The relevant details obtained in this way will now be considered more closely.

Second Home Development in Overstrand: Some General Trends[2]

The first case study has as focus the development of a very basic geography of second homes in the southern parts of the Western Cape Province, an established second homes location (see Visser, 2003a). The aim was to develop an overall impression of the scale of second home distributions in the area, as well as an indication of where the owners of these properties reside permanently relative to the second home location. In addition, this general background was employed as a way by which to ascertain a range of issues and research foci that could be worked into the more detailed investigations in the case studies that would follow.

The Overstrand District Municipality, which stretch from Rooiels in the west to Franskraal in the east, consists of a number of former fishing villages, mostly established in the early 1800s. Many of these towns have now developed into settlements ranging 200 formal housing units (Rooiels) to as many as 12,800

(Hermanus) (figure 7.3). The area has four main urban centers focused on Gansbaai, Hangklip-Kleinmond, Hermanus, and Stanford. The whole stretch of towns and hamlets has since the mid-twentieth century been host to second homes owners, although this trend has developed most strongly over the past fifteen to twenty years (Visser, 2003a). Given that no official second homes data exits, the actual trends cannot be calculated. However, the property rates-based data makes it possible to ascertain the distribution of second homes in the study area and mapped in figure 7.3, as well as providing insight into where the second homeowners reside permanently (see table 7.1). While this information is very general, a number of tentative observations can be made and some preliminary conclusions drawn. First, it was found that approximately 36 percent (n=8,312) of properties in the region, as a whole, were in all likelihood used as second homes. These properties are unevenly distributed along the coastline. As would be expected the larger towns have a higher incidence of second homes properties. However, the proportion of second homes to primary residences varied as it is clear that in some of the smaller towns larger proportions of second homes occur. For example, 53 percent of the Hangklip-Rooiels areas' properties are second homes. So too, in the Gansbaai area, 50 percent of all properties are second homes. On the other hand, in the largest town—Hermanus—only 28 percent of the housing stock is used as second homes, although the town has the greatest number of second homes, the survey having identified no fewer than 3,603 such properties. The towns with proportionally the largest number of second homes are Pearly Beach, where all 504 properties are second homes and Rooiels with 86 percent of the 190 properties being second homes. The Mount Pleasant area in Hermanus has the smallest proportion of properties acting as second homes, with a mere 1.8 percent used for such purposes. Furthermore, it was found that Standford, which is not located on the coast, has only 107 second homes (10.2 percent of all properties).

Second, the distance of the second homes from the primary place of residence varied significantly. However, it was clear that these second homes properties in all likelihood fulfilled different functions. A majority of owners' primary residence was within one hour traveling distance from the second homes. This is to suggest that these second homes probably act as weekend homes. This is particularly the case when looking at towns such as Rooiels and Betty's Bay where the majority of owners live permanently in the Cape Town metropolitan region. On the other hand, approximately 20 percent of the owners resided permanently in locations that were beyond the three-hour traveling-time boundary. In this case these properties are most likely to be holiday homes. These owners resided in nearly all parts of South Africa. However, a large proportion of owners reside permanently in Gauteng.

Third, despite the variation in locations in which second homeowners reside, some general trends can nevertheless be discerned. The rates data revealed not

Figure 7.3
Distribution of Second Homes in the Overstrand Municipality

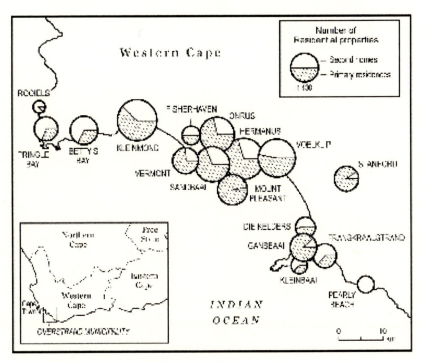

only from which town or city second homes owners come but also the neighborhood. The data revealed that the second homeowners are wealthy, with nearly
all of the elite neighborhoods of Johannesburg and Cape Town, for example,
represented in the listing. Moreover, most of these neighborhoods are predominantly former "white group areas" and it is thus very likely that most of these
owners are white South Africans. Whereas, not part of this investigation, closer
scrutiny of the data also suggests differences within that category, with some
areas in the Overstrand area having larger concentrations of white persons from
predominantly Afrikaans—or English-speaking parts of, for example, Cape
Town. There also appears to be potential links between particular second home
locations and specific neighborhoods in the second homeowner originating areas. This might suggest that family or friends in the primary place of residence
influences the decision of where a particular second home investment might be
made, or even the act of acquiring a second home in the first place. However, not
all addresses point to predictable higher-income areas, with some lower income
areas included and surprising even former "black group area" neighborhoods.
Fourth, although popular press statements proclaim that foreign landowner-
ship in South Africa has placed price pressure on the local residential property

Table 7.1
Second Home Owners Area of Origin by Distance

Town	Total Number of Residential Properties	Total Number of Second Homes	<1 hour	<2 hours	<3 hours	>3 hours (SA)	Overseas	Other (Rest of Africa)
Eastcliff	961	230	96	31	1	85	10	6
Kleinrivier	48	15	7	4	1	3	0	0
Hermanus	272	52	12	4	0	18	8	9
Fisherhaven	572	294	203	30	1	47	6	7
Vermont	1222	314	188	44	1	59	10	12
Stanford	1042	107	72	7	2	22	4	0
Onrus	2060	594	403	83	2	38	37	31
Voelklip	2411	1145	498	216	29	364	33	3
Sandbaai	2138	668	324	159	11	149	7	16
Mount Pleasant	1428	26	7	1	0	18	0	0
Mooisig	33	11	1	1	0	3	1	5
Northcliff	729	94	30	18	6	35	3	1
Westcliff	843	160	55	23	5	54	8	14
De Kelders	725	380	174	83	6	103	9	2
Gansbaai	1242	154	67	49	1	33	2	0
Franskraal	924	596	282	181	19	106	4	0
Kleinbaai	404	251	134	78	3	35	1	0
Pearly Beach	504	504	340	85	7	52	5	8
Pringle Bay	874	603	378	91	2	108	19	2
Kleinmond	2700	1014	416	256	28	275	24	1
Rooiels	190	165	116	17	1	26	1	2
Betty's Bay	1371	941	655	120	6	132	23	0
Totals	22693	8312	4458	1581	132	1765	215	119

market (cf. Visser, 2003a) less than five percent of the properties are owned by foreigners. In this small cohort a number of countries are represented, although these second homes owners tend to be from The Netherlands, Germany, the United Kingdom, and United States of America—all countries ranking among South Africa's main tourist generating regions.

Fifth, it was discerned from the data that those towns that have high proportions of second homeownership were also those areas with the least diverse urban economies, and generally smaller. Excellent examples of this trend relate to Betty's Bay, Pearly Beach, Pringle Bay, and Rooiels that all have second homes which account for more than 60 percent of the permanent housing stock. This would suggest that the transient nature of second homeowners might explain the lack of diverse economic activity, and hence large proportions of permanent residents. Moreover, the location of relatively speaking larger towns such as Gansbaai, Hermanus, and Standford, means that second homes owners might use these service centers for goods and services and thus have an economic impact at a different location to the one in which the second home is located.

From these brief remarks a number of potential research foci, already identified in the opening section of the paper can be outlined:

- What is the incidence of second homes in South Africa?
- What types of second homes are found in South Africa in terms of, for example, Marsden's categorisation?
- What are the linkages between the consumption of leisure space through second home development and the production of other types of economies that underpin new or different forms of migration, be it labor migration, retirement migration, and so on?
- Who are the second homeowners and why have they invested in these properties, and in particular areas of the country?
- What are the economic impacts of second home development and how do they contribute to the development of the host communities; and
- What is the relationship between host communities and second homeowners?

Against the backdrop of these questions the objective of the section that follows is to ascertain in what way these issues are reflected in the case study areas.

Second Home Development: Three Detailed Studies

The aim of this section is to expand upon the very general findings presented in the previous section. Here attention turns to detailed analysis of the historical development of second home locations, who the property investors are, why they make these investments, and how those decisions impact upon the host communities.

Second Homes Development—Clarens[3]

Clarens is located 35 kilometres from Bethlehem in the eastern Free State, situated within a valley characterised by vertical sandstone cliffs. The town is accessible by road form Gauteng and Bloemfontein, by means of a three hour car journey. Clarens was established in 1912 and subsequently developed as a retirement town for farmers in the area. It retained much of its original character until the mid–1980s never exceeding 200 inhabitants (Marais, 2004 and see also table 7.2). Besides Clarens' role as a retirement center, the servicing of the farming sector comprised its main economic purpose. Commercially, only one convenience store and the agricultural cooperative were in operation in Clarens. Higher-order, commercial activities were conducted in nearby Bethlehem.

The retirement culture of the town was shattered in 1985 when Mr Bruce Weyers, a Gauteng businessperson, started to buy properties in Clarens (also see Marais, 2004). His vision was that the high natural amenity value of the area

Table 7.2
The changing population size of Clarens, 1985-2002

	Clarens	Kgubetswana	Total
1985	200	5	205
1991	276	1224	1500
1996	587	1949	2536
2002	620	3000	3620

Source: Marais, 2004

would enable tourism development in future. He was soon joined by another entrepreneur, Mr Robert Crowther, who shared this optimism (interviews 1, 2, and 3). At the time properties were sold for as little as R2,000. The newly acquired properties were generally rented out on a short-term basis to enterprising independent tourists, with Clarens retaining its small-town characteristics typical of the Free State. Real changes to the character of Clarens would come from a different source. In 1990 the Lesotho Highlands Water Scheme required the construction of a tunnel from Katse Dam in Lesotho to the Ash River just outside Clarens. Clarens was chosen as the living quarters for the teams involved in the construction of the tunnel. This resulted in the construction of sixty-three new housing units, which extended the formal housing stock of the town by 25 percent. In addition, a more extensive infrastructure was developed, including well-designed tarred roads connecting Clarens to a number of destinations in the region, a better water supply, electricity, and telecommunications links. A further contributing factor was the large number of foreign contractors who took up residence in Clarens, including international workers and engineers from a number of European countries.

It should also be mentioned that the large population growth of Kgubetswana (the town's black township) between 1985 and 1991 can also directly be attributed to this development. The influx of these persons changed the character of this Afrikaans-dominated small town. Secondly, the new inhabitants immediately created a larger and more diverse market, for example, in terms of the types of food and eateries required. Consequently, besides the development of accommodation infrastructure to service this larger population, a significant impact was caused by the development of restaurants and taverns (there was no such establishments in Clarens prior to this event) to cater for the leisure needs of these workers. The subsequent completion of the Lesotho Highlands Water Project (or specifically the tunnel component thereof) in 1994 inevitably meant that international workers left Clarens, temporarily plunging the town into recession, in the main because its extended economic infrastructure had largely been developed around the needs of the international labor migrants (interviews 4 and 5). However, this crisis provided an opportunity for resourceful entrepreneurs who proceeded to buy up large numbers of properties and to market the town as a unique leisure hide-away (interview 2). In the wake of these marketing drives a small number of bed-and-breakfast and self-catering establishments started to develop. In addition, artists were enticed to take the opportunity to work from this picturesque setting, opening galleries and studios at prices unheard of in South Africa's main metropolitan areas (interview 4). Moreover, the "select" tourist trade provided a ready market for selling art, as well as craft products.

In the wake of these successes, the existing restaurant offering broadened, and outdoor recreational services and facilities, such as fly-fishing, hiking, horse-riding, and so on, were established. In turn, the expansion of economic activity underpinned the migration of art and leisure entrepreneurs to Clarens, expanding the local tourism product, which in turn stimulated greater tourist flows. Presently, Clarens has forty-four bed-and-breakfast establishments, as well as a range of (flexible) self-catering facilities providing 3,000 bed spaces. It also has nineteen art galleries and eight restaurants (interview 3). Other activities include golf, river rafting, abseiling, mountain biking, quad biking, clay-pigeon shooting, and 4x4 trails. It is currently estimated that Clarens hosts as many as 30,000 tourists a month (Marais, 2004).

With all this development taking place in Clarens, leisure seekers also grew increasingly acquainted with the area and its recreational diversity. Investors seeking such amenities become interested in buying properties to serve as second homes. Currently, Clarens is home to 3,620 residents, living in 650 residential units, of which 281 are permanent houses, forty-seven are second homes, constituting 16.7 percent of the permanent housing stock in Clarens. This proportion is not stable and it is important to note that the status of second homes in Clarens, as indeed elsewhere, is in constant flux. What is important to note, however, is that the size of the second home housing stock is not constant but is enlarging with the key target market, which is comprised of second home investors and jointly enlarging the formal housing stock by some 40 percent (interview 3). Moreover, this will bring the total number of second home properties to no less than 40 percent of the total formal housing stock. While Clarens might once have been a small, quiet retirement town, it has increasingly become a site of intensive leisure consumption involving a transient community of second homeowners. It is because of their expanding numbers relative to other types of residents, that it is necessary to better understand who these investors are and what impacts their presence holds for Clarens. The question, then, arises as to who the second homeowners of Clarens are, why they have invested in the area and how they use the properties they have purchased.

All second homeowners in Clarens are white, mostly male (73 percent), English speaking (77 percent) South Africans (table 7.3). Given that this age and gender cohort in the Eastern Free State is predominantly Afrikaans-speaking, Clarens has an uncharacteristic English-speaking base. The educational level of the second owners is high, with 49 percent having completed tertiary education. With regard to the ages of the household members it is evident that these households are predominantly established family units mainly comprised of adults in their middle-age, or approaching retirement. Concerning the economic profile of the owners, and given their high educational level, it is not surprising that the majority are upper-middle to upper-level income earners (table 7.3).

It is generally argued that second homeowners seek out properties that are located relatively close to their permanent place of residence so as to achieve maximum equilibrium between work and leisure time (Chaplin, 1999). In different contexts of modes of transport, the relevant distance between the first and second homes might vary. Being an average three-hour drive from Bloemfontein, Johannesburg, and Durban, Clarens is ideally located for the development of second homes intended for use over weekends and during holiday periods. The empirical evidence supports this view, with Gauteng comprising the primary place of residence of 77 percent of second homeowners (table 7.4).

The purchase dates of second homes in Clarens vary. Thirty-two percent of second homeowners bought their properties before 1990. Fifty-four percent bought their properties between 1990 and 2000, during a period in which buying a second home in Clarens became popular, and lastly, 14 percent of second homeowners bought their second homes after 2000. The reasons for buying a second home in Clarens also vary. Twenty-five percent of the owners purchased their properties for their aesthetic value; two percent bought second homes because doing so was a popular trend; and nineteen percent acquired their second homes because purchasing such properties was seen as a potentially profitable investment. As one respondent pointed out "The first home that I bought was in 1986, R70,000 … and the same house was recently assessed for R1,220 000" (interview 3). As might be imagined, such growth certainly constitutes a good investment return, especially in view of the fact that property values in rural towns in the Free State province have generally declined in real terms over the past decade (Marais, 2004). Twenty-nine percent of the respondents bought their second homes with the intention of retiring to Clarens at some time in the future—a fact that corroborates an established trend that investigators such as Coppock (1977) verified decades ago. Only six percent bought their second homes on the basis of the presence of family and friends in the town and region. As seen in table 7.5, 86 percent of the respondents are sole owners of their second homes, while 14 percent are not. Of the latter, 25 percent share their properties with business associates and 75 percent with relatives. Sixty-eight percent of the respondents bought their properties for under R100,000, 14 percent for between R100,001 and R200,000 and 18 percent for over R200,000. This might suggest that during the initial influx of purchases of second homes, original inhabitants started to sell their properties for higher

Table 7.3
Socio-Economic Profile of Second Home Owner Respondents

	Clarens	De Waterkant	Zinkwasi
Gender			
Male	73	n/a	70
Female	27	n/a	30
Age			
19-30	15	0	2
31-40	11	0	35
41-50	24	50	45
51-60	25	50	5
>60	25	0	13
Marital Status			
Married/partnered	95	90	90
Single	0	5	2.5
Widower/widow	5	0	2.5
Divorced	0	5	5
Home language			
English	77	65	78
Afrikaans	23	10	22
Other	0	25	0
Academic qualifications			
Grade 12	23	n/a	25
Diploma	26	n/a	18
Bachelor's degree	23	n/a	32
Master's degree	18	n/a	5
Doctoral degree	5	n/a	5
Other	5	n/a	10
Personal annual income			
Under R100 000	14	0	5
R100 000-R200 000	18	0	15
R200 001-R300 000	14	0	20
R300 001-R400 000	18	0	20
Over R400 000	36	100	40
Age of household members			
<6	9	n/a	3
6-12	9	n/a	8
13-18	11	n/a	7
19-30	11	n/a	24
31-40	7	n/a	4
41-50	17	n/a	24
51-60	18	n/a	14
>60	18	n/a	6

Table 7.4
Spatial and Economic Distribution of Second Homes Owners Respondents

	Clarens	De Waterkant	Zinkwasi
Place of permanent residence			
Greater Durban	0	0	60
Greater Johannesburg	77	25	40
Other (South Africa)	13	25	0
Europe	0	50	0
Distance from second home in kilometres			
<100	0	5	50
100-300	27	0	10
301-500	68	0	0
>500	5	95	40
Purchase date			
<1990	32	10	11
1990-2000	54	40	66
>2000	14	50	23
Reason for buying second home			
Aesthetic value	25	0	28
Poplar trend	2	0	2
Good investment	19	100	38
To retire to one day	29	0	6
Family and friends	6	0	15
Location perfect in relation to permanent residence	19	0	11

prices. This might explain why 14 percent and 18 percent of respondents paid more than R100,000 and R200,000, respectively. Current property prices typically range from R500,000 to R1 million. Thus, all these second homeowners have gained significantly from their investments in Clarens.

In terms of the temporality of second home use, it was found that owners mostly reside in Clarens during the Christmas season and Easter (April), and to a lesser extent during the June and July winter school recess. For the remainder of the year, visits are structured by work and school commitments, with long weekends being taken at least once a month. As seen in table 7.6, the December holiday sees owners staying for ten days on average, usually from the week running up to Christmas through to the first week after New Year. Eighty-two percent of the second homeowner respondents do not rent out their property for the periods during which they are not in Clarens. Only 18 percent rent out their properties, usually during the periods between school holidays, for example during February and March; during May; and from September or October to November (table 7.6)

Table 7.5
Residential Characteristics of Second Home Residents

	Clarens	**De Waterkant**	**Zinkwasi**
Sole owner			
Yes	86	30	75
No	14	70	25
Shared ownership			
Business associates	25	100	50
Friends	0	0	10
Relatives	75	0	40
Market value of property when bought			
<R100 000	68	0	0
R100 000-R300 000	14	10	14
R300 001-R600 000	18	40	60
>R600 001	0	50	26
Renovated home on acquisition			
Yes	32	100	100
No	68	0	0
Used local builder			
Yes	100	100	100
No	0	0	0
Material used from the area			
Yes	86	100	0
No	14	0	100
Amount spent on renovations			
<R100 000	26	0	40
R100 001-R200 000	32	0	60
R200 001-R300 000	16	0	0
>R300 000	26	100	0
Percentage of consumables bought in location			
0	10	0	15
20	47	0	10
40	5	0	15
60	14	0	12.5
80	24	0	12.5
100	0	100	35

Given these general demographic features, along with the use of second home properties, the question arises as to how these properties impact upon Clarens. Second homes in this town evidently fall within the ambit of Marsden's (1977) four-part categorisation of this phenomenon. Clearly, these are supplementary accommodation units that are privately owned, for the purposes of leisure during weekend and holidays for family and non-paying guests. Many of these properties also hold investment value for the owners and might be used as places of retirement in future. This function holds a range of positive and negative implications for Clarens.

Box 7.1 summarises a selection of positive and negative impacts associated with second home development in Clarens. As can be seen, the positive impacts may be regarded as a positive investment return for second home investors. This situation has not, however, come about at the expense of the local community through the pricing out of the original residents, as the retirement character of the town means that these residents have long since "passed on." Other positive impacts relate to the generation of employment through the renovation and redevelopment of existing properties and, currently, the development of new properties. In addition, leisure activities have been established in the form of restaurants, taverns, and outdoor activity organizers. These, in turn, have

Table 7.6
Average Number of Days Visited in a Year by Month

	Clarens	De Waterkant	Zinkwasi
January	6	n/a	6
February	3	n/a	2
March	3	n/a	2
April	5	n/a	7
May	3	n/a	2
June	5	n/a	5
July	4	n/a	6
August	3	n/a	2
September	3	n/a	4
October	3	n/a	3
November	3	n/a	4
December	10	n/a	11
Total over a year	**51**	**n/a**	**54**

Box 1
Impacts of Second Home Development in Clarens

Positive impacts	Negative impacts
Older residents have gained substantially as property prices have increased substantially, with average prices of between R500 000 and R1 million (Interview 2, 3, 5).	Property mobility of the permanent residents working in the Clarens economy is strained as they are competing with incomes generated in urban economies that are far larger, and in which higher salaries are paid (Author's survey).
Significant renovation is undertaken upon acquiring the second home, providing employment for local builders.	As second home owners acquire properties in the formerly "white" area of Clarens, the racially-based cleavages in the property market are inadvertently maintain (Author's survey).
Second home owners are dependent upon hired assistance to maintain their homes. Thus, employment was created in all cases in a region that has very few alternative economic opportunities.	The wage levels are low as there are few alternative employment opportunities for the host community (Author's survey).
A large financial contribution is made to the local authority through the rates and taxes bill. As the property owners use their properties infrequently, charges for services have high "profits" owing to underutilisation, providing opportunities for the poorer community in the town to have higher level services which they could not otherwise afford.	The employment created through second home use is often irregular leading to underemployment (Author's survey).
The leisure activities pursued by second home owners during their visits to Clarens have led to the development of many restaurants, taverns and leisure activities such as golfing and fishing, providing a range of employment opportunities.	The economic base of Clarens is changing to service the needs of the relatively wealthy and is increasingly neglecting the provision of affordable, as well as appropriate goods and services for the poorer segments of the community (Author's survey).
The acquisition of foodstuffs and household goods by second home owners generate an income stream for the Clarens region (Interviews 1, 2, 3, 4, 5).	

stimulated the in-migration of a number of entrepreneurs. Moreover, the local authority has a significantly increased rates base owing to more properties being developed and the fact that price-related property rates and taxes have increased considerably.

Negative impacts associated with second home development in Clarens are only now starting to emerge. The most important impact, so often seen elsewhere, relates to property-price increases. This impact means that there is no chance of property mobility for permanent residents working in this economy and entering the housing market. This holds true for both the permanent white and black residents of Clarens. However, this factor is certainly more pertinent for the owners of property in the township, as the better-quality housing is located in the formerly white areas, which are also the focus of second home investment. This situation inadvertently reinforces racially-based cleavages in the property market.

A second issue arising from second home development, but which is in fact linked to the broader development of the tourism economy of Clarens, relates to the types of labor markets that prevail. The pressure on the value of property is driven from outside the region, in the main by investors usually residing in Gauteng, or who have relocated from there to Clarens. Those working in Clarens do not have incomes comparable to those earned in Gauteng, and hence cannot compete in the local property market. In addition, while the white population have migrated to Clarens with investment capital in hand, those living in the townships migrated there either because they worked on the Lesotho Highlands Water Scheme, or owing to displacement from surrounding farms. As they are, in the main, wage laborers, filling the more rudimentary positions at tourism related enterprises, they do not earn anything near what is necessary to own property outside of the township. Thus, they are spatially confined to the township with no hope, in terms of the current economy of Clarens, of systematically starting to engage the "white" residential areas of Clarens.

It has also been noted that the cost of living in terms of buying basic foodstuffs is higher in Clarens. Thus, those who have the lowest means cannot buy goods in Bethlehem at lower unit costs. Should they seek to do so, they would have to pay the taxi fare in order to travel to Bethlehem. The fact that second homeowners buy their main supplies elsewhere, acts as a disincentive for potential food-retail entrepreneurs, since the most lucrative market does not, in the main, buy goods locally. On the other hand, the market that is less mobile is the very market that does not have adequate buying power to justify retail investment (interview 2).

Second Home Development in Zinkwasi[4]

Zinkwasi is located on the South bank of the Zinkwasi lagoon, 80 kilometres north of Durban along the KwaZulu-Natal coast (figure 7.2). Although the lagoon has been known to both the Zulu inhabitants and the colonial settlers for some time, the physical development of the settlement only started in 1903. The properties developed in Zinkwasi were initially exclusively intended as second homes for holiday use (Interview 6). These developments were slow-paced. As seen in table 7.7, it took a century for the village to reach 394 dwellings, housing approximately 1,200 people (Mellett, 2003). An indication that these properties were not permanently inhabited is the fact that the first convenience store was only opened in 1968; and the village still has no church, an unusual circumstance in the South African urban context. Indeed, for most of its existence, this village has been a small urban settlement, consisting of a community of people who never permanently lived in the area. Despite the lack of permanent residents, the families who own properties in the area know one another well (Mellett, 2003). Indeed, some of the families have used their second homes over a period covering four generations. As the expansion of the town was slow, new families moving to the area became integrated into the "holiday community." Indeed, many of those who invested in Zinkwasi were introduced to the village by existing owners who invited them for a holiday there.

The expansion of Zinkwasi only started to gain momentum during the late 1980s when roads leading to the village, as well as the resurfacing and expansion of the national road some 8 kilometres away, drastically improved access to the village. Commercially, too, the establishment of a small holiday resort, a restaurant, as well as a nursery and fresh produce supply, drew more attention to the village. However, on this front, development has not expanded any further, as higher-order commercial activities were, and still are, conducted in nearby Stanger, or Durban. During the past two decades Zinkwasi has slowly become home to permanent residents, who have either retired there, or commute to work in Stanger or Durban. Consequently, the proportion of second homeowners to permanent residents has declined, although the actual number of second homes has in fact increased. Currently, 196 of the 394 dwellings in Zinkwasi are used as second homes.

Table 7.8
An Overview of the Number of Housing Units in Zinkwasi

Year	Number of units	Number of people
1903	1	No data
1906	2	No data
1920	3	No data
1960	27	No data
1970	86	120
1980	120	750
1990	246	800
2004	394	1200

All second homeowners in Zwinkwasi are white, mostly male (70 percent), English speaking South Africans (table 7.3). The educational level of the second homeowners is high, with 75 percent having completed tertiary education. Of this group, as many as 23 percent are in possession of postgraduate degrees. With regard to the ages of the household members, it is evident that these households are predominantly established family units in which the adults are in their early middle-age, with teenage children. Concerning the economic profile of the owners, and given their high educational level, it is not surprising that the majority are upper-middle to upper-level income earners (table 7.3). Only 20 percent have an annual income of less than R200,000. All owners in the latter category are persons who inherited their second homes.

Being an hour's drive from Durban, two hours from Pietermaritzburg and six hours from Johannesburg, Zinkwasi is an ideal location for the development of second homes, both as weekend retreats and holiday homes (table 7.4). The purchase dates of second homes in Zinkwasi vary considerably. The fact that the village started as a second home destination, means that it started off with all properties fulfilling a second home function. In time (specifically over the past decade) it has been transformed into a village that has permanent residents too.

As the road networks connecting Zinkwasi with Stanger and Durban improved, increasing numbers of people decided to live in the village on a permanent basis. As can be seen in table 7.4, the 1990s marked a major expansion in second homeownership, with 66 percent (129 dwellings) of second homes having been purchased during the 1990s and 23 percent (45 dwellings) since 2000. The reasons for buying a second home in Zinkwasi vary, with 38 percent of owners having acquired their properties because purchasing such properties was seen as a potentially profitable investment. Indeed, undeveloped beach-side plots of half an acre, which cost R1,700 in the early 1960s, will currently cost R600,000. Unlike second homes in Clarens, and in contrast to many second home development trends elsewhere along the South African coast (see Visser, 2004a), only 6 percent of respondents bought their second homes with the intention of retiring to Zinkwasi. The main reason for this is the high temperatures and humidity, particularly in summer, which are experienced negatively by older persons. Interestingly, none of the respondents bought their second home because of its proximity to their permanent place of residence, even though 60 percent have a primary residence within two hours' drive.

As seen in table 7.5, 75 percent of the respondents are sole owners of their second homes, while 25 percent are not. Of the latter, 50 percent share their properties with business associates and 40 percent with relatives. The high percentage of shared family ownerships relates to the fact that most of the initial developers of the second homes placed the properties in trust for future generations. Indeed, 27 percent of all the second homes are held in family trusts. The oldest of these homes is the very first house built in Zinkwasi, owned by the Balcomb Family

Trust. Of those owners who did not obtain ownership through inheritance, 14 percent bought their properties for under R300,000, 60 percent for between R300,001 and R600,000 and 26 percent for over R600,000. Current property prices typically range from R800,000 to R2 million (Mellett, 2003). Thus, all of these second homeowners have gained significantly from their investments in Zinkwasi. The estate agents servicing the area, however, expect a significant escalation in property prices. The reason is that the village only has 521 plots of land, with only 100 left in the market, with scarcity increasing the potential asking price. Moreover, the town's water supply comes from boreholes. This limits the number of households that the area can sustain, making densification impossible too. In addition, the town is now in the middle of a conservancy, which has led to the demarcation of a specific urban edge curtailing the expansion of housing development. Finally, as many of the second home properties have been in family trusts, and as more homes are likely to be placed in trusts, nearly 30 percent of the existing building stock is highly unlikely to come onto the market, thus increasing property scarcity and, consequently prices.

In terms of the temporality of second home use, it was found that owners mostly reside in Zinkwasi during the Christmas season and Easter (April), and to a lesser extent during the June and July winter school recess. For the remainder of the year, visits are structured by work and school commitments, with long weekends being taken at least once a month. As can be seen in table 7.6, the December holiday sees owners staying for eleven days on average, usually from the week running up to Christmas through to the first week after New Year. Very few of the respondents rent out their property for the periods during which they are not in Zinkwasi. Those who do occasionally rent out their property typically do so during school holidays.

At a general level the observation can be made that second homes in Zinkwasi fall within the ambit of Marsden's (1977) four-part categorisation of this phenomenon. Clearly, these are supplementary accommodation units that are privately owned, for the purposes of leisure during weekends and holidays for family and non-paying guests. Many of these properties also hold investment value for the owners and might be used as places of retirement in future.

This function holds a range of positive and negative implications for Zinkwasi (box 7.2). As can be seen in box 7.2, the positive impacts for the second homeowners, as in the case of Clarens, include a significant increase in the value of their properties. Moreover, as in Clarens, properties were re-developed to suit the needs of the new owners. In this respect, a significant amount of capital was invested in Zinkwasi. All the participants employed a gardener and domestic worker, in addition to the ordinary obligations of paying the monthly rates, electricity fees, refuse removal fees, and water and security bills. In contrast to the situation in Clarens, hired workers are employed on a full-time basis, while the wages earned are significantly higher. Likewise, the local authority has gained substantially, as the rates base (linked to the value of the properties) has increased significantly. By virtue of the fact that Zinkwasi developed as a second home location, its impacts on the host community might be expected to be different.

After all, the host community first consisted only of second homeowners. In many ways this village is an artificial urban form—it has no economic base—as its development never followed the logical urban development process. In many ways this was, and remains, a wealthy "island" community, not reflecting the usual socio-economic variations of a small town, and certainly not typical of South Africa.

However, second home development in Zinkwasi can also be interpreted as holding negative implications, the following comprising some of the most frequently observed. The first relates to the workforce that supports the functioning and maintenance of second home properties (table 7.8). Although the survey did not consistently record whether or not accommodation was provided for domestic and garden-maintenance workers, it is highly unlikely that all of these workers would be live-in workers, especially the gardeners. As low-cost housing was never developed in Zinkwasi, the poorest members of this community are expected, as is often the case in South Africa, to travel the furthest distances to work, in most cases from Darnell and Stanger. Secondly, there is no diversified economy in Zinkwasi. This holds implications for the local laborers on adjacent farms, who will not be able to engage in any other economic activity close by, except agriculture, or domestic work. Moreover, workers cannot disengage from their current jobs as farm laborers, as they have nowhere to stay in Zinkwasi since all the properties have been developed for the wealthy.

Second Home Development in De Waterkant[5]

The De Waterkant neighborhood, a historic area that forms part of the Green Point suburb, is nestled between two arterial routes (Somerset Road and Strand Street), connecting Cape Town's Central Business District (CBD) with the Atlantic seaboard suburbs of Three Anchor Bay and Sea Point (figure 7.2). De Waterkant was home to a racially mixed community before being declared a white group area, with the neighborhood's "non-white" residents being removed between 1969 and 1973. Loader, Dixon, Napier, and Waterkant Street, among others, were "emptied out" to make way for whites (Kotze, 1998). From the 1970s onward, De Waterkant was a "bohemian" area with many owners and tenants "involved in the arts" and with "a strong gay overtone" (cf. Visser 2003b, 2003c). At the beginning of the 1990s a process of gentrification was established with a significant inflow of middle-class professional men (Visser 2003c: 128). The development of De Waterkant as a site for second homes was in many ways not apparent at the time. The area was in close proximity to the CBD that was at that stage in a cycle of decline. The area consisted of relatively small properties, and the neighborhood was unknown to the broader public (Visser, 2003c).

Box 7.2
Impacts of Second Homes Development in Zinkwasi

Positive impacts	Negative impacts
Residents have gained substantially as property prices have increased substantially, with average house prices of between R800 000 and R2 million.	The town has no economic base. It is essentially a neighbourhood (Author's survey).
Significant renovation is undertaken upon acquiring second homes, providing employment for local builders.	Persons who work as support staff have no place to live near their place of work. Hence, the poorest in this community have to commute to work (Author's survey).
A large contribution is made to the local authority through the rates and taxes bill. As the property owners use their properties infrequently charges for services have high "profits", providing opportunities for the poorer community in the town to have higher-level services which they could not otherwise afford.	Development of the town will only be aimed at benefiting the top-end of the property market and the town will retain its racialised and un-integrated socio-economic characteristics (Author's survey).
Second home owners are dependent upon hired assistance to maintain their homes. Employment is created in all cases, in an area that has very few alternative economic opportunities.	

Table 7.8
Average Maintenence Costs of Properties

	Clarens	De Waterkant	Zinkwasi
Domestic worker	140	n/a	826
Electricity	130	n/a	505
Gardener	155	n/a	590
Rates/taxes	330	550	349
Refuse removal	48	n/a	143
Security	45	n/a	203
Water	49	n/a	302
Management fees	n/a	9600	n/a
Totals	**897**	**11500**	**2918**

In time, however, a co-ordinated re-development of large parts of the area was spear-headed by a hospitality and property management firm, *Village and Life*, led by a local resident, Mr Maree Brink (interview 10; interview 11). The purpose of this company was to provide high-quality tourist accommodation, using investors' second homes in a coordinated manner. Indeed, they introduced "hassle-free" second homeownership to De Waterkant, while generating a return on investment for the owners, and a business opportunity for themselves. *Village and Life's* business model is that of a company which is closely involved in the locations and properties in which it operates, through a range of different, yet complementary activities, which include typical tourism functions, on the one hand, and typical property-investment functions on the other. This involvement entails a number of services which continuously present income opportunities to the company but which also generate a range of economic linkages that are highly beneficial to the economy within which the company operates.

This company started off as a very small concern involving only three participating properties, and employed only one person. To aid the expansion of this small company a private banking service was launched in 1997, as a unique property investment service for individuals investing in the area. In addition, the company launched *Village and Life Interiors*, which specialises in the preparation of properties for furnished letting, according to detailed specifications and standards developed over previous years (interview 10; interview 11). The company now manages 190 properties in four "villages" along Cape Town's Atlantic Seaboard, fifty of which are located in De Waterkant.

Second homes in De Waterkant are in the main, owned through legal entities such as businesses and family trusts. The directors of the trusts are mainly white men. Their permanent places of residence, as opposed to the domiciles of the legal entities, are in Europe (50 percent), particularly in United Kingdom (40 percent of the European total), Germany (15 percent and the Netherlands (15 percent), as well as South Africa (mainly Gauteng). Irrespective of their country of origin, the owners are wealthy and generally in their middle-age (interview 10; interview 11) (table 7.3). The purchase dates of second homes in De Waterkant vary and, owing to the legal entities in which these homes are held are transferred, clear analysis in this regard is almost impossible. Indeed, as many as 70 percent of second homes are held in business trusts, of which the members are all business associates. However, in broad terms an analysis of the property registers reveals that investment in the areas has escalated dramatically in the past eight years, with 40 percent of second homes having been purchased in the 1990s and 50 percent thereof, since 2000. Whereas there is some variation as to why second homeowners purchase their properties in the other case-study areas, the key motivation in De Waterkant is investment return. Property prices have increased significantly over the past decade from R300,000 to R1.5 million for a two-bedroom unit. Not surprisingly, Village and Life market their properties with the promise of high investment return potential (City of Cape Town, 2003).

An additional reason for investment in De Waterkant is that they also generate a constant income stream through use as tourist accommodation. In terms of the temporality of second home occupation, it was found that the owners themselves use the properties repeatedly throughout the year, although generally in the shoulder and off-peak season (April-October), so as to keep the properties open for tourists' use and hence maximise their rental returns (table 7.6). As far as tourist use of the properties is concerned, the summer season (November to March) sees a near—100 percent occupancy rate, with a 60 percent occupation occurring during the remainder of the year (Du Plessis, 2001; Lategan, 2003).

Second homes in De Waterkant fall within the ambit of Marsden's (1977) four-part categorisation. Clearly, these properties serve as commercial holiday homes, owned as an investment and usually let and managed by an agent. All of them hold investment value for their owners. However, there is no intention on the part of the owners to use these homes as retirement properties, or to relocate to De Waterkant at some time in the future. As seen in box 7.3, this investment function holds a range of positive and negative implications for De Waterkant.

First, second home development in De Waterkant has led to an inflow of capital through property purchasing in the area by investors from outside of Cape Town and indeed, from outside of South Africa. Further inflows directly associated with this ownership shift relate to property financing, legal fees, and estate agent fees. A second important impact relates to the local economy of Cape Town, through the preparation of properties for use as tourist accommodation. The use of units for tourist accommodation implies a range of direct costs, representing the main recurrent income stream to both the owners of participating properties and *Village and Life* as a company. However, a range of investments in fittings and fixtures precede the use of the properties for tourist accommodation purposes. At current prices these fixtures and fittings, which are additional to the purchasing costs, amount to R196,000 for a two-bedroom unit and R362,000 for a three-bedroom unit. These "prescribed items" are sourced and fitted by Village and Life property services, providing benefits in terms of economies of scale and unit uniformity for key items. What is important about these "prescribed goods" is that they are all locally sourced, a fact that Village and Life is at pains to point out (interview 12).

A third impact relates to the employment of these properties as accommodation for tourists. There are numerous linkages to the local economy via service fees, such as those charged for cleaning, booking and consumables. Considered in monetary terms, 56 percent of the room rate is directed into the local economy. Indeed, the monthly maintenance cost of a second home participating in *Village and Life* is approximately R11,500 (interview 11; Village and Life, 2003a). A fourth economic impact relates to the labor force required by the company to facilitate its various functions. In total, Village and Life employs over 120 permanent employees at its head office and the three "villages," a fact that in

Box 7.3
Impacts of second homes development in De Waterkant

Positive impacts	Negative impacts
Residents have gained substantially as property prices have increased substantially, with average house prices of between R1.3 and R3.5 million.	Property prices have increased dramatically, placing price pressure on the adjacent neighbourhoods (Interview).
Capital inflows to the Cape Town economy through property financing, legal fees and estate agent fees.	Economic opportunities created are limited to the skilled and those with start-up capital. There is little opportunity for employment that directly benefits the less skilled (Author's survey).
Large investments are made through the preparation of properties for tourist accommodation.	The surrounding area has been redeveloped, largely owing to the gentrification of De Waterkant. The opportunities created are, however, high-end service-based employment, providing little opportunity for less-skilled persons (Author's survey).
Large amounts of money are spent on the furnishing of the properties.	The scale of second home prevalence has cleared the neighbourhood of most of its former residents, creating an area with very few permanent residents and little in the way of local community (Author's survey).
Very substantial income is generated from the letting of properties for short-term high-end tourist accommodation, generating employment for a range of different skills categories elsewhere in the South African economy.	The large number of tourists is challenging the gay-coded nature of De Waterkant, thereby threatening the maintenance of space where discrimination against the homosexual communities is minimised (Author's survey).
Significant employment is generated and is relatively well-paid. There is also some evidence of a career path for certain categories of employment (Interview 10).	The area reinforces and maintains the race and gender division of South Africa, particularly in terms of inequities in the division of labour (Author's survey).
Second home development has consolidated the redevelopment of a historic neighbourhood (Interview 11, Author's survey).	
A large number of restaurants, bars, interior and lifestyle businesses have been established because of second home development in the area (Author's survey).	

itself also has important economic impacts. Fifth, the activities of *Village and Life* have had an important impact on the urban form of De Waterkant. Although the neighborhood was already gentrified prior to the formation of *Village and Life*, the involvement of this company has led to greatly enhanced coherence in the manner in which this historical area has been redeveloped. Buildings that were at risk of being destroyed owing to their age, high maintenance costs, and the basic configuration of living spaces, have been preserved.

Sixth, the most significant point about the second home development system in De Waterkant relates to the productive nature thereof. What differentiates these second homes from those in Clarens and Zinkwasi, is the fact that constant economic activities are generated by their use as tourist accommodation. The very essence of the *Village and Life* involvement in De Waterkant lies in the fact that the properties do not remain vacant over long periods, but are productively used to generate income, not only for the owners, but also for the company and its employees, as well as for a range of goods suppliers and service providers.

There are, however, potential difficulties that may affect the host community of De Waterkant and the larger Green Point area in which it is located, and possibly also Cape Town in general. The most important of these relates to property price increases. These increases have been part of the larger property-related growth phase in Cape Town in general. However, it is fair to argue that the desirability of property for second home-use has put pressure on the housing stock in a more general sense. In this context it is important to note that the *Village and Life* hospitality concept promotes the conversion of property for second home use and, therefore, continuously removes housing stock for the usual residential purposes from the housing market in this very central area of Cape Town. Moreover, *Village and Life* is operating in other parts of Cape Town, too, so these concerns have spread out from De Waterkant to a larger residential property market. Such activity inevitably has a "knock-on" effect on the adjacent areas of Green Point, where more and more properties are being re-developed and property prices have risen significantly (Visser 2003b, 2003c). Such issues inevitably point to concerns over the social and economic exclusion of Capetonians who have lived in these neighborhoods in the past. The Village and Life hospitality concept does not provide much opportunity for anyone other than the already wealthy to benefit from its development. Indeed, the more extensive this company's activities, the greater the potential for exclusion that could emerge on a number of fronts.

A second important negative impact is that the type of development taking place is leading to a range of development interests that cannot easily incorporate or accommodate other types of land uses or business in, or in close proximity to, De Waterkant. Private capital is increasingly determining the type and nature of development, leading to the exclusion of local and provincial governments and related institutions. Whereas this is of lesser importance in the neighborhood itself, it constitutes a more serious issue in terms of development along the area's periphery. De Waterkant's fashionable status, not only as a tourist accommodation area but also as a leisure area, has stimulated development around it. Currently, there is a wave of high-end service-based businesses in the area. These businesses are expanding deeper into Green Point, placing increased pressure on the property market. This leads to increased rent, which in turn pushes out those who can least afford long commutes to work in central Cape Town.

Moreover, De Waterkant has a number of gay facilities, and thus constitutes a leisure space that has come to function as a site for gay identity formation and consumption over the past ten years (Visser 2003c). The influx of tourists who stay in De Waterkant, and who also use many of these leisure spaces, has led to these facilities being increasingly populated by the wealthy. Whereas distinct class, gender, and racial biases that are decidedly not favorable to working-class, female, or black persons have developed within the gay scene (Visser 2003c), this current trend in development serves to strengthen such exclusion. Moreover, the space has largely lost its gay-coding, which in turn fragments the gay scene, certainly in terms of class and inadvertently, in the South African context, in terms of race and gender.

Discussion and Conclusions

Although the in-depth case studies were carried out in diverse geographic settings, this section aims to suggest that commonalities might be identified, both among the in-depth case study areas, but also linked to the questions raised in the Overstrand investigation. Furthermore, it is argued that second home development in South Africa reflects at least some similarities to development concerning second homes in the post-industrialized North, judging from international debates.

First, it is important to note that the three in-depth case studies clearly fell within the ambit of Marsden's four-part categorisation of second homes. In the case of Clarens second homes are used as supplementary accommodation units that are privately owned, for the purposes of leisure during weekends and holidays for family and non-paying guests. Many of them also hold investment value for the owners and might be used as places of retirement in future. In the case of Zinkwasi, second homes are supplementary accommodation units that are privately owned, for the purposes of leisure during weekends and holidays for family and non-paying guests. In the case of De Waterkant, second homes are commercial holiday homes, owned as an investment and usually let and managed by an agent. All of these homes hold investment value for their owners. However, these owners have no intention of using these properties for retirement purposes nor do they intend to relocate to De Waterkant at some time in the future.

The second point, directly linked to the first, is that it transpires, although very tentatively, that different types of consumption-led migration underpin the development of second homes in South Africa. In addition, debates in respect of production-led migration linked to second home development also surfaced. For example, in this investigation the case of Zinkwasi pointed to temporary holiday migration, a phenomenon that is found in countless other second home locations elsewhere in the world. On the other hand, the Clarens case study demonstrated that second home development could also be linked to weekend use, and potential retirement migration. In terms of production-led migration, the Clarens example also pointed to the migration of labor to this town in the wake of its development as a second home location. In this respect, then, it may tentatively be concluded that there is suggestive evidence that the processes that underpin consumption-led migration in the "northern" second home debates are of direct relevance to the understanding of second home development in South Africa. It can also be argued that some evidence exists to demonstrate that second home development also generates processes of production-led migration directly linked to these properties (see Hall and Müller, 2004).

A further set of conclusions that may be drawn are more specific to the local context, although they reflect issues commonly encountered in the international second home discourse. A third point then, is that in terms of the ownership base there is a distinctive demographic profile that clearly represents the presence of an elite in the South African context (see Halseth, 2004). The owners are overwhelmingly white, wealthy professional men in their middle-age, in settled family units with teenage or adolescent children. The permanent places of residence are not diverse, since Gauteng was the permanent home to the vast majority. As Gauteng is the economic heartland of South Africa, this factor, too, seems quite predictable. The remainder of the second homeowners are largely from the main metropolitan areas of South Africa. A further point, considered in terms of the total number of second home units investigated in the three case studies, was that overseas ownership was relatively small in extent, and in this investigation such ownership was confined to the Cape Town case study. Overseas ownership in this location seems logical as it is the premier overseas leisure tourist-destination and potential international second home investors are likely to have been exposed to that city and its investment opportunities at some time in the past. From this, it may be concluded that, for both national and international investors, tourism activity in the past has underpinned the decision to invest in second home properties at a later stage.

Fourth, in terms of the economic impacts of second homes on the host communities, different impacts were recorded for different locations. Three different kinds of impacts were discerned, and as a result no general conclusion is possible. This is probably the case because only three random case studies were conducted. Given broader and more numerous investigations in other parts of the country, more distinctive trends might emerge. However, a common denominator in terms of economic impacts can be identified, relating to the clear manner in which property prices have increased significantly owing to second home investor activity. This impact sets off a chain of different impacts, starting with commissions earned by the estate agents, the taxes paid to the central government through transfer duties and other property transfer costs. Increases in the property values lead to higher property rates and taxes, as these are price-related. Further immediate economic impacts relate to renovation and adaptation of the second home properties, entailing significant capital inputs. In this regard, however, it was clear that those properties that are used in a commercial manner require significantly larger inputs than those that are mainly used by the owners and their families. This also suggests a possible conclusion that commercial second home properties developed in the manner of *Village and Life* cause larger economic impacts than those properties that are earmarked for exclusive personal use. Moreover, the impact of renovation and adaptation on the local economy is greater in larger urban areas, such as cities, and this seems to minimise leakages from the host community. In this respect the case studies support the argument of Müller and Hall (2004) that second home tourism often forms an important contributor to the local economy and particularly to local service suppliers.

Fifth, the difference in the ways in which properties are used underpinned differences in the type of lasting economic impacts that can be linked to second home development. Foremost in this respect is employment creation. In terms of the non-commercial second homes, the properties in Clarens led to the creation of employment, but of a low quality and particularly low remuneration. In addition, the gendered nature of domestic labor is clearly maintained through such employment. Similarly, this is also the case in Zinkwasi, although workers were slightly better paid. Moreover, the fact that the locality started off as a dedicated second home location, undermined the development of other types of economic activities and resulted in a total lack of properties for less wealthy persons. Indeed, Zinkwasi, as a place to live, is fundamentally exclusionary of all but the wealthy (cf. Halseth, 2004). In terms of the commercial second homes of De Waterkant, a number of different employment types have been created, and are significantly better paid. Moreover, these employment opportunities are not affected by seasonality. In addition, there are opportunities to progress from one kind of work to another. Although the residential market left in the wake of De Waterkant's development is certainly also exclusionary of all but the very wealthy, its setting in a metropolitan area means that at least there are other housing options for those who work in De Waterkant.

Sixth, currently there appear to be no problems between second home investors and the local host communities. Having said that, it is nevertheless difficult to determine whether second homeowners socialize with the local population and act as ambassadors for the host community, promoting their produce and virtues as found by Quinn (2004) and Flognfeldt (2004). In part, this is owing to the particular case studies investigated. In terms of Clarens, the profile of the former residents, along with the relatively slow in-migration of second homeowners over a period of more than a decade, helped to prevent antagonism between the host community and new owners. Also, the dismal economic position in which many local residents found themselves in the past has apparently made them more accepting of the second home investors' presence. While second home development was not the intention of the local authorities, they have attracted high-profile tourists by default (cf. Hall, 2004), through allowing investors to develop the areas. However, recent debates are said to have developed between second homeowners who use their properties on a more permanent basis, particularly retirees, and those who use their properties more infrequently. Here the focus of the debate is on the magnitude of new developments that are in progress or in the planning stages. Typical of debates seen elsewhere, the core focus relates to the loss of the "rural feel" of the town (cf. Aronsson, 2004). In terms of Zinkwasi no disagreements have arisen between second homeowners and permanent residents. In this case, however, such disagreements are unlikely as the town started off as a second home location. Moreover, the fact that there are very clear limits to the future physical development of this town, also makes such disagreement less likely. In the case of De Waterkant no real conflicts could be identified, again mainly because the neighborhood is primarily a place of second home investors. Although there was evidence of conflicts earlier in the 1990s, when the shift from a neighborhood with permanent residents to one that is mainly used for holiday leisure occurred, those inhabitants have apparently either adjusted to their new realities, or have moved out of the area, in the process gaining substantial profits from their properties' capital gains.

Seventh, a significant impact relates to the amalgam of the general impacts set out above. In terms of individual impacts, second home development does seem to have been a rather benign process in the case study areas. However, there is a key issue that arises from these impacts—that of exclusionary urban spaces—which is anything but positive (cf. Halseth, 2004). This exclusion presents itself in different ways, the most obvious being the absence of a range of "others." In the case of Zinkwasi, the exclusion holds the implication that the area's function provides no opportunity for the surrounding communities to engage in any other economic activity. Moreover, there is nowhere to stay, as Zinkwasi is home to no one but the rich. The same might be said of Clarens, but at a different level. While the township provides accommodation for some members of the serving classes, it provides no urban services for that population. Expensive foodstuffs and entertainment are the only options in the town, other than an expensive journey to Bethlehem some 35 km away for goods and services that are better priced. Either way, the poor lose.

Moreover, there is also an exclusion of the artistic and entertainment entrepreneurs of Clarens, who, while not poor, are not as wealthy as the patrons who support their business ventures. Price competition from second home investors frustrates the ability of the persons to enter the Clarens property market, with the result that they are denied the opportunity to hold property in the town that is, after all, their primary home. In De Waterkant, the nature of exclusion is somewhat different and is perhaps less of an issue—since it is the relatively wealthy who are excluded by the wealthy. However, once again the issue of the serving class who are servicing the second home investors comes to the fore, as these people do not have the resources to compete in that property market. Perhaps the final and most crucial observation is that the cost of those spaces created through second home development in South Africa results in the maintenance of race and class segregation. Moreover, it also keeps out other less wealthy, non-nuclear families and non-white persons. This factor would not be an issue if it was only encountered in these case study areas, but clusters of second homes very literally cover hundreds of kilometres of coastline, and an increasing number of locations in South Africa's interior. Herein lies the urgency of the need to come to a far better understanding of second home development in South Africa.

Finally, in conclusion, from the three case studies reviewed in this paper, the evidence tentatively suggests that second homes in South Africa exhibit similarities to those in other parts of the world. For example, it is possible to use general categorisation schemas found in the international second home discourse, in the South African context. Moreover, those processes underpinning the development of second homes in developed countries also appear to be at play in South Africa. Likewise, the case studies also highlighted that, at least at the general level, certain issues concerning the impacts of second home development found elsewhere are of relevance to the South African situation. Whether second home development in South Africa is, to echo Coppock (1977), a curse or a blessing, is difficult to determine from the material presented here. At best this investigation merely points to the tremendous difficulty of judging whether second home development is desirable or not in the local context. Providing a clearer statement in this regard would call for significantly more research.

Notes

1. The chapter is an adaptation of research first published in Current Issues in Tourism and Urban Forum.
2. For an in-depth analysis of second home development in Overstrand, see De Wet et al., (2005).
3. For an in-depth analysis of second home development in Clarens, see Hoogendoorn and Visser (2004).
4. For an in-depth analysis of second home development in Zinkwasi, see Mellett (2003).
5. For an in-depth analysis of second home development in De Waterkant, see Visser (2004).

References

Aronsson, L., 2004: Place attachment of vacation residents: between tourists and permanent residents, in C.M. Hall and D.K. Müller (Eds.), *Tourism, Mobility and Second homes: Between Elite Landscapes and Common Ground*, Channel View, Clevedon, 75-86.

Chaplin, D., 1999: Consuming work/productive leisure: the consumption patterns of second home environments, *Leisure Studies*, 18(1), 41-45.

City of Cape Town, 2003: Rate-payers roll, Cape Town.

Coppock, J.T., 1977: Second homes in perspective, in J. T. Coppock, (Ed.), *Second Homes: Curse or Blessing?*, Pergamon, London.

Flognfeldt, T., 2004: Second homes as part of a new rural lifestyle in Norway, in C.M. Hall and D.K. Müller (Eds.), *Tourism, Mobility and Second Homes: Between Elite Landscapes and Common Ground*, Channel View, Clevedon, 233-243.

De Wet, C.N., Kotze, N., Jacobson, J.N. and Visser, G., 2005: Second homeownership in South Africa, Unpublished report, Department of Geography, University of the Free State, Bloemfontein.

Gallant, N., Mace, A. and Tewdwr-Jones, M., 2004: Second homes: a new framework for policy, *Town Planning Review*, 75, 287-308.

Gallant, N. and Tewdwr-Jones, M., 2001: Second homes and the UK planning system, *Planning Practice and Research*, 16(1), 59-69.

Gartner, W., 1987: Environmental impacts of recreational home developments, *Annals of Tourism Research*, 14, 38-57.

Goodall, B., 1987: *Dictionary of Human Geography*, Penguin, Harmondsworth.

Hall, C.M., Keen, D. and Müller, D., 2003: Second homes—curse or blessing? Twenty-five years on, Paper presented at the IGU Regional Conference of the International Geographical Union, Durban 4-7 August 2002.

Hall, C.M. and Muller, D.K. (Eds.), 2004: *Tourism, Mobility and Second Homes: Between Elite Landscapes and Common Ground*, Channel View, Clevedon, 3-14.

Halseth, G., 2004: The "cottage" privilege: increasingly elite landscapes of second homes in Canada, in C.M. Hall and D.K. Müller (Eds.), *Tourism, Mobility and Second Homes: Between Elite Landscapes and Common Ground*, Channel View, Clevedon, 35-54.

Hoogendoorn, G. and Visser, G., 2004: Second homes and small-town (re)development: the case of Clarens, *Journal of Family Ecology and Consumer Science*, 32, 105-115.

Marais, L., 2004: From small town to tourism Mecca: the Clarens fairy tale, in C.M. Rogerson and G.Visser (Eds.), *Tourism and Development Issues in Contemporary South Africa*, Africa Institute of South Africa, Pretoria, 420-435.

Marsden, B., 1977: Holiday homespaces of Queensland, in J. Coppock (Ed.), *Second Homes: Curse or Blessing?*, Pergamon, London, 57-73.

Mellett, R., 2003: The distribution and economic impact of second home development in Zinkwasi. Unpublished Report, Department of Geography, University of the Free State, Bloemfontein.

Müller, D.K. and Hall, C.M., 2004: The future of second home tourism, in C.M. Hall and D.K. Muller (Eds.), *Tourism, Mobility and Second Homes: Between Elite landscapes and Common Ground*, Channel View, Clevedon, 273-278.

Müller, D.K., Hall, C.M. and Keen, D., 2004: Second home tourism impact, planning and management, in C.M. Hall and D.K. Müller (Eds.), *Tourism, Mobility and Second Homes: Between Elite landscapes and Common Ground*, Channel View, Clevedon, 15-32.

Phillips, M., 1993: Rural gentrification and the processes of class colonization, *Journal of Rural Studies*, 9, 123-140.

Phillips, M., 1998: Investigations of the British rural middle class: part 2, fragmentation, identity, morality, and contestation, *Journal of Rural Studies*, 14, 427-443.

Quinn, B., 2004: Dwelling through multiple places: a case study of second homeownership in Ireland, in C.M. Hall and D.K. Müller (Eds.), *Tourism, Mobility and Second Homes: Between Elite landscapes and Common Ground*, Channel View, Clevedon, 113-130.

Riebsame, W., Gosnell, H. and Theobold, D., 1996: Land use and landscape change in the Colorado Mountains 1: theory, scale and pattern, *Mountain Research and Development*, 16, 395-405.

Rogerson, C.M., 2002: Tourism: an economic driver for South Africa. in A. Lemon, and C.M. Rogerson (Eds.), *Geography and Environment in South Africa and its Neighbours*, Ashgate, Aldershot, 95-110.

Rogerson, C.M. and Visser, G. (Eds.), 2004: *Tourism and Development Issues in Contemporary South Africa*, Africa Institute of South Africa, Pretoria.

Sharpley, R. and Telfer, D.J. (Eds.), 2002: *Tourism and Development: Concepts and Issues*, Channel View, Clevedon.

Village and Life 2003a Introduction to our investment service. http://www.villageandlife. com, viewed on 20 November 2003.

Village and Life 2003b Investment information, http://www.villageandlife.com, viewed on 20 November 2003.

Visser, G., 2003a: Visible, yet unknown: reflections on second home development in South Africa, *Urban Forum*, 14, 379-407.

Visser, G., 2003b: Gay men, leisure space and South African cities: the case of Cape Town, *Geoforum*, 34, 123-137.

Visser, G., 2003c: Gay men, tourism and urban space: reflections on Africa's "gay capital," *Tourism Geographies*, 5(2), 168-189.

Visser, G., 2004a: Second homes: reflections on an unexplored phenomenon in South Africa, in C.M. Hall and D.K. Müller (Eds.) *Tourism, Mobility and Second Homes: Between Elite Landscapes and Common Ground*, Channel View, Clevedon, 196-214.

Visser, G., 2004b: Second homes and local development: issues arising form Cape Town's De Waterkant, *GeoJournal*, 60, 256-271.

Visser, G. and Rogerson, C.M., 2004: Researching the South African tourism and development nexus, *GeoJournal*, 60, 201-215.

Williams, A.M. and Hall, C.M., 2000: Tourism and migration new relationships between production and consumption, *Tourism Geographies*, 2(1), 5-27.

Interviews

Interview 1: Mrs E. Meijer, Municipal worker, interviewed on 29 July 2003.

Interview 2: Mr R. Growther, Former mayor of Clarens and private developer, interviewed on 30 July 2003.

Interview 3: Mr B. Weyers, Property developer and estate agent, interviewed on 29 July 2003.

Interview 4: Anonymous, Art gallery manager, interviewed on 29 July 2003.

Interview 5: Anonymous, Former Clarens resident, interviewed on 30 July 2003.

Interview 6: Anonymous, Black worker at the Lesotho Highlands Water Project, interviewed on 29 July 2003.

Interview 7: Anonymous, Black worker at restaurant, interviewed on 29 July 2003.

Interview 8: Mrs A. Curry, Estate agent servicing Zinkwasi, interviewed on 14 July 2003.

Interview 9: Mr G. Prentice, Zinkwasi resident, interviewed on 15 July 2003.

Interview 10: Mr J. Lategan, Director—Finance, Village and Life (pty) Limited, Cape town, interviewed on 1 July 2003.

Interview 11: Ms J. du Plessis, Marketing manager, Village and Life (Pty) Limited, Cape Town, interviewed on 7 May 2001.

Interview 12: Ms B. Steiner, Personal assistant to Director—Finance, Village and Life PTY) Limited, Cape Town.

8

Creative Industries and Urban Tourism: South African Perspectives

Christian M. Rogerson

Richards and Wilson (2006a) categorize under four major headings the multiple different strategies used by cities in "developing distinction in tourism." First, is the construction of major new landmarks or flagship developments that aim to become symbolic icons for a city's identity (Evans, 2003). Alongside such international examples as Bilbao's Guggerheim Museum, African illustrations would include the Nelson Mandela Bridge in Johannesburg and the proposed Mandela "Liberty" statue at Port Elizabeth harbor. Second, is the attraction of mega-events or expositions that is now a standard strategy that many cities compete fiercely to employ (Garcia, 2004; Kurtzman, 2005; Richards and Wilson, 2006a), including also developing world cities such as Cape Town (Padayachee, 1997; Hiller, 2000; Hall, 2004). "Thematization" is viewed as the third basis for strategies for urban regeneration and involves cities seeking to distinguish themselves by focusing on a specific theme, such as culture, sport, arts, or entertainment and marketing themselves variously as "cultural capital" or "24 hour cities" (Law, 1992, 1993; Swarbrooke, 1999, 2000; McCarthy, 2002). The final category is that of "heritage mining" through which cities attempt "to re-develop themselves through the revalorisation of cultural heritage, usually with an emphasis on the built heritage" (Richards and Wilson, 2006a). In the developing world, Havana provides one of best examples of this strategy for urban tourism promotion (Colantonio and Potter, 2006).

The success of these various different approaches towards tourism-led urban regeneration has been observed to be both spatially and temporally uneven, with some cities enjoying periods of revitalisation, which are often followed, however, by a need for further re-invention or refreshment through the development of newer tourism products. At the heart of the difficulty of applying tourism-led regeneration strategies is that "nothing succeeds like success" (Richards and Wilson, 2006a). As a consequence, there is a common and ever-increasing tendency for cities to borrow, adapt, and copy regeneration ideas from other successful cities (Harvey, 1989). Thus, as more and more cities compete in producing and reproducing themselves as spaces for tourism consumption, tourism-led strategies of regeneration tend to employ "the same formulaic mechanisms" which in turn leads to the serial reproduction of culture (Richards and Wilson, 2006a). Accordingly, as culture is utilised as a means of social and economic regeneration, the cultural tourism market becomes flooded with "identikit" new cultural attractions and heritage centers (Smith, 2005a; Richards and Wilson, 2006b).

In addressing this dilemma of the serial reproduction of culture and of the need for developing new urban tourism products, one of the most fashionable approaches is viewed as via the encouragement and nurturing of "creativity," "creative industries," and "creative tourism" in cities (Smith, 2005a, 2005b; Richards and Wilson, 2006a, 2006b). As Smith (2005b: 23) reflects, creative industries are used increasingly "as tools for the regeneration and transfiguration of urban spaces of consumption." The aim in this discussion is to profile the emerging relationship between urban tourism and creative industries in Africa through the experience of Johannesburg, South Africa's leading economic city. Two sections of material are presented. First, the current debates taking place in the developed world are explored around the linkages between "creative industries" and urban tourism. Against this backcloth, attention moves to introduce a perspective from South Africa, in particular through the record of Johannesburg.

Creativity, Creative Tourism, and Creative Industries

In a recent international survey of tourism, culture and urban regeneration, Smith (2005b: 33) asserts that "the role of creativity in the development of cities and tourist spaces is of increasing importance." Within a wider setting, it was observed that "the theme of creativity is currently of great significance, not just for tourism and leisure, but in terms of social and cultural development more generally" (Smith, 2005a: 3).

The term "creative tourism" has been increasingly applied as an extension of "cultural tourism" (Richards, 2005; Richards and Wilson, 2006a, 2006b). It was defined by Richards and Raymond (2000: 18) as "tourism that offers visitors the opportunity to develop their creative potential through active participation in courses and learning experiences which are characteristic of the holiday destination where they are undertaken." The emergence of creative tourism is viewed sometimes as, in part, a reaction to dissatisfaction with cultural tourism products in recent years (Smith, 2005a). In particular, such disappointments concern "the lack of involvement and participation available to tourists and the relatively standardised nature of the product" (Richards, 2005: 15). Creative tourism is "active rather than passive, about learning rather than looking, about self-development as well as economic development" (Richards, 2005: 17-18). The activity of creative tourism potentially can draw upon local skills, expertise, traditions, and the uniqueness of places (Binkhorst, 2005; Richards and Wilson, 2006a). Beyond the well-known creative tourism experiences of gastronomy and wine holidays, the creative tourist can learn through participation also about arts and crafts, design, health, languages, or sport (Meethan and Beer, 2005; Richards, 2005). Above all, the essential foundation for developing creative tourism "is to identify those activities that are closely linked to a specific region" (Richards, 2005: 19). As has been demonstrated by the experience of Nelson, New Zealand, the growth of creative tourism can be forged through linkages made with local "creative industries" (especially arts and crafts) and assisted by support from local government as part of destination management initiatives (Zahra, 2005).

The concept of "creative industries" represents "a quite recent category in academic, policy, and industry discourse" (Cunningham, 2003: 1). It has been argued that the formal origins of the concept can be found in the Blair Labour Government's establishment of a Creative Industries Task Force (CITF) after its election in Britain in 1997 (Flew, 2002). The Creative Industries Mapping Document, which was prepared by the newly constituted Department of Culture, Media and Sport (1998), defined creative industries "as those activities which have their origin in individual creativity, skill, and talent and which have the potential for wealth and job creation through generation and exploitation of intellectual property." The boundaries of "creative industries" are not always tightly defined. Wood and Taylor (2004: 389) go so far as to argue that defining creative industries "is a task fraught with methodological and semantic challenges." The U.K. CITF identified as many as thirteen different sectors that were to be encompassed within the framework of "creative industries" (table 8.1).

As Flew (2002: 5) asserts, "such listings inherently carry an ad hoc and pragmatic element to them." Likewise, Cunningham (2003: 1) criticizes the CITF listing as "eclectic." In a more analytical fashion, the economist Caves

Table 8.1
Creative Industries in the United Kingdom

• Advertising	• Interactive Leisure Software
• Architecture	• Music
• Arts and Antique Markets	• Television and radio
• Crafts	• Performing Arts
• Design	• Publishing
• Designer Fashion	• Software
• Film	

Source: Department of Culture, Media and Sport, U.K.,1998

(2000: 1) sought to define creative industries in the following terms: "Creative industries supply goods and services that we broadly associate with cultural, artistic, or simply entertainment value. They include book and magazine publishing, the visual arts (painting and sculpture), the performing arts (theater, opera, concerts, dance), sound recordings, cinema, and TV films, even fashion and toys and games." Since 2000, several other researchers have sought to modify these definitions and offer varying sectoral listings of creative industries; most frequently, these lists include film and television, arts, crafts, music, media, and designer fashion; sometimes, they extend to include even the activity of tourism as a whole rather than just "creative tourism" (Evans, 2005).

The scholarship on creative industries essentially builds upon earlier thinking on "cultural industries" (Flew, 2002) and in particular of the challenges raised by Richard Florida's (2002) book, *The Rise of the Creative Class*. The major contribution of Florida (2002) was to unsettle conventional notions of culture and creativity "as frivolous and derivative, as something that is nice to have, but not important to nuts and bolts economic development" (Leslie, 2005: 403). Indeed, Florida's work (2002) demonstrates that creativity and culture can have economic benefits and that creativity and economy are inextricably woven together. In recent years, research interest concerning the development of creative industries has burgeoned and a vibrant set of debates has emerged particularly around creativity, clusters, and industrial districts (Landry and Bianchini, 1995; Scott, 1996; Caves, 2000; de Berranger and Meldrum, 2000; Hall, 2000; Bilton and Leary, 2002; Florida, 2002; Santagata, 2002; Caves, 2003; Flew, 2003; Turok, 2003; Brecknock, 2004; Santagata, 2004). In particular, Scott (2004: 463) draws attention to the growth of the new creative economy and of rising levels of optimism surrounding "cultural-industrial districts" as "drivers of local economic development at selected locations, above all in large cosmopolitan cities, but also in many other kinds of geographical contexts." Creative industries are characterised by, *inter alia*, extensive networking, self-help, and collaboration, "flat hierarchies" and partnerships, and the domination of small and micro-enterprise (Evans, 2005; Meethan and Beer, 2005). Another common feature is a locational preference among certain segments of creative industries for central or inner-city locations rather than peripheral areas (Newton, 2003).

Despite definitional controversy, over the last few years creative industries and creative districts, undoubtedly, "have become a major new consideration in urban economics and city politics" (Brecknock, 2004: 1). At a national level, the creative industry of designer fashion came under the spotlight in both the United Kingdom and New Zealand during the 1990s. Unprecedented attention was accorded to designer fashion by the media and national government in campaigns such as "Cool Britannia." Moreover, it has been observed that fashion was assigned "the dual tasks of economic development and re-branding New Zealand as a creative talented nation" (Bill, 2005: 7). For some scholars, whole cities are now called upon to re-invent themselves as "creative cities" (Landry,

2000). In particular, the English town of Huddersfield, a former woollen mill town, has sought to transform itself through its Creative Town Initiative (Wood and Taylor, 2004).

Policy initiatives to support or nurture the category of creative industries have been launched by several cities including Brisbane, Berlin, Barcelona, Dublin, Helsinki, Manchester, Milan, Tilburg, and Toronto (Hall, 2000; Flew, 2002; Cunningham, 2003; Scott, 2004; Leslie, 2005). In addition, the Canadian city of Montreal aims to position itself as "a design metropole" (Leslie, 2005). Many cities plan strategically to enhance the growth and development within cities of "creative spaces" (Dabinett, 2004; Scott, 2004; Evans, 2005). It has been pointed out, however, that some of the most well-known creative districts—such as Soho in New York City or Montmartre in Paris—were never planned; rather "they emerged spontaneously from currents of dissent, conflict, and collision present in cities of disorder" (Leslie, 2005: 405).

A critical set of international debates are beginning to surface concerning the "local conditions" which facilitate the development of "creative clusters" and of "creative cities" (Landry and Bianchini, 1995; Hall, 2000; Landry, 2000; Bell and Jayne, 2003; Brecknock, 2004; Masters et al., 2005). In an important contribution, Pratt (2004) argues that creative clusters are formally a set of business clusters. Internationally, Evans (2005) considers that creative industries are now identified as an economic cluster. For localities that host significant concentrations of these creative industries, Wu (2005: 3) stresses that the "beneficial impacts are tremendous" especially in respect of local growth potential. Commonly, creative industries are added to a list of "leading edge" or "growth sectors" such as financial services, ICT, or high-technology, which signals the strength and potential of a local economy (Evans, 2005).

Several factors are identified as important influences upon the emergence of dynamic creative clusters, including local innovation capacity, availability of venture capital, the role of institutions in mediating collaboration, an appropriate skills and knowledge base, and targeted public policies (Wu, 2005). For Meethan and Beer (2005) creative industries thrive on innovation, mobility and flexibility. The growth of "creative spaces" and "creative industries" is also viewed as linked critically to the factor of market demand. Sustaining the development of creative industries, Evans (2005: 7) argues, requires a growing local economy, affluence, and investor confidence. From the international experience it is contended that "cities need to build institutional and political mechanisms that nurture creativity and channel innovation" in order to sustain creative clusters (Wu, 2005: 7). In addition, considerable significance is attached also to the imperative for increased collaboration between the different creative industries sectors. Nevertheless, it is recognized that the greatest scope for growth and innovation exists between creative industries and other sectors, including tourism (Evans, 2005: 7). It is against this backcloth that the discussion turns to review the South African record.

Creative Industries in the Developing World: South African Experiences

Tourism is one of two sectors with the highest strategic priority for economic development planning in contemporary South Africa (Mlambo-Ngcuka, 2006). Recent national level investigations have disclosed, however, that the long-term competitiveness of South Africa's tourism economy is contingent upon addressing several barriers to innovation in the industry as well as the imperative for identifying new drivers for growth, particularly as regards new product development and enhancement of current products (Monitor, 2004; Department of Trade and Industry, 2005a). It can be argued that for South Africa one source for potential innovation in tourism products, as yet untapped, is through the making of stronger linkages between tourism and local creative industries. This section reviews national and local policy initiatives towards creative industries.

The Record of Policy Debates in South Africa

The terminology of the "creative city" was first introduced into the lexicon of South African development scholarship by Dirsuweit (1999) in her work on culture and economic development in Johannesburg. Nevertheless, by 2005 it could be observed that the term "creative industries" had been little utilised in national level policy debates on South African economic development. One possible reason for neglect was suggested by Minty (2005: 5) as a consequence of the fact that "the creative industry in South Africa—and thus to a large extent the symbolic economy—is the least transformed in the country." Moreover, at present, there exists little systematic published research on the organization or workings of so-termed "creative industries" in South Africa. Indeed, there has been no real parallel in South Africa to the British Creative Industries Task Force, or to the emergence of the sorts of vibrant discussions that operate at national level in Australia, New Zealand, or the U.K. about harnessing the developmental potential of creative industries.

That said, what has emerged in post-apartheid South Africa is a growing recognition of the significance of the parallel (and sometimes overlapping) notions of "cultural industries" (Dirsuweit, 1999; Minty, 2005). The importance of promoting cultural industries in South Africa and their potential for economic development was signalled in 1998 by the appearance of a series of reports produced by the Cultural Strategy Group (1998a, 1998b) for the (former) Department of Arts, Culture, Science, and Technology. The category of "cultural industries" was defined broadly to incorporate music, the visual arts, the publishing sector based on creative writing of literature, the audio-visual and media sector, performing arts, the craft sector (including traditional African art, designer goods, and souvenirs); cultural tourism, and, the cultural heritage sector. In addition, the Cultural Strategy Group (1998a) also included within cultural industries the sectors of design and fashion that were seen as "sectors where creative input is a secondary but critical means of enhancing the value of other products whose marketability and effectiveness would otherwise be lessened."

The series of research reports generated by the Cultural Strategy Group are highly relevant for the creative industries. The core objective of the Cultural Industries Growth Strategy (CIGS) was of "integrating arts and culture into all aspects of socio-economic development" (Newton, 2003: 25) in South Africa. In particular, the Cultural Strategy Group produced detailed reports and recommendations for supporting the craft (Cultural Strategy Group, 1998b), film and video (Cultural Strategy Group, 1998c), music (Cultural Strategy Group, 1998d), and publishing (Cultural Strategy Group, 1998e) industries. Taken together, this body of research identified major problems currently facing the development of the core segments of South African cultural industries. Key cross-cutting issues for enterprise growth were recognized as a lack of adequate skills, difficulty of market access, and a lack of innovative product development (Create SA, 2005). While differentiated for the various sectors under investigation, the major suggested strategic interventions included:

- Education and training to improve skill levels
- Market development and facilitation of market access
- Co-ordination of government initiatives
- The development of partnerships at all levels to implement joint projects; and,
- Advocacy for cultural industries (Newton, 2003)

Overall, the so-termed "Creative South Africa" initiative sought to introduce and demarcate "cultural industries as an important sector in its own right" (Cultural Strategy Group, 1998a: 7) in terms of national policy debates. The results of this project were directed explicitly at National Government and sought to forge awareness within Government about the potential of cultural industries for growth, job creation, and enterprise development. Since 1998 it must be observed that there has occurred little movement in terms of national support initiatives for so-termed cultural industries. In large measure this is because core responsibility has rested with the little-resourced Department of Arts and Culture (DAC). The limited available support from DAC has been channelled towards developing public-private partnerships and initiatives using culture as a tool for urban regeneration with a special poverty relief allocation which seeks at "providing access to skills and markets as a tool for urban regeneration, rural development, and job creation" (Department of Arts and Culture, 2004: 4).

The greatest success of the Creative South Africa initiative has been recorded in terms of strategic awareness-raising among policy-makers within national government. In 2002 the Integrated Manufacturing Strategy (IMS) was issued by South Africa's Department of Trade and Industry (DTI). The IMS constitutes a collective government position aimed to coordinate a set of actions across government and geared primarily at improving competitiveness across the national economy. The IMS takes off from the government's Microeconomic Reform Strategy which set forth a vision for a restructured and adaptive economy characterised by growth, employment equity, built upon the full potential of persons, communities and geographic areas (Machaka and Roberts, 2003). Of greatest significance is that the DTI identified a cluster of nine "priority sectors" for accelerated development. These nine sectors were selected on the basis of their potential contribution to the economy in terms of growth, equity, and employment creation. It is significant that cultural industries was identified as a priority economic sector alongside, inter alia, agro-processing, business process outsourcing, and information technology enabled services; chemical and allied industries; clothing, textiles, leather, and footwear; information and communication technologies; electronics; tourism; and, transport industries (automotive, aerospace, marine, and rail).

In December 2005 government issued a significant discussion document on developing a national shared growth initiative, titled the *Accelerated and Shared Growth-South Africa* (ASGISA) (Department of Trade and Industry, 2005b). This initiative seeks to boost the national growth rate for the period 2004-2014 to at least 6 percent as well as to enhance "the environment and opportunities for more labour-absorbing economic activities" (Mlambo-Ngcuka, 2006). Among the several dimensions of this initiative, designed to achieve balanced and sustainable growth for the period 2004-2014, is the identification, once again, of priority sectors. These are viewed as those sectors in which the country "has a range of comparative economic advantages which, if fully exploited, would lend themselves to higher rates of economic growth" (Department of Trade and Industry, 2005b). One of the nine sectors, seen as "medium-term priority" is that of creative industries (Mlambo-Ngcuka, 2006). Within "creative industries" existing policy thinking currently is directed towards two foci: 1) supporting greater linkages of the craft industry with tourism, and 2) supporting the film and television production industry (Department of Trade and Industry, 2005b).

By end-2005, however, only limited progress regarding actual policy initiatives for direct support of cultural industries (or the creative sector) could be observed. Of striking concern was the minimal progress made for direct national government support interventions for business development among cultural industry entrepreneurs through the national institutional framework for small business development (Newton, 2003). Indeed, the most progress in terms of implementation was recorded not at national level but at certain provincial and local tiers of government in South Africa. For example, Western Cape Province and the City of Cape Town have taken certain pro-active initiatives in support of the cultural sector as a vehicle for local economic development, albeit the approach so far adopted has been criticised as so far "relatively unsophisticated and piecemeal" (Minty, 2005: 6). In addition, within Cape Town, South Africa's leading center for international tourism, few linkages seemingly have been made between the cultural and creative sector and new tourism product innovation.

Creative Industries: The Johannesburg Experience

The Economic Development Unit of the City of Johannesburg has recognized officially the role and potential of creative industries for contributing towards the goals of *Joburg 2030*, the city's blueprint for economic development over the next three decades (Rogerson, 2005). Indeed, it is significant that the terminology of "creative industries" is now used widely in planning documents issued by the city and its associated development agencies (see e.g., City of Johannesburg, 2005a; Johannesburg Development Agency, 2005).

The recognition of creative industries is the latest chapter in the implementation of *Joburg 2030*, one important element of which includes support for targeted strategic sectors of the urban economy (Rogerson, 2005). During 2005, alongside new support programs for business process outsourcing call centers, ICT, freight and logistics, and sport, it was announced that the Economic Development Unit of Johannesburg would support actively also the sector of "creative industries." A Sector Development Programme would be prepared for creative industries and focused on sector clustering and support. The Sector Development Programme is a vital component of *Joburg 2030* and is aimed at the removal of constraints and inefficiencies and the harnessing of opportunities in the targeted sectors as well as provision of relevant information to sector participants. The overall goal of the Programme is to enhance the competitiveness of the sectors and attracting and retaining investment in these sectors, thereby growing the city's economy as a whole (Rogerson, 2005).

The background to this announcement of support was the undertaking during 2003 of a series of scoping studies that linked to the key potential sectors for future development that had been identified in the *Joburg 2030* analysis. Nine sectors were looked at in detail, viz.,

- Financial and business services;
- Information and Communications Technology;
- Retail and wholesale trade;
- Professional equipment manufacture;
- Other Equipment manufacture;
- Food and Beverages;
- Biotechnology;
- Automotive Parts; and
- Creative Industries.

The Creative Industries Sector scoping study for Johannesburg built upon the foundations of the national cultural industry study of the Cultural Strategy Group (Newton, 2003). Essentially, the definitions used by the Cultural Strategy

Group (1998a, 1998b) were applied to re-name the sector in Johannesburg as "creative industries." The focus of the scoping investigation was thus primarily upon the segments of TV and film—in which (along with Cape Town) Johannesburg is the major national center—music, performing arts, visual arts, crafts, and design. Critically, the research highlighted that the "Johannesburg creative industries sector dominates the national profile" (Newton, 2003: 42) and that the sub-sectors that dominate the local landscape are "craft, performing arts, visual arts, music, and film" (Newton, 2003: 47).

In common with the emerging national picture of cultural industries, it was demonstrated that the sector of creative industries in Johannesburg is characterized by a high level of small and micro-enterprises, "the sole proprietors of which are predominantly the producers of creative products or content" (Newton, 2003: 33). In the majority of cases, particularly in micro-enterprise, the proprietor fulfils a set of multi-tasking roles as producer, agent, marketer and retailer. The products of the Johannesburg creative industries economy are overwhelmingly targeted at local markets. Indeed, the majority of products and services were consumed within the creative sector itself. None the less, mirroring the strategic position of creative industries in the value chains of other sectors, it was recorded that "the major private sector markets for creative industry products are the tourism, services and retail sectors" (Newton, 2003: 51).

The creative industries sector was found to exhibit signs of growth in terms of new business start-ups and by a profile of enterprises that was dominated by business start-ups occurring after South Africa's 1994 democratic transition (Newton, 2003: 44). A significant finding across creative industries as a whole was that their estimated annual turnover figure of R50,000 indicated that the sector contains a large element of what would be described as "survivalist" enterprises. Moreover, the survey of creative industries in Johannesburg disclosed that 51 percent of enterprises reported they worked across between two to five of the different spectrum of activities that comprise the "sector" of creative industries. In common with the earlier work of Dirsuweit (1999), it was shown that creative industries exhibited a locational tendency towards geographical clustering in parts of the city. Finally, while white-ownership was strong in the "commanding heights" of the sector—in terms of the largest and dominant enterprises—it was observed that in Johannesburg, black economic empowerment was advancing in creative industries, unlike the laggard situation as recently reported in Cape Town (Minty, 2005).

The scoping study made a series of recommendations to Council for development of the sector. The most significant recommendations were as follows:

- Branding an image for Johannesburg's creative industries so that additional demand is generated;
- Addressing the chronic skills shortages in the sector;
- Enhancing networks and alliances such that the capacity of the cluster is strengthened to rapidly respond to new demands;

- Developing a strong business development infrastructure in terms of providing a business-friendly foundation of physical space, telecommunications, policy support and funding mechanisms; and,
- Dealing with the high levels of crime and urban decay in the inner city that act as deterrents to tourists and the audiences of creative industries.

The City of Johannesburg's creative industries consolidated sector support initiative was announced by the Economic Development Unit in 2005 (City of Johannesburg, 2005a). The central goal is described as "to support both cultural workers with talent but limited institutional support, as well as emerging companies with an entertainment industry focus" (City of Johannesburg, 2005a). There are four elements that comprise the support initiative.

- First, is the establishment of an innovative project styled the Johannesburg Art Bank, which draws upon parallel models already successfully operating in Canada and Australia (City of Johannesburg, 2005b). The objective of this project is to furnish support and supplement the income of Johannesburg-based contemporary artists by creating a market for their work over a five-year period (City of Johannesburg, 2005b). The bank functions by purchasing visual art works from local artists and then leases these to companies "who can refresh their office displays every two years at a fraction of the full cost of buying new art" (City of Johannesburg, 2005a).
- Second, the city has launched a Creative Industries Seed Fund which will "provide support to promising creative industries that could benefit both from the provision of business skills and up-front financial assistance to take a viable creative industry business-plan into implementation." This project operates as a competition amongst learners who recently have completed learnerships in craft operations management, music business management or cultural entrepreneurship.
- Third, the Economic Development Unit has initiated support for a facility that is targeted "to incubate start-up filmmakers" (City of Johannesburg, 2005a). More specifically, the Film and Video Incubator is aimed at support of new entrepreneurs in the film industry. The project is anchored upon a "dedicated facility where start-up filmmakers are provided with office space, office infrastructure and specialised equipment at subsidised rentals for approximately eighteen to twenty-four months" (City of Johannesburg, 2005a).
- Finally, the City is funding a Johannesburg National Arts Festival Fringe Project as a basis for defining appropriate support for a performing arts incubator. This initiative supports selected performing arts companies that have already put on productions at the annual national arts festival (held at Grahamstown) to perform these shows in Johannesburg, thus helping them gain national exposure as well as deepening local demand for quality productions (City of Johannesburg, 2005a).

Although the Sector Development Programme for creative industries represents the first co-ordinated explicit support from the city for creative industries, it must be recognized that other significant support interventions have been introduced outside of the Programme. Three developments are of especial note.

- First, is support for the Art City project that involved a joint initiative by the Council with a cell phone company to develop art murals on major inner city buildings. During mid-2002 the inner city of Johannesburg began to be transformed into a large art gallery with nearly seventy large murals displayed on the side of a range of buildings (Davie, 2002a). The project aimed to showcase the inner city "as the hub and cultural center of Africa's world class city" and to further enhance the role of tourism in the city (Davie, 2002b). The beginning of the display of art works coincided with the World Summit for Sustainable Development and ran until the Cricket World Cup held in March 2003.

- Second, the Newtown Cultural Precinct is a tourism-related project that was a joint initiative between the city and the Provincial Government and geared to promote a cluster of creative industries and more especially cultural industries that might enhance the area's tourism potential (Dirsuweit, 1999). The planned cultural district represents a cluster of creative activities, entertainment and related industries for the promotion of tourism (Blue IQ, 2002). Through the promotion of cultural tourism and the making of a cultural district, this historic area of Johannesburg, which contains several museums, theaters and heritage sites, is set to be transformed into "the creative capital of South Africa" (Blue IQ, 2002). In 2005 the provincial government's involvement with the Newtown project was terminated with responsibility passed to the Johannesburg Development Agency (JDA). The JDA views the re-development of Newtown as a major regeneration initiative and seeks to galvanize "major investment, particularly in the creative industries, culture and tourism" (Johannesburg Development Agency, 2005: 17).

- Finally, assistance has been provided by Council, through the activities of the Johannesburg Development Agency, for the development in the inner city of a "fashion district" (Johannesburg Development Agency, 2004). This support was for establishing a hub for fashion design as part of re-invigorating the city's clothing economy not on the basis of mass-produced goods but of individual fashion items using an African design (Cachalia et al., 2004; Rogerson, 2004). Central to the vision has been the notion of promoting the "Urban Edge of African Fashion," capturing the spirit and vision of a fashion-oriented, trendsetting, and outward looking district (Johannesburg Development Agency, 2004: 5). In terms of creative industries, this project is highly significant for it goes beyond the group of activities that are the targets of support under the Creative Industries Sector Support Programme.

Conclusion: A Developing Nexus

In South Africa the strengthening of policy support for creative industries with new product development and innovation in tourism represents a future challenge that must be addressed. A first step has been made in the encouraging strategic policy thinking of national government's Accelerated and Shared Growth Initiative for South Africa that contains the important commitment to strengthen the industry linkages of the craft sector with tourism (Department of Trade and Industry, 2005b).

Over the past decade, it is evident that a solid foundation for establishing a nexus between creative industries and tourism has been established. The "discovery" by national government of the economic potential of "cultural industries" can be attributed mainly to the important advocacy work and research produced by the Cultural Strategy Group and the Creative South Africa Initiative. Since 2000, however, the major policy innovations for supporting creative industries have been undertaken at provincial and local level as part of wider urban economic development initiatives. The City of Johannesburg must be acknowledged as particularly pro-active in this respect by according recognition and growing support to the creative industries sector.

Looking ahead, in terms of further development, it can be argued that what is required is to expand more deeply the linkages between the emerging creative industries sector and tourism developments taking place in the city. Indeed, the first signs of this linkage already are in evidence through changes occurring in urban tourism planning for the city (Monitor, 2005). It is significant that Johannesburg is beginning to re-position itself for tourism not just as a retail and business tourism "Mecca" but instead around a cultural theme (ComMark Trust, 2005). The "new" Johannesburg cultural product recognizes that alongside the city's historical, political and entertainment assets and significance in the anti-apartheid struggle and associated monuments, the city is a cosmopolitan center with valuable tourism assets for music, dance, fashion, theater, and the arts (Monitor, 2005). The "creative" city of Johannesburg is beginning on a pathway that should lead to more significant linkages and synergies forged, over the next decade, between creative industries, tourism, and economic regeneration.

Acknowledgements

Thanks are extended to the National Research Foundation, Pretoria for research funding support under Gun Award 205464.

References

Bill, A., 2005: "Blood, sweat and tears": disciplining the creative in Aotearoa New Zealand, Unpublished paper, College of Design, Fine Arts and Music, Massey University.

Bilton, C. and Leary, R., 2002: What can managers do for creativity?: brokering creativity in the creative industries, *International Journal of Cultural Policy*, 8, 49-64.

Binkhorst, E., 2005: The experience economy and creativity, towards the co-creation tourism experience?, Paper presented at the ATLAS Annual Conference 2005: Tourism Creativity and Development, Barcelona, 2-4 November.

Blue IQ, 2002: *Blue IQ: The Plan for a Smart Province – Gauteng*, Blue IQ, Johannesburg.

Brecknock, R., 2004: Creative capital: creative industries in the "creative city," Unpublished paper, Brecknock Consulting Australia, Brisbane.

Cachalia, F., Jocum, M. and Rogerson, C.M., 2004: 'The urban edge of African fashion': the evolution of Johannesburg's planned fashion district, in D. McCormick and C.M. Rogerson (Eds.), *Clothing and Footwear in African Industrialisation*, Africa Institute of South Africa, Pretoria, 527-546.

Caves, R., 2000: *Creative Industries: Contracts Between Art and Commerce*, Harvard, Cambridge.

Caves, R., 2003: Contracts between art and commerce, *Journal of Economic Perspectives*, 17, 73-83.

City of Johannesburg, 2005a: Five-Year Review, Unpublished draft report of the Johannesburg Economic Development Unit.

City of Johannesburg, 2005b: Joburg 2030 Joburg Art Bank, Unpublished report presented to the city Finance Strategy and Economic Development Committee 5 November.

ComMark Trust, 2005; Tourism overview, available at www.commark.org.za

Colantonio, A. and Potter, R., 2006: *Urban Tourism and Development in the Socialist State: Havana During the 'Special Period'*, Ashgate, Aldershot.

Create SA, 2005: About CREATE SA, available at www.createsa.org.za

Cultural Strategy Group, 1998a: Creative South Africa: A Strategy for Realising the Potential of the Cultural Industries, Unpublished report for the Department of Arts, Culture, Science and Technology, Pretoria.

Cultural Strategy Group, 1998b: Cultural Industries Growth Strategy: The South African Craft Industry Report, Unpublished report for the Department of Arts, Culture, Science and Technology, Pretoria.

Cultural Strategy Group, 1998c: Cultural Industries Growth Strategy: The South African Film sector report, Unpublished report for the Department of Arts, Culture, Science and Technology, Pretoria.

Cultural Strategy Group, 1998d: Cultural Industries Growth Strategy: The South African Music sector report, Unpublished report for the Department of Arts, Culture, Science and Technology, Pretoria.

Cultural Strategy Group, 1998e: Cultural Industries Growth Strategy: The South African Publishing sector report, Unpublished report for the Department of Arts, Culture, Science and Technology, Pretoria.

Cunningham, S., 2003: From cultural to creative industries: theory, industry and policy implications, Unpublished paper, Creative Industries Research and Applications Centre, Queensland University of Technology, Brisbane.

Dabinett, G., 2004: Creative Sheffield: creating value and changing values?, *Local Economy*, 19, 414-419.

Davie, L., 2002a: Turning the city into an art gallery, available at www.goafrica.co.za/joburg_june_2002/art.stm

Davie, L., 2002b: Jo'burg art gallery, available at www.goafrica.co.za/joburg_oct_2002/oct2_art.stm

De Berranger, P. and Meldrum, M.C.R., 2000: The development of intelligent local clusters to increase global competitiveness and local cohesion: the case of small businesses in the creative industries, *Urban Studies*, 37, 1827-1835.

Department of Arts and Culture, South Africa 2004: *Strategic Plan 1 April 2004-31 March 2007*, available at www.dac.gov.za

Department of Culture, Media and Sport, U.K., 1998: *Mapping the Creative Industries*, available at www.culture.gov.uk/creative/creative_industries.html

Department of Trade and Industry, South Africa 2005a: *Tourism Sector Development Strategy*, Trade and Investment South Africa for DTI, Pretoria.

Department of Trade and Industry, South Africa, 2005b: *A Growing Economy that Benefits All: Accelerated & Shared Growth Initiative for South Africa (ASGI-SA): Discussion Document*, DTI, Pretoria.

Dirsuweit, T., 1999: From fortress city to creative city: developing culture and the information-based sectors in the regeneration and reconstruction of the Greater Johannesburg Area, *Urban Forum*, 10, 183-213.

Evans, G., 2003: Hard-branding the cultural city – from Prado to Prada, *International Journal of Urban and Regional Research*, 27, 417-440.

Evans, G., 2005: Creative spaces: strategies for creative cities, in J. Swarbrooke, M. Smith and L. Onderwater (Eds.), *Tourism, Creativity and Development: ATLAS Reflections 2005*, Association for Tourism and Leisure Education, Arnhem, 7-10.

Flew, T., 2002: Beyond *ad hocery:* defining creative industries, Unpublished paper presented to the Second International Conference on Cultural Policy Research, Te Papa, Wellington, 23-26 January.

Flew, T., 2003: Creative industries: from the chicken cheer to the culture of services, *Continuum: Journal of Media and Cultural Studies*, 17, 89-94.

Florida, R., 2002: *The Role of the Creative Class,* Basic Books, New York.

Garcia, B., 2004: Urban regeneration, arts programming and major events, *International Journal of Cultural Policy*, 10, 103-118.

Hall, C.M., 2004: Sport tourism and urban regeneration, in BW Ritchie and D. Adair (Eds.), *Sport Tourism: Interrelationships, Impacts and Issues,* Channel View, Clevedon, 192-205.

Hall, P., 2000: Creative cities and economic development, *Urban Studies*, 37, 639-649.

Harvey, D., 1989: From managerialism to entrepreneurialism: the transformation in urban governance in late capitalism, *Geografiska Annaler* 71B, 3-17.

Hiller, H.H., 2000: Mega-events, urban boosterism and growth strategies: an analysis of the objectives and legitimations of the Cape Town 2004 Olympic Bid, *International Journal of Urban and Regional Research*, 24, 439-458.

Johannesburg Development Agency, 2004: *Development Business Plan JDA 009: Fashion District Development,* available at www.jda.co.za

Johannesburg Development Agency, 2005: *Business Plan 2005-06,* JDA, Johannesburg.

Kurtzman, J., 2005: Economic impact: sports tourism and the city, *Journal of Sports Tourism*, 10, 47-71.

Landry, C., 2000: *The Creative City: A Toolkit for Urban Innovators*, Earthscan, London.

Landry, C. and Bianchini, F., 1995: *The Creative City*, Demos, London.

Law, C.M., 1992: Urban tourism and its contribution to economic regeneration, *Urban Studies*, 29, 599-618.

Law, C.M., 1993: *Urban Tourism: Attracting Visitors to Large Cities*, Mansell, London.

Leslie, D., 2005: Creative cities?, *Geoforum,* 36, 403-405.

Machaka, J. and Roberts, S. 2003: The DTI's new "Integrated Manufacturing Strategy"?: comparative industrial performance, linkages and technology, *South African Journal of Economics*, 71, 1-26.

Masters, T.A., Russell, R., and Brooks, R., 2005: Creativity and regeneration: economic impacts of creative arts in rural and regional Victoria, Australia, Paper presented at the ATLAS Annual Conference 2005: Tourism Creativity and development, Barcelona, 2-4 November.

McCarthy, J., 2002: Entertainment-led regeneration: the case of Detroit, *Cities*, 19, 105-111.

Meethan, K. and Beer, J., 2005: Economic clustering, tourism and the creative industries in Plymouth: developing a practical tool for impact assessment, Paper presented at the ATLAS Annual Conference 2005: Tourism Creativity and development, Barcelona, 2-4 November.

Minty, Z., 2005: Breaching borders: using culture in Cape Town's Central City for social change, *Isandla Development Communication* 2 (8/9), Isandla Institute, Cape Town.

Mlambo-Ngcuka, P., 2006: Media Briefing on Background Document: A Catalyst for Accelerated and Shared Growth-South Africa, 6 February, available at www.info.gov.za/speeches.

Monitor, 2004: *Global Competitiveness Project: Summary of Key Findings of Phase 1,* South African Tourism, Johannesburg.

Monitor, 2005: *Final Report to ComMark Trust on the Feasibility Assessment of Cultural Tourism in Johannesburg,* available at www.commark.org.za

Newton, M., 2003: Joburg Creative Industries Sector Scoping Report, Unpublished Report for the Economic Development Department, City of Johannesburg.

Padayachee, T., 1997: Olympics or not, the bid makes a difference: Cape Town 2004, *Urban Forum*, 8 (1), 109-116.

Pratt, A.C., 2004: Creative clusters: towards the governance of the creative industries production system, *Media International Australia incorporating Culture and Policy*, 112, 50-66.

Richards, G., 2005: Creativity: a new strategic resource for tourism, in J. Swarbrooke, M. Smith and L. Onderwater (Eds.), *Tourism, Creativity and Development: ATLAS Reflections 2005*, Association for Tourism and Leisure Education, Arnhem, 11-22.

Richards, G. and Raymond, C., 2000: Creative tourism, *ATLAS News,* 23, 16-20.

Richards, G. and Wilson, J., 2006a: Developing creativity in tourist experiences: a solution to the serial reproduction of culture, *Tourism Management*, 27, 1209-1223.

Richards, G. and Wilson, J., 2006b: Tourism, creativity and development, Unpublished mimeo paper.

Rogerson, C.M., 2004: Pro-poor local economic development in post-apartheid South Africa: the Johannesburg fashion district, *International Development Planning Review*, 26, 401-429.

Rogerson, C.M., 2005: Globalization, economic restructuring and local response in Johannesburg—the most isolated "world city," in K. Segbers, S. Raiser and K. Volkmann (Ed.), *Public Problems—Private Solutions?: Globalizing Cities in the South*, Ashgate, Aldershot, 17-34.

Santagata, W., 2002: *Creativity, Fashion, and Market Behavior*, Working Paper No. 5/2002, International Centre for Research on the Economics of Culture, Institutions and Creativity, Department of Economics, University of Turin.

Santagata, W., 2004: *Cultural Districts and Economic Development,* Working Paper No. 1/2004, International Centre for Research on the Economics of Culture, Institutions and Creativity, Department of Economics, University of Turin.

Scott, A.J., 1996: The craft, fashion and cultural products industries of Los Angeles: competitive dynamics and policy dilemmas, *Annals of the Association of American Geographers*, 86, 306-323.

Scott, A.J., 2004: Cultural-products industries and urban economic development: prospects for growth and market contestation in a global context, *Urban Affairs Review*, 39, 461-490.

Smith, M., 2005a: Introduction, in J. Swarbrooke, M. Smith and L. Onderwater (Eds.), *Tourism, Creativity and Development: ATLAS Reflections 2005*, Association for Tourism and Leisure Education, Arnhem, 3-6.

Smith, M., 2005b: Tourism, culture and regeneration: differentiation through creativity, in J. Swarbrooke, M. Smith and L. Onderwater (Eds.), *Tourism, Creativity and Development: ATLAS Reflections 2005*, Association for Tourism and Leisure Education, Arnhem, 23-38.

Swarbrooke, J., 1999: Urban areas, in J. Swarbrooke, *Sustainable Tourism Management*, CABI Publishing, Wallingford, 172-182.

Swarbrooke, J., 2000: Tourism, economic development and urban regeneration: a critical evaluation, in M. Robinson, R. Sharpley, N. Evans, P. Long and J. Swarbrooke (Eds.), *Developments in Urban and Rural Tourism*, Centre for Travel and Tourism, Sheffield Hallam University and University of Northumbria, Sunderland, 269-285.

Turok, I., 2003: Cities, clusters and creative industries: the case of film and television in Scotland, *European Planning Studies*, 11, 549-565.

Wood, P. and Taylor, C., 2004: Big ideas for a small town: the Huddersfield creative town initiative, *Local Economy*, 19, 380-395.

Wu, W., 2005: *Dynamic Cities and Creative Clusters*, World Bank Policy Research Working Paper 3509, Washington, DC.

Zahra, A., 2005: Destination management obstacles to creativity and a creative response from local government in New Zealand, Paper presented at the ATLAS Annual Conference 2005: Tourism Creativity and Development, Barcelona, 2-4 November.

9

Gay Tourism in South Africa:
The Cape Town Experience

Gustav Visser

"Cape Town—Now voted one of the top three
Gay Travel Destinations and certainly one of
the most beautiful places in the world" (www.
ourway.co.za, 2005).

Until recently gay tourism was largely invisible to tourism researchers
(Ryan and Hall, 2002: 102-103). Nevertheless, gay tourism was a discernible
trend in Europe during the late nineteenth and early twentieth centuries, and
metropolitan cities such as New York were host to a large gay leisure scene
that drew visitors from across the U.S. (Graham, 2002). It was, however, not
until the impact of the human-rights movements of the late 1960s and 1970s
filtered through Western societies that this cohort became an identifiable tourism
market segment (Graham, 2002). Moreover, the commodification of different
types of identity has led to the consolidation and expansion of gay leisure and
tourism (Stuber, 2002). The body of research focused on the gay male tourist
is still relatively small, but is growing rapidly. A persistent theme in this corpus
of research relates to the "urban" focus of gay tourism (Cox, 2002). Indeed,
gay tourism, both in terms of its historical development (cf. Graham, 2002)
and its contemporary manifestations (cf. Clift, Luongo and Callister, 2002),
has largely been portrayed as an urban phenomenon, with the leisure facilities
of "gay Meccas" such as Amsterdam, Berlin, New York, San Francisco, and
Sydney forming the backbone of these destinations' gay tourism infrastructure
(Cox, 2002). Similarly, in South Africa, the development of a gay tourism
system has been underpinned by the gay leisure infrastructure of the country's
metropolitan regions (Visser, 2003a; 2003b).

The demise of apartheid witnessed two important events in terms of the
way of thinking about gay tourism in South African cities: the introduction of

the country's progressive constitution, and the increase in tourist flows. The constitution enshrines a range of human rights, including that of sexual orientation/preference. This has led to a visible gay and lesbian community, which has created spaces for leisure and recreation, particularly in large metropolitan areas. On the whole, the "materialization" of homosexual rights has taken the form of dedicated leisure spaces largely focused on the needs of relatively wealthy, white gay men (Visser, 2003a; 2003b). As yet, the impact of the constitution remains minimal particularly in the case of black gays and lesbians, who continue to experience high levels of social marginalization and violence at the hands of a homophobic, patriarchal society (Van Zyl and Steyn, 2005). In addition, class and racial discrimination still prevents black men and women from attaining meaningful membership of the larger "gay and lesbian community" (see Visser, 2003a; 2003b; Van Zyl and Steyn, 2005 for accounts of extensive investigation in this respect). A second outcome closely related to the demise of apartheid is the large-scale expansion of the South African tourism system, with Cape Town as the main beneficiary (Visser, 2003a; 2003b). As Cape Town has developed into Africa's premier leisure tourist destination, it has subsequently also emerged as a popular destination choice for gay male tourists.

This chapter investigates the development of gay male tourism in South Africa. Particular attention is drawn to the Cape Town gay tourism system, since Cape Town is currently the only city in Africa that has an international gay tourism profile. Indeed, tourism activity in that city pursues both the domestic and international gay travel market. In addition, the chapter aims to demonstrate how sexuality—one of our key human-status characteristics—impacts on the urban tourism system of Cape Town. In particular, the investigation aims to show the impact of sexual identity in the (re)shaping of the urban form, and also to identify the challenges that such redevelopment holds for both the local gay host community and the city at large.

Gay Men and Tourism Clusters

Gay men use space to adopt separate identities. This process often occurs away from the home and the workplace, encouraging the consumption of leisure space (Hughes, 1998). It is argued (Hughes, 1997; 2002; 2003) that urban areas facilitate the assumption of a gay identity in many ways, not least through the concentration of gay leisure places available. Binnie (1997) suggests that such leisure-related freedom has been widely embraced as a validation of gay identity, if only as a reaction to a more general powerlessness. Moreover, as argued by Knopp (1995), the use of space may have the effect of transforming that space so that it becomes coded as "gay."

Tourism by gay men may be the ultimate manifestation of the use of space in order to demarcate separate identities (Hughes, 1998). Cox (2002) develops this idea further, pointing out that gay tourism to these "gay coded leisure clusters" from small urban areas to "metropolitan" gay areas plays a significant role in learning how to be gay or in finding different ways in which to express and develop a gay identity. Studies of gay leisure spaces interpret the clustering of such activity as part of a homosexual challenge to the heterosexual coding of public space, empowering those who are currently excluded and disenfranchised (Binnie and Valentine, 2000). Gay spaces provide community and territory, as well as a sense of order, to a diverse and geographically scattered community (Pritchard et al., 1998).

Not only do gay leisure spaces tend to cluster together, however; so, too, does tourism activity in a more general sense. It has been suggested that tourism in a city is related to a combination of its primary and secondary tourism elements. It is usually argued that the "activity place" is composed of attractions that characterize most cities, such as museums and historic sites, whereas the leisure setting is the physical and socio-cultural context within which the attractions are set: the overall spatial structure of the city and its ambience (Jansen-Verbeke, 1994). The secondary elements, according to Jansen-Verbeke, include shops, cafés, restaurants and bars, hotels and entertainment.

Primary elements that are proximate to each other, as clusters, may have a greater appeal to the tourist than non-proximate elements. Several tourist clusters, spatially separate and with distinct features, may exist in a city to give it polycentricity (Hughes, 1998). The identification of clusters ultimately depends on tourist use. These elements are, however, usually consumed by both tourists and local residents. The overlapping use of gay leisure clusters and primary, as well as secondary, tourism elements, may also cause a city to be transformed in whole or in part, both materially and symbolically (Hughes, 1998). It is at the intersection of the overlapping use of urban space that this chapter aims to demonstrate the impact that this process has had on the De Waterkant district of Cape Town's Central Business District (CBD) periphery.

Gay Leisure, Tourism, and Cape Town

Apartheid South Africa was a heteropatriarchal society superimposed onto a racially segregated space (Elder, 2002). This feature was most acutely seen in the structuring of the country's urban areas, which had clearly-defined tourism and leisure geographies in which inter-racial contact was minimized to the extreme. While homosexual lifestyles fell beyond the parameters of apartheid heteropatriachy, white, middle-class men, by virtue of their privileged racial and class position in this societal framework, claimed and asserted their identity through leisure and tourism consumption within the apartheid urban spatial structure (Visser, 2003b). As a consequence, a white, middle-class gay leisure space economy developed in most of South Africa's main metropolitan areas.

In post-apartheid South Africa gay leisure facilities are found across the South African urban hierarchy, but the main focus still falls upon the main metropolitan areas. However, in providing an overview of gay leisure space, it has to be conceded that the gay leisure infrastructure reflected in travel brochures and guides, inevitably ignores those places of leisure which, although they may have gay patronage and although they may be gay-friendly, are not regarded as key role-players in a particular gay leisure scene. Consequently, spaces of gay leisure and recreation in many smaller cities and towns are not recorded here, and thus evade the investigatory gaze. In addition, the more liminal spaces of gay or gay-friendly township shebeens, bars, and public spaces such as parks and beaches, which arguably provide the backbone of gay leisure in South Africa, are not included. However, as the chapter focuses on gay tourism, it needs to be borne in mind that the liminal spaces of gay leisure cannot be included, since tourists who seek out gay (or gay-friendly) destinations are significantly influenced by the formal, visible, gay infrastructure that a country, city or town has to offer. Tables 9.1 provide some insight into the distribution of South Africa's key gay leisure facilities. This table reveals two important features of the South African formal gay leisure scene. Firstly, it is not very extensive; and secondly (not surprisingly, and in line with the experience elsewhere in the world), the leading metropolitan areas host the largest number of gay leisure facilities. Moreover, it is clear that two cities—Cape Town and Johannesburg—significantly dominate gay leisure facility provision. While both cities have near-identical offerings in terms of leisure facilities, the distinguishing feature relates to the significantly greater occurrence of gay-only, or gay-friendly tourist accommodation. In this very important respect Cape Town differentiates itself from Johannesburg and strongly emerges as South Africa's key gay travel destination.

Cape Town has been the principal beneficiary of the post-apartheid tourism boom (Visser, 2003a; 2003b). It is now the most important leisure tourism destination (for overseas leisure tourists) on the African continent. As part of a strategy to diversify and grow tourism arrivals the regional tourism authority has identified those niche markets which hold the most potential in the context of the city's tourism product offering. These include sport, cultural, cruise-liner, eco- and MICE tourism (Visser, 2002). Echoing national government priorities, the overall goal is to provide opportunities for both small and large businesses. One market niche that encompasses the consumption of one or more of these target areas is the gay tourism market (Tebje, 2004). This particular niche started to draw attention towards the mid-1990s and has attracted considerable support since the early 2000s (Tebje, 2004). The main reason for pursuing the gay market is based on this cohort's apparently higher income and spending levels. It must, however, be noted that there are many questions concerning the survey-technique biases that support these claims. As a consequence, our view of this market is skewed in terms of class (middle-class), race (white), and gender (male). Nevertheless, available market research (admittedly in the context of these constraints) suggests that these tourists travel further, are well-off, have double incomes and do not have children (Heard and Ludski, 2001: 71; Van Niekerk, 2005).

It has been estimated that the American gay travel market displays the general characteristics mentioned above, and comprises 26 million tourists, while

Table 9.1
Gay Tourism Infrastructure in Metropolitan South Africa

Gay facilities	Cape Town	Durban	Greater Johannesburg	Pretoria
Bars	7	3	7	1
Night clubs	3	2	4	3
Saunas (gay men only)	2	0	2	1
Massage Studios (gay men only)	3	1	2	2
Guest houses/hotels (exclusively gay)	5	0	0	0
Guest houses/hotels (advertised as gay friendly)	22	3	3	1

Source: Exit (2005); Gay Page (2005); Pink Map (2005)

Europe's gay market is considered to be even larger (IGLTA, 2001). While these statistics are, at best, the result of informed guesswork, it has to be stressed that in the context of a long-haul destination, the demographic characteristics of tourists from Australasia, Europe and North America traveling to cities such as Cape Town and to South Africa more generally, would imply, by default, that the likely tourist cohort would be wealthier. Moreover, South Africa's tourism industry and, indeed, the policy environment shaping its tourism planning and promotion strategies generally, do not, on the whole, enter into competition with budget resorts and destinations (South African Tourism, 2003; Visser, 2003a; 2003b).

Although only a fraction of both the international gay and "straight" markets visit South Africa, there is obviously much that could potentially be gained from targeting this market niche. Of the current one million overseas tourists visiting Cape Town, about ten percent would be gay males (Fine, 2001). Awareness of the gay market is already well established in the wider leisure sector (Binnie and Valentine, 2000). Despite the growth and profitability of the gay male market, as well as the intense contemporary inter-place competition for tourists, Cape Town remains the only South African, and indeed, the only African destination that is actively exploiting the potential of gay tourism.

Owing to varying data given by different sources, the information concerning the size of the gay tourist market varies considerably. Similarly, the size of the gay tourist market that patronizes Cape Town cannot be accurately estimated. It is, however, possible to provide some insight into the most common basic features of gay tourists visiting Cape Town by analyzing the guest registers of gay men-only tourist accommodation establishments. Drawing on a five-year (November 2000 – November 2005) analysis of visits paid to Cape Town's premier gay tourist accommodation establishment, the *Amsterdam Guest House* (winner of the DIVA award for the best gay hospitality establishment in South Africa), a relatively accurate profile of the countries of origin of gay tourists can be presented.

Table 9.2 shows that over a five-year period, gay male tourists from no fewer than forty-seven countries visited Cape Town. It is clear that overseas tourists constitute the most important market segment for South African gay tourist accommodation establishments, with domestic visitors accounting for only 16.5 percent of all guests. The relatively low incidence of domestic gay travelers can probably be explained by two factors. Firstly, room rates are relatively high (R600-R1000 per room) for South African tourists, and secondly, more than 50 percent of the domestic tourism market to the Cape Town region falls into the Visiting Friends and Relatives market segment. Consequently, these tourists do not primarily engage the formal tourist accommodation system. In terms of the international gay visitor, it is evident that there is a high concentration of tourists from only a handful of tourist-generating regions, primarily comprising the United Kingdom (19.7 percent), Germany (16.3 percent), the U.S. (13.3 percent), and the Netherlands (7 percent). This finding is, however, not unexpected, as these countries represent the key overseas tourist-generating regions for South Africa in general. In terms of the domestic gay male market, Table 9.3 reveals that most of the visitors came from the Gauteng province (76.6 percent), South Africa's economic heartland and, by virtue of its population size, the home province of the largest concentration of gay men in the country.

Gay-friendliness, Place Promotion, and Gay Tourism

It is now commonly agreed that the popularity of South Africa as a gay destination has been influenced by its liberal post-apartheid constitution (Visser, 2003a: 175). In stark contrast to other African countries, South Africa's constitution has come to invest a key role in the protection of gay and lesbian rights, setting the context for the development of a gay leisure market, on the foundation of which a niche tourism market has developed. Against this backdrop, the importance of Cape Town as Africa's leading gay-friendly tourist destination has been developed through increased exposure in the international gay press, for example, in the *Spartacus International Gay Guide* (published by Bruno Gmunder Verlag, Berlin). In the late-1990s the British mainstream press also took note of the "gay-friendly" character of Cape Town, which has consistently been voted one of the top three gay travel destinations in the world over the past five years (Our Way, 2005).

This was, and remains, the main response to one of the first changes witnessed in the development of gay tourism infrastructure in post-apartheid Cape Town—specialized organizations that have emerged to promote Cape Town as "gay-friendly." In this respect organizations such as the Gay and Lesbian Association of Cape Town: Tourism, Industry and Commerce (GALACTTIC)—and

Table 9.2
Countries of Origin of Gay Travellers to Cape Town

Country of origin	Number	Percentage (region)	Percentage (total)	Percentage (all overseas visitors)
Europe				
Austria	5	1.7	1	1.1
Belgium	12	4.1	2.5	2.2
Czech Republic	2	0.6	0.04	0.02
Denmark	3	1	0.06	1
Finland	1	0.3	0.02	0.3
France	20	6.8	4.2	6.1
Germany	77	26.5	16.3	13.4
Greece	2	0.6	0.04	0.04
Ireland	2	0.6	0.04	1.8
Italy	4	1.3	0.08	2.6
Malta	1	0.3	0.02	0.01
Netherlands	33	11.3	7	6.3
Norway	5	1.7	1	0.9
Poland	2	0.6	0.04	0.3
Portugal	1	0.3	0.02	1.5
Spain	8	2.7	1.6	1.3
Sweden	4	1.3	0.08	1.5
Switzerland	15	5.1	3.1	1.8
United Kingdom	93	32	19.7	23.8
Sub-Total	**290**	**100**	**61.6**	**n/a**
Americas				
Canada	9	11.8	1.9	1.8
Dominican Republic	1	1.3	0.02	0.001
Mexico	2	2.6	0.04	0.01
Paraguay	1	1.3	0.02	0.01
USA	63	82.2	13.3	9.9
Sub-Total	**76**	**100**	**16.1**	**n/a**
Middle East				
Dubai	1	16.6	0.02	0.03
Israel	2	33.3	0.04	0.79
Saudi Arabia	2	33.3	0.04	0.1
Sub-Total	**6**	**100**	**1.2**	**n/a**
Australasia and Far East				
Australia	10	76.9	2.1	3.7
Hong Kong	1	7.6	0.02	0.6
Japan	1	7.6	0.02	1.1
Thailand	1	7.6	0.02	0.3
Sub-Total	**13**	**100**	**2.8**	**n/a**
Africa				**(All African visitors)**
Egypt	1	16.6	0.02	0.07
Kenya	2	2.3	0.04	0.4
Malawi	1	1.1	0.02	1.9
Mauritius	2	2.3	0.04	0.3
Namibia	3	3.4	0.06	4.8
South Africa	78	90.6	16.5	-
Sub-Total	**86**	**100**	**18.3**	**n/a**
Total	**471**	-	**100**	**100**

Source: Author's survey (every fifth entry from Amsterdam Guest House guest register)

Table 9.3
Provinces of Origin of Gay South African Travellers to Cape Town

Province of origin	Number	Percentage
Eastern Cape	2	2.6
Free State	5	6.4
Gauteng	60	76.9
KwaZulu-Natal	11	14.1
Total	**78**	**100**

Source: Author's survey (every fifth entry from Amsterdam Guest House guest register)

numerous websites (for example *ourway.co.za, capetownpride.co.za*, and *gay-info.co.za*)—provide much information to the gay tourist.

An analysis of tour operators' tour itineraries (for example those of Our Way Travel and Safari, as well as Friends of Dorothy Tours) demonstrates the degree of tourist motivation that is generally pitched at a number of different holiday experiences. The advertised travel programs certainly do not only encompass stereotypical beach and nightclub holidays involving the sun-seeking and romance that are so typical of many of the Mediterranean gay resorts. Rather, these travel programs also include what Clift and Forrest (1999) refer to as "personal development and activity" tour programs, which are designed to reflect the fact that the holiday experience involves traveling around, sight-seeing and a broadening of experience. Our Way Travel and Safari (2005, no page numbers), for example, placed an advertisement that was worded as follows:

> Not only has Cape Town established itself as the gay capital of Africa but she is also famous throughout the world for her majestic mountain setting, and the many places and sights that both the city and the Cape Peninsula offer the tourist. Over the centuries, visitors have marveled, not only at the peninsula's natural splendor, but also at the cultural diversity of the "Mother City"'—the blending of Eastern, African and Western ways of life, which is constantly evident in architecture, dress and local customs. Its legendary hospitality and friendly (hot!) guys combined with a scenic diversity including Table Mountain and sandy white beaches, not to mention the exciting gay nightlife and value for money shopping, truly make this HEAVEN ON EARTH!

These features are repeatedly encountered in other web-based advertising. Currently, there is a significant difference between the promotion of Cape Town as a gay tourist destination and that of, for example, Amsterdam. The key focus is the broader destination experience of nature, culture and history, in a societal environment that is tolerant of gay men. The motivating elements, however, remain those that are listed among Jansen-Verbeke's "primary tourism elements" (Table 9.4).

Table 9.4
Tourism Product of Cape Town

Primary elements	Secondary elements
Historical	Shopping
Including Cape Dutch buildings, Constantia, South African parliament, the Castle, Robben Island, V&A Waterfront	Cafés
	Coffee shops
	Restaurants
	Guest houses
Cultural	Hotels
Including museums, Winelands, "Malay Quarter," Townships	Entertainment facilities
	Bars
Environmental/Outdoors	Clubs
Including Table Mountain, Beaches, Cape Peninsula National Park, Kirstenbosch Gardens, Chapman's Peak	

Sources: Based on De Villiers (2001); Hughes (1998); Jansen-Verbeke (1994); Ozinsky (2001); The Pink Map (2005)

Although tourism has often depended on natural attractions to draw visitors, a more recent phenomenon has been the creation and development of major festivals/events that serve as a magnet to draw specific audiences to a region. Similarly, a key theme in the development of gay destinations is the role of festivals and events. Events such as the Sydney Mardi Gras have played a pivotal role in promoting destinations as gay-friendly. These events draw considerable numbers, provide a massive cash injection into the local economy, serve to unite people from gay communities all around the world and act as a testing ground for future visits. In Cape Town, the Mother City Queer Project Party (MCQP party) has emerged as a popular fixture on the international gay events calendar. Having been in existence for eleven years, the event has proved so popular that special packages are now organized by tour operators. Two 2005 tour packages included the "Mother City Queer Project Theme Party and Safari" and the "Pink Loerie Garden Route Tour" (Our Way Travel and Safaris, 2005). The organizers of these events, along with the package tour operators, argue that international gay tourists and locals alike focus on specific events, and not only on events within a particular city, province or country, in choosing where they travel. While it is difficult to confirm, this conclusion seems to be justified by the way in which the event has grown, particularly in terms of its international following.

The first party in 1994 drew 1,000 people, while in 2004, the event attracted 8,000 revelers, of whom 1,000 were from overseas countries. These events do not only impact upon Cape Town; the travel itineraries of the packaged tours reveal that these tourists are also directed to other urban areas of South Africa, including a number of coastal towns, as well as Johannesburg. In addition, a three-day safari in the North-West Province is included.

A similar event, though not aimed specifically at the international gay tourism market, is the annual Pink Loerie Mardi Gras held in Knysna. This event was initiated by two gay enterprise owners to promote Knysna and stimulate the local economy, in an attempt to overcome a vexatious business cycle they referred to as "suicide May." The first Pink Loerie Mardi Gras was held in May 2001. Since then the event has become ever more popular, with extensive support from the gay and lesbian community. A key point is that an enlargement of the "gay experience" of Cape Town is now taking place, with a view to the inclusion of other urban areas in the Western Cape Province. This trend has become particularly noticeable in the "Pink Map," a key tourism information resource for gay travelers that now includes a number of guesthouses around the Western Cape. Not only does this broaden the travel experience of the tourist; it also reinforces the idea that South Africa is gay-friendly.

Besides the development of specialist literature, media exposure, travel/leisure agencies and party events, the main impact of the growing gay tourism market—particularly in Cape Town—has been the expansion of local gay leisure facilities.

Gay Infrastructure and De Waterkant

The existence of a core gay population is often the primary catalyst for the development of a gay-friendly tourist destination (Cox, 2002). Pritchard et al. (1997; 2000) argue that while the gay market may be important to the local economy and the socio-cultural life of many destinations, the popularity of cities such as Amsterdam and Sydney is mostly owing to their substantial gay infrastructure. Even if some gay travelers were not attracted to the gay scene per se, gay services and facilities still remain an attractive offering and an important signal of gay friendliness. Cape Town is at an advantage because it has a well-established gay-infrastructure comprising bars, clubs, restaurants, accommodation, tour operators, and literature.

Gay space in the form of physical leisure facilities exists throughout Cape Town. Since the early-1990s a specific "gay cluster" has, however, taken shape in De Waterkant, an area located on the Cape Town CBD periphery and in close proximity to established tourism clusters such as the Cape Town CBD and the V&A Waterfront (see Visser 2003a; 2003b for a review of the historical development of De Waterkant) (figure 9.1). Currently, explicitly gay-oriented leisure facilities in Cape Town include seven bars, three nightclubs, two sauna complexes, three massage studios and eight gay cinemas. Not all these facilities are located in the De Waterkant area. Of these facilities, all five of the bars are located on three adjacent street blocks (figure 9.2). The nightclubs are located on Somerset Road, while the massage studios and saunas are nearby. Since the mid-1990s a number of restaurants geared towards the gay market have also opened in close proximity to the other facilities, servicing both the local gay leisure market, and the increasing number of gay male tourists.

The village does not only encompass the leisure facilities of De Waterkant but also the surrounding residential area. A synergistic relationship has developed between the homeowners of the area and the leisure facilities of the gay village. As can be seen in table 9.5, there is a significant amount of gay-friendly tourist accommodation in Cape Town (and some gay-friendly tourists accommodation elsewhere in the province table 9.6). Most of this accommodation is located in the De Waterkant and City Bowl areas. In the case of De Waterkant, property owners have created a privately-held tourism and hospitality company—Village and Life. The concept entails the purchase of properties as second homes by individuals, with the company letting these properties as tourist accommodation

Figure 9.1
De Waterkant's Location in Central Cape Town

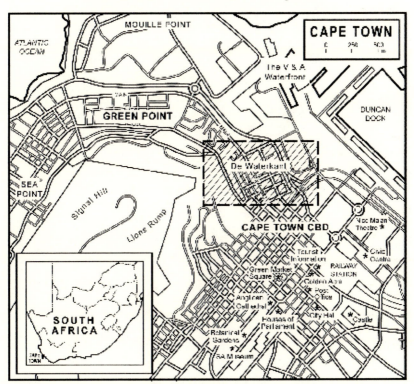

Figure 9.2
Gay leisure infrastructure of De Waterkant

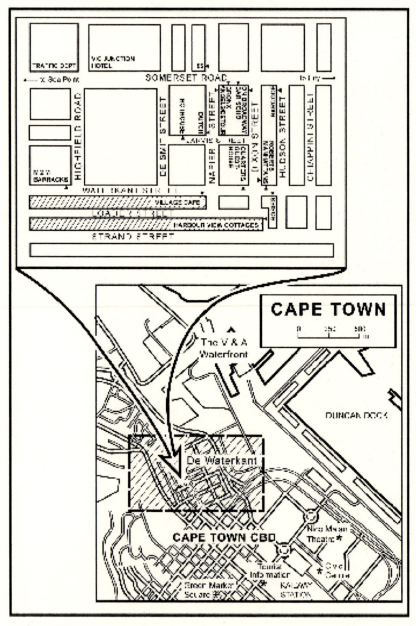

Table 9.5
Gay Tourist Accommodation in Cape Town

Area	Gay-owned/ managed	Exclusively gay	Gay-friendly	Totals
City Bowl and Sea Point	6	4	1	11
Camps Bay and Clifton	1	0	2	3
De Waterkant	2	0	3	5
Southern Suburbs	2	1	1	4
V&A Waterfront	0	0	4	4
Totals	**11**	**5**	**11**	**27**

Sources: Our Way Travel and Safari (2005); The Pink Map (2005)

Table 9.6
Gay Tourist Accommodation in the Western Cape (Excluding Cape Town)

Area	Gay-owned/ managed	Exclusively gay	Gay-friendly	Totals
Cape Winelands	3	0	1	4
Cape West Coast	2	0	0	2
Cederberg	1	0	2	3
Cape South Coast	1	0	2	3
Route 62	2	0	0	2
Garden Route	3	0	5	8
Totals	**12**	**0**	**10**	**22**

Sources: Our Way Travel and Safari (2005); The Pink Map (2005)

during those times when the owners are not resident. The neighborhood has become part of the tourism system together with adjacent facilities which were first developed for the local gay leisure market but which have now been closely integrated into the tourism system. Importantly, however, there is a significant clustering of gay leisure facilities in De Waterkant that has consolidated its identity as Cape Town's gay village.

The type of development is welcomed by owners of a range of businesses, not only in De Waterkant, but also those in close proximity to the clusters of gay-friendly and exclusively gay guesthouses in the City Bowl and Sea Point. Most of these businesses host patrons who have been referred to their establishments by the gay-oriented accommodation sector, often providing some type of special deal for these guests. As a result of the initial focus of the gay accommodation on De Waterkant and the development of a synergistic relationship between complementary service providers seeking out the wealthy sectors of the gay market, as well as the proximity of this accommodation to the gay leisure cluster, a self-reinforcing relationship has developed, in which the urban fabric has undergone intensive and continued redevelopment. Key role-players, such as Village and Life, have been very positive about their impact on the area, pointing out that the often run-down properties of the past have been restored; that the area has seen a significant drop in crime; and that it is very clean and tidy (Du Plessis, 2001).   More recently, the area has seen further redevelopment, particularly over the past three years. Arguably the key development has been the "Cape Quarter," which is a business complex consisting of shops, a number of restaurants and some offices. Indeed, De Waterkant has seen the last vestiges of the former light industrial base along Somerset Road being reworked into up-market shops mainly focused on designer furniture and interior accessories.

On the whole the area has become part of a historical and cultural tourism cluster on the Cape Town CBD periphery, serving the dual purpose of a space for gay leisure, as well as tourism consumption. The location of De Waterkant between the increasingly redeveloped and attractive Cape Town CBD and the highly successful V&A Waterfront, has led to the increased consolidation of what might be interpreted as a "tourism arch." The impact of these developments has moved beyond De Waterkant and can also be seen along Somerset Road, extending towards both the Waterfront complex and the CBD—both of which comprise established tourism and leisure clusters.

Gay Leisure and Tourism in Cape Town

The overlapping use of gay leisure and tourism space has led to a number of consequences that impinge upon the seemingly unqualified success of gay tourism and its contribution towards the urban form. The impact of gay tourism on urban areas in the Western Cape is differential, being particularly pronounced in Cape Town's De Waterkant area and of little or no consequence elsewhere in the province.

First, an outcome of the touristification of De Waterkant has been a loss of the permanent local neighborhood population. Very few of the properties in the area are now used for residential purposes. Simply put, these properties have become very expensive, with the best return on investment now being the use of the residential property stock for business purposes such as tourist accommodation. Moreover, the constant presence of tourists has, in some ways, degraded the neighborhood in terms of its desirability as a permanent place of residence. In large part this once-gay neighborhood first became something akin to a type of "gay resort." Subsequently, it would appear that the "degaying" of the area is now in progress. Although the "loss" of a gay neighborhood could be interpreted as a negative consequence, it should be kept in mind that South African cities have never had a "gay ghetto." Indeed, the "normalization" of this area in terms of the sexuality of those who frequent the area does not appear to be problematic. The local gay press, for example, has not responded negatively to this trend at all. Perhaps gay identity, as far as middle-class, white men are concerned, in the South African context, is just not so closely tied to the desire for the consolidation of an exclusive urban space for one "sexuality type." Alternatively, perhaps the local gay community has not yet come to reflect upon the loss of such a dedicated gay space.

Secondly, and in direct relation to the forgoing, it would appear that the former gay identity of De Waterkant has been sufficiently "normalized" to the extent that the whole area is now integrated with heterosexual eateries and shops, and now even includes non-gay bars and clubs. Indeed, there are two "straight" nightclubs alongside two key gay venues. Moreover, the gay restaurants, the *Manhattan Café* and the dinner theater *On Broadway*, are well supported by the heterosexual community, in particular overseas tourists. This observation opens the way for a range of possible debates concerning the "integrity" of gay culture which might appear to be threatened by various "forces," such as tourism, leading to "degaying," and the "erosion" of gay identity (cf. Pritchard et al., 2000). Again, what is of interest is the fact that the "local" gay community (comprising white middle-class men) does not appear to be concerned about this development.

However, it is possible that gay tourists do experience this trend negatively. Although the De Waterkant tourist accommodation units were initially very popular with gay tourists, they have increasingly become popular with the heterosexual overseas tourist market too. There is a noticeable shift in tourist accommodation marketing away from "gay-friendly." Whereas eighty-two guesthouses marketed themselves as "gay-friendly" in 2001 and only three marketed themselves as being for "gay men only," there are now five exclusively gay guesthouses, and only eleven "gay-friendly" guesthouses in the immediate area. The main growth in gay-friendly, or exclusively gay tourist accommodation has taken place nearly exclusively outside of the gay village.

Third, the marketing of Cape Town and the Village as the Gay Capital of Africa is problematic, even to those who benefit from it and support the idea generally. Gay service providers warn that De Waterkant is probably one of the smallest gay villages in the world, yet it is receiving disproportionate advertising attention in leading gay travel guides. The advertising drives glamorize the village beyond what it can possibly offer. However, while these are certainly valid concerns, Cape Town's marketing campaigns targeting gay men, demonstrate that the main focus remains that of Cape Town's more general tourism offering of historical, cultural and natural attractions. A more problematic aspect of the gay village is, however, the increasing use of the space by heterosexual tourists and leisure seekers. Whereas currently, there appears to be little resistance to this trend among the local gay community, not all gay tourists might be equally accepting of such developments.

Fourth, not all urban residents are tolerant of the idea that Cape Town is an explicitly marketed gay destination; and as a result, this idea has been met with some resistance. As De Waterkant started to take shape as a gay village, the local press was inundated with debates focusing on the active promotion of the city as a favored destination for gay tourists. Also in Knysna the establishment and development of the Pink Loerie Mardi Gras was met with similar debates and disapproval. However, it would appear that the potential beneficial impacts of gay tourism have come to overshadow the initial resistance. In the case of Knysna, the Mardi Gras has seen very significant buy-in from local tourism service providers, to the extent that, when it was rumored that the event might be cancelled owing to its low profit margin for the organizers, the heterosexual tourism industry quickly mobilized support to retain the staging of the event. Also, despite some very negative remarks from the Durban mayor concerning gay tourism some years ago, the success of Cape Town in drawing white, gay male tourists has been the catalyst for the development of niche-tourism development strategies in KwaZulu-Natal. The provincial government's initial strategy for engaging the homosexual traveling public has suggested, as a direct consequence, that this province should focus on other cohorts internal to the gay travel market. To avoid direct competition with Cape Town, it is suggested that, as Cape Town focuses on white, gay males, KwaZulu-Natal should focus on white lesbians and, more generally, on the black gay and lesbian market (Seymour, 2003).

Fifth, the process of gay tourism development, including the establishment of complementary spaces primarily for wealthier white men, potentially holds implications for the relationship between gay men and women. It is clear that De Waterkant and the surrounding neighborhoods are primarily aimed at catering for the relatively wealthy, white gay man. The marketing of gay male tourism to Cape Town, superimposed on the existing gay male dominance of De Waterkant, means that this area is promoted as a wealthy, gay male leisure space. This problematises the marketing of gay travel to "gay-friendly" Cape Town, in the sense that this space is not inclusive of lesbian or black visitors, both domestic and international. It is neither gender-inclusive, nor does it accommodate income differences. Thus, instead of the development of a "gay space" for all, gay male space has been developed in a way that amplifies gender differences—potentially straining relations between these subsets of the broader lesbian, gay, bisexual and transgender community. Likewise, this holds true for race and, inevitably in the South African context, class; and this has implications for the actual and potential participation of certain societal segments in the "gay village" in particular, and gay Cape Town more generally.

Finally, this process of change alludes to a litany of processes that accompany urban renewal in terms of race and class in South Africa. Within a post-apartheid context, the gender-race matrix still underpins the economic and social marginalization of black and colored communities and women of all races.

This apartheid legacy has not changed significantly since the early-1990s; and in De Waterkant, it seems to have been reinstated in the form of relatively homogeneous wealthy white gay male leisure spaces. The historically disadvantaged communities remain excluded from the consumption of the facilities of this area, largely owing to the supply of gender-, race-, and class-specific facilities, and services. This exclusion cuts across the whole spectrum of South African society—including poorer white males/lesbians as a whole black South Africans, as well as most of the colored community. Also, in terms of the division of labor internal to these spaces, the support-system of this playground for the wealthy, white gay male is provided by the poor women and men from the far-off corners of the colored and black Cape Flats of Cape Town. Thus, underneath this "liberated space" of gay expression lies a far more complex and "un-liberated" socio-economic system.

Conclusion

Cape Town has emerged as a destination for wealthy gay men. A part of the city has been physically, and to some extent, symbolically transformed by gay patronage. In many ways, the conclusion of this chapter echoes key findings by Hughes (1997) concerning the impact of gay tourism on the urban form of Amsterdam. As is the case of his findings, there is little evidence that Cape Town has, or is in the process of developing, a gay residential concentration similar to that of cities such as New York or San Francisco. On the contrary, Cape Town has a district of gay leisure facilities, which is increasingly becoming associated with tourism. Moreover, the touristification of the residential component of De Waterkant makes such a development seem even more unlikely. Physically, De Waterkant has been transformed over the past decade and a half by the existence and development of dedicated gay facilities and their use by sectors of the local gay community. These facilities are little different from other leisure or tourist facilities—mainly comprising bars, cafés, restaurants, night-clubs, and so on. There is little that is distinctively gay about the area, and its activities do not generally contrast very much with those of any other urban area that has undergone significant levels of gentrification, urban renewal, or tourism development.

There has also been a symbolic transformation of De Waterkant in terms of its status as Africa's gay capital. However, in contrast to Hughes' (1998) conclusion that the core elements of the Amsterdam tourist product for the gay tourist do not coincide with the core tourism elements identified by Jansen-Verbeke (1994), this is not the case in Cape Town. Gay tourists travel to Cape Town mainly for its natural, cultural and historical attractions. Thus, gay tourists to South Africa are, in many important respects, no different from their fellow heterosexual tourists. Irrespective of the motivation of gay men in their decision to travel to South Africa, the impact of the overlapping use of gay leisure space and gay tourism functions has had a dramatic effect upon the urban form of Cape Town's De Waterkant area. As is the case of gay villages elsewhere, gay leisure consumption, along with expanding tourism consumption, has had a positive impact in terms of stimulating and expanding urban renewal.

In some ways this constitutes a positive development. However, serious issues do arise regarding the potential displacement of the main local gay leisure functions of this area owing to increased tourism activity, as well as the area's increased popularity with heterosexual leisure and tourism visitors. This exclusion is not only problematical in terms of the gay tourism-leisure binary, but certainly also in terms of class, race, and gender. In fact, directly echoing the concerns of Elder (2002), this entails the creation of a particular kind of homo-masculine space. The result is that the promotion of Cape Town as "Africa's gay capital," and its current linkages to urban development in De Waterkant, inadvertently betray the celebrated and marketed constitutional protection of sexual orientation. De Waterkant ultimately welcomes the empowered gay man, as well as an increasing number of heterosexual patrons, while in the same stroke marginalizing the already disempowered of Cape Town.

References

Binnie, J., 1997: Coming out of geography: towards a queer epistemology? *Environment and Planning D: Space and Society*, 15, 223-237.

Binnie, J. and Valentine, G., 2000: Geographies of sexuality—a review of progress, *Progress in Human Geography*, 23, 175-187.

Cape Review, 2001: Moseing a-long, *Cape Review*, Cape Town, July, 42-44.

Clift, S. and Forrest, S., 1999: Gay men and tourism: destinations and holiday motivations, *Tourism Management*, 20, 615-625.

Clift, S., Luongo, M. and Callister, C. (Eds.), 2002: *Gay Tourism: Culture, Identity and Sex*, Continuum, London.

Cox, M., 2002: The long-haul out of the closet: the journey from smalltown to boystown, in S. Clift, M. Luongo, and C. Callister, (Eds.), *Gay Tourism: Culture, Identity and Sex*, Continuum, London, 155-173.

De Villiers, J., 2001: Gay tourism guide, Interviewed on 26 June 2001, Cape Town.

Du Plessis, J., 2001: Marketing manager of Village and Life Ltd., interviewed on 7 May 2001, Cape Town.

Elder, G., 2002: Somewhere, over the rainbow: the invention of Cape Town as a "gay destination," Unpublished paper, Department of Geography, University of Vermont.

Exit, 2005: *Exit*, December 2005/January 2006, 188, Highland Publications, Johannesburg.

Fine, A., 2001: Religious groups hoist red flag over pink rand, *Business Day*, March 2, 12.

Gay Pages, 2005: *Gay Pages*, Summer 2005, Associated Business Network, Johannesburg.

Graham, M., 2002: Challenges from the margins: gay tourism as cultural critique, in S. Clift, M. Luongo, and C. Callister, (Eds.), *Gay Tourism: Culture, Identity and Sex*, Continuum, London, 17- 41.

Heard, J. and Ludski, H., 2001: Pink rand quietly helps to put tourism in black, *Sunday Times—Business Times*, 13 March, 7.

Hughes, H.L., 1997: Holidays and homosexual identity, *Tourism Management*, 18, 3-7.

Hughes, H.L., 2002: Gay men's holidays: identity and inhibitors, in S. Clift, M. Luongo, and C. Callister, (Eds.), *Gay Tourism: Culture, Identity and Sex,* Continuum, London, 174 -190.

Hughes, H.L., 2003: Marketing gay tourism in Manchester: new market of urban tourism or destruction of "gay space"?, *Journal of Vacation Marketing* 9(2), 152-163.

IGLTA, 2001: International Gay and Lesbian Travel Association, http://www.igta.org 25 (March).

Jansen-Verbeke, M., 1994: The synergy between shopping and tourism: the Japanese experience, in W. Theobald, (Ed.), *Global Tourism: The Next Decade*, Butterworth-Heinemann, Oxford, 347-362.

Knopp, L.,1995: Sexuality and urban space: a framework for analysis, in D. Bell and G. Valentine, (Eds.), *Mapping Desire*, Routledge, New York, 149-161.

Our Way Travel and Safari, 2005: Our Way Travel and Safari, http://www.ourway.co.za.

Ozinsky, S., 2001: Pink marketing—an investigation into gay tourism marketing in the Western Cape, Paper presented at the Tourism Summit, Cape Town, 28-30 March.

Pritchard, A., Morgan, N.J., Sedgley, D., Khan, E. and Jenkins, A., 1998: Research out to the gay tourist: opportunities and threats in an emerging market segment, *Tourism Management,* 19, 273-282.

Pritchard, A., Morgan, N.J., Sedgley, D., Khan, E. and Jenkins, A., 2000: Sexuality and holiday choices: conversations with gay and lesbian tourists, *Leisure Studies*, 19, 267-282.

Ryan, C. and Hall, C.M., 2002: *Sex Tourism: Marginal People and Liminalities*, Routledge, London.

Seymour, J., 2003: *Engaging the KwaZulu-Natal gay and lesbian tourism market: Tourism KwaZulu-Natal's initial gay and lesbian tourism strategy,* Tourism KwaZulu-Natal, Durban.

Stuber, M., 2002: Tourism marketing aimed at gay men and lesbians: a business perspective, in S. Clift, M. Luongo, and C. Callister, (Eds.), *Gay Tourism: Culture, Identity and Sex,* Continuum, London, 88-124.

Tebje, M., 2004: South Africa's promotion to the gay market, The Tourism Network, available at www.tourismknowledge.com.

The Pink Map, 2005: *The Gay Guide to Cape Town and Surrounds*, Mail and Guardian, Johannesburg.

Van Niekerk, R., 2005: Pink money, gay media, corporate marketing, *Gay Pages*, (Summer) 56-59.

Van Zyl, M. and Steyn, M., 2005: *Performing Queer: Shaping Sexualities 1994-2004 – Volume One*, Kwela Books, Cape Town.

Visser, G., 2002: Gay tourism in South Africa: issues from the Cape Town experience, *Urban Forum*, 13, 85 - 94.

Visser, G., 2003a: Gay men, tourism and urban space: reflections on Africa's 'gay capital', *Tourism Geographies*, 5, 168-189.

Visser, G., 2003b: Gay men, leisure space and South African cities: the case of Cape Town, *Geoforum*, 34, 123 -137.

10

Township Tourism in Africa: Emerging Tour Operators in Gauteng, South Africa

Irene Nemasetoni and Christian M. Rogerson

South Africa's tourism industry is highly concentrated and dominated by a small elite group of large and mostly locally-owned tourism enterprises, which dominate the tourism economy (Rogerson and Visser, 2004). Nevertheless, in common with the situation in Australia and the United Kingdom (Thomas, 1998, 2000, 2004a), the greatest number of tourism enterprises in South Africa would be classified as small, medium or micro-enterprises (SMMEs) (Rogerson, 2005a). One recent investigation concerning the organization of the South African tourism industry described the tourism cluster as comprising "a complex interaction of a large number of players, with a few large players and numerous SMMEs" (Monitor, 2004: 44). In the accommodation sub-sector, leading enterprises are Sun International, Protea and Southern Sun whereas in travel and touring the importance of Rennies, Thompsons Travel, Avis or Imperial Car Rental, among others, is evident. Overall, the local tourism economy can be conceptualized as a three-tiered hierarchy of enterprises. At the apex are the operations of the elite group of large enterprises, which are responsible for, inter alia, the country's major travel and tour agencies, transportation, hotels, casinos and conference centers. The greatest share of the business hierarchy is represented by the activities of, at least, two different kinds of SMMEs (Rogerson, 2005a). The middle tier is formed by groups of established, almost predominantly white-owned SMMEs which operate a host of different establishments from travel and touring companies, restaurants, small hotels, self-catering and resorts, game farms, bed and breakfasts or backpacking hostels. The lowest tier or rung in the South African travel and tourism industry is represented by the emerging black-owned tourism economy which constitutes a mix of formally registered micro-enterprises as well as a mass of informal tourism enterprises. Currently, this segment of emerging black-owned tourism enterprises is the center of much discussion in the context of national government policy goals for transforming the ownership structure of tourism, by expanding the involvement of black entrepreneurs (Rogerson, 2003, 2004a, 2004b, 2004c).

The aim in this chapter is to present recent findings on the challenges that face a particular group of these emerging tourism small firms or small, medium and micro-enterprises (SMMEs) in South Africa. More specifically, the focus of attention falls upon the segment of emerging black-owned tour operators within a context of the growth of the distinctive segment of "township tourism." Within the existing literature on tourism small firms the major focus so far has been upon the accommodation sub-sector (see Thomas, 2004a). By contrast, there is remarkably little research on the tour-operating sector, especially in the developing world. In South Africa the only material that exists on black tour operators is some descriptive business case studies which relate aspects of the history and development of two of the more established operating companies, viz., Grassroute Tours in Cape Town (Milner, 2004) and Jimmy's Face-to-Face Tours in Soweto (Ramchander, 2004).

In this analysis, two major sections of discussion are provided. In the first section, the key themes of research and debate in international scholarship on tourism small firms are reviewed. This discussion provides the essential background context for the presentation and analysis of the results of a survey, which was completed in 2004, of black-owned travel and tour operating enterprises based in the metropolitan areas of Gauteng province, at the heart of which is Johannesburg, South Africa's largest city. The majority of these emerging small enterprises are engaged in the activity of township tourism, a new and growing tourism product in post-apartheid South Africa that involves taking groups of mainly international tourists to visit the focal points of the anti-apartheid struggle. In addition, in common with *favela* tourism in urban Brazil (see Jaguaribe and Hetherington, 2004), township tourism also involves taking visitors to areas of poverty within the urban townships of South Africa.

Research on Developing Small Enterprises in Tourism

In terms of the existing research on entrepreneurship in tourism and on the operations of tourism small firms, it must be observed that the bulk of scholarship relates to developed rather than developing countries (Rogerson, 2004a). Existing analysis on the micro-development and organization of tourism activities and of small service providers at the destination level is "very much concentrated in Western European countries, particularly the U.K." (Ateljevic and Doorne 2004: 6).

In the developed world, it is contended that tourism small firms can be distinguished broadly into groups of "lifestyle enterprises" that are set up to provide owner-managers with an acceptable income at comfort levels of activity and "entrepreneurial small businesses" driven by the growth motives of the Schumpeterian type of entrepreneur (Buhalis and Paraskevas, 2002; Ateljevic and Doorne, 2003, 2004; Shaw and Williams, 2004; Thomas, 2004b). The significance of social, "lifestyle" or non-economic factors in tourism entrepreneurship within developed countries is a significant finding that is raised by several scholars (Williams et al., 1989; Ateljevic and Doorne, 2000, 2003; Shaw and Williams, 1990, 2004; Hall and Rusher, 2004; Morrison and Teixeira, 2004; Shaw, 2004; Getz and Carlsen, 2005; Getz and Petersen, 2005; Lynch et al., 2005). In terms of their business development, small tourism firms "encounter difficulties related to: lack of financial resources and management skills; limited access to expertise in core business disciplines; and life-style motivations that create long-term economic problems" (Ateljevic and Doorne, 2004: 6). Several managerial characteristics have been identified as distinguishing the operations of small tourism firms from those of larger enterprises (Page et al., 1999). Among the most important of these features are a short-term business horizon, often limited knowledge of the business environment, and "owner-managed structures in which attitudes, personal qualities (i.e. leadership skills) and experience influence the way tasks are managed" (Ateljevic and Doorne, 2004: 7).

By contrast to the surge of new research and analysis on small tourism firms in the North, the literature on small tourism firms in the South or developing world is relatively undeveloped (Rogerson, 2004a, 2005a). Useful contributions are contained in the edited collections by Dahles and Bras (1999a) which interrogates the role and activities of small entrepreneurs participating in the Indonesian tourism economy and by Dahles and Kuene (2002) concerning tourism entrepreneurship and small tourism enterprises in Latin America and the Caribbean. Within a developing world context it is now widely accepted that the common economic objectives of increased earnings, foreign exchange, investment, job opportunities as well as the minimization of adverse social and cultural effects might be best achieved through the promotion of small tourism firms rather than large enterprises (Rodenburg, 1980; Dahles and Kuene, 2002; Roe et al., 2004).

Despite such assertions, at present, there is only a limited volume of detailed empirical work on tourism entrepreneurship in the South with notable works for Ghana (Gartner, 1999, 2004), India (Kokkranikal and Morrison, 2002), Indonesia (Dahles and Bras, 1999b; Dahles, 2000, 2001; Hampton, 2003), Malaysia (Hamzah, 1997), Melanesia (Douglas, 1997), and Namibia (Shackley, 1993). In terms of the kinds of tourism small firms that have been under investigation, the central focus has been upon issues that challenge the development of the small accommodation sub-sector. The transport sub-sector is little researched with the most relevant studies concerning houseboats in Kerala as a means of achieving sustainable tourism in India (Kokkranikal and Morrison, 2002) and the education and training needs for Kenya's tour operating sector (Mayaka and King, 2002).

From Indonesian research, Hampton (2003) avers that small tourism firms can be viewed as a form of "pro-poor tourism" with important implications for local development. Indeed, the emergent body of scholarship on pro-poor tourism stresses the importance of maximizing linkages with, and correspondingly the local developmental potential of, small emerging tourism enterprises (Ashley et al., 2000, 2001; Ashley and Roe, 2002; Bah and Goodwin, 2003; Roe et al., 2004; Mitchell and Ashley, 2006). Lastly, there exists a notable range of writings on the activities of survival level enterprises in the "informal sector of tourism" across the developing world (Oppermann and Chon, 1997). Examples are works that deal with beach masseurs, craft trading, street guiding and providers of informal accommodation (Wahnschafft, 1982; Crick, 1992; Timothy and Wall, 1997; Dahles, 1998; Dahles and Bras, 1999a, 1999b; Bah and Goodwin, 2003; Hampton, 2003).

A major finding of research in the South is that the growth prospects of small firms in tourism frequently are severely constrained by the power and competitive dominance enjoyed by large tourism enterprises (Britton, 1982a, 1982b, 1987). As a result, the most promising opportunities for small firms occur not in the activity of mass tourism but instead in alternative "niche" forms of tourism or low-budget tourism such as backpacking (Hampton, 2001, 2003). As many kinds of alternative tourism occur in peripheral regions, it has been recommended that local control and local small enterprise development in tourism in such areas might be supported by the provision of special government fiscal and monetary incentives to enable local entrepreneurs to own and operate small tourism establishments (Tosun, 2005). Overall, a common conclusion from research on small tourism enterprises in both developed and developing countries is that tourism firms require institutional assistance to overcome their intrinsic disadvantages and to avert business failure (Wanhill, 2000; Bah and Goodwin, 2003; Ateljevic and Doorne, 2004; Wanhill, 2004).

The Challenges of Developing Small Tourism Firms in South Africa

One of the major policy commitments made by the democratic government in South Africa after the 1994 political transition was to support the upgrading and role of the SMME economy. The Centre for Development and Enterprise (2004: 35) recently observed: "South Africa's adoption of more market friendly economic policies during the 1990s coincided with powerful international championing of the market in development debates," including growing policy support for SMMEs. Accordingly, a new framework and institutional support for SMME development was introduced and slowly implemented from 1995. The workings, performance and impacts of this new national pro-SMME framework have been investigated by several researchers (Berry et al.., 2002; Kesper, 2002; DTI, 2004; Rogerson, 2004d). In addition, a number of analytical studies have been undertaken on the problems and challenges that have confronted specifically the growth and upgrading of manufacturing SMMEs (Kesper, 2001; Rogerson, 2001a, 2001b; Kesper, 2002; Rogerson, 2005b).

Despite the fact that tourism has been identified by South Africa's Department of Trade and Industry (DTI) as one of the strategic priority sectors for promotion, at present, there has been little attention devoted to issues surrounding the development of tourism SMMEs (Visser and Rogerson, 2004; Rogerson, 2005a). In common with the international experience, the existing literature is dominated by studies of the accommodation sub-sector and especially of white-owned bed and breakfast establishments or small guesthouses (Visser and Van Huyssteen, 1997, 1999; Nuntsu et al., 2004). Research on transformation and changing the ownership profile of the South African tourism economy provided the context for one detailed study of bed and breakfasts operated in the townships by emerging black entrepreneurs (Rogerson, 2004c). Overall, there is only a limited literature that explores the conditions of small-scale and informal tourism entrepreneurs operating in South Africa's black townships (see Rogerson, 2004e; Thomas, 2005).

Township Tourism and Emerging Tour Operators

The first opportunities for the development of black-owned tour operating enterprises occurred with the post-apartheid transition and South Africa's re-integration into the global tourism economy after many years of international sanctions. With the post-1994 "Mandela boom" of a wave of new international tourism arrivals, occasioned by interest in South Africa's peaceful democratic transition, the black townships emerged as new sites for tourism development and focal points for new tourism products. The townships contain important sites for heritage and political tourism (Ashworth, 2004).

The emergence of "township tourism" is largely a phenomenon of the post-apartheid period. Township tourism brings visitors to the sites of significance to the anti-apartheid movement as well as improving tourists' understanding of poverty issues of historically oppressed communities. Indeed, because of its features, township tourism has been termed a South African variant of "justice tourism" (Scheyvens, 2002). Until 1994 heritage tourism in South Africa essentially was synonymous with "white heritage" and reflected exclusively the needs and interests of the country's white minority (Goudie et al., 1999). Moreover, throughout the apartheid period, high levels of political violence made the black townships "no-go" zones for international tourists. With political transition and the accompanying re-birth of South Africa's tourism economy, the townships have become more accessible and opportunities have opened for black South African communities to recount their stories of their struggles against apartheid to a receptive audience after decades of having their voices repressed by a hostile government (Scheyvens, 2002). Around Johannesburg and Cape Town, in particular, township tours have become increasingly popular among international visitors. In townships such as Soweto, Alexandra and Khayelitsha, township tours have seen considerable growth, albeit off a low base. In particular, the number of tourists visiting Soweto township is recorded as doubling between 2000-2005 reaching approximately 2000 visitors a day.

The mushrooming growth of township tourism thus provides the context for potential economic opportunities for local entrepreneurs to enter the ground tour operating business, an activity that traditionally has been the domain of established white South African entrepreneurs (Milner, 2004; Ramchander, 2004). It is critically important to understand whether township tourism can offer local people real opportunities for economic empowerment (Scheyvens, 2002; Rogerson, 2004e). In order to address this issue, a total of forty structured interviews were undertaken during 2004 in and around the black townships close to Johannesburg. Themes of concern in the interviews were to examine the origins, development and current problems of business development of these emerging black tourism entrepreneurs (Nemasetoni, 2005).

Tour Operators and Enterprise Development

At the outset it must be acknowledged that there is no comprehensive listing or data source that allows a firm estimate of the actual size of the black owned travel and tour economy in Gauteng. The national body, the Southern African Tourism Services Association (SATSA), is not a government organization but instead an association of private sector businesses which provide tourism products and services. SATSA functions as an industry spokesman and lobby organization. Although SATSA maintains a database of registered members, this includes the providers of all forms of accommodation, tourism services (including exhibitions, security, restaurants) as well as tour operators as part of a wider category of transport providers (including air or water charters). The provincial tourism authority, the Gauteng Tourism Authority (GTA), is not a regulatory authority but has compiled a list of black tour operators, albeit this list is admitted to be incomplete and contains names of tour operators that are no longer in business.

Enquiries directed at the national Department of Environmental Affairs and Tourism (DEAT), the Tourism Enterprise Programme and the Gauteng Tourism Authority (GTA) confirmed that there is no formal set of government regulations that controls the registration of tour operators in South Africa. Indeed, the GTA and DEAT refer potential tour operators to the guidelines and procedures that are in place for registration as tour operator by SATSA. This organization charges an annual fee of R2 850 for membership as well as a non-refundable application fee of R627. The SATSA guidelines for new tour operators specify several requirements that should be considered. The four major requirements for tour operators are:

- An Operating License to be obtained from the Operating License Board
- Professional Driving Permit issued by the Traffic Department, Department of Transport
- The Operator must be a qualified Tour Guide from an accredited institution or use a qualified guide.
- Finally, the potential tour operator must have a passenger liability insurance cover, which SATSA recommends a minimum of R5 million insurance cover for a vehicle that carries five to seven persons.

Taken together the compliance costs for these regulations and membership costs are quite burdensome for aspirant black tour operators, many of whom thus seek to operate outside of SATSA registration.

A profile of emerging black tour operators and their enterprises can be gleaned from the forty survey respondents interviewed in 2004 (Nemasetoni, 2005). The majority of tour operators were over forty years in age with a considerable number in the fifty-one to sixty age group; only a small proportion of entrepreneurs would be classed as youthful. In terms of gender of business owner, 61 percent of businesses were owned by men; 13 percent by women and 26 percent by joint husband and wife teams. Although the vast majority of businesses are in individual or family ownership, a small proportion of tour operating enterprises are owned by partnerships of three or more individuals. On the whole, respondents were well-educated and over 70 percent of the sample had completed post-secondary school qualifications, including a number with University degrees. Moreover, nearly 80 percent of the sample had undertaken accredited training courses in tourism as tour guides, which is one of the formal requirements for a tour operator.

Three-quarters of businesses run by black tour operators are based in the home; only 25 percent of the sample operate their businesses from offices outside their home. The length of establishment of businesses discloses that tour operation is a phenomenon largely of the post-apartheid era. The longest established enterprise had been in operation for eight years and the majority of businesses (60 percent) functioning for at least five years. In common with the pattern observed in the township accommodation sub-sector (Rogerson, 2004c), there was a surge of new business establishments in tour operation during 2002 when the World Summit on Sustainable Development was held in Johannesburg. An analysis of the reasons for start-up of businesses discloses that the majority would be classed as run by growth-oriented or opportunistic entrepreneurs. In common with the financing of small businesses as a whole, the most common sources for start-up capital for the tour operating enterprise were through own savings, severance or retrenchment packages or the sale of property.

The motivation for profit and wealth generation in the context of potential opportunities in a growing tourism economy coupled with the desire for self-employment underpinned the largest number of business start-ups in tour operation. Typically, one interviewee remarked: "I saw an opportunity since the new government came into being and I began to see a flood of tourists coming into South Africa to bring opportunities to us." The majority of interviewees indicated that they had prior experience or knowledge of tourism before setting up their tour-operating enterprise. For example, two respondents reported that they had worked for travel agencies, in one case for a period of twelve years after which "I felt I had enough experience to operate my own company in an industry I understood." Nevertheless, entry into tourism was recorded from prior work in a diverse range of occupations including banking and retailing. Two tour operators were former owners respectively of a construction company and a cigarette distribution enterprise.

The push of retrenchment was also an important basis for the search for an alternative income source. In the words of one tour operator: "I became redundant at my job and I had often been asked to take delegates on tours of Soweto. From this I learned the trade and when I was fired from my job I decided to start my own company." In another similar case history it was stated: "I used to work for a company where I was required to take company executives on various business excursions to various localities. I learned the trade and I was attracted to continue with the job when my former employees fired me."

In terms of the choice of tourism for new business development many survey respondents indicated that they had prior exposure to tour operators through work, friends or acquaintances. The largest share of the Gauteng interviewees had worked previously in the transport sector as owners of taxis. The shift from taxi-operator to tour operator was frequently a response to the high levels of violence that affects the taxi industry. The following selection of responses illustrates the different pathways of entry into tourism by black tour operators.

- "My friend worked for Jimmy's Face-to-Face some time ago. I was always with him when he worked for that company. I saw how it operated and I began to have an interest in it. After some time, I considered starting my own business."
- "I own taxis and used some of the money saved to start the business."
- "A friend of mine worked for a white-owned tour operating company and asked me to accompany him to Sun City to collect tourists. I saw the amount of money made in a single tour. For some time I worked as a pirate operator to learn the trade and thereafter I left my job and started my own.
- "When I was working at Wits University, I was often asked to take international guest professors to places like Kruger and I developed the skills and interest in the business."
- "A group of six taxi owners started saving money for insurance purposes. By 1997 we had accumulated R40 000 and we did not know what to do. We then decided to invest the money in a tourism business."

For 70 percent of tour operators, the tour business is their major source of household income. In the remainder of our sample, the tour operator business is a supplement to another business, most commonly the taxi industry but even in one case to an income earned from working as an on-air producer at a radio station.

The 40 surveyed enterprises provided a total of ninety-nine employment opportunities, an average of 2.5 persons per business with the largest enterprise employing 8 persons. In terms of the nature of these employment opportunities, the major share is in respect of tour guides either on a freelance or full-time basis or the hiring of drivers. Clearly, a high proportion of the employment generated by the tour enterprises is on a part-time or casual basis and dependent upon work load. It was observed that nearly 40 percent of enterprises were, however, single person enterprises that did not have any regular employees. The fragile basis of many of these businesses is exposed by the finding that 37 percent of black tour operators do not even own any transport vehicle and instead hire vehicles as and when needed. By contrast, the group of more established tour operators have transport fleets of three to four vehicles.

Challenges and Constraints

The survey disclosed that the segment of emerging black tour operators is confronted by an array of challenges in terms of its further expansion. Overall, the interviews revealed that the two core problems of tour operators concern access to sources of finance and access to markets and marketing support (Nemasetoni, 2005).

Of the surveyed enterprises 50 percent stated that access to finance for vehicle purchase was the major constraint on the expansion of their business both at the time of start-up and at present. It was observed that at start-up most entrepreneurs used their own savings or funds from retrenchment pay-outs in order to finance their business. Often the resources of family were drawn up as one respondent reported: "I used a loan from my family to fund the business." Amongst entrepreneurs, awareness levels were high of existing government support programs for small business development. But, access to the national programs operated by Ntsika and Khula was minimal and these organizations viewed as "least helpful" by surveyed entrepreneurs (Nemasetoni, 2005: 75). Although several tour operators had lodged formal applications for support, no support from these public-sector organizations had been secured. The frustrations and difficulties experienced by emerging tour operators in obtaining access to finance are captured in the following interview responses:

- "I had difficulty accessing funds. The initial application to Ntsika had a complete business plan that was written with the help of consultants that were recommended by Ntsika. The business plan was turned down because it was of poor quality but they did not tell us what was weak about the plan."

- "Funding is the major constraint. We tried to apply for funding with Khula but they referred us to banks that informed us they do not fund tourism companies for vehicles."

The lack of support from commercial banks for vehicle financing has been of critical concern. With no direct access to funding support through national government support programs for small business, the entrepreneurs' lack of collateral or credit track record emerges as a blockage for enterprise development. Typically, the tour operators complained "because I did not have collateral, it was impossible to get a loan from the bank." Likewise, other respondents stressed that even with a business plan in hand, the bank's remained reluctant to provide funding support. In the words of one interviewee "although we had a business plan in place, banks were unwilling to fund us for vehicles."

Overall, the two organizations that were identified as providing some assistance for the emerging tour operators were the provincial tourism authority (GTA) and the Tourism Enterprise Programme (TEP). The Gauteng Tourism Authority provided funding support for tour operators to participate at local tourism trade shows or exhibitions, most importantly the annual tourism Indaba. In addition, GTA funding was accessed for the design and production of marketing material, including publicity brochures and business cards. Likewise, support for marketing was also obtainable from the largely private sector funded TEP that represents "an important indirect player in terms of indirect funding support for tourism SMME development in South Africa" (Rogerson, 2004f: 243).

Tourism represents an economic sector that is a marketing-intensive. Issues of access to markets and support for marketing emerge as the second critical set of challenges for emerging tour operators. The competitive power and dominance of the tour operating business by established enterprises is understood as a major constraint on the market penetration of emerging tour businesses. The responses of several interviewees highlighted recurring concerns about information access and the marginal role played by black tour operators.

- "It is difficult to penetrate the market because white people are still dominating the industry."
- "The industry is dominated by white role players because they have access to information and they become a barrier to black-owned companies that are growing."
- "The industry is white dominated and white operators do not want to deal with black tour operators."
- "There are about six companies that package South Africa across the world and there are about 200 or so white tour operators that are making money. Below that there are about 600 black tour operators. Next year

the majority of them [Businesses operated by black tour operators] will be dead and will be replaced by new ones."

The enormous difficulties faced by new enterprises in breaking into existing markets were expressed by several interviewees:

- "I was unable to access the market because large established companies are mostly preferred."
- "It took between eighteen to twenty-four months to establish a client base."
- "We were unable to break the market barrier particularly to foreign markets because we were unknown."
- "Lack of access to profitable markets and marketing—most people see you as a taxi service not a tour operator."
- "To penetrate a market that is already dominated by established players is not easy and to make an impact when you are new or as an individual is difficult."
- "Tourism operates as a cartel with close dealings and associations in which big businesses have greater control."

The competitive strength of the established white tour operators was acknowledged in terms of their information access and marketing abilities that give them access to international tourists. For black tour operators across Gauteng the market of international tourism is the anchor for their businesses. The majority of interviewees stated that international tourists comprise between 70-95 percent of their clientele; the remainder is mainly what is described as 'corporate South Africa." It was evident that the leisure market of domestic South African tourism is of only minor significance for most black tour operators.

In a situation of constrained access to markets, limited funds for marketing and lack of support from established enterprises, the majority of black tour operators become marginalized in a situation of large firm dominance of the tour operating industry as a whole. Essentially, many black tour operators become geographically confined to undertaking the occasional township tour and to the receipt of small contracts from white tour operators. The situation was aptly captured by one interviewee: "White people are able to market their products abroad and they get the most of the cake. It leaves very few crumbs for black operators."

Conclusion

Small tourism firms are recognized as a significant component of tourism economies, including those of developing Africa (Dieke, 2003: 292). In South Africa, as in most of the developing world, the largest segment of enterprises in tourism would be regarded as small firms (Rogerson, 2005a). Belatedly, the research agenda of tourism is beginning to acknowledge the importance of understanding issues around entrepreneurship and small enterprise development as well as tourism policy-making (Thomas, 2004a; Thomas and Thomas, 2005). In the developing world, the structural environment for tourism small firm development is marked by the power and dominance of large enterprises, especially in the mass tourism market (Britton, 1982a, 1987). The marginal role played by the small firm economy in tourism is mitigated only partially by the growth of "niche" or "alternative" forms of tourism, such as township tourism.

Against this backdrop, the South African record of township tourism experience offers a useful case study in the problems of emerging small firms in tourism. As a result of apartheid, the country's black entrepreneurs were excluded from participation in the tourism economy and the developing South African tourism economy of the 1970s and 1980s was built-up and consolidated through the expansion of large locally owned tourism enterprises. More recently, a tier of white-owned small enterprises has emerged in the services of accommodation, tour agency and tour operation. In the changed environment of post-apartheid South Africa, national government has recognized the need to address the structural environment of tourism and the imperative to transform the ownership structure of the industry, including through support for new initiatives encouraging black entrepreneurship in tourism. Key themes in national tourism policy are transformation and the promotion of black economic empowerment in tourism, which will be achieved in part through promoting new entrepreneurship in the tourism economy. The results of this research on emerging black tour operators in Gauteng represent a cautionary tale in that they point to a set of serious challenges that need to be confronted in order to attain the government's objectives for transformation through small enterprise development.

Acknowledgements

The research reported here was supported by the South Africa Netherlands Research Programme on Alternatives in Development (SANPAD), which is thanked for generous funding assistance.

References

Ashley C. and Roe D., 2002: Making tourism work for the poor: strategies and challenges in southern Africa, *Development Southern Africa,* 19, 61-82.

Ashley, C., Boyd, C. and Goodwin, H., 2000: *Pro-poor Tourism: Putting Poverty at the Heart of the Tourism Agenda*, Natural Resources Perspectives No. 61, Overseas Development Institute, London.

Ashley, C., Roe, D. and Goodwin, H., 2001: *Pro-Poor Tourism Strategies: Making Tourism Work for the Poor*, Pro-Poor Tourism Report No. 1, Overseas Development Institute, London.

Ashworth, G.J., 2004: Tourism and the heritage of atrocity: managing the heritage of South African apartheid for entertainment, in T.V. Singh (Ed.), *New Horizons in Tourism: Strange Experiences and Stranger Practices*, CABI Publishing, Wallingford, 95-108.

Ateljevic, I. and Doorne, S., 2000: "Staying within the fence": lifestyle entrepreneurship in tourism. *Journal of Sustainable Tourism,* 8, 378-392.

Ateljevic, I. and Doorne, S., 2003: Unpacking the local: a cultural analysis of tourism entrepreneurship in Murter, Croatia, *Tourism Geographies,* 5, 123-150.

Ateljevic J. and Doorne S., 2004: Diseconomies of scale: a study of development constraints in small tourism firms in central New Zealand, *Tourism and Hospitality Research,* 5, 5-24.

Bah, A. and Goodwin, H., 2003: *Improving Access for the Informal Sector to Tourism in The Gambia,* Pro-Poor Tourism Working Paper No. 15, London, Overseas Development Institute.

Berry, A., von Blottnitz, M., Cassim, R., Kesper, A., Rajaratnam, B. and van Seventer, D.E., 2002: *The Economics of Small, Medium and Micro Enterprises in South Africa,* Trade and Industrial Policy Strategies, Johannesburg.

Britton, S.G., 1982a: The political economy of tourism in the Third World, *Annals of Tourism Research,* 9, 331-358.

Britton, S.G., 1982b: International tourism and multinational corporations in the Pacific, in M. Taylor and N. Thrift (Eds.), *The Geography of Multinationals,* Croom Helm, London, 252-274.

Britton, S.G., 1987: Tourism in small developing countries, in S. Britton and W.C. Clarke (Eds.), *Ambiguous Alternative: Tourism in Small Developing Countries,* University of South Pacific, Suva, 167-194.

Buhalis, D. and Paraskevas, A., 2002: Conference report: Entrepreneurship in tourism and the contexts of experience economy, *Tourism Management,* 23, 427-428.

Centre for Development and Enterprise, 2004: *Key to Growth: Supporting South Africa's Emerging Entrepreneurs,* Centre for Development and Enterprise, Johannesburg.

Crick, M., 1992: Life in the informal sector: street guides in Kandy, Sri Lanka, in D. Harrison (Ed.), *Tourism and the Less Developed Countries,* Chichester, Wiley, 135-147.

Dahles, H., 1998: Tourism, government policy and petty entrepreneurs, *South East Asian Research,* 6, 73-98.

Dahles, H., 2000: Tourism, small enterprises and community development, in G. Richards and D. Hall (Eds.), *Tourism and Sustainable Community Development,* Routledge, London, 154-169.

Dahles, H., 2001: *Tourism, Heritage and National Culture in Java,* Curzon, Richmond.

Dahles, H. and Bras, K. (Eds.), 1999a: *Tourism and Small Entrepreneurs: Development, National Policy and Entrepreneurial Culture—Indonesian Cases,* Cognizant Communication, New York.

Dahles, H. and Bras, K., 1999b: Entrepreneurs in romance: tourism in Indonesia, *Annals of Tourism Research,* 26, 267-293.

Dahles, H. and Keune, L. (Eds.), 2002: *Tourism Development and Local Participation in Latin America,* Cognizant Communication, New York.

Dieke, P.U.C., 2003: Tourism in Africa's economic development: policy implications, *Management Decision,* 41, 287-295.

Douglas, N., 1997: Melanesians as observers, entrepreneurs and administrators of tourism, *Journal of Travel and Tourism Marketing,* 6, 85-92.

DTI (Department of Trade and Industry), 2004: *Annual Review of Small Business in South Africa—2003,* Enterprise Development Unit, Department of Trade and Industry, Pretoria.

Gartner, W.C., 1999: Small scale enterprises in the tourism industry in Ghana's Central region, in D.G. Pearce and R.W. Butler (Eds.), *Contemporary Issues in Tourism Development,* Routledge, London, 158-175.

Gartner, W.C., 2004: Factors affecting small firms in tourism: a Ghanaian perspective, in R. Thomas (Ed.), *Small Firms in Tourism: International Perspectives,* Elsevier, Amsterdam, 35-51.

Getz, D. and Carlsen, J., 2005: Family business in tourism: state of the art, *Annals of Tourism Research,* 32, 237-258.

Getz, D. and Petersen, T., 2005: Growth and profit-oriented entrepreneurship among family business owners in the tourism and hospitality industry, *International Journal of Hospitality Management,* 24, 219-242.

Goudie S.C., Khan F. and Kilian D., 1999: Transforming tourism: black empowerment, heritage and identity beyond apartheid. *South African Geographical Journal,* 81, 22-31.

Hampton, M.P., 1998: Backpacker tourism and economic development, *Annals of Tourism Research,* 25, 639-660.

Hampton, M.P., 2003: Entry points for local tourism in developing countries: evidence from Yogyakarta, Indonesia, *Geografiska Annaler,* 85B, 85-101.

Hamzah, A., 1997: The evolution of small-scale tourism in Malaysia; problems, opportunities and implications for sustainability, in M. J. Stabler (Ed.), *Tourism a n d Sustainability: Principles to Practice,* CAB International, Wallingford, 199-217.

Jaguaribe, B. and Hetherington, K., 2004: *Favela* tours: indistinct and mapless representations of the real in Rio de Janeiro, in M. Sheller and J. Urry (Eds.), *Tourism Mobilities: Places to Play, Places in Play,* Routledge, London.

Kesper, A., 2001: Failing or not aiming to grow?: manufacturing SMMEs and their contribution to employment growth in South Africa, *Urban Forum,* 12, 171-203.

Kesper, A., 2002: Tracing trajectories of successful manufacturing SMMEs in South Africa, Unpublished PhD dissertation, University of the Witwatersrand, Johannesburg.

Kokkranikal, J. and Morrison, A., 2002: Entrepreneurship and sustainable tourism: the houseboats of Kerala, *Tourism and Hospitality Research,* 4, 7-20.

Lynch, P., Morrison, A. and Thomas, R., 2005: Lifestyle labels and concepts: "in search of the hairy arsed yeti," Paper presented at the ATLAS 2005 Annual Conference, Tourism, Creativity and Development, Barcelona, 2-4 November.

Mayaka, M. and King, B., 2002: A quality assessment of education and training for Kenya's tour-operating sector, *Current Issues in Tourism,* 5, 112-133.

Milner, L., 2004: Grassroute tours, in A. Bennett and R. George (Eds.), *South African Travel and Tourism Cases,* Van Schaik, Pretoria, 108-114.

Mitchell, J. and Ashley, C., 2006: *Can Tourism Help Reduce Poverty in Africa?,* Briefing Paper, Overseas Development Institute, London.

Monitor, 2004: *Global Competitiveness Project: Summary of Key Findings of Phase 1,* South African Tourism, Johannesburg.

Morrison, A. and Teixeira, R., 2004: Small business performance: a tourism sector focus, *Journal of Small Business and Enterprise Development,* 11 (2), 166-173.

Nemasetoni, I., 2005: Contribution of tourism towards the development of black-owned small, medium and micro-enterprises (SMMEs) in post-apartheid South Africa: an evaluation of tour operators, Unpublished MA Research Report, University of the Witwatersrand, Johannesburg.

Nuntsu, N., Tassiopoulos, D. and Haydam, N., 2004: The bed and breakfast market of Buffalo City (BC), South Africa: present status, constraints and success factors, *Tourism Management,* 25, 515-524.

Oppermann, M. and Chon, K-S, 1997: *Tourism in Developing Countries,* International Thomson Business Press, London.

Page, S. J., Forer, P. and Lawton, G.R., 1999: Small business development and tourism: *terra incognita?, Tourism Management*, 20, 435-459.

Ramchander, P., 2004: Soweto set to lure tourists, in A. Bennett and R. George (Eds.), *South African Travel and Tourism Cases*, Van Schaik, Pretoria, 200-210.

Rodenburg, E., 1980: The effects of scale in economic development: Tourism in Bali, *Annals of Tourism Research*, 7, 177-196.

Roe, D., Goodwin, H. and Ashley, C., 2004: Pro-poor tourism: benefiting the poor, in T.V. Singh (Ed.), *New Horizons in Tourism: Strange Experiences and Stranger Practices*, CABI Publishing, Wallingford, 147-161.

Rogerson, C.M., 2001a: Growing the SMME manufacturing economy of South Africa: evidence from Gauteng province, *Journal of Contemporary African Studies,* 19, 267-291.

Rogerson, C.M., 2001b: Addressing the support needs of SMME manufacturers in South Africa, *Africa Insight*, 31 (2), 51-60.

Rogerson, C.M., 2003: Tourism and transformation: small enterprise development in South Africa, *Africa Insight,* 33 (1/2), 108-115.

Rogerson, C.M., 2004a: Tourism, small firm development and empowerment in post-apartheid South Africa, in R. Thomas (Ed.), *Small Firms in Tourism: International Perspectives,* Elsevier, Amsterdam, 13-33.

Rogerson, C.M., 2004b: Black economic empowerment in South African tourism, in C.M. Rogerson and G. Visser (Eds.), *Tourism and Development Issues in Contemporary South Africa*, Africa Institute of South Africa, Pretoria, 321-334.

Rogerson, C.M., 2004c: Transforming the South African tourism industry: the emerging black-owned bed and breakfast economy. *GeoJournal*, 60, 273-281.

Rogerson, C.M., 2004d: The impact of the South African government's SMME programs: a ten year review (1994-2003), *Development Southern Africa*, 21, 765-784.

Rogerson, C.M., 2004e: Urban tourism and small tourism enterprise development in Johannesburg: the case of township tourism, *GeoJournal*, 60, 249-257.

Rogerson, C.M., 2004f: Financing tourism SMMEs in South Africa: a supply-side analysis, in C.M. Rogerson and G. Visser (Eds.), *Tourism and Development Issues in Contemporary South Africa*, Africa Institute of South Africa, Pretoria, 222-267.

Rogerson, C.M., 2005a: Unpacking tourism SMMEs in South Africa: structure, support needs and policy response, *Development Southern Africa* 22, 623-642.

Rogerson, C.M., 2005b: SMME development in peripheral regions: manufacturing in Free State Province, South Africa, *Urban Forum*, 16, 36-56.

Rogerson, C.M. and Visser, G. (Eds.) 2004: *Tourism and Development Issues in Contemporary South Africa*, Africa Institute of South Africa, Pretoria.

Scheyvens R., 2002: *Tourism for Development: Empowering Communities,* Prentice Hall, Harlow.

Shackley, M., 1993: Guest farms in Namibia: an emerging accommodation sector in Africa's hottest destination, *International Journal of Hospitality Management*, 12, 253-265.

Shaw, G., 2004: Entrepreneurial cultures and small business enterprises in tourism, in A.A. Lew, C.M. Hall and A.M. Williams (Eds.), *A Companion to Tourism*, Blackwell, Oxford, 122-134.

Shaw, G. and Williams, A.M., 1990: Tourism, economic development and the role of entrepreneurial activity, in C.P. Cooper (Ed.), *Progress in Tourism: Recreation and Hospitality Management* Vol. 2. Belhaven, London, 67-81.

Shaw, G. and Williams, A.M., 2004: From lifestyle consumption to lifestyle production: changing patterns of tourism entrepreneurship, in R. Thomas (Ed.), *Small Firms in Tourism: International Perspectives,* Elsevier, Amsterdam, 99-113.

Thomas, R., 1998: An introduction to the study of small tourism and hospitality firms, in R. Thomas (Ed.), *The Management of Small Tourism and Hospitality Firms*, Cassell, London, 1-16.

Thomas, R., 2000: Small firms in the tourism industry: some conceptual issues. *International Journal of Tourism Research*, 2, 345-353.

Thomas, R. (Ed.), 2004a: *Small Firms in Tourism: International Perspectives*, Elsevier, Amsterdam.

Thomas, R., 2004b: International perspectives on small firms in tourism: a synthesis, in R. Thomas (Ed.), *Small Firms in Tourism: International Perspectives*. Elsevier, Amsterdam, 1-12.

Thomas R. and Thomas, H., 2005: Understanding tourism policy-making in urban areas, with particular reference to small firms, *Tourism Geographies*, 7, 121-137.

Thomas, W.H., 2005: *"Second Economy" Paths into South African Tourism Business*, Research Report 1, Centre for Tourism Research in Africa, Cape Peninsula University of Technology, Cape Town.

Timothy, D. and Wall, G., 1997: Selling to tourists: Indonesian street vendors, *Annals of Tourism Research*, 24, 322-340.

Tosun, C., 2005: Stages in the emergence of a participatory tourism development approach in the developing world, *Geoforum*, 36, 333-352.

Visser, G. and Rogerson, C.M. 2004: Researching the South African tourism and development nexus, *GeoJournal*, 60, 201-215.

Visser, G. and Van Huyssteen, K., 1997: Guest houses—new option for tourists in the Western Cape Winelands. *Acta Academica* 29(2), 106-137.

Visser, G. and Van Huyssteen, K., 1999: Guest houses: the emergence of a new tourist accommodation type in the South African tourism industry. *Tourism and Hospitality Research* 1, 155-175.

Wahnschafft, R., 1982: Formal and informal tourism sectors: a case study of Pattaya, Thailand, *Annals of Tourism Research*, 9, 429-451.

Wanhill, S., 2000: Small and medium tourism enterprises, *Annals of Tourism Research*, 27, 148-163.

Wanhill, S., 2004: Government assistance for tourism SMEs: from theory to practice, in R. Thomas (Ed.), *Small Firms in Tourism: International Perspectives*. Elsevier, Amsterdam, 53-70.

Williams, A.M., Shaw, G. and Greenwood, J., 1989: From tourist to tourism entrepreneur, from consumption to production: evidence from Cornwall, England. *Environment and Planning A*, 21, 1639-1653.

Part 3

Urban Tourism Experiences across the South African Urban Hierarchy

11

Urban Tourism in Cape Town

Gordon Pirie

Cape Town is one of few South African (and African) cities to which several of the world's most popular travel guide publishers have devoted entire books. Cape Town is the only African city in the Lonely Planet city travel guide series. Cape Town features with Cairo, Johannesburg, Marrakesh, Mombasa, and Nairobi in the Rough Guide series. The only African cities in the London-based TimeOut city guides are Nairobi, Johannesburg, and Cape Town. America's Fodor mini-guides cover Cairo, Cape Town, Johannesburg, Fez, and Marrakesh. The high profile of Cape Town on the real and virtual shelves of major booksellers is matched by the profusion of websites dedicated to the city and surrounds. In early 2006, a web-search using "Cape Town" and "tourism" as keywords tracked approximately 5.6 million web pages. The count for Johannesburg was 2.3 m, Cairo 1.9 m, Durban 1.3 m, and Nairobi 1.25 m. For a city of its size, Cape Town is heavily pre-scripted.

Travel opinion surveys conducted in the new century confirm Cape Town's popularity as a tourist destination. The surveys also confirm ("brand") familiarity with the city's name and image. In October 2002, Cape Town was voted fifth (and the top city) in the BBC television list of "fifty places to see before you die." For the second year in a row, Cape Town was top long-haul destination in the U.K. 2004 Trends and Spends Survey. In 2003, a U.S.-based travel magazine ranked the city fifth behind Sydney, Florence, Bankgok and Rome (Travel & Leisure, July 2003). For the fifth consecutive year, Cape Town was voted best Africa/Middle East destination by the same magazine, and eighth best city in the world (fifth in 2004)(Travel & Leisure, July 2005). In September 2003 the U.K. *Sunday Times* newspaper voted Cape Town "the world's hottest winter spot." A year later, the British Airways onboard magazine *Highlife* reported that airline staff voted Cape Town "the best city in the world for eating out." The view from Table Mountain was voted second only to that from the Corcovado in Rio de Janeiro.

In a fiendishly competitive global tourism market in which proliferation of annual awards may be engineered deliberately, their durability, meaning, and value needs careful decoding. However passing and superficial the good news, Cape Town tourism interests recite it with alacrity. Agents relish evidence that thirty thousand British people polled by an overseas professional survey organisation rated Cape Town their favorite foreign (and only non-European) city for the second year in succession (*Daily Telegraph*, 8 October 2005). Rating world cities according to ambience, friendliness, culture/sights, restaurants, accommodation, and shopping, 28,000 readers of an upmarket travel magazine voted Cape Town the best city in Africa and the Middle East (Conde Nast, October 2005). A British Internet travel agency reported Cape Town the seventh most popular destination for short breaks (*Burger*, 1 April 2005). The accolades were not just from foreign sources. In 2005, a South African market research agency found that Cape Town was South Africans' favorite destination, leading Durban by a considerable margin (*Sunday Times*, 25 September 2005).

Cape Town's geographical identity in these ratings is likely to be fluid. In all instances it is likely to include the central city and peninsular Cape Town. The latter includes the smart Atlantic suburbs and associated beaches, harbors and scenic coastal roads, as well as Cape Point, the False Bay fishing villages and beaches, the Constantia wine lands and Kirstenbosch botanic gardens. In the minds of some respondents, Cape Town may also include the formal and shanty townships on the Cape Flats, and the northern suburbs' wine lands. Many respondents are likely to bracket Cape Town with the historic towns of Stellenbosch and Franschoek and their wine lands.

Whichever way "Cape Town" is configured in the minds of travel survey respondents, it is useful to think of a metropolitan place comprising approximately 3.5 million people. More than just a container, however, it is a place that has been imbued (slightly erroneously) with specific situational glamour. Geographical niceties aside, Cape Town is at the southern tip of a continent and at an oceanic divide. These senses give the city locational and experiential cache: the hemispheric vastness in all compass directions is palpable and magnetic (45 percent of visitors to Cape Town trek to Cape Point). Tourist marketers like mythologizing that Cape Town is the only city in the world where one can watch the sun rise and set over a different ocean. The city has a romance too as anchor of a century of ambitious, imaginative, transcontinental Cape-to-Cairo projects and journeys. At a less grand geographical scale (and less grandly also because of poor railway station facilities), Cape Town is also the start and end point of luxurious long-distance train journeys undertaken mainly by well-heeled tourists from overseas. A private company (Rovos Rail) serves southern African tourist destinations using restored historic rolling stock; the state-owned, legendary "Blue Train" links Cape Town to Johannesburg and Pretoria. In the IT age, the city now features as a jumping off point too for web-based community projects promoting continental route tourism (Visser, 2004a).

Capturing and reflecting Cape Town's uniqueness has preoccupied artists of various persuasions for centuries. For modern tourism purposes, distillation of the city's essence has been reduced to public opinion surveys.[1] The massive, memorable outline of Table Mountain and its flanks has become iconic, and image-makers have devised a sketch line logo of the mountain skyline as a way of branding the city. It has been more difficult grinding out tourism management capacity and integrating it with out-of-town tourism initiatives. A succession of private and public tourism bodies in the early-2000s presented fragmented tourism information at best. The hiatus ended in 2004, when, under the auspices of a unified provincial and city tourism authority, Cape Town started being marketed officially under the controversial but holistic "Cape Town Routes Unlimited" badge which includes attractions in outlying regions. Indicatively, the Cape Town Pass, instituted in 2004, gives visitors discounted access to fifty selected attractions and activities in and around Cape Town as well as the Peninsula and the Wine lands. Administrative and environmental boundaries are made porous: tourism publicity merges the urban and the rural faster even than the visible dissolution of the countryside.

Perhaps the key phenomenon with which Cape Town's marketers have grappled in the past decade has been the soaring number of visitors. Like all South African tourist magnets, Cape Town's international rating soared in the 1990s during the successful transition to democratic rule and the Republic's re-entry to the world trade and travel map. First-time and return visitor and investor numbers increased; tourism demands and linked service industry opportunities swelled. One of the world's most spectacular small coastal cities woke up to a new future and a new floating population of close on 1 million international visitors annually, the majority of them in the southern hemisphere summer.

Familiar with only modest visitor volumes and demands, people in a city renowned for its easygoing way of life have taken some years to adjust to and tool up for service beyond just beach hotel accommodation and catering. Significant new opportunities arose in construction, niche accommodation, car renting, coach transport, tour guiding, personalised touring, trip management, holiday planning and facilitation services, and marketing. The tourist product range expanded. Cape Town was being used by more visitors than ever as the platform for easy-to-access local sea and mountain tourism (e.g., hiking, fishing, surfing, boat charter, beach horse riding, birding, climbing, abseiling, kayaking, hang gliding, whale watching), extreme sports (e.g., wild surfing, shark-cage diving) and sports tourism (e.g., golf; round-Peninsula cycling and running). The city makes a fine place for urban tourism and is also part of any industrial[2] and architectural touring (e.g., Cape Dutch and colonial). Impromptu vineyard touring has long been a staple ingredient of a visit to Cape Town, but private and tailored shopping and gourmet culinary and wine tasting tours are a mark of the maturing local tourist economy. Success bred success and sophistication.

Refined segmentation has also occurred. Ten private schools have been established for teaching English to foreigners. In the specialised gay travel market, a holiday planning and facilitation service has emerged to offer tours, transport and accommodation exclusively by lesbians for lesbians. "Wanderwoman" is the preferred tour operator for "The Lavender Meander," a lesbian road tour. Health tourism is no longer just about spas and sunny beaches, but has grown to include medical treatment packaged with pampered post-operative leisure. The cleverly named "Mediscapes" company markets plastic surgery (cosmetic and reconstructive; dental and laser eye surgery) using a slogan that plays on Cape Town's reputation for fine food and its dominant landmark (rather than its terminal position on the continent); the surgeons "waiting for you at our table" charge rates less than half those in Britain. Mediscapes offers optional consultation in London or Scotland before travel to Cape Town. Unlike in accommodation and catering where vendor greed in 2004 reportedly backfired in 2005, there has been no tourist outcry yet about extortionate and opportunistic medical and hospital fees.

A great deal of tourist consumption in Cape Town is conspicuous; that much is plain to any hungry, homeless, daring street youth. Some of the visitor wealth is now vested semi-permanently in the city. Riding the weak Rand currency at the turn of the century, international tourists who fell in love with the city made hay of low property prices and snapped up bargains, especially along the Atlantic coastal strip. British, German, and Dutch investors helped fashion this "African Riviera" with its dry-summer Mediterranean climate and pristine sand beaches. Purchase, occupation, lease and rental of ostentatious dormitory villas by a global elite of international nomads (Low, 2003) has spawned yet another tourism sub-sector, namely, residential property advice, selection, purchasing and management services. The arrival in town of a German realtor, and high-profile local tie-ups with foreign (especially British) realtors such as Christie's Great Estates, Knight Frank, Sotheby's and Savill's International have "globalized" residential real estate in Cape Town and driven property marketing to a new pitch. Sale of second and holiday homes to foreigners and up-country residents has not been uniformly welcomed, of course: it has further inflated the booming residential property market, and priced out many local Capetonians.[3]

The double-sided nature of tourism is not unique to Cape Town; all cities in the South particularly have to confront and attempt to balance tourism benefits and costs. In Cape Town, as in all South Africa, public authorities, non-profit agencies and private entrepreneurs are conscious of the imperative of using tourism as a lever to assist job creation, social upliftment, transformation, and economic growth. Many tourists, too, may be presumed to be acutely aware of their privileges and the potential developmental effect of their expenditure. A high number of the many working-age, college-educated, European, English-speaking visitors in Cape Town's tourist mix between 1999 and 2003 (tables 11.1 and 11.2) will know about the ambiguities of tourism before leaving home, and will know about the democratic but divided country and society they will be visiting. If not, the descent into Cape Town airport and the road trip from the airport sensitises tourists quickly to the deep socio-economic and spatial inequalities in Cape Town.

As tourist guide books never tire of noting, the unavoidable N2 highway that joins the airport to the tourist traps in formerly "white" Cape Town plunges visitors speedily and involuntarily into a close-up view of the shacks which hundreds of thousands of Africans occupy on the featureless Cape Flats. Nearby, the more substantial homes inhabited by the poor stratum of colored Capetonians only serve to accentuate the depths of African poverty. Occasionally, tourist coaches, cabs and taxis will have to plough through thick smoke from tens of tightly packed, flammable shelters set ablaze by accidentally overturned open-flame stoves and heaters. Happily, stone throwing and vehicle hi-jacking by damaged and disillusioned township youths is a less frequent occurrence than in the 1990s. Talk is that the new apartment blocks alongside the motorway are partly humanitarian re-housing, and partly re-imaging in advance of the FIFA World Cup 2010 visitors. A new public housing estate would certainly render shanty accommodation less continuous and would help validate travel market spin. A patch of walk-up apartments will reduce the shock of seeing shack-living and will create a more favorable first impression. As less fortunate Capetonians and their spokespeople note, however, hiding urban realities from tourists is a deceit. Overseas visitors will be shocked by levels of poverty in otherwise magnificent Cape Town, and they should be for as long as shocking inequalities persist. Tourists from Africa (approximately 5 percent of the foreign total) and domestic tourists are less appalled by what they see, partly because of familiarity, and partly because, as repeat visitors, they have seen it before (tables 11.2 and 11.3).

Table 11.1
Social Profile of Cape Town Tourists, 1999-2003

		International (%)	Domestic (%)
Age (years)	18-25	13.7	16.7
	26-35	25.4	25.0
	36-50	29.2	36.7
	51-65	22.5	16.2
	65 +	8.9	5.2
Education	Post-school qualification	45.7	34.3
Marital status	Married, no children	35.2	25.7
	Married, children	14.5	37.3
	Not married	26.8	20.2

Source: Cape Town Convention Bureau, 2004

Table 11.2
Proportion of Cape Town Tourists by Origin, 1999-2003

Foreign	%	Domestic (province)	%
United Kingdom	35.9	Gauteng	46.6
Germany	14.9	KwaZulu-Natal	21.3
Netherlands/Belgium	12.2	Eastern Cape	11.5
France	2.4	Western Cape	5.0
Italy	0.9	Free State	5.0
Other Europe	11.1	Mpumalanga	4.5
(EUROPE TOTAL)	*(77.4)*		
North America	12.6	North West	2.6
Australasia	3.8	Northern Cape	2.6
Africa	5.0	Limpopo	2.3
	100.0		100.0

Source: Cape Town Convention Bureau, 2004

Cape Town's tourist portal was meant to have been different. It was to have been reassuring, glorifying and inspirational. Before the 1960s, when most overseas visitors arrived in Cape Town by ocean liner, they would be greeted first by Table Mountain appearing on the horizon, and then by the sight of a fine, modern town of European design coming into view. The lofty city plan of the 1940s provided for elegant boulevards sweeping down to the docks and giving grand vistas of the City Hall and Parliament. Even in the early-1900s, "scars" on the urban landscape, such as District Six "slum," were to have been eradicated from the tourist gaze by having the railway operator fix low train fares that would entice the working classes away (Coetzer, 2003: 121, 203). Apartheid achieved what free-market railway economics did not. State-owned railway construction and train-fare subsidy eventually enabled forced relocation of a significant number of the centrally resident urban poor, ironically to land astride the corridor that air-age tourists would use.

Few tourist arrivals in Cape Town are by sea; far from the northern hemi-sphere short-break cruise ship routes, its harbor is also hamstrung by vessel size limitations, high winds, plodding and archaic customs procedures, and poor onward land transport (Vos, 2004). Only nine cruise liners docked in Cape Town in 2000/01; all the cruise liners that put in at South African ports in 2001 carried only 8,707 passengers in total and not all ships stopped at Cape Town. Cruise liner visits to Cape Town have increased since, but the pre-conditions for a flourishing tourism cruise market in Cape Town are circular and are unlikely to alter fundamentally in the near future: substantial infrastructural re-invest-ment depends on an assured high-season market, and more cruise ships will only book Cape Town after port upgrades.

Table 11.3
Cape Town Visitor History, 1999-2003

	International	Domestic
	%	%
First-time visitors	74.2	37.4
Second time	12.3	18.4
Three or more times	13.4	44.0
	100.0	100.0

Source: Cape Town Convention Bureau, 2004

First impressions of Cape Town depend, in part, on the mode of transport and route taken. Passenger rail service has tailed off dramatically since the 1980s, but the looming presence of Table Mountain will be similar from the windows of trains, road vehicles and aircraft. In the immediate foreground, the incidence and unfolding sequence of industrial estates, shopping centres, suburbs and townships will vary, but from all directions the 3,000 ft massif has a commanding presence.

Styled variously as the "Cape of Good Hope" and the "Cape of Storms," the compelling natural environment of Cape Town has always drawn travellers. Within a short radius, under mostly sunny skies, there are beaches, mountains, planted forests and indigenous gardens, and dramatic panoramic views. From 1908 when the city council was first granted funds to produce a guidebook advertising the city, scenic drives have been punted vigorously. The route taken now by open-top tourist buses is little changed from the course mapped out seventy years ago in the Cape Peninsula Publicity Association's pamphlet "The Motorists Paradise." The increased traffic congestion—and road rage—is a clear difference.

Less visceral, the sense of what Cape Town is as a tourist destination has been changing. The notion of the 'city beautiful' remains a prime motif just as it was in the two publicity films of the Cape Peninsula screened in 1934 at the Empire Exhibition at Wembley in London. There, a set of seventy-four photographs displayed by the City of Cape Town depicted the city and peninsula as "predominantly picturesque and part of a grand European tradition" (Coetzer, 2003: 56). Decades of publicity in the monthly railway magazine cultivated the same image (see Foster, 2003). Here lies the change. Apart from ugly intrusions that have rendered parts of the built environment hideous, the tourist city is no longer entirely conceived, presented or desired as non-African. Those N2 shanties belie that mirage. Overseas tourists especially seek out and enjoy the encounter with Africa in Cape Town. Diluted and of questionable provenance it may be, but as even the most casual survey of carry-on luggage aboard outbound aircraft confirms, travel trophies and trinkets are conspicuously African.

The African-ness of Cape Town is a contentious and sensitive point for tourists and tourism marketers. A cynical view is that the city attracts overseas visitors precisely because it is the least African city in South Africa (and therefore probably the least African city on the continent). The suggestion is that Cape Town is a European fantasy—that it is teeming Africa tamed. The epithet "Australia without the jet lag" is meant to refer to South Africa's attractiveness because of the physically less fatiguing journey, but it can be read more subtly as reference to a psychically less discomforting journey from the North to recognisable, ordered territory away from the heart of a dark continent. Had European heritage been obliterated in the North and better preserved in the post-colonial South, the argument that visiting Cape Town is a nostalgic trip into the European past would be more convincing. Domestic African tourists diagnose Cape Town's marginal African-ness differently, reporting that the city (the only one in South Africa where Africans are in a demographic minority) is unwelcoming. Were the travel experience strange rather than hostile, more South Africans might want to visit just because Cape Town is the most unusual city in their own country.

Leveraging on the unquestionably (South) African attraction of seeing the "big five" animals in their wild habitat, Cape Town tourism publicity trumpets its own "big six" attractions.[4] These also happen to be six of South Africa's top ten tourist attractions, and they afford Cape Town a big slice of the country's overseas travel market: in 2002, approximately 976,000 (53 percent) of international visitors to South Africa came to the Western Cape either directly or as a diversion (Cape Town Convention Bureau, 2004).

The city's favorable positioning within reach of non-stop commercial airline service from Europe is a considerable advantage, although this is undercut by the political economy of licensing direct flights, a sore point in Cape circles. But, at the southern-most apex of the lucrative domestic airway triangle whose other two points are Johannesburg and Durban, Cape Town airport is well served by shuttle operators (including no-frills carriers), and is one of the best value flight destinations in South Africa for domestic and foreign travellers.

In order of popularity that is the same for foreign and domestic tourists, the 'big six' Cape Town attractions are the Victoria and Alfred Waterfront, Robben Island, Table Mountain, the Constantia Vineyards, the Castle of Good Hope, and the National Botanic Gardens at Kirstenbosch. A greater proportion of foreign than local tourists visit these top sites (table 11.4), a pattern that conforms with the higher proportion of domestic visitors who make repeat visits to Cape Town (table 11.3).

The Victoria and Alfred (V&A) is a classic inner city urban waterfront revitalisation project that provides upmarket retailing, entertainment and accommodation in a safe, aesthetically pleasing, heritage environment (Worden, 1994; Worden and van Heyningen, 1996; Dodson and Killian, 1998). Billed as the crowning jewel in the national property portfolio, heavy footfall at the

Table 11.4
Annual Average Percentage of International and Domestic Tourists Visiting Cape Town's Top Tourist Sites, 1999-2003

Sites	International	Domestic
V & A Waterfront	85.8	78.2
Table Mountain	67.7	47.9
Cape Point	52.0	36.3
Kirstenbosch Gardens	40.6	25.1
Good Hope Castle	24.2	20.2
Robben Island	30.6	14.7

Source: Cape Town Convention Bureau, 2004

ten-year-old V&A makes it the country's most visited site. Within a short drive, five-year-old Century City "shoppertainment" complex competes for tourists. Domestic travellers especially are most likely to be attracted by its fake architectural exoticism and amnesic seduction, if not by proprietary coach transport to and from dedicated drop-off and collection spots around a complex whose surface area approximates that of the entire Cape Town CBD (Marks and Bezzoli, 2001).

Unlike the downtown districts of South Africa's other principal cities, central Cape Town (transformed in this century especially by various upgrade initiatives), has become a tourist trap in its own right. Its multiple access points make accurate visitor counts impossible, but estimates are that 90 percent of tourists spend some time in the central city for heritage and cultural purposes, and for shopping. Compact, and suited to strolling, the city offers a diversity of accommodation, facilities, attractions and sights. In the CBD alone, there are an estimated fifty-eight hotels and guesthouses; the 252 restaurants, bars and cafés include many of the best in South Africa. The central city's fine architectural heritage includes an eclectic collection of Cape Dutch, Victorian and Edwardian design commercial, government and residential buildings. The many restored Art Deco buildings are a photogenic trademark of the central city and were a draw for an international conference of period historians in 2003. Museums and art and craft shops abound.

Pre-constructed walking, motor bus (and horse-bus) tour routes written up extensively in all city guides include visits to the city's (some say the nation's) premier cultural precinct.[5] This comprises the Parliament buildings, the Slave Lodge, the historic "Company Gardens," the "People's Cathedral" (St George's), an art gallery and museum, a branch of the national library, the Great Synagogue and the Jewish Museum. Guided waking tours (one offers guides in English, German, and French, but not in any indigenous African language)[6] like to stress the South African miracle that is the passage from oppressive, racist history to a democratic present. Alluding to the title of Nelson Mandela's autobiography, the "Footsteps to Freedom" city walk is one of several that exposes visitors to residues of the national past in the city, but that also enables visitors "to absorb the charisma and African energy of Cape Town."

South Africa's oldest city can indeed be used as a convenient window on colonial, apartheid, and post-apartheid South Africa. Tours through famed District Six and Bo Kaap, and tour bus stops at their respective museums, give insight into the iniquities visited on thousands of anonymous inner-city residents in spaces that have diametrically opposed apartheid histories and startlingly different contemporary visualities. Other sites associated with well-known South African personalities tap into public memory and, in a halo effect, offer tourists a sense of presence and connectedness. St George's Cathedral, forever linked to Emeritus Archbishop Desmond Tutu, appeared regularly on TV screens as the place where anti-apartheid protestors gathered, held vigils and sought sanctuary. Cape Town's Grand Parade will long be associated with Nelson Mandela's first public appearance and address after his release from prison in 1990 and with his first speech as president of the new South Africa in 1994.

Enhanced recognition and celebration of (central) Cape Town's past jigsaws nicely with heritage tourism. Heritage discoveries persist. One such is a new precinct and trail being designed for a central city site where recent construction unearthed over 2,000 human skeletons believed to be of the city's seventeenth/ eighteenth century poor and under-classes such as sailors, servants, slaves, and indigenous people. The proposal is to commemorate these citizens in a project that will include re-interment in St Andrew's churchyard. A formless and forlorn adjacent public plot will become a memorial square, and walls of memory/interpretive panels will be positioned along an upgraded and partially pedestrianized route leading past nine forgotten eighteenth/nineteenth century church cemeteries to the site of a Dutch colonial coastal fortification. Prestwich Memorial Place will strengthen the tourist axis between the central city and the V&A, and will reinforce the self-narration of Cape Town's past as one of exploitation and hardship, and its present as one of respect and honour.

Those strands of displayed, photographed urban life have been partially worked out in a nearby district of particular appeal to gay tourists. De Water-kant, a heavily gentrified district, has become the city's gay "quarter" and is, by default, the hub of South Africa's—and Africa's—gay tourism (Visser, 2002; 2004b). More than any other single place in Cape Town, De Waterkant may be what respondents have in mind when rating the city among the world's top ten gay destinations. Like the Bo Kaap where a minority group (but a much bigger, settled one) live in a photogenic space, De Waterkant is also a tourist trap, figuratively and literally. The aestheticization of the "Malay" quarter involves persistent but crude, over-determined, re-assertion of a fictionalised heritage linked to slavery and exile (Ward, 1997). Misrepresentation is also afoot in De Waterkant's quaint Chelsea-like streets. In its own way, this district too is an urban struggle space. It can be thought of as an island bastion at which charges of "seaside sodomy" were directed at the turn of the century, and where retaliation kept alive the marketing of Cape Town as a gay capital in the wake of acrimonious public exchanges about the accuracy, form, and desirability of such publicity (Bennett, 2004).

But the tolerance of gay culture in Cape Town conceals complex layerings of inclusion, indignity and dispossession. The sheer presence of De Waterkant and the hosting of perhaps 25,000 gay visitors annually on holiday and at feathered festivals is apt to overstate normality. Tourism pamphlets fail to project a nuanced history. One oversight is of a past that was once polyglot, sexually raw and probably transgressive on the edges of a dockland. Another oversight is of a more recent and shameful racist past during which mixed-race residents were evicted by apartheid planning from the hilltop cottages on Loader Street sought after and fought after for bijou retreats. More recently, the superior buying power of wealthy British and German gay men especially has effectively excluded middle-class gay Capetonians (Visser, 2003a). Distortions persist in the way that Cape Town's "pink" marketers fail to differentiate Cape Town's gay past or present from other urban gay centres in the world. Apart from stereotyping homosexuality, publicists follow uncritically a global model and present De Waterkant as a contiguous, safe community space in Cape Town. Yet the monopoly space obscures all lesbian lives and struggles there and elsewhere in the city, and denies other local worlds of gay men who are black and / or poor (Visser, 2003b; Elder, 2004, 2005).

No outcast space in Cape Town has ever been as assiduously cultivated as a tourist blind spot as Robben Island. The reality of the former guano island, leper colony and maximum security prison has come to light in the last decade; South Africa's Alcatraz has been propelled to UN World Heritage status and ensured a steady stream of curious, humbled visitors on political pilgrimage. Unsettling and inspiring by turns, the Island is the best known of Cape Town's many sites of "trauma tourism"; the Holocaust Centre and the townships are others. The Island provokes introspection on tourist voyeurism and the commoditisation of suffering and punishment (Bologna, 2000; Strange and Kempa, 2003).

Appropriately, Robben Island is accessed via the Nelson Mandela gateway that is at the end of a marked V&A walk that tells "stories of bravery, slavery, tragedy & triumph." Nearby, statues of four of South Africa's Nobel Peace Prize winners (including Mandela and Tutu) stand in newly-opened Nobel Square, a space of contemplation that draws many tourists and their cameras and helps remind rapacious consumers of other realities. A little way off, but on a tourist track, Cape Town's version of Johannesburg's Constitution Hill is likely to become a huge tourist attraction too: the Desmond Tutu Peace Centre will house display spaces, a conference centre and a leadership development school.

From Robben Island, the sight of Cape Town and Table Mountain is one of the most beautiful, tantalising and achingly poignant to be had anywhere. Albeit with a very different emotional charge, this view approximates the one seen by tourists at the end of a sea voyage. It emphasises the compact city's stunning location in an amphitheatre formed by Table Mountain, Signal Hill, Lion's Head, and Devil's Peak. The proximity of Cape Town to such a landscape, and to its unique assemblage of flora, underwrites a significant form of peri-urban ecotourism. Table Mountain National Park, reaching as far south as Cape Point, generates 4.5 million visitors annually. Declared South Africa's sixth world heritage site in 2004, this urban edge resource is home to a fine-leafed plant ('fynbos') that forms the smallest of the world's six floral kingdoms, but the most diverse in species and the most concentrated geographically. The display of indigenous vegetation in Kirstenbosch botanic gardens on one slope of Table Mountain—and the tranquillity there—is a major tourist attraction (table 11.4). The flat top mountain has lodged long and deep in the public imagination (van Sittert, 2003); the measure of its place in contemporary consciousness is the local and international media coverage of fires that devastated the slopes in January 2006. The culpability of one British tourist and the death of another were not surprising statistically.

Many of the 15 million visitors who have used the seventy-five-year-old cable car facility to ascend Table Mountain ventured no further than the hoist station from where they gazed down at the city and its suburbs, and photographed a sunset. A fresh corps of cable car passengers will be tourists participating in the new-guided mountain trail. Short, inexpensive trails are intended for Capetonians, especially day-trippers from disadvantaged communities. An up-market three-day Hoerikwagga ("Sea Mountain") urban-mountain walking trail is targeted at tourists. Served by porters, it entails sleeping in smart, catered camps. The trail takes in Robben Island, central city highlights, an overnight stay in a restored washhouse, and an extended hike on the mountain. The contribution of the programme to black economic empowerment is via training of guides recruited from Cape Town's disadvantaged African and colored communities. A public works programme has also funded training and work for 420 township residents in path building (136km), clearance of alien vegetation, and stone masonry.

Tourist use of outdoor Cape Town has been marred by criminality. In 2005, thirty-three variously violent (racially indiscriminate) assaults were made on visitors to Table Mountain, Lion's Head, and Signal Hill. Sixty-strong patrols of visitor safety guards failed to stop the actions of individuals and armed gangs (*Cape Times*, 16 December 2005). Other incidents occurred in the Waterfront, in the city centre, and on beaches. In 2005 there was a steady stream of press reports about muggings and snatchings by vagrants, street children and professional criminals.

Wherever it occurs in Cape Town, violence understandably deters and destabilises city tourism (George, 2001, 2003a, 2003b). Such, fortunately, has not been the case recently in township tourism where there was only one reported incidence of violence in 2005. On this occasion, four men boarded a tour coach in Khayelitsha township and stole personal possessions at gunpoint. The startled and traumatised passengers were among a party of 700 visiting German travel agents (*Cape Times*, 1 December 2005). The incident, headline news in the local press, posed worrying questions about the adverse effects on future inbound German tourism. It raised questions about authentic tourism experiences, about the partitioning of Cape Town into safe and unsafe tourist spots, about site-selective (cultural/heritage) tourism, about the ownership, delivery and packaging of township tourism, and about the notion of responsible tourism.

Tourism into the city's sprawling commuter townships on the Cape Flats is among the best known and the least known. Constituting an informal and little known segment, an estimated one million domestic tourists annually stay in private homes in the Cape Flats with friends and relations (Rule, et al., 2004; Wamema, 2005). Far better known is the township sightseeing component of commercially guided touring outside central Cape Town (McEachern, 1997; Resnick, 1997; Goudie, et al., 1999; Bologna, 2000). The genealogy of this so-called cultural tourism includes different varieties of apartheid-era touring: "officially" organized soft-soap trips to Cape Flats townships constructed as ethnic villages in the city, and "unofficial" (NGO- or politically-organized) conscientizing trips for foreign funders, international "struggle junkies" and local whites.

Ethno tourism—if such it is—has grown significantly, but in the process it has also become a contested element of Cape Town tourism: not only is its typology debateable, but its conflation with townships is problematic. The 2005 Lonely Planet DVD on Cape Town makes the point well: the video includes trance dancing in Khayelitsha and a township house-building project, but it also films a spring queen carnival in a central city arena, the Cape minstrels working the downtown streets,[7] and a *halaal* picnic on the seafront.

The purpose of township tourism is simple: tourists like to see the places where the majority of Capetonians live (between 20 percent and 25 percent of Cape Town's tourists book a township tour; a very high percentage would be foreigners). Some tourists enjoy more than a superficial coach journey and like to engage with township life more directly than through a camera lens. They elect to meet residents, buy local food and other products, join in cultural activities, and lodge overnight. The practice of township touring has evolved largely into a drive back through time across what survives of the "forever *hamba*'[8] landscape of sequential township establishment. Charting the "social cartography of apartheid's dispossession and oppression" (McEachern, 1997: 142-143), many township tours start at the District Six Museum and trace outward from there the geography of forced removals into the colored townships (such as Athlone, Bonteheuvel, Crossroads, and Mitchell's Plain). Dock Location, Windermere and Ndabeni are gone, fathomable only via astute literary tourism, but the establishment of existing African townships (such as Langa, Nyanga, Guguletu, and Khayelitsha) is traceable. Other tours into the newer, disconnected Atlantic townships of Masiphumelele and Imizamo Yethu necessarily follow a different narrative. Conveying the complex spatiality and synchrony of (re)settlement to an interested but lay audience is a considerable challenge. Narrative accounts by local tourist guides project a subjective authenticity, even if they contain exaggerations, gaps and inaccuracies, as some recorded evidence shows (Dondolo, 2002). Tour guiding is but one possibility for black-owned small tourism businesses which, in Cape Town, are largely short of experience, training, awareness, business plans, capital, support, and partners (Quesada, 2005).

A township tour will generally give a view of densely populated places characterised by visible unemployment, absence from school, make-do private housing, public hostels, and small scale manufacture and trade. A tour itinerary typically includes stops at places such as markets, empowerment and training centres, self-help communal gardens, taverns or shebeens, spaza shops, soup kitchens, nourishment centres, crèches, churches, and charitable organisations. The companies and private tour operators who visit Langa list in their publicity the open air meat market, beer tasting, a guided walk, a visit to a herbalist/traditional healer, "traditional" dinner with a family, a jazz evening, and a "sunset cruise on a donkey cart." Operators advertise a few township B&Bs/guesthouses, and even a visit just to see what one looks like. "Meet the people, feel the warmth, discover the truth!" announces one publicity flyer. The promise is that tourists will discover and experience the (forgiving) spirit, ingenuity, and dynamism in the rainbow nation.

Several tour operators include sites of struggle in their itinerary. In September 2005 a memorial wall was unveiled in Athlone to honour anti-apartheid demonstrators killed and wounded by police in the infamous "Trojan Horse" incident. In Langa, tourists can see the taxi rank site which, in 2001, was unofficially re-named Sobukwe Square to commemorate the political leader's address to migrant laborers there in 1960, and the apartment block from which a famous 1960 anti-pass march to the City started. In Guguletu, the modest cross where Amy Biehl, a young visiting American, was butchered in 1993 is a poignant stop. Another is the strikingly harsh memorial to seven innocent men trapped and murdered by police in 1986. These trenchant sites of significance resonate in a way that the sweeping and detached view from a Khayelitsha dune top lookout never has since its establishment in 2004 (Dyssel, 2006).

Setting aside logistical challenges, a study of the difficulties confronting township tour guides in 1996 found guides adept at tracing startling and fine gradations of inequality. Guides endeavoured to present to visitors the "normality" of township life (in opposition to their pathologized representation in the media), but also to tell visitors about the historical atrocities and pain that created the townships. In the process, however, guides struggled with contradictory elements. Tours intended as un-staged township encounters were inescapable public performances of sameness and difference (McEachern, 1997) between guide, visitor and visited. Some performance might involve tour guides fore-fronting the solidarity struggle of their subjects while staying silent about the internal struggle politics of township tour guiding and routeing.

A study of three different Cape Flats' township tours in the 1990s disclosed diverse scripts. One tour guide celebrated multiculturalism in the rainbow nation, rode roughshod over complexities of "exotic indigenous" cultures, and focused on the "Black-exotic" of sangomas, shebeens, and spazas. He repackaged the township into an unthreatening, aestheticised, uncritical, charming narrative about African resilience, vitality, and creativity. Another tour proved more au-thoritative politically and exposed the more mundane daily experiences of racial-ized poverty. A third tour, led by former ANC activists, visited sites of resistance, demonstrations and marches, and questioned progress in the rainbow nation. On this tour, perhaps, there would have been a chance to query how "despite being one of the homicide and rape capitals of the world, Cape Town managed to represent itself as one of Africa's most popular tourist cities" (Robins, 2000: 417). The tour should not have been among those which, in 2001, neglected the police station, church, and pass office that Langa residents regarded as key cultural spaces, and which ignored the exhibition of Cape township histories at the Sivuyile Centre in Guguletu (Dondolo, 2002).

There is nothing about Cape Town that exempts it from the general dif-ficulties of constructing and delivering a "two cities" tour. A township tour is a spatially visible expression of pro-poor tourism and has become a signature of tourist sensitivity, solidarity and social conscience. But difficulties abound, and in a tourism industry that is still racialized in a city that is still racialized, the very concept of a township tour is problematic. Reification of racial divides is hard to avoid. It is difficult to escape essentializing discourses and images, to resist reductive and homogenising speech, and to navigate actualities and representations (Robins, 2000). Like ethno-tourism generally, tours can easily caricature people and situations and offend all parties. Exotic and indigenous are confused. Authenticity is easily compromised; style, safety, sanitisation and shallowness can win the day.

Township touring is unquestionably fraught, but perhaps no more so than other less questioned forms of tourism. Its distinctiveness as a category may be ephemeral, a matter of time and place. But town planners, urban historians, and geographers will always be fascinated by Cape Town's townships as specific places. General interest among a broader public may flag: as South African soci-ety normalises and the past recedes, visitors might balk more at objectification, othering and spectatorship. Humanitarianism may continue to motivate earnest and welcome links with specific institutions and individuals, but would dissolve tourism-voyeurism. Specialisation may indeed be one way of sustaining tourist visits into townships. The product is likely to always appeal to an educational niche market among leisure tourists; growth might reside among segments of Cape Town's undeveloped business tourism market. Some of the generalised township offerings may graduate into more specialized—even designer—tours constructed around a particular theme of interest to visiting specialists such as conference delegates. Special focus tours of medical interest might include visits to hospitals and clinics concerned with, for example, HIV/AIDS. Educational tours would focus on schools. Vernacular architecture might make a themed tour. Culturally themed tours might focus on dance, music, and artwork such as pottery and weaving, beadwork, wirework, and scrap-metal work. Indeed, in a city where accusations of philistinism mostly address absent European cultural forms (literary, theatre, ballet, dance, opera, painting, sculpture, recitals, concerts), township culture may come to define mainstream cultural tourism. A space to watch in this regard is the defunct Athlone power station, centrally located and accessible.[9]

The development of business tourism in Cape Town has lagged (table 11.5) for the obvious reason that the city was only ever the economic heart of South Africa more than a century ago, and only one of two international gateways to that heart for only fifty years longer. The city has retained its position as the business centre of the Western Cape, but its vital commercial statistics pale beside those of the national powerhouse in Gauteng. Where Cape Town does lead in entrepreneurialism, it is in tightly defined niche activities around which business tourism coalesces. Winery tourism is an outstanding example. Tourism associated with film production (advertising, documentary, and feature) is a recent development: Cape Town is reputedly the fifth busiest film production venue in the world. In 2003/2004 the City issued permits for 900 film-shooting days (compared to San Francisco's 980). The effect in the central city is palpable: studios, production units and film schools have sprung up and streets are regularly cordoned off. For a city rated among the eight most creative cities in the world (*Newsweek*, April 2002), a sub-categorisation of business tourism would record numerous professional work-play visits hinged on filming, design, media, publishing, and arts and crafts such as jewellery work.

In the past, modest numbers of "working tourists" in Cape Town have been accommodated in gracious old family hotels such as the famed Mount Nelson Hotel (1899) and the beachfront Winchester Mansions (1920s). The recent

Table 11.5
Principal Trip Purposes: Annual Average Percent of Tourists, 1999-2003

	International	Domestic
Visit friends & relatives	20.5	32.7
Holiday / leisure	49.2	57.9
Business / educational	9.2	11.7
Special interest	17.1	9.4
Specific attraction	14.3	9.1

Source: Cape Town Convention Bureau, 2004

construction of venues dedicated to the work/rest needs of the modern business tourist has capacitated Cape Town for the lucrative MICE tourism market and enabled it to compete better with Johannesburg and Durban for business tourism. Quality hosting increased significantly in the 1990s with the provision of forty conference and function rooms at the V&A. Facilities there seat more than 2,200 conference delegates simultaneously and provide banquet seating for more than 2,700 people. Opened in June 2003, the even larger R566m Cape Town International Convention Centre (CTICC) has been used for exhibits, trade shows, fashion events, musical and sports performances, and conferences. In its first seven months, the CTICC hosted 290,000 visitors at 196 events. In 2004, a joint meeting of the International Congress and Conference Association and the International Association of Conference and Visitor Bureaux, and a workshop of the web-based "Best Cities" organisation, brought hundreds of influential tourist-business tourists to Cape Town.

The boost given by the CTICC to the city's event hosting capacity and image was such that in 2005 the International Congress and Convention Association ranked Cape Town thirtieth on the list of world convention cities, joint with Vancouver, Glasgow and Sydney.[10] There were no other African cities in the top-100 list; Cairo, Johannesburg and Durban each accommodated less than ten formally-rated international conferences in 2004. In 2004 Cape Town staged more than half such congresses held in South Africa. In 2005 the CTICC hosted 367 events, fifty more than in the previous year. Visitor numbers swelled by 70,000. Among several major conferences scheduled for 2006 is the International Bicycle Planning Conference, Velo Mondiale, an event for which Cape Town outbid Bogota, New Delhi, Osaka, and Beijing in 2002. The meeting is the first such to be held in the southern hemisphere. Other major conferences booked at the CTICC will set new records.[11] However clichéd, e-postcards and travel mementos sent and taken home by returning business tourists export images of Cape Town that are invaluable generators of leisure tourism. Tackiness is avoidable: the wire art model of Table Bay that is on display in the World's Most Beautiful Bays Museum in Toronto manages to break the mold and promote indigenous craft.

The commercial ripple effect from the CTICC has been and will be considerable (Ingram, 2004). During its construction, CTICC contributed R1.2bn to the central city, and created 4,000 direct jobs, (August 2003). Projections are that in the first ten years of its life, the CTICC will inject R11.2bn into the Western Cape economy, and that by 2012 it will have yielded R1.03bn in tax, created 15,000 jobs and generated R5.6bn in indirect household income. If the CTICC does indeed generate 200,000 new visitor bed nights by 2012 (and an additional 570,000 new visitor bed nights from induced tourism), the net foreign exchange earnings of R3.3bn will catalyse more than R1bn in ancillary new tourism and leisure investments in the area (Cape Africa, Vol. 2, 2001). The direct and indirect contributions made by the CTICC to Cape Town's economy will be enhanced from early 2007 when exhibition space will increase by 1,200m². Floors in a new 12,000m² office tower started selling at the end of 2005. Negotiation has started with government for acquisition of the adjacent dockside Customs House, an underused office tower block.

Four new quality hotels have been built across the road from the CTICC.[12] Four upmarket hotels had already opened in the 1990s at the V&A within a short drive. Other hotels in the neighbourhood have been extended and modified.[13] Since 2000, more than 1,000 rooms have been added to the stock of short-term accommodation in fifty-eight hotels and guesthouses in the central city and 1,600 more rooms are being provided in six new hotels under construction. Hotel building has sustained 39,000 construction jobs. The new hotels in design and under construction include one in the shell of the vacant Huguenot Memorial Hall adjacent to the Gardens. A fifth up-market V&A hotel with adjacent time-share units and island chalets will be built in 2006 in the Marina, a gated residential community nestling round the edges of the historic harbor.

Crowning the provision of new tourist accommodation in central Cape Town is a 180-room six-star hotel that is being retro-fitted into the historic Reserve Bank building at prestigious Rhodes-Mandela place. Conversion of exquisite Art Deco commercial buildings in central Cape Town has already created a range of boutique hotels.[14] Luxurious accommodation is also mushrooming in historic private homes in suburbs close to the inner city. Self-catering loft apartments in renovated buildings, and new-build studio apartments, provide alternative interesting private-rent accommodation downtown. They all succour heritage tourism. At the inexpensive end of the short-term accommodation scale, the nineteen backpacker lodges in Cape Town cater for that thriving tourist sector (Visser, 2003c). Government's information website boasts that Cape Town is probably the most popular backpacker destination in the world, and has more hostels than any other city.

Despite significantly increased tourism capacity, Cape Town continues to wrestle and juggle episodic and seasonal visitor numbers.[15] The sheer physical shape of a city hemmed in by seas and mountains puts considerable pressure on streets and parking in peak season. Surplus out-of-season accommodation and staffing is an unwanted diseconomy. Marketing the winter attractions of Cape Town to consumers is a clear priority for producers. As regards accommodation, friends and families continue to absorb hordes of summer holiday-makers (table 11.5) as they always have. But the pressure mounts. Two sport-tourism events deliver a sharp shock on two separate weekends each year when the city is besieged by some 12,000 entrants into the Two-Oceans ultra- and half-marathon, and approximately 40,000 entrants into the world's largest timed bicycle challenge (around the Peninsula). The cost-benefit ratio of the deluge might not be all that different from lesser events such as the annual extreme wave surfing competition, and various regular national football, rugby and cricket tournaments. Cape Town hosted matches in the World Cup Rugby and Cricket tournaments, and, thanks to a new domed stadium, is likely to host a semi-final match in the 2010 Soccer World Cup.

Cape Town's attempts to grasp single city, mega-tourism events include, most notably, the unsuccessful bid in 1996 to host the 2004 Olympic Games. The failed bid for the 2010 Gay Games was of a lesser order. Linking the Olympic bid strongly to urban social transformation elevated the city's bid above rival South African cities, but claims about its infrastructural capacity were probably inflated—the incapacitating effect of a series of electrical power cuts in the city during 2005 (and their damaging effect on tourism) is salutary. Despite failure, the Olympic bid helped raise Cape Town's profile, drew the attention of prospective visitors, and created a favorable image (Padayachee, 1997; Hiller, 2000). Lesser sporting events continue to dazzle sports fanatics passing through Cape Town en route to coastal golf tournaments and, not least, en route to trans-oceanic destinations: in 2005/2006 competitors and support teams for the quadrennial Volvo Ocean Race (round-the-world) are estimated to have pumped more than R225 million into the local economy during their brief stopover. The windfall would have been enhanced during simultaneous preparations for the start of the eleventh yacht race across the South Atlantic. The 2007 World Squash Master's championships will be less spectacularly monetised sport tourism, but one that nonetheless promotes South Africa's "Mother City."

This favorite moniker of Cape Town has maternal connotations that have some traction in contemporary South African tourism. Millions of tourists have "discovered" the city in the last decade, and the reproduction and nurturing of tourism in such an intrinsically captivating place seems assured. Urban tourism in Cape Town is well established and well regarded. Positive referrals multiply geometrically. But, as sports competitors know well, complacency is folly, exhaustion can set in, and ratings have to be re-earned continually. Imagination will be needed to refresh, reinvent and re-script a tourism product and experience that is so palpably tied to stunning but static site and situation.

Even if they wished to, tourism marketers could not easily remodel the dramatic geographical staging. Yet this elemental facet of tourism in Cape Town is under pressure from the volume of human visitors. Tourists are re-making Cape Town in other ways too. They reinforce spatial enclaves, help to reproduce symbolic boundaries between privileged and underprivileged, producers and consumers, wealthy and poor, and destabilize and even twist the categories of outsider (resident) and insider (visitor). The challenge is to confront and deal with what post-apartheid Cape Town is (in danger of) becoming, and to recognise the limits of its mothering. Writing in a travel magazine whose readers rank the city so highly (Travel & Leisure, February 2003), one of South Africa's most astringent commentators, Riaan Malan (an outsider seduced into residing in Cape Town), remarked that one of the planet's "most stylish tourist destinations" was already "a city of delusions, a generically Western whites-only moon base in Africa."

Acknowledgement

Thanks to Mark Boekstein for the Convention Bureau statistical source, for a text reference, for answering queries, and for checking the penultimate version.

Notes

1. 2001/02 sample surveys and interviews probing the sources of international visitor information and tourist expectations, (dis)likes, memories and images are analysed in detail by Prayag (2003).
2. In Cape Town, Green Point lighthouse (South Africa's oldest: 1824) had 832 visitors in 2003 & 2004.
3. On the specific effect in the historic Waterkant enclave, see Visser (2004a).
4. Cape Town's Grand West Casino concedes the hold of wilderness in South African tourism by advertising its product as 'the best game watching in Africa'.
5. Walking trails beyond central Cape Town include four historic walks in Wynberg, one through Witteboom, a previously coloured group area that has a Malay orientation. A new venture targeted at car-hire tourists is pre-recorded in-car audio guides triggered by in-vehicle sensors and road-side transmitters.
6. The first language of Cape Town's international tourists is English (53%), German (18%), French (5%). For domestic visitors the proportions are English (52%), Afrikaans (33%), Xhosa (2%) (Cape Town Convention Bureau, 2004).
7. The century-old minstrel-parade along the CBD streets at New Year (Martin, 1999; Baxter, 2001) is a unique cultural expression in South Africa, but not a tourist attraction on the scale of city carnivals like Rio de Janeiro's.
8. An Anglo-Zulu phrase connoting the ceaseless chasing away of Africans.
9. Launching a Cape Flats Tourism Framework document, a senior city tourism official likened the prospect to Bilbao's Guggenheim Museum, the London Eye and Sydney's Opera House (Cape Argus, 14 December 2005), but better parallels are London's Tate Modern and Johannesburg's Turbine Hall.
10. The world's top 100 convention cities included Barcelona (1), Vienna (2), Singapore (3), Rio de Janeiro (27), Melbourne (29), Brisbane (34), Montreal (35) and Shanghai (36).
11. 2006: International Congress of Local Government Leaders; Planning Africa 2006; Airports Council International World Annual General Assembly & Exhibition; World Autism Congress; Annual Convention of the Society of International Urologists (6,000 delegates); 2009: International Diabetes Federation Conference (10,000 delegates); Federation of Gynaecologists and Obstetricians (8,000 delegates).
12. Arabella Sheraton (500 beds); Cullinan; Holiday Inn; Protea (North Wharf).
13. The Capetonian; Tulbagh; Protea (Jetty Square & Victoria Junction).
14. Metropole; Urban Chic; Cape Heritage; Hippo.
15. Indicatively, the number of weekly international flights using Cape Town airport dropped from 54 in summer to 26 in winter 2005 (Business Day, 17 August 2005). Facilitating air charters into Cape Town by northern hemisphere holiday operators may not shift their winter escape packages and may simply increase the 15% of international tourists who travel on organised tours to Cape Town.

References

Baxter, L. M., 2001: Continuity and change in Cape Town's Coon carnival: the 1960s and 1970s. *African Studies*, 60, 87-106.

Bennett, A., 2004: The Cape of Storms, in A. Bennett, and R. George, (Eds.), *South African Travel and Tourism Cases*, Van Schaik, Pretoria, 39-49.

Bologna, S., 2000: The Construction of South African Heritage: a Study of Tourism to Robben Island and Cape Town Townships, Department of Anthropology, University of Cape Town.

Cape Town Convention Bureau 2004, 1999-2003: Trends & Outlook Cape Town.

Coetzer, N. R., 2003: The Production of the City as a White Space: Representing and Restructuring Identity and Architecture, Cape Town 1892-1936, Unpublished DPhil. Thesis, University College London, London.

Dodson, B. and Killian, D., 1998: From port to playground: the redevelopment of the Victoria and Albert waterfront, Cape Town, in D. Tyler, Y. Guerrier, and M. Robertson, (Eds.), *Managing Tourism in Cities*, Wiley, New York, 139-162.

Dondolo, L., 2002: The Construction of Public History and Tourist Destinations in Cape Town's Townships: A Study of Routes, Site and Heritage. Unpublished MA dissertation, University of the Western Cape.

Dyssel, M., 2006: "Elevating" township tourism: Khayelitsha's Look Out Hill, in S. Cornelissen, I. Demhardt, A. van Niekerk and W. Thomas, (Eds.), *Tourism in South Africa's Western Cape: A Reader* (in press).

Elder, G., 2004: Love for sale: marketing gay male (p)leisure space in contemporary Cape Town, South Africa in J. Seager, and L. Nelson, (Eds.), *Companion to Feminist Geography*, Blackwell, Oxford, 578-589.

Elder, G., 2005: Somewhere, over the rainbow: Cape Town, South Africa, as a "gay destination," in L. Ouzgane, and R. Morrell, (Eds.), *African Masculinities,* Palgrave, New York, 43-59.

Foster, J., 2003: "Land of Contrasts" or "Home we have always known"?: the SAR&H and the imaginary geography of White South African nationhood, 1910-1930, *Journal of Southern African Studies*, 29, 657-680.

George, R., 2001: The impact of crime on international tourist numbers to Cape Town, *Crime Prevention and Community Safety*, 3(3), 19-30.

George, R., 2003a: Tourists' fear of crime while on holiday in Cape Town, *Crime Prevention and Community Safety*, 5(1), 13-26.

George, R., 2003b: Tourists' perceptions of safety and security while visiting Cape Town, *Tourism Management*, 24, 575-585.

Goudie, S. C., Khan, F. and Killian, D., 1999: Transforming tourism: Black empowerment, heritage and identity beyond apartheid, *South African Geographical Journal*, 81, 22-31.

Hiller, H. H., 2000: Mega-events, urban boosterism and growth strategies: an analysis of the objectives and legitimations of the Cape Town 2004 Olympic bid, *International Journal of Urban and Regional Research*, 24, 439-458.

Ingram, Z., 2004: Cape Town International Convention Centre, in A. Bennett, and R. George, (Eds.), *South African Travel and Tourism Cases*, Van Schaik, Pretoria, 50-57.

Low, I., 2003: Space and reconciliation: Cape Town and the South African City under transformation, *Urban Design International*, 8(4), 223-246.

Marks, R. and Bezzoli, M., 2001: Palaces of desire: Century City, Cape Town, and the ambiguities of development, *Urban Forum*, 12, 27-47.

Martin, D. C., 1999: *Coon Carnival: New Year in Cape Town, Past to Present*, David Philip, Cape Town.

McEachern, C., 1997: From surveillance to the tourist gaze: township tours in the new South Africa, in P. Ahluwalia, and P. Nursery-Bray, (Eds.), *Post-colonialism: Culture and Identity in Africa*, Nova Science Publishers, Commack, NY, 135-151.

Padayachee, T., 1997: Olympics or not, the bid makes a difference: Cape Town 2004, *Urban Forum,* 8(1), 109-116.

Prayag, G., 2003: An Investigation into International Tourists' Perceptions of Cape Town as a Holiday Destination: One Destination—an Unforgettable Experience, Unpublished MBusSc. Thesis, University of Cape Town.

Quesada, L. L., 2005: The Role of Provincial Government Support in the Development of Black-Owned Small Tourism Business in the City of Cape Town, Unpublished MComm Thesis, University of the Western Cape, Bellville.

Resnick, L., 1997: The other side of the sun: a guided tour to Cape Town's townships, *Journal of African Travel-Writing,* 2, 16-20.

Robins, S., 2000: City sites: multicultural planning and the post-apartheid city, in S. Nuttall and C-A. Michael, (Eds.), *Senses of Culture: South African Cultural Studies,* Oxford University Press, Cape Town, 408-415.

Rule, S., Viljoen, J., Zama, S., Struwig, J., Langa, Z. and Bouare, O., 2004: Visiting friends and relatives: South Africa's most popular form of domestic tourism, in C. M. Rogerson, and G. Visser, (Eds.), *Tourism and Development Issues in Contemporary South Africa,* Africa Institute of South Africa, Pretoria, 78-101.

Strange, C. and Kempa, M., 2003: Shades of dark tourism: Alcatraz and Robben Island, *Annals of Tourism Research,* 30, 386-405.

van Sittert, L., 2003: The bourgeois eye aloft: Table Mountain in the Anglo urban middle class imagination c1891-1952, *Kronos,* 29, 161-190.

Visser, G., 2002: Gay tourism in South Africa: issues from the Cape Town experience, *Urban Forum,* 13, 85-94.

Visser, G., 2003a: Gay men, leisure space and South African cities: the case of Cape Town. *Geoforum,* 34, 123-137.

Visser, G., 2003b: Gay men, tourism and urban space: reflections on Africa's 'gay capital." *Tourism Geographies,* 5, 168-189.

Visser, G., 2003c: The local development impacts of backpacker tourism, *Urban Forum,* 14, 264-293.

Visser, G., 2004a: The world wide web and tourism in South Africa, C.M. Rogerson, and G. Visser, (Eds.), *Tourism and Development Issues in Contemporary South Africa,* Africa Institute of South Africa, Pretoria, 335-354.

Visser, G., 2004b: Second homes and local development: issues arising from Cape Town's de Waterkant, *GeoJournal,* 60), 259-271.

Vos, K., 2004: Starlight cruises, in A. Bennett and R. George, (Eds.), *South African Travel and Tourism Cases,* Van Schaik, Pretoria, 211-220.

Wamema, J., 2005: Accommodating Domestic Tourists in Township Environments: A Comparative Study of Kampala (Uganda) and Cape Town (South Africa), Unpublished M Public Admin. Thesis, University of the Western Cape, Bellville.

Ward, K., 1997: "Captive audiences": remembering and forgetting the history of slavery in Cape Town, South Africa, in P. Ahluwalia, and P. Nursery-Bray, (Eds.), *Postcolonialism: Culture and Identity in Africa,* Nova Science Publishers, Commack, NY, 153-173.

Worden, N., 1994: Unwrapping history: the Cape Town Waterfront, *Public Historian,* 16(2), 33-50.

Worden, N. and van Heyningen, E., 1996: Signs of the times: tourism and public history at Cape Town's Victoria and Alfred Waterfront, *Cahiers d'Études Africaines,* 36(141/142), 215-236.

12

Urban Tourism in Durban

Robert Preston-Whyte and Dianne Scott

For over a century, Durban has been recognized as a primary tourism destination (Swanson, 1964) with visitors from the hinterland and overseas drawn by the balmy subtropical climate, warm seas and inviting beaches to a city presided over by Africa's largest and busiest harbor (KwaZulu-Natal Tourism Authority, 2006a). These initial features provided the catalyst for the early development of the beachfront, mimicking similar developments in Britain, and branding the city with images and narratives of "sun, sand, and surf" (Grant, 1992; Preston-Whyte, 2001). "If Johannesburg has a business culture and Cape Town has a culture culture, Durban has a beach culture," proclaims South African Travel Experiences (2006:1), thereby underlining the iconic nature of the seaside.

From 1900 to 1980, urban tourism, which was largely restricted to the beachfront, saw successive phases that echoed Butler's (1980) tourist area cycle of evolution. Initially, beachfront development was shaped and inspired by British cultural hegemony. After World War II, the invasion of visitors from the industrial heartland in the interior of South Africa, as well as the segregation of beaches by race in accordance with apartheid policies, led by the 1970s, to a decline in visitor numbers as many English-speaking visitors and Durban residents began to view the beach as a vulgar, shabby, and tasteless place (Holford and Kantorwich, 1968: Grant, 1992). Given the "pariah status" of South Africa during this period, international tourists were not available to swell visitor numbers (Rogerson and Visser, 2004), and by the early-1980s the decline in domestic tourism market precipitated the City Council to begin a thorough beachfront refurbishment. This renovation positioned the beaches to accommodate a new wave of tourists when the beaches were racially desegregated in December 1989 (Preston-Whyte, 2001).

Urban tourism in contemporary Durban has expanded beyond the turbulence of the 1990s, when grime and avoidance by white tourists were linked to racial constructions in the media and elsewhere (Durrheim and Dixon, 2001). Eleven years into democracy, the integration of South Africa into the global economy, institutional initiatives in marketing strategy and transformation policy, public-private ventures, and the cultural and environmental assets of the city, have led to an increasingly sophisticated and expanded set of urban tourist opportunities and drivers, although the beachfront remains the primary destination.

Many of these drivers are common to other urban centers, some in direct competition with Durban for the international and domestic tourism market. For Durban, the warning signals are clear. Since 1997, a decline in domestic tourist numbers and tourism revenue has been recorded in KwaZulu-Natal, attributed largely to issues of "grime, personal safety, and "tired" products" (Deloitte and Touche, 2002: 35). The report notes that foreign tourism to KwaZulu-Natal appears to have grown, "but not to the extent that it has increased in other areas of South Africa" (Deloitte and Touche, 2002: 2). The report by Monitor Group and Durban Unicity (2000), commissioned by the Durban Unicity to undertake a long-term economic strategy for the city, echoes the Deloitte and Touche report in noting that currently, tourism is "sluggish" and "is increasingly attracting lower value customers" (Monitor Group and Durban Unicity, 2000: 14). This means that for Durban to compete successfully with other urban centers, tourism and city planners, and their political masters, will need to make strategic choices about which tourists they wish to attract, what they can be offered, and how they will contribute to reconstruction and development. These are difficult decisions to make because they lie at the heart of debates about political transformation, equity, and social justice. Unwise decision-making and tourism planning may serve to exacerbate the generally poor economic performance of Durban that has stagnated over the last ten years (Monitor Group and Durban Unicity, 2000).

In a market where tourists are "spoilt for choice" (Deloitte and Touche, 2002: 2), the nature of drivers are important because they provide an understanding of how tourism in the city is informed by environmental considerations, local and global networks, the nature of tourism demand, government interventions, and private-public development strategies. The nature and success of existing and emergent destinations in the city then needs to be assessed. We attempt this by discussing three types of tourism spaces. These are, firstly, urban tourism sites that have been planned, developed, or orchestrated into spaces that are ordered and controlled, secondly, potential tourism spaces that are avoided by tourists because of dysfunctional social conditions and perceptions of insecurity, and finally, emerging "third spaces" where there is spontaneous integration of different identities and culture.

Urban Tourism Drivers

Urban tourism in Durban has come a long way since the first democratic election in 1994. Domestic and international demand for the consumption of beach and cultural resources has moved in step with improved linkage to the global economy and increasing levels in domestic expendable income. Rogerson and Visser (2004: 5) note that, "building on the 'Mandela' boom associated with the new democracy," the events associated with global terror have led to the "re-assessment of South Africa as a relatively 'safe' and neutral destination for international tourism." However, rumblings of discontent expressed by media reports and letters complaining of beachfront, grime and threats to personal safety (Delport, 2001; Sithole, 2001; Barford, 2005), coupled with declining domestic tourism and tourism revenue (Deloitte and Touche, 2002), have prompted extensive research funded by the KwaZulu-Natal Tourism Authority. This is intended to inform policies to reverse negative perceptions and implement "plans to make the city the world's playground" (Goldstone, 2005a). This means taking a critical look at the principal tourism drivers that we identify as the natural and built environment, globalization, tourist demand, policy-driven imperatives, and public-private partnerships.

Natural and Built Environment

Surveys carried out by the KwaZulu-Natal Tourism Authority are consistent in locating Durban as the country's premier seaside resort and the destination of the majority of visitors to the province. The natural and built environment is a powerful driver that facilitates a year-round visitor season. Spring and winter months are mild, dry, and usually cloudless, while summer months are hot and humid with cooling sea breezes. The seven kilometre-long sandy beach is developed into twelve shark-protected swimming beaches (figure 12.1) with associated changing facilities, life guards and parking. Five beaches, Umhlanga Rocks Main Beach, Bay of Plenty Beach, Addington Beach, South Beach, and Anstey's Beach, meet international standards of safety, amenities, cleanliness, and have been awarded the coveted Blue Flag status (Booth, 2005; Zulu, 2005). Water temperatures range from 20^0C to 28^0C making the sea attractive to swimmers in all seasons. Well-developed waves make Durban an internationally-recognized surfing destination while, depending on wind direction and season, the sheltering effect of the Bluff on Addington and South Beach can result in almost waveless sea conditions. Such variety accommodates both board surfers, swimmers who enjoy a more confrontational and robust encounter with the waves, and those who have a preference for swimming in calmer water.

Swimming and surfing conditions at many resort towns along the Kwa-Zulu-Natal coastline equal those at Durban. Additional drivers are therefore needed to make Durban a pre-eminent urban tourist destination. These include the availability of luxury hotels and an abundance of sophisticated restaurants and shopping opportunities that are embedded in a cultural setting that is rich in heritage and variety. However, as other coastal resorts expand their tourism marketing, identify and grow niche demand activities and learn to placate

Figure 12.1
Location of Beaches and Other Tourist Attractions in Durban

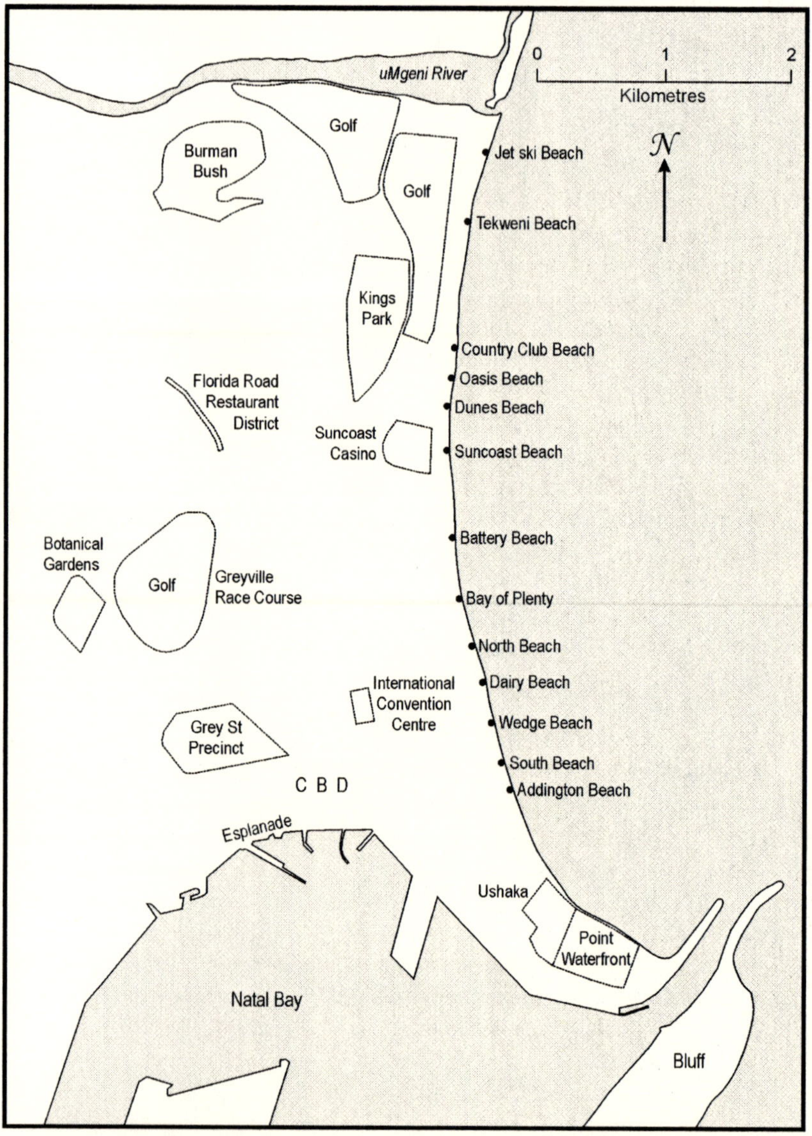

tourist fears about crime, personal safety, and corruption, Durban is in danger of losing much of its appeal for sectors of the current tourism market that are sensitive to these issues.

With the expansion of the size of the eThekweni Municipal boundary in 2000, beach areas to the north, such as Umhlanga Rocks and Umhloti, and to the south in Amanzimtoti, have added additional beach nodes that are being developed as tourist attractions (figure 12.2).

Globalization

The process of globalization and its impact on Durban accelerated after 1994 with the demise of isolationist policies associated with the apartheid regime. This has impacted on almost every facet of urban life, and transformed the city into a region that is rich in the attributes demanded by foreign tourists:

Figure 12.2
**The Extent of the eTekweni Municipality and Beach and Town
Locations beyond Durban**

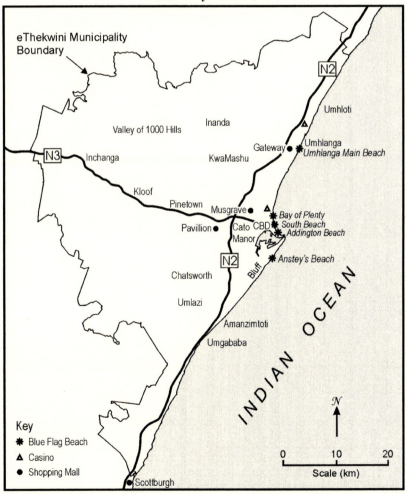

good and varied restaurants (Preston-Whyte, 1999), up-market shopping malls such as "Gateway—Theatre of Shopping" (Michel and Scott, 2005: 105) an international convention center, luxury hotels, the capacity to host world-class sporting events and excellent beach facilities. To contrast the homogenizing effect of global influences, distinctive local charm is offered in the form of township tours, Indian and African cultural sites and the transformation of a Victorian-Edwardian constructed inner city, much of which still remains, into an African and Indian urban environment that is rich in ethnic color.

That much of this transformation has taken place in the last decade, says something about the confidence that investors and municipal planners have in the future. It can be argued that much of the entrepreneurial daring and development confidence in the city results from the government's neo-liberal macro-economic policy designed to boost investor confidence. The cornerstone of this policy is the GEAR (Growth, Equity and Redistribution Programme) strategy, which is focused on attracting global investment, while a sound monetary policy, which has succeeded in bringing inflation under control, is an added incentive (Nel et al. 2003).

Over the last five years, municipal initiatives, in partnership with private developers, have instigated pro-growth developments in close proximity to the beachfront zone and integrated with it (Nel et al. 2003). These developments recognize the global trend towards the increasingly influential social construction of local places as destinations to be gazed upon (Urry, 1990; 1995) and consumed by "new tourists" (Poon, 1990) and "post-tourists" (Urry, 1990; 1995). That Durban is not immune from the influence of ideas on "theme cities" (Sorkin, 1992), urban waterfronts (Goss, 1996) and public entertainment spaces (Cybriwsky, 1999), is demonstrated by recent public-private sector beachfront developments that embody these developments. The post-modern aestheticization of the built environment has played an important role in changing the face of the tourism environment with the creation of themed entertainment and retail complexes along the beachfront (Jacobs, 1998).

However, urban tourists need more than promotional and imaging strategies that duplicate a multitude of other destinations in a homogeneous global world. Marketers and tourists alike need the differentiating power of an icon. In recognition of this deficiency, the KwaZulu-Natal Tourism Authority has enthusiastically branded KwaZulu-Natal as the Kingdom of the Zulu, with Durban envisioned as the kingdom's playground and gateway to the Kingdom (KwaZulu-Natal Tourism Authority, 2006b).

Unfortunately, Durban still lacks a recognizable icon that can compete with Cape Town's Table Mountain and its wine lands and reputation for cultural sophistication. Like Auckland in New Zealand, that markets itself as the "City of Sails," Durban could be presented as the 'City of Beaches." Instead, a politically-driven vision embraces the potential of cultural tourism. The dubious impact of political logic in tourism marketing aside, Durban's ability to attract international tourists is hampered by the absence of long-haul air linkages. Runway length at Durban International Airport cannot be extended to accommodate larger passenger aircraft and the long-delayed King Shaka International Airport is still far from complete (Chamber Digest, 2002).

Tourist Demand

Although the natural drivers have changed little since the development of the ocean frontage, from 1900 onward cultural drivers have responded to political and economic change (Grant, 1992; Preston-Whyte, 2001) in ways that have influenced tourist demand. In the Monitor Group and Unicity (2000) survey, it is reported that domestic tourists, categorised into emerging tourists, young up-and-coming, fast-paced, established-and-settled, and older folks, far surpass the number of international tourists. The "emerging" tourists are higher in number than all other categories. However, they remain a relatively short time in the city and spend little money. Although international tourists number far less, their spending power is far higher, up to R2000 per day (Monitor Group and Durban Unicity, 2000).

Since 1994, the transformation of South African society has changed the pattern of tourism demand in Durban, and this is reflected in the emergent needs of the new black tourist and the growth of the black middle-class. In terms of numbers of visitors, if not in per capita contribution to the economic welfare of the city, these visitors elevate the Durban beachfront to the primary tourist destination in the city. A survey revealed that 80.4 percent of tourists select the beach as their recreation of choice (Monitor Group and Durban Unicity, 2000).

While white domestic and international tourists also visit the beaches, although in smaller numbers, this group also show an interest in wildlife, heritage and nature tourism, and use Durban as a springboard to these destinations within the city and province. For example, 19.6 percent show an interest in visiting an African cultural village and 13.7 percent visit Indian temples (Monitor Group and Durban Unicity, 2000). Durban's tourist strength appears, therefore, to be in attracting different types of tourists. By providing something for everybody (Monitor Group and Durban Unicity, 2000), the city seems able to meet most demands.

In recognition of the arrival of the emergent black tourist, both domestic and from other African countries, as well as international tourists, Durban has positioned itself as a tourist destination within the Kingdom of the Zulu. As the "gateway to Africa" the rich variety of tourist opportunities are marketed by drawing attention to the city's international conference facilities, sporting fixtures, Indian cultural footprints, African cultural experiences in the Valley of a Thousand Hills, black townships, shopping facilities, and, of course, the beach.

The dynamism and volatility of tourism is an abiding characteristic of the tourist industry. While city entrepreneurs and municipal tourism managers continually seek to attract tourists by skilful marketing and adroit product development, tourists possess the luxury of a smorgasbord of choice. Given that the goal of the average urban tourist is to relax and enjoy what the city has to offer, issues of transformation, black economic empowerment, and municipal governance are not their concern until their health, comfort, safety, or security is perceived to be at risk. Then tourists decide to visit more congenial locations in other cities, often advised by tourist operators who are equally conscious of the need to keep customers satisfied.

Sadly, Durban has had a bad press about crime and grime. Despite valiant efforts by the municipality to green the city, regulate informal pavement vendors and control litter, the beachfront and inner city is still perceived to be dangerous and dirty (Delport, 2001; Barford, 2005; Sookha and Naidu, 2005). An easily-tested indicator of public fear and insecurity is the number of tourists visible on the beachfront and in the inner city after dark. Given that hotel managers warn their clients about the dangers of venturing outside (Allen and Brennan, 2004), it is not surprising that these spaces are utterly empty and desolate once the sun has set. An exception to this is the Surfing Festival held every July, when the central beachfront is illuminated, night surfing competitions are held and the public spaces of the promenade are leased out to small retail outlets.

Policy-Driven Imperatives

At a national level, tourism was viewed as a driver for economic growth only after 1994 when it was included in the reconstruction and development goals of the new democratically elected government. This policy-driven imperative was followed in 1996 by a White Paper on the Development and Promotion of Tourism (South Africa, 1996) and the Tourism in GEAR Strategy Document (South Africa, 1998). The effect of these policies was to kick-start the marketing and management of tourism in Durban and the rest of the province through the development of the KwaZulu-Natal Tourism Authority.

The management of tourism, which is concerned with the planning process and the control of tourism development, took place against a background of earlier concern over the deterioration of the Durban beachfront and coastal and seaside resources in general. Change for the Durban beachfront came in the early-1980s as a product of political upheaval in the City Council (Preston-Whyte, 1987) and the appointment of a Beach and City Steering Committee. The outcome was an exercise in post-modern reconstruction that attempted to reconstruct the pre-World War II beachfront landscape. A start was also made on the development of policies for coastal zone management by the Council for the Environment (1989; 1991) and, in 1998, a Green Paper on Coastal Policy (Coastal Management Policy Programme, 1998) followed, in 2000, by a White Paper on Sustainable Coastal Development (Coastal Management Policy Programme, 2000).

The concept of "responsible tourism" in which government and business are expected to cooperate in the development, management and marketing of the tourism industry with a high priority placed on the incorporation of local communities, is a central theme of national and local policy goals. Such concepts form part of the hegemony of post-apartheid transformational planning and inform black economic empowerment strategies and beachfront and city planning (Rogerson and Visser, 2004).

Public-Private Partnerships

One of the key outcomes of the adoption of the GEAR imperatives for economic growth of the city, along with privatisation, is the engagement in public-private partnerships for economic development. The driving effect of public-private sector involvement in tourism development in Durban has led to the creation of uShaka Island and Point Waterfront, the International Convention Centre, Suncoast Casino, and proposed new Small Craft Harbour (Nel et al. 2003).

These initiatives send several important signals. The first is about confidence. Unlike public tax-based financing, private organisations are more careful about the return on their investments, and are unlikely to become involved in high-risk developments. This means deeper research into profitability, sustainability, global trends, and tourist behavior. The second signal is about balanced objectives. While private ventures place a strong emphasis on consumption and the ensuing profits, the public sector tends to view its responsibilities around issues of social and environmental impact, political transformation, and equity and associated policy and regulations. Given South Africa's previous discriminatory legislation, this is an important consideration.

In general, public-private partnerships are dominated by large pro-growth developments. This is in line with GEAR policy that also envisages the alleviation of poverty through creation of a new group of entrepreneurs who would set up small, medium and micro-scale enterprises (SMMEs) that would lead to a "trickle down" effect and reduce poverty. Unfortunately, this class of operators or service providers in the tourism sector is largely absent in Durban causing Nel et al. (2003) to note the dominance of pro-growth initiatives in Durban, as opposed to pro-poor. The only evidence of provision for small-scale operators is the construction of thatched shelters along the beachfront for crafters who sell their local and globally produced wares.

Emergent and Languishing Tourism Spaces

The globalization-localization relationship is a useful integrative tool with which to appreciate and assess the impact on urban tourism of global capitalism, economic restructuring, and social change (Chang and Huang, 2004). The relational nature of the two scales reflects, "a deepening enmeshment of the local and global such that the impact of distant events is magnified while even the most local developments may come to have enormous global consequences" (Held et al., 1999: 15). Such ideas form part of the approach adopted by planners, marketers and the media in presenting Durban as a blend of cosmopolitan connections and local allure.

Yet, on a daily basis, newspapers, radio, and television reports remind their audiences of the dangers they face from muggers and hijackers. These reports impact on tourists in various ways, from avoidance of Durban to watchful participation (Hammond, 2005). For the perceptive tourist there is an additional tension brought about by an awareness of moral issues that are endemic to tourist areas. Allen and Brennan (2004: 158) comment on this problem:

> Our tourist, sitting on the beach in the early evening sun …is brought, potentially, face to face with the suffering of others, with the need to make a living for the beachfront workers, legal, and low-paid, or illegal with wide variations in income, such as the prostitutes and their pimps. If necessary, the economics of survival may require exploiting the international tourist who, worldwide, has the aura of an "easy touch."

Crime and perceptions of security are central problems confronting tourism development in Durban, and their impact is well understood by city planners and tourism entrepreneurs. The challenge facing these officials is the construction of safe, reassuring, and predictable tourist spaces, without resorting to unacceptable exclusionary tactics. This is a difficult task indeed, particularly in a city characterised by a history of separation and inequity and sharply bounded cultural differences and wide disparities in income. For that reason we have chosen to examine three different categories of tourism space in Durban defined by order and control, fear, and disorder and so-called "third spaces."

Spaces of Order and Control

One of the key characteristics of post-modern cities is the increasingly insecure nature of urban life causing walls and security devices to structure and control the spaces through which city dwellers move. While these "carceral cities" (Davis, 1990; Mabin, 1995) are a global phenomenon, in South African cities, spaces of fear are exacerbated by the high levels of crime caused by unemployment and poverty.

Public spaces, which should be open to all citizens, particularly if they form a key tourist attraction, are often "secured" in order to create a safe place for tourists. Jacobs (1961) argues that, "safe public spaces manage to produce a network of relationships which balance people's rights to privacy and their coexistent desire for degrees of contact, excitement or assistance" (cited in Pile et al., 1999: 107). Thus these spaces must have the "magical" capacity to "bring large

number of strangers together and transform their presence into a "safety asset'"
(Pile et al., 1999: 108). Natural surveillance is a soft form of social control, so
where there are a number of people, the space would be safe. This is the same
as the concept of "eyes on the street" (McLaughlin and Muncie, 1999). The
concept of safety in numbers is, therefore, an important key to securing the
Durban beachfront. This has led to the use of specific areas for hosting events,
which, by attracting crowds, creates relatively safer spaces.

The Durban beachfront is the primary tourism zone in the city. As a public
space it is free for all to use. This is unlike other tourist spaces in the city, where
tourist activities take place in private secure spaces, such as shopping malls,
Indian temples, bird parks, and the like. However, city dwellers and tourists
who enter the beachfront zone have to negotiate "the fears, dangers, risks,
and pleasures" associated with being in the company of strangers (Pile et al.,
1999:106). In the multicultural environment of Durban, one of the "pleasures"
that tourists come to enjoy is the cultural variety evident in public spaces such
as the beach. The beachfront promenade facilitates this activity with plans
underway to enable visitors to walk virtually from Country Club beach to the
Point. The main aim of this development is to provide tourists with, "minimum
involvement but maximum reassurance" (Pile et al., 1998: 107).

Tourists are not the only people attracted to the beachfront as a public space.
Tourism spaces, particularly if they are public spaces, are key areas attracting the
unemployed to find opportunities for informal employment. There are a large number of car guards employed along the Durban beachfront providing an important
security service to visitors. Another growing informal activity, which is adding
character to the beachfront, is the creation of sand sculptures by sand artists.

Features of the "carceral city" (Davis, 1990; Mabin, 1995) in which attempts
are made to order and control beachfront space, occur through the privatisation
of public spaces by leasing them to private organisations as a public-private
venture. Faced with the realities of increasing poverty, high levels of urban
crime and an increasing gap between the rich and the poor, the privatisation
of public space is a strategy in which business takes on the responsibility of
providing safe and predictable tourist spaces, and thereby ensures their profitability (Zukin, 1995).

A public-private partnership is formed where public space is leased to private sector companies to operate their business activities. The business, and the
buffer zone around it, become safer through constant use and the employment
of security guards, and improved surveillance. In this way the space becomes
peopled and used, and the private sector operation has a vested interest in securing "good order" through creating a "lively and convivial" active space (Pile et
al., 1999: 109). The engagement of a public sector partner to secure and manage
a zone of public space provides the capacity to make the space safer.

Restaurants that operate along the beachfront promenade, which have seating
areas on the promenade, provide an example of such spaces. A large develop-

ment of this kind is the Suncoast Casino situated on the beachfront, where a public-private agreement with the city has resulted in the Casino managing the security of the area by employing security guards. This includes "privatizing" the promenade and adjacent dunes and beach. For a nominal sum, patrons who sit on the grassed dunes in front of the casino, occupy a controlled and secure public space. Even more secure is the uShaka Marine world, where visitors pay to enter a simulated marine environment and snorkel with the fish. The latest development, the first of its kind on the beachfront, is a small restaurant, spanning the boardwalk and the beach at North Beach, where tourists can enjoy their meals on the sand.

In terms of beachfront planning, the eThekweni Municipality is slowly demolishing a number of old leased facilities to make way for new developments that form part of the beachfront development plan and the inner city renewal plan undertaken through the Inner Thekwini Regeneration and Urban Management Programme (iTrump) (eThekweni Municipality, 2004). Examples are relics of modernist tourist venues from the 1960s and 1970s such as the restaurant at Blue Lagoon, and the Sea World and Cineland sites at South Beach. They are to be replaced by developments regarded as more appropriate to the time, such as the beach amphitheater in the old Sea World site (Goldstone, 2005b)

Another strategy to secure and order beachfront space is the establishment of "bridging activities" to keep people in the area and thereby "crowd out" socially disruptive elements. This strategy operates reasonably successfully for the duration of specific events. Examples include international surfing competitions with the concomitant temporary establishment of large numbers of small retail outlets on the promenade that remain open at night, night surfing events which requires the beach and surf to be illuminated, and the Hari Krishna religious festival.

In high season, December/January, July and Easter, additional policing is introduced with police on horseback as a form of social control. Policed spaces reinforce the idea of "rule-governed" spaces where accepted norms dictate who may do what in that space. Private security guards are also employed around the beachfront restaurants and along the uShaka promenade. Although this is a public space, there is a "soft ordering" via surveillance techniques and policing to weed out those who are perceived to constitute a threat to the safety of visitors. However, a degree of "benign disorder" is crucial so that castle builders, mime-artists, and cultural dancers can contribute to the vitality of these spaces (Pile et al., 1999).

One of the key and growing attractions for foreign tourists is to experience the material products of African culture. The craft sellers on the Durban beachfront, who previously offered their wares on pavements, have been confined to controlled spaces above North Beach. Thatched "Africanized" shelters are available for vendors who must have valid permits to operate. This management and regulation of informal sector activities is part of the broader policy of the eThekweni Municipality to control the informal economy and regulate its spatial location.

An often-neglected group, who also need to cope with problems of crime and insecurity, are the beachfront residents. The response to this problem in most beachfront residential apartments is the installation of their own controlled spaces with underground or secure parking and security guards at the entrance who check visitor credentials. These apartments effectively become gated communities.

Away from the beachfront, ordered spaces that are frequently visited by urban tourists are restaurants and shopping malls. In addition to security, restaurant patrons seek good food that is efficiently served in spaces constructed to create an ambience that facilitates social interaction and a sense of well-being. Until the late-1980s, such spaces were located mainly along the beachfront, in the CBD or in hotels. However, the gradual deterioration of the business district, accompanied by perceptions of insecurity and loss of identity by whites, led to the flight of restaurants to shopping malls and restaurant areas in the suburbs (Preston-Whyte, 1999). Contemporary tourists seeking a restaurant experience would look in the Florida Road area where restaurants have clustered, attracted by the charm of Victorian and Edwardian architecture, tree-lined roads, and parking watched over by regulated car guards. Musgrave Shopping Centre, Gateway Mall, and The Pavilion provide other restaurant clusters in secure surroundings.

The location of shopping malls outside of the central business district has been a worldwide phenomenon, driven by the availability of space and flight from the perceived disorder of the city center (Michel and Scott, 2005). The origin of Durban malls is no different. Since the development of the Musgrave Shopping Centre in the 1970s, and its early success as a destination for shoppers who no longer wished to frequent the city center, other malls have been developed, each bigger and more splendid than the previous one. The Pavilion proved a considerable attraction forcing the refurbishment of the Musgrave Centre. This was followed by the Gateway Mall which would rank as a tourist attraction anywhere in the world.

Spaces of Fear and Disorder

Our sense of insecurity and safety is not a given condition but is a set of dynamic and "spatially situated relational understandings and reflective judgements which have to be constantly renewed in daily encounters" (Pile et al., 1999: 107). By reputation or from personal experience, there are places of fear and disorder that local visitors and tourists avoid. While spaces of order and control attract tourists, there are many spaces that have tourist potential but fail to succeed because of real and perceived security problems. These spaces acquire their reputation from media reports and word of mouth experiences.

Around 1994, the beachfront received bad press about being a dangerous and unsafe space. However, this reality and perception has slowly changed and only certain parts of the beachfront at certain times and seasons now remain as spaces of fear and disorder. A further factor that has impacted on the use and safety of public spaces in the inner city and beachfront is the growth and legalisation of the informal sector that uses public space predominantly for trading. The eThekweni Municipality's Inner City Renewal Planning process has been putting in place a range of measures to secure the inner city and beachfront area and regulate informal activity. Notable success has been achieved, for example, in the Warwick Junction area.

Point Road, historically a "red-light district" leads to the Point Waterfront. It is perceived to be a space of fear and disorder and this may account for the lacklustre performance of this area by night. Here the squalid streets, vandalised buildings, presence of the homeless, drug dealers and prostitutes has made the area a "no-go" area, through which visitors have to travel to reach the revitalised Point Waterfront. Similar perceptions of insecurity as a tourist area are associated with the "back of beach" streets of the beachfront.

Spaces of fear also vary temporally and seasonally. At night, the entire beachfront is deemed unsafe, judging by the lack of visitor activity. Similar perceptions prevail in certain areas in the low season when there are fewer people. The streets behind the beachfront hotels, the inner city, and the Grey Street area with its colorful Indian shops, the Workshop area and the Victoria Embankment by night are all perceived to be relatively unsafe (Sookha and Naidu, 2005).

Third Spaces

While urban tourists may be influenced by concerns for personal safety to seek spaces of order and control, the experiences of individual tourists would be greatly diminished if they lacked the opportunity of transcending, even for a short time, the world of binary opposites structured around the conflicting world of them and us, danger and safety, freedom and control, nature and culture.

But how and where are such experiences to be found? Pile et al. (1999: 106) note the "delicate balancing act of assessing and negotiating the fears, dangers, risks, and pleasures associated with the presence of strangers in public places." This negotiation of fear and safety places the tourist and local user of public space in a "third space" (Soja, 1996). This is a space of challenge, risk and excitement, where the person leaves the safety of their known reality and puts them in the position of a new experience or encounter that will transform them.

It takes courage to engage with the new and as yet unknown. There are spaces in the city where this can occur, and the beachfront is such a place. Since 1994, spaces such as the beachfront, have been major sites where multicultural engagement and mixing can occur in an uncontained and organic way. Many visitors to the uShaka and Point beaches have noted that they visited this area for that reason (Scott and Oelofse, 2005).

Many writers have recognized the beach as a marginal space between land and sea where a sense of ecstasy and freedom draws on attributes from nature and culture to transcend these opposites in a way that is neither physical nor spiritual, but something in-between (Dutton 1983). Drawing on the anthropological work of Van Gennep (1909) and Turner (1974), Shields (1991) sees the beach as a occupying a cultural margin between liminality and carnival, while Fiske (1989) is concerned with the semiotic interpretation of the beach as a marginal space that is open to a range of different meanings and interpretations. Novelists such as William Golding (1954) and Alex Garland (1997) have used the setting of the beach to great effect in capturing the liminality of the beach "as a way of proceeding from the known to the unknown" (Nisbet, 1969: 4), "from the accepted symbols of the profane to the elusive, ambiguous and powerful symbols of the sacred" (Preston-Whyte, 2004: 350).

Tourists encounter and experience these marginal spaces as events, situations or opportunities in ways that are emphatically individual. For many people, the act of stepping from the paved road onto the sandy beach may be accompanied by, ... a feeling of upliftment, a frisson of awareness, a holistic sensation in which action and consciousness are merged at the moment of crossing into what we can call a liminal space (Preston-Whyte, 2004: 349).

This in-between space is recognized by religious groups and individuals who frequently use the Durban beaches as means for seeking spiritual succour (Preston-Whyte, 2004). The feeling of occupying a marginal space, free from the constraints and tensions of everyday life, also attracts groups who combine a search for identity, usually racially or culturally defined, with the need to foster socially unifying experiences (Preston-Whyte, 2001). Surfers, too, are familiar with the ecstasy of a liminal experience associated with the thrill and excitement of a successful run on a challenging wave (Farmer, 1992; Preston-Whyte, 2002; Ford and Brown, 2006)

While the beach is a powerful source of liminality for those searching for the magic of the memorable tourist experience, it is not the sole location in Durban. The Suncoast, and Sibaya Casinos constitute spaces of order and compulsion in which patrons wait in expectation for the moment of the big win, when they briefly will enter a limbo-like space in which ecstasy and excitement can be expressed without social or cultural restraints.

Concluding Comments

Tourism in Durban is the product of a range of drivers that have combined to shape the urban leisure industry into one of the most vibrant in South Africa. Lured by a benign and attractive beach environment and supported by adequate hotel accommodation, demand for Durban as a resort city has grown since 1994, particularly amongst black tourists. The beach is the primary destination although up-market shopping malls, chic restaurants and beckoning casinos bare testimony to the process of globalization.

While Durban has the reputation of being an "African" city that accommodates the recreation demand of many black visitors, the tourist industry is concerned by the city's poor international profile and the loss of high-income visitors to other destinations. Tourism planners are acutely aware of the need to enhance Durban's first world facilities, without detracting from the development needs of emerging black entrepreneurs. The result has been a series of public-private partnerships such as the International Convention Centre, Suncoast Casino, the uShaka Island and Point Waterfront development, and proposed Small Craft Harbour (Nel et al., 2003).

While policy imperatives feature black economic empowerment, and public-private partnerships signal confidence in the future, tourism demand amongst upper-income visitors is unlikely to grow until perceptions of crime are laid to rest. The power to create (or destroy) urban tourism lies in the hands of municipal decision-makers who must confront three issues. First, municipal decision-makers must recognize the existence of the fearful tourist. Allen and Brennan (2004) believe that Furedi's (2002) ideas expressed in *Culture of Fear* are worth examining as a starting point to any debate on fear:

> The evaluation of everything from the perspective of safety is a defining characteristic of contemporary society. When safety is worshipped and risks are seen as intrinsically bad, society is making a clear statement about the values that ought to guide life...Risk has become big business. Thousands of consultants provide advice on "risk analysis" and "risk management" and "risk communications." The media too has become increasingly interested in the subject, and terms like the "risk society" and "risk perception" now regularly appear in newspaper columns. ... There is a definite, anxious consensus that we must all be at risk in one way or another. Being at risk is treated as if it has become a permanent condition that exists separately from any particularly problem. Risks hover over human beings (Furedi, 2002: 4).

While the affluent (particularly white) visitor to Durban may wrestle on the one hand with conflicting feelings of guilt and remorse when confronted with poverty, and, on the other hand, a socially-constructed sense of risk, many will opt for survival in the face of perceived risk. This not only diminishes enjoyment in the holiday experience but leads to moral degeneration by eroding faith in others.

Secondly, potential tourists must be able to trust in the ability of those in positions of power to provide spaces of order and control. Trust reduces the fear of the unknown and the complexity of cross-cultural interactions, and by enhancing confidence in institutional structures may lead to levels of "altruistic trust" (Mainsbridge, 1980) where morally corrosive distrust in individuals is replaced by giving them the benefit of the doubt. Urban tourism development cannot be sustainable without trust in the action, authority, efficacy, and impartiality of public officials and the police service. Years of significant improvement towards upgrading the city to make it more appealing to visitors can be destroyed by a single report of violent crime directed towards a tourist.

Thirdly, lessons could be learnt from the strategies employed by successful coastal resorts worldwide. The mantra in these cases seems to have a common theme: the privatization of public space, the exclusion of those likely to threaten tourist perceptions of safety and security, and competent and visible policing. This last recommendation is probably the most difficult for contemporary politicians to sanction given its association with the heady whiff of elitism. Such spaces of order and control need to be developed sensitively allowing for the collective and impartial absorption of identities that pass for racial differences in South Africa.

Nel et al. (2003) point out that South African government policy obliges municipalities on the one hand to engage in social and economic development, and on the other, to stimulate economic growth and integration with the global economy. The development of the Durban beachfront and the decisions that impact on the growth of tourism in this space mirror these tensions. There in particular, city planners will have to carry out a careful balancing act between creating a globally marketable destination and addressing negative perceptions around issues of safety, security, and overcrowding.

References

Allen, G. and Brennan, F., 2004: *Tourism in the New South Africa: Social Responsibility and the Tourist Experience,* I.B. Taurus, London.

Barford, R., 2005: Beach crowds raises hackles, *Sunday Tribune,* 18 December, 4.

Booth, H., 2005: Deep blue sea, *South African Garden and Home,* December, 140-143.

Butler, R.W., 1980: The concept of a tourist area cycle of evolution: implications for management of resources, *Canadian Geographer,* 24, 5-12.

Chamber Digest (KwaZulu-Natal Region), 2002: *Durban Poised for Growth,* Durban Chamber of Commerce, Durban.

Chang, T.C. and Huang, S., 2004: Urban tourism: between the global and the local, in A.A. Lew, C.M. Hall, and A.M. Williams, (Eds.), *A Companion to Tourism,* Blackwell, Oxford, 223-234.

Coastal Management Policy Programme, 1998: *Coastal Policy Green Paper: Towards Sustainable Coastal Development in South Africa,* Department of Environmental Affairs and Tourism, Cape Town.

Coastal Management Policy Programme, 2000: *White Paper for Sustainable Coastal Coastal Development in South Africa,* Department of Environmental Affairs and Tourism, Cape Town.

Council for the Environment, 1989: *A Policy for Coastal Zone Management in the Republic of South Africa—Part 1: Principles and Objectives,* Joan Lotter Publications, Pretoria.

Council for the Environment, 1991: *A Policy for Coastal Zone Management in the Republic of South Africa – Part 2,* Academica Publications, Pretoria.

Cybriwsky, R., 1999: Changing patterns of urban public space: observations and assessments from the Tokyo and New York metropolitan areas, *Cities,* 16, 223-231.

Davis, M., 1990: *City of Quartz,* Verso Books, London.

Deloitte and Touche Consortium, 2002: KwaZulu-Natal Tourism Authority tourism product development strategy, available at: http://www.kzn.org.za/kzn/kznta/93.xml. (accessed 24 January 2006).

Delport, D., 2001: Nice from far…but it could be nicer, *Sunday Tribune*, 16 December, 3.

Durrheim, K. and Dixon, J., 2001: The role of place and metaphor in racial exclusion: South Africa's beaches as sites of shifting racialization, *Ethnic and Racial Studies*, 24, 433-450.

Dutton, G., 1983: *Sun, Sea, Surf, and Sand,* Oxford University Press, Oxford.

eThekwini Municipality 2004. Area Based Management and Development, Annual Business Plan, 2004/2005, eThekweni Municipality, Durban.

Farmer, R.J., 1992: Surfing: motivations, values and culture, *Journal of Sport Behaviour,* 15, 241-257.

Fiske, J., 1989: *Reading the Popular*, Unwin Hyman, London.

Ford, N. and Brown, D., 2006: *Surfing and Social Theory: Experience, Embodiment and Narrative of the Dream Glide,* Routledge, Oxford.

Furedi, F., 2002: *Culture of Fear: Risk Taking and the Morality of Low Expectation,* Continuum, London.

Garland, A., 1997: *The Beach*, Penguin Books, London.

Golding, W., 1954: *The Lord of the Flies*, Faber and Faber, London.

Goldstone, C. 2005a: Beach upgrade planned, *The Mercury*, 12 October,1.

Goldstone, C., 2005b: Developments to transform Durban into a mega city, *The Mercury,* 13 October, 9.

Goss, J., 1996: Disquiet on the waterfront: reflections of nostalgia and utopia in the urban archetypes of festival marketplaces, *Urban Geography*, 17, 221- 247.

Grant, L., 1992: An Historical Geography of the Durban Beachfront, Unpublished MSc thesis, University of Natal, Durban.

Hammond, P., 2005: Gangsters at work in Durban. Available at: http://www.christian-action.org.za/firearmnews/2005-01_GangstersAtWorkInDurban.htm, (accessed 24 January 2006).

Held, D., McGrew, A., Goldblatt, D., and Perraton, J., 1999: *Global Transformations: Politics, Economics and Culture*, Polity, Cambridge.

Holford, W. and Kantorwich, R., 1968: A plan for central Durban in its regional setting, City Engineers, Durban.

Jacobs, J., 1998: Staging difference: aestheticization and politics of difference in contemporary cities, in R. Fincher, and J. Jacobs, (Eds.), *Cities of Difference*, Guilford, New York, 252-278.

KwaZulu-Natal Tourism Authority, 2006a: Durban harbor, available at: http://www. durban.kzn.org.za/durban/about/129.xml (accessed 24 January 2006).

KwaZulu-Natal Tourism Authority, 2006b: The Zulu kingdom, available at: http://www. kzn.org.za/kzn/ (accessed 24 January 2006).

Mabin, A., 1995: On the problems and prospects of overcoming segregation and fragmentation in South African cities in the postmodern era, in S. Watson, and K. Gibson, (Eds.), *Postmodern Cities and Spaces,* Oxford, Blackwell, 187-198.

Mainsbridge, J., 1980: *Beyond Adversary Democracy,* Basic Books, New York..

Mclaughlin, E. and Muncie, J., 1999: Walled cities: surveillance, regulation and segregation, in S. Pile, C. Brooks, and G. Mooney, (Eds.), *Unruly Cities: Order/Disorder*, Routledge, London, 103- 148.

Michel, D. and Scott, D. 2005: The La Lucia-Umhlanga ridge as an emerging edge city, *South African Geographical Journal*, 87, 104-114.

Monitor Group and Durban Unicity, 2000: *Durban at the Watershed,* Monitor Company Inc., Durban.

Nel, E., Hill, T. and Maharaj, B., 2003: Durban's pursuit of economic development in the post-apartheid era, *Urban Forum*, 14, 223-243.

Nisbet, R.A., 1969: *Social Change and History: Aspects of the Western Theory of Development*, Oxford University Press, London.

Pile, S., Brooks, C. and Mooney, G. (Eds.), 1999: *Unruly Cities: Order/Disorder,* Routledge, London.

Poon, A., 1994: The "New Tourism" revolution, *Tourism Management*, 15(2), 91-92.

Preston-Whyte, R.A., 1987: A case study of public and press reaction to an environmental decision, *International Journal of Environmental Studies*, 30, 23-28.

Preston-Whyte, R.A., 1999: Restaurant trends in Durban, *Tourism Geographies*, 1, 443-459.

Preston-Whyte, R.A., 2001: Constructed leisure space. The seaside at Durban, *Annals of Tourism Research*, 28, 581-596.

Preston-Whyte, R.A., 2002: Constructions of surfing space at Durban, South Africa. *Tourism Geographies*, 4, 307-328.

Preston-Whyte, R.A., 2004: The beach as a liminal space, in A.A. Lew, C.M. Hall and A.M. Williams, (Eds.), *A Companion to Tourism*, Blackwell Publishing, Oxford, 349-359.

Rogerson, C. and Visser, G. (Eds.), 2004: *Tourism and Development Issues in Contemporary South Africa,* Africa Institute of South Africa, Pretoria.

Scott, D. and Oelofse, C., 2005: Beach User Survey, Durban Small Craft Harbour Social Impact Assessment, University of KwaZulu-Natal, Durban.

Shields, R., 1991: *Places on the Margin: Alternative Geographies of Modernity,* Routledge, London.

Sitole, M., 2001: Dreaming of a white Christmas, *Sunday Tribune*, December 16, 24.

Soja, E., 1996: *Thirdspace: Journeys to Los Angeles and other Real-and-Imagined Places*, Blackwell, Malden, MA.

Sookha, B. and Naidu, R., 2005: City hit by rising crime: unsafe CBD fast becoming no-go area for shoppers, *Daily News*, 24 November, 7.

South African Travel Experiences, 2006: Available at: http://wwwsouthafrica.info/plan_trip/holiday/cities/durban.htm. (accessed 24 January 2006).

South Africa, 1996: *White Paper on the Development and Promotion of Tourism in South Africa,* Department of Environmental Affairs and Tourism, Pretoria.

South Africa, 1998: *Tourism in GEAR Tourism Development Strategy: 1998-2000,* Department of Environmental Affairs and Tourism, Pretoria.

Sorkin, M. (Ed.), 1992: *Variations on a Theme Place,* Noonday Press, New York.

Swanson, M., 1964: The Rise of Multicultural Durban: Urban History and Race Policy in South Africa, 1830-1939, Unpublished PhD Dissertation, Harvard University.

Turner, B.S., 1984: *The Body and Society,* Blackwell Ltd., Oxford.

Urry, J., 1990: *The Tourist Gaze: Leisure and Travel in Contemporary Societies*, Sage Publications, London.

Urry, J., 1995: *Consuming Places,* Routledge, London.

Van Gennep, A., 1909: *The Rites of Passage*, Routledge and Kegan Paul, London.

Zukin, S., 1995: *The Cultures of Cities*, Blackwell, Cambridge, MA.

Zulu, X., 2005: Blue flag status for five beaches, *The Mercury*, 18 October, 5.

13

Tourism Promotion in "Difficult Areas": The Experience of Johannesburg Inner City

Christian M. Rogerson and Lucy Kaplan

In common with many international cities, tourism has been identified as potentially one of the most important sectoral drivers for the economic regeneration of Johannesburg, Africa's aspirant "world class" city (Rogerson, 2004a, 2004b, 2005). Over the past decade, significant spatial shifts have occurred in the Johannesburg tourism economy with the emergence of a group of new tourism spaces to surpass the traditional or old tourism spaces of the city. During the 1970s and 1980s the major spatial focus for tourism activity in Johannesburg was the inner city, which encompassed a cluster of high grade hotels, restaurants and retailing complexes serving a mixture of both business and leisure tourists. As a consequence of the decentralization of offices and retailing in Johannesburg, rising crime and physical decay, the inner city tourism economy went into a spiral of decline that was symbolized most dramatically in the 1990s by the mothballing of tourism accommodation and subsequent closure of the city's flagship Carlton Hotel (Rogerson, 2002). Currently, the inner-city of Johannesburg fits well the characteristics of what is defined as a "difficult area" for tourism development. Difficult areas are viewed as those that have only a small tourism base in terms of receipts, areas which might be regarded as unsuitable for tourism development because of "poor image"; and, in need of infrastructural improvement (see Buckley and Witt, 1985, 1989; Hope and Klemm, 2001)

The aim in this chapter is to present the results of a recent analysis of the changing potential of tourism in Johannesburg inner city. It will be argued that the inner city of Johannesburg, albeit potentially a "difficult area" for tourism development, does have a number of positive assets that can be harnessed to provide the basis for the revival of tourism activity, more especially as part of wider sets of ongoing initiatives for economic and physical regeneration (City of Johannesburg, 2004). This chapter is organized into four uneven sections of discussion.

- First, as context, the international record of promoting tourism in inner cities, in particular linked to wider objectives and programs of economic regeneration, is surveyed.
- Second, a review is undertaken of wider strategic initiatives for growing tourism in Johannesburg and of specific initiatives around inner city regeneration.
- Third, an historical analysis is presented of shifts in the tourism economy of inner-city Johannesburg over the last fifteen years.
- Four, a detailed profile is given of the current state of tourism in Johannesburg inner-city. This analysis draws upon a review of existing documentation and importantly from the findings of focused interviews that were conducted during 2004 with key stakeholders and tourism product owners concerning tourism developments in the inner city.

Inner-City Tourism: The International Record

Tourism in cities and tourism promotion of inner-cities is not a new phenomenon (Hoffman et al., 2003). In seeking to promote tourism in the inner city of Johannesburg one can learn from the experience of many other cities – mainly in Western Europe and North America - which have sought to undertake similar types of tourism development. In particular, the experience of Johannesburg finds close parallels with the promotion of urban tourism as part of programs to meet wider objectives of economic and physical regeneration (Law, 1991, 1992, 1993, 1996). For Chang and Huang (2004: 226-227) the re-emergence of the city as a tourist lure is explained as part of a wider "sea change in consumer demand at a global level" with escalating demands by tourists for urban sights and heritage cities.

Tourism as a Tool for Urban Regeneration

As a result of global economic restructuring and the decline of traditional manufacturing activities in many cities of the developed world, many urban governments have turned to tourism as one element of strategies for economic regeneration, restructuring and local economic development (Law, 1996; Beauregard, 1998; Coles, 2003). For Hoyle (2001), urban tourism is set to be a major twenty-first century industry.

In understanding the phenomenon of urban tourism, Fagence (2004) argues that it must be acknowledged as the outcome of complex, interlocking decisions made by the investment and development "industry," public agencies and governments of various kinds and at different levels. De-industrialization and global economic restructuring provided the impetus for former manufacturing cities to re-construct and re-invent themselves as centers of consumption (Judd, 1995; Ioannides, 2003). As Scott (2004: 463) emphasizes, across urban Western Europe and North America, the cultural-products industries, including tourism, are "significantly on the rise of late and they are notably visible as drivers of local economic development." In addition, the notion of the city as spectacle has been harnessed for purposes of local development with many urban areas seeking to revive their fortunes by presenting themselves as offering a spectacular consumptive experience (Crewe, 1991; Garcia, 2004).

For cities confronted by the challenges of the service economy and information age, tourism provides an opportunity to re-position themselves and re-define their essential functions (King, 2004). Several potential benefits are associated with tourism-based regeneration. These include:

Economic benefits: There are a range of direct and indirect effects, such as job creation and other wider economic benefits, the profits of which, it is hoped, "will encourage further investment leading to a virtuous cycle of growth" (Law, 1991: 50).

Improved image: Localities that are externally perceived as important and interesting visitor destinations (as a result of marketing and tourism-led physical and environmental improvements) "tend to be significantly better placed to attract new businesses and industries as well as an appropriate workforce" (Karski, 1990: 15). The enhancement of image is often a critical benefit for tourism-led regeneration (Bradley et al., 2002; Han et al., 2003; Chang and Huang, 2004).

Improved quality of life for residents: Tourism based regeneration also includes improvements and better access for local residents to new leisure facilities. In association with this trend, as the tempo of visitor flows is increased, residents may gain civic pride that might have a further knock-on effect for environmental improvements (Law, 1996).

The essential basis of tourism-led economic regeneration is the development and promotion of new or enhanced tourism products or attractions in cities (Hoyle, 2001; Pearce, 2001). Based upon the existing international experience, at least eight different tourism-led approaches towards attaining goals of urban revitalization are recognized (see Law, 1993; Page, 1995; Swarbrooke, 1999, 2000). These strategies are summarized in table 13.1. It must be noted that the particular strategy or mix of strategies for any individual city is clearly influenced by the character of its specific tourism resources that can be harnessed for tourism marketing and promotion.

Leisure tourism is the most common focus for tourism strategies that link to economic regeneration, particularly of inner-cities (Law, 2000). In some cities the essential focus has been upon entertainment-based regeneration through ca-

Table 13.1
Tourism-Led Approaches to Urban Regeneration

Visitor-attractions: new physical attractions, such as waterfront developments, new museums or casinos are used to attract tourists.

Cultural attractions: expanding and using cultural attractions, such as the arts, theatre or music in order to attract visitors.

Events: creating new festivals or attracting 'mega-events' such as major festivals and sports events.

Leisure shopping: developing new shopping-retailing complexes.

Promoting the City as a host venue: attracting local and international fairs, conferences and exhibitions.

Nightlife: improving nightlife in order to attract particularly younger tourists for clubbing as part of creating a 24-hour city.

Industrial attractions: redeveloping industrial attractions and related retail outlets.

Local food and drink: promoting distinctive local cuisine

Source: Based upon Swarbrooke 1999, 2000

sinos or sports with the U.S. city of Detroit a classic example (McCarthy, 2002). Cultural heritage management has been an important aspect of promoting new inner city tourism in Asian cities such as Singapore (Chang, 2000) and Hong Kong (McKercher et al., 2005). The English cities of Manchester and Liverpool provide good examples of the linkages that are forged between the making of "tourism cities" and of inner-city regeneration. In the case of Manchester the development of new sports facilities, a new Chinatown development and Gay Village as well as the encouragement of entertainment (clubs) as part of a "24 hour city" policy have all contributed to tourism and leisure-led regeneration (Law, 2000; Hughes, 2003). In Liverpool, arts and cultural products to attract tourism have been the foundation for inner-city regeneration initiatives (Couch and Farr, 2000). The growth of tourism in Harlem in inner-city New York is a further example of tourism that is linked to inner-city regeneration (Hoffman, 2000). The assets of Harlem for tourism development have been its "cultural capital" as a focus of African-American history and culture as well as the area's entertainment attractions and special significance for jazz (Hoffman, 2003).

For many cities, the focus within urban tourism promotion has been to capitalize upon their potential for business travel and tourism (Swarbrooke and Horner 2001). The English city of Birmingham provides, perhaps, the best example of urban regeneration that is linked to targeted promotion of business tourism and of the meetings tourism market. In the case of Birmingham the key basis for selling the city for conference tourism was the development of an American style convention center to complement the city's existing National Exhibition Centre (Bradley et al., 2002). As noted by one observer, Birmingham "has now, arguably eclipsed London as the U.K.'s top business tourism event destination" (Swarbrooke, 1999: 176). Another good example of inner-city tourism that has been boosted by business travel is Adelaide, South Australia where once again the building of a new convention center has been critical. Finally, using examples from Canada and Australia, Hall (2002) draws attention to the potential for business travel in relation to the function of national capital city.

Investment in Secondary or "Soft" Elements

It is clear from a cross-section of experience of tourism in European inner cities that successful urban tourism is not guaranteed merely by the possession of a good set of tourism resources or assets (Pearce, 1998; Russo and van der Borg, 2002). Rather, tourism development requires also that attention be accorded to addressing the intangibles of "visitor-friendliness" and to a number of basic conditions regarding the quality of hospitality including communication with the public, the "atmosphere" of the place, accessibility of tourism products, and safety issues (Law, 1996; Russo and van der Borg, 2002).

In surveying a range of international case studies of cities that have variously sought to link the development of inner city tourism to issues of economic and physical regeneration, an important observation can be made about the importance of geographic and conceptual clustering. As has been argued, successful inner city tourism in Western Europe and North America has been anchored upon an appropriate blend of two sets of tourism resources. First, are the primary elements that are those which attract people and consist variously of museums, art galleries, concert halls, entertainment, historic buildings, and special events (Jansen-Verbeke, 1985, 1986). Secondary elements that enhance these attractions or assist in the process of attracting tourists include shopping, accommodations, and restaurant facilities (Law, 1992, 1996). Most successful urban tourism developments have seen the spatial clustering of these primary and secondary resources into tourism districts. Indeed, a common approach towards tourism-led economic regeneration has been through the planning of "tourism precincts," which represent concentrations or clusters of tourist-related land uses, activities and visitation within fairly definable boundaries (Pearce, 1998; Hayllar and Griffin, 2005). Tourism precincts generally evince a distinctive character by virtue of their mixture of land uses, such as restaurants, attractions and nightlife, their physical and architectural fabric or connections to particular cultural or ethnic groups within cities (Jansen-Verbeke, 1986; Conforti, 1996).

The creation of tourism districts or clusters has several advantages (Scott, 2004). These clusters can be based around business activities, entertainment districts, museums, cultural districts or quarters. Clusters allow the use of shared infrastructure, public transport and access roads and lead to greater visibility of tourism resources or products. Moreover, the physical proximity of a number of tourism products provides visitors with an opportunity to engage in multiple activities in a short period of time (Law, 2000). In cases of cities where there does not occur a number of attractions within close proximity, the most appropriate strategy is that of routing. The development of themed routes to attract visitors and tourists is a means to make dispersed facilities "appear" as a cluster with the explicit intention of drawing more visitors as a result of these themed routes (Van Aalst and Boogaarts, 2002).

The Johannesburg Planning Context

At one level, the promotion of tourism as part of the regeneration of in inner city Johannesburg must be part of wider strategic planning for the growth of tourism in Johannesburg as a whole (Rogerson, 2004b). In addition, planning for tourism in the inner city must be located within and linked to other ongoing strategic initiatives relating to the economic and physical regeneration of the inner city (figure 13.1). The wider strategic planning interventions that impact upon tourism in inner-city Johannesburg are discussed here.

Joburg 2030

The most significant city development framework for Johannesburg is that provided by the important *Joburg 2030* document which was issued by the city's Corporate Planning Unit (GJMC, 2002). By 2030 the core goals are to elevate Johannesburg into the ranks of 'world cities' with a strongly outward-oriented economy, specialized in the service sector, and exhibiting strong economic growth that delivers increasing standards of living and quality of life to all the city's inhabitants. Of central significance in the strategic planning proposed for the city is the endorsement of targeted or selected sectoral interventions that would be made by the city authorities in order to enhance economies of localization (Rogerson, 2005). The analysis identifies the high-skill and knowledge-based financial and business services sector as that sector which ranked most strongly on the basis of relative attractiveness and competitiveness for augmenting the future economic development of Johannesburg. Nevertheless, what is significant also is that tourism was identified among the small group of other targeted sectors (Rogerson, 2004a).

It was argued that the city's tourism industry and economy "is substantially large in absolute and relative terms, and exhibits sufficient growth potential that it is an important sector for the overall economy of the city." Overall, tourism was viewed as a sector that can "become a more important player in the City's economy" (GJMC, 2001: 72) and thus was selected for targeting.

Figure 13.1
Location of the Inner-City Area of Johannesburg

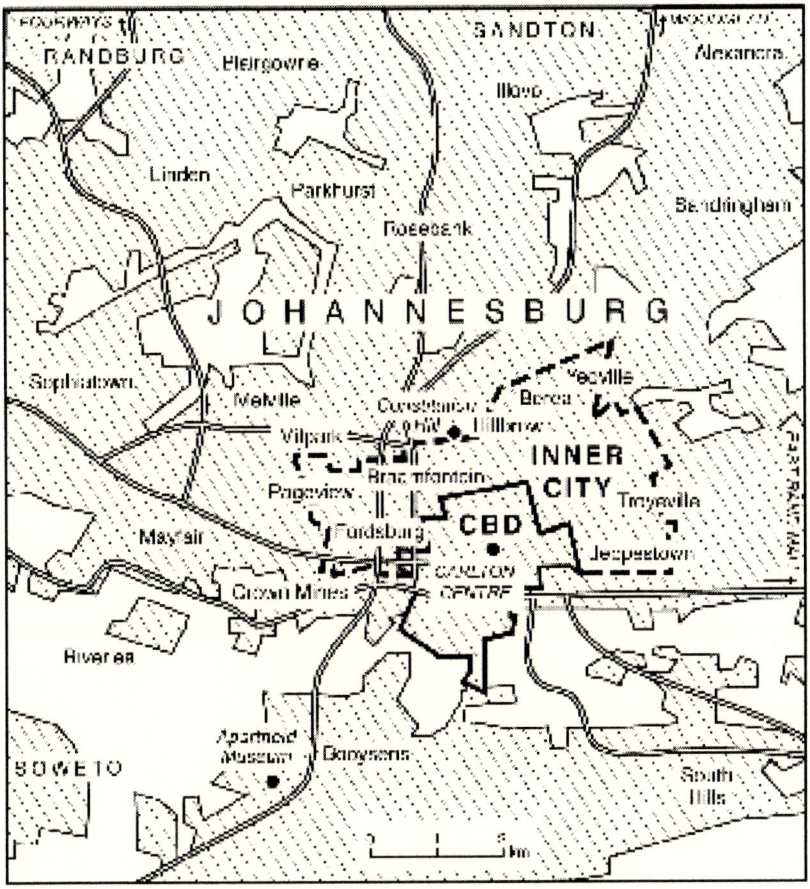

The Johannesburg Inner City Regeneration Strategy Business Plan

The Johannesburg Inner City Regeneration Strategy Business Plan 2004-2007 was published by the City of Johannesburg in March 2004. The importance of this Business Plan is that it serves to synchronize the efforts of all agencies—local, provincial, and national government, the private sector, NGOs and civil society—under the leadership of the City of Johannesburg for the active regeneration of the inner city. The Business Plan captures all the ongoing major inner city development initiatives seeking to "encourage improved coordination of efforts and mobilization of resources, better institutional management and identification of areas for attention" (City of Johannesburg, 2004a: 3).

The key elements from the Inner City Regeneration Strategy business plan and Business Plan that impact upon the development of an Inner City Tourism Strategy are twofold. First, the strategic importance of the inner city as an economic asset to the wider planning goal of developing Johannesburg as a world-class African city is highlighted. Second, a five-pillar strategy (figure 13.2) is at the heart of this strategic framework and seeks to raise and sustain private investment (City of Johannesburg, 2004a).

The first pillar seeks to address the problem of sinkholes that are defined as either "properties that are slummed, abandoned, overcrowded, poorly maintained" or "used for illegal or unsuitable purposes" (City of Johannesburg, 2004a). The second pillar is that of intensive urban management which "involves focusing efforts to ensure effective by-law enforcement, management of informal trading, regular or improved delivery of services and utilities and maintenance of the public realm." Private examples of such intensive urban management are seen as the City Improvement Districts and CCTV surveillance programs whereas public-sector initiatives include the work of the Inner City Task Force (City of Johannesburg, 2004a). The third pillar is primarily a function of the city's utility companies and concerns "the maintenance and improvement of service delivery infrastructure, including roads, street signs and robots, water, sanitation and power networks and waste collection points." The fourth pillar is the promotion of so-termed "ripple pond investments" which are defined as "catalytic, concerted investments in property that create confidence for further investment in adjacent areas." The examples of such ripple pond investments would be either private sector or public sector led initiatives such as the Braamfontein Regeneration, Constitution Hill or the Newtown Cultural Precinct. The final pillar relates to targeted support for select

Figure 13.2
The Five Pillars of the Johannesburg Inner-City Regeneration Strategy

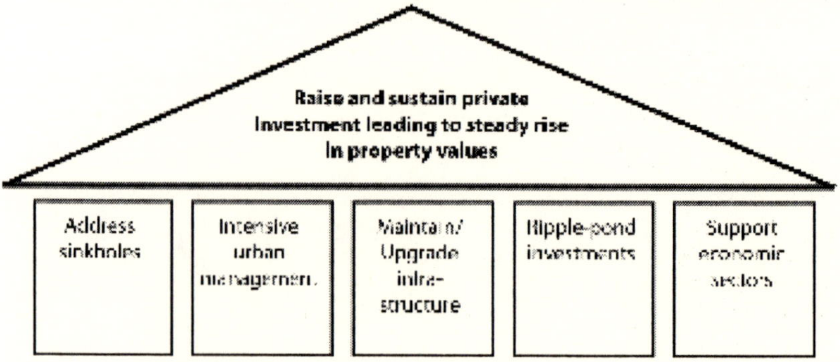

Source: City of Johannesburg, 2004a: 10.

economic sectors of activity that "are of current or potential importance to the gross geographic product of the inner city" (City of Johannesburg, 2004a). Examples of these initiatives would encompass The Business Place that supports youth entrepreneurs and the nurturing of the inner-city Fashion District (Rogerson, 2004c).

The Johannesburg Tourism Strategy

In 2001 the city prepared a Tourism Strategy, which currently (January 2005) is in a process of updating (GJMC, 2001). It is made clear in interviews conducted in this research, however, that the process of updating and revision will not change in any way the key conclusions from the 2001 analysis or affect the strategic directions identified in the 2001 Strategy (Saunders, 2004).

The Tourism Strategy recognizes that Johannesburg does not possess a competitive advantage for the promotion of leisure tourism. Indeed, in terms of South Africa's nine provinces, Gauteng is ranked last in terms of leisure tourism but significantly first as a destination for business travelers. Of these business tourists, 66 percent spent at least two nights in Johannesburg with 89 percent coming to the city on general business and the remaining 11 percent for the purpose of attending a conference or exhibition. The Tourism Strategy identifies two major growth areas as drivers for Johannesburg's future tourism economy based upon an analysis of the city's competitive advantage. The first of these is the general area of business tourism with a special focus on the MICE sector of meetings, incentives, conferences and exhibitions (Rogerson, 2004b). Regional tourism and the strengthening of Johannesburg's role as a major shopping hub for sub-Saharan represents the second policy focus.

In terms of overall support for tourism from the metropolitan level of government, the city's tourism development strategy identifies a set of important development interventions (GJMC, 2001, 2002). It is recognized that the key contribution the Council can directly make to tourism in Johannesburg is to undertake activities that increase the flow of tourists in the city. Three potential areas for intervention and support are noted. First, to increase aggregate demand through marketing and other city promotional initiatives in order to increase visitor arrivals. In terms of retail tourism, the marketing of the city is to be intensified prior to planned promotional retail tourism weeks. Another critical element of this city marketing for tourism is to be focused on the strategy of 'landing the big one' as regards large international conferences. In this respect, it is estimated that a conference such as the World Summit on Sustainable Development generates in a single five-day period as much value as three months of average MICE and general business tourism in Johannesburg (Viljoen, 2004). Second, to address issues raised as barriers to visitation, the most important is known to concern issues of crime and safety of tourists in Johannesburg (Ferreira and Harmse, 2000). By addressing crime, the Council would be indirectly assisting tourism development in the city. Finally, the role of infrastructure development is critical in particular for MICE and cross-border retail tourism. Few facility gaps are seen currently as of urgent need in terms of the city's strength for MICE tourism other than issues of upgrading. In retail tourism, however, proposals have been made for designating a potential retail hub that would concentrate the goods and services most frequently sought out by African cross-border shoppers.

The Gauteng Tourism Authority's Tourism Marketing Plan 2001-2006

As with the city's tourism strategy, the provincial tourism marketing plan of Gauteng for 2001-06 seeks to reinforce metropolitan Johannesburg's competitive base as "an economic hub with world class business infrastructure and facilities" (Gauteng Tourism Authority, 2003). The plan focuses particularly on growing the domestic business market, inter alia, by "adding value to the overall business experience by focusing on strategies and initiatives aimed at extending length of stay, motivating the consumption of diverse products, influencing perceptions (particularly of Johannesburg) and developing strategic partnerships with demand generators" (KPMG, 2001: 6).

In line with the City's focus on maximizing the impacts of regional tourism flows, the GTA sees that the "African business market is a lucrative one" and represents "the core base to build upon in relation to the strength of existing travel patterns and product consumption" (KPMG, 2001: 8).

It is significant that GTA marketing recognizes that "the growth of the MICE market is a strategic priority for creating both international and domestic awareness, positioning the city (Johannesburg) as the preferred "meetings destination" strengthening the provincial tourism product and creating strategic local, provincial and national market and product linkages" (KPMG, 2001: 14). It is within this context of wider tourism planning for Gauteng and for Johannesburg in particular that a tourism promotion strategy for the inner city must be situated.

The Historical Decline and Changing Face of Tourism in Johannesburg Inner City

Until the early-1990s Johannesburg inner city was one of the major focal points for tourism enterprises within the GJMA (Rogerson, 2002). Historically, the inner city developed as a cluster for business tourism as well as for specialist shopping and entertainment activities. Of particular importance was the group of hotel, retail and travel-related enterprises that concentrated in the CBD, particularly around the Carlton Hotel (figure 13.1). In addition, the Berea and Hillbrow areas traditionally also functioned as important zones for accommodation and tourism entertainment.

Over the past fifteen years the inner city tourism economy weakened and has been overtaken by the momentum of newer decentralized tourism nodes in the northern parts of Greater Johannesburg (figure 13.1). Localities such as Sandton, Rosebank, and Fourways are the city's "new tourism spaces" that have benefited from the growth-taking place in the overall tourism economy of Johannesburg (Rogerson, 2004b). The weakening of the cluster is linked to the exodus of office and retail activities to decentralized property nodes, such as Sandton and Rosebank (Rogerson, 1995), and accelerated by an associated rise in levels of crime and violence in the inner-city, which has negatively impacted upon tourism. By the early-1990s demand for four or five-star hotel accommodation in Johannesburg inner-city was collapsing as the focus for international tourists and the business tourism economy gravitated spatially from the inner-city to Rosebank and increasingly towards Sandton (Rogerson, 2002). In an examination of tourists' perception and risk of crime in South Africa it was concluded that "most foreign visitors stay away from Central Johannesburg because its crime reputation scares people" (Ferreira and Harmse, 2000: 84). Indeed, it was recorded that in 1995 the occupancy levels at the Carlton had fallen to 35 percent (as compared to the Sandton Sun which was operating at occupancy levels of 80 per cent or better) and "it is only once the Sandton Sun has no vacancies left that people book into the Carlton" (Hunter et al., 1995: 132).

The decline and changing nature of the tourism economy of the inner-city can be attributed to several factors. First, is the influence of office and retailing decentralization and the exodus from the inner city of such activities to Sandton and Rosebank (Rogerson, 1995). In the 1995 Johannesburg Inner-City Strategic Framework analysis it was observed that "the widespread perception that the inner-city hotels are located in an "unsafe" environment and that once a person has checked into one of these hotels he/she basically becomes a prisoner within that building, to a large extent accounts for the poor performance of these hotels" (Hunter et al., 1995: 131). Indeed, a comparison of occupancy levels of inner-city Johannesburg hotels with those outside the city disclosed stark differences in occupancy (Hunter et al., 1995). Another signal of the demise of the tourism economy of the inner city was relocation from there of many restaurants to newer decentralized retailing areas (Hunter et al., 1995: 135).

Since the early-1990s there has been a strong tendency amongst many smaller and older hotels in Johannesburg inner city to change their emphasis from being establishments offering predominantly accommodation to becoming liquor-dominated establishments. Another element of readjustment has been the voluntary downgrading of several establishments in order to enhance occupancy levels. The lack of investment in new tourism products and the disinvestment from the CBD of leading hotel chains have been further manifestations of the spiral of decline. In 1993 the downgrading took place of the five-star Johannesburg Sun International (built only in 1986) to a three-star Holiday Inn Garden Court as an adjustment in response to the shifting inner-city tourism market (Mlangeni, 1997). Most importantly, the demise of the Johannesburg inner-city tourism cluster is marked by the progressive rundown and subsequent closure during April 1998 of the city's prestigious and former five-star Carlton Hotel, an icon of Johannesburg (Shevel, 1998).

As early as the mid-1990s it was evident that certain important changes were occurring in the nature of visitor flows and patterns of tourism into Johannesburg inner city. First, it was observed in 1995 that "whereas in the past most of the hotels catered almost solely for the white sector of the domestic and international market, there has been a substantial shift away from this trend, particularly for those hotels located in the inner city" (Hunter et al., 1995: 132). The nature of this shift was explained thus: "Hotel managers in the city report that insofar as a domestic trend existed years ago for whites to come to the city center over weekends either for social reasons, shopping or to attend sporting or other events, this trend has to a large extent been taken over by the African sector of the population which has the financial means to do so" (Hunter et al., 1995: 133).

The inner city tourism economy has witnessed the replacement of leisure tourism with MICE tourism. In particular, there has been a repositioning towards attracting the MICE market for particularly those hotels situated on the borders of the CBD. Indeed, the search for "niches" in business tourism was reflected in the Devonshire Hotel establishing itself as a business/corporate hotel, the Parktonian attracting "a large proportion of people from the development industry" and the (former) Karos Johannesburger securing "all the business which stems from the trade unions including business lunches and conferences" (Hunter et al., 1995: 133). It should be noted that in a context of the rapid growth of the MICE sector of business tourism, the CBD was poorly positioned in terms of competing for this growing market, not least due to the "limited range of small scale conference facilities" that were recorded as operating there (Hunter et al., 1995: 138).

Finally, another important shift that was increasingly in evidence concerns the appearance and substantial growth in the 1990s of flows of regional tourists, and especially of cross-border shoppers from other parts of sub-Saharan Africa (Rogerson, 2004d). The stream of regional tourists from other countries in sub-Saharan Africa was first noticed in the early 1990s. In 1992 it was observed that: "A visit to Johannesburg's bus and long-distance mini-bus terminuses indicate the high levels of business which residents of neighboring states bring to Johannesburg as travelers cram in huge quantities of consumer and electrical goods" (City of Johannesburg, 1992: 11).

Overall, therefore, the precipitate decline of the tourism economy of Johannesburg inner city was part of broader processes of spatial change taking place across the city. The dramatic weakening of this "old" tourism space of Johannesburg was manifest in a situation of under-investment in existing tourism plant, lack of investment in new tourism products, disinvestment strategies by leading hotel chains, the downgrading of some establishments and the closure or mothballing of others. All these shifts were occurring against the backdrop of, and linked inseparably to, several fundamental shifts in the character of tourism flows into the inner city.

The Current State of Johannesburg Inner City's Tourism Economy

The discussion turns now to examine in greater detail the present state of the tourism economy of Johannesburg's inner city. The analysis here is drawn from the results of interviews that were conducted with tourism product owners and stakeholders during the period March-April 2004. Other relevant documentary source material supplements these findings. The research on tourism in the inner city sought to investigate the following themes, inter alia, current trends in terms of the nature of tourism flows, the purpose of tourism and origins of tourists; and, opportunities and constraints on the "new" tourism economy of the inner city.

The Size and Profile of the Johannesburg Tourism Market

Accurate statistics on visitor attractions, tourism flows into Johannesburg and of the importance of tourism to the urban economy are difficult to obtain. For the purposes of this study, statistics have been drawn from two sources. First, a set of unpublished research work collated on behalf of the Johannesburg Tourism Company and reported in an interview by the Chief Executive Officer (Viljoen, 2004). Second, is baseline research conducted in 2002 for the City Department of Marketing and Tourism (Haley Sharpe Southern Africa, 2003).

According to the Johannesburg Tourism Company total annual visitor numbers to (Greater) Johannesburg are estimated as 6.2 million (Viljoen, 2004). This number is broken down as follows 3 million domestic tourists, 2 million regional tourists or visitors from sub-Saharan Africa, and 1.2 million, international tourists from long-haul destinations, mainly in Western Europe. Other key features of the Johannesburg tourism economy are that average tourism spend is calculated at R1,300 per trip to Johannesburg. The highest estimated spend is from international visitors, a value of R2,400 per trip. By contrast, the average spend by domestic tourists visiting Johannesburg from other parts of South Africa is estimated as R500-700, and is lower because the majority of tourists are staying with friends or relatives. No reliable estimates can be gleaned, however, on patterns of spending in Johannesburg by the large group of cross-border shoppers (Viljoen, 2004). Finally, South African Tourism's recent Domestic Tourism Growth Strategy 2004-2007 stresses that 60 percent of all domestic tourism in South Africa is intra-provincial, meaning that the majority of domestic travel within Gauteng is generated from within Gauteng (Rule et al., 2004; South African Tourism, 2004).

Gauteng has a higher percentage of business tourists (both international and domestic) than the rest of South Africa and a lower percentage of leisure tourists. Another important point, for the purposes of this study, is the high number of

Table 13.2
Key Findings from Inner City Accommodation and Conference Providers

Tourism Product	Nature of Tourism	Origin of Tourists	Comments
Devonshire Hotel	95 percent MICE Tourism, mainly conferences for unions and Government	95 percent is South African	No business from health tourism, leisure or cross-border shoppers. Occupancies are lowest at weekends.
KwaDukuza Egoli Hotel and Conference Centre	Predominantly MICE Tourism to attend conferences but also a significant flow of cross-border shopping tourists	Largest flows are Regional tourists from neighbouring African states and domestic South African visitors for conferences. Very few international tourists.	Month end is busiest for regional tourists involved with cross-border shopping. Malawi is a notable source for cross-border shoppers.
Johannesburger Hotel	Most visitors are cross-border shoppers or MICE tourists attending conferences.	Two-thirds of visitors are regional tourists from neighbouring African states. South Africans are major flow of business tourists.	Occupancies are strongest at month end including flow of local visitors.
Mariston Hotel	Mainly Residential use with only a small number of "day rooms."	All domestic South African	Converted to residential use for Technikon students rather than tourists
Orchidea Hotel	MICE Tourism for conferences	Majority of visitors are South African although there are a small flow of regional tourists from Africa	Strongest occupancies are at month end. In addition to conferences, the hotel is used for functions such as weddings and matric dances.
Parktonian Hotel	85-90 percent is MICE Tourism mainly for conferences. Rest is Leisure Tourism. Most conferences are for Unions, Government or Corporates in the Surrounding Area.	80 percent are South African. Next in significance are regional African visitors.	The conference tourism is overwhelmingly South African with regional tourists and international visitors mainly for sports or cultural events
Pyramid Conference Centre	All activity is MICE tourism in terms of day conferences as no accommodation is available. Most business is from corporates, especially banks, and from provincial government.	99 percent of visitors are South African	In four years of operations, most business is corporate training meetings or budgeting meetings.
Springbok Hotel	Vast majority (80-90 percent) of visitors are cross-border shoppers with occasional business tourists attending conferences	Vast majority of visitors are regional African tourists especially from Zambia, Zimbabwe and Botswana.	None

Table 13.2 (cont.)

Sunnyside Park Hotel	All activity is MICE and Business Tourism. The majority is linked to conferences or individual business travellers of corporates, NGOs or Universities in the locality.	80 percent is South African, 20 percent regional tourists (business) from Africa.	Despite its location, there are almost no health tourists. Leisure tourism is virtually nil.
Troyeville Hotel	Most visitors are residents working in South Africa on short-term contracts of two weeks or more	80-90 percent of visitors are Portuguese speakers from Mozambique or Portugal. 10 percent of visitors are South African.	Although this is a tourist hotel, it is functioning effectively as a residential hotel.

Source: Author survey

one-day trips to Central Gauteng. According to the national Domestic Tourism Survey 11 percent of the estimated 55 million one-day trips undertaken in South Africa during 2000/2001 were to Central Gauteng, which approximates to nearly 6 million one-day trips per annum (Rule et al. 2001).

Overall, this available data underlines the sectoral importance of tourism as a contributor to the economy of contemporary Johannesburg. Furthermore, it serves to reinforce the significance of strategic initiatives that are set to promote tourism in the city as part of wider economic development programs in the city (Rogerson, 2004a, 2005).

Major Market Segments of Inner City Tourism

The current trends in terms of tourism in the inner city are disclosed by the interviews that were conducted with nine hotels operating in the inner city and one dedicated conference center (figure 13.3). These findings are summarized in table 13.2.

The interviews make clear that there is currently little or no international market for the hotels and conference centers within the inner city. In addition, there is little or no leisure market (whether international or domestic) for overnight stays within the inner city. This is evidenced by the extremely low weekend occupancy rates as reported by the various hotels.

The main market for hotels within the inner city is made up by visitors from neighboring African countries and by the domestic MICE market, i.e. domestic travelers who are in Johannesburg for meetings, training courses or conferences. In broad terms those hotels within the CBD such as the KwaDukuza Egoli and the Johannesburger rely mainly on regional tourists while those situated in the Braamfontein and Parktown areas (the Devonshire, the Sunnyside and the Parktonian) rely mainly on the domestic MICE market. The major markets for domestic conferences and meetings within the inner city are government—mainly

Figure 13.3
Location of Inner City Accommodation and Conference Providers

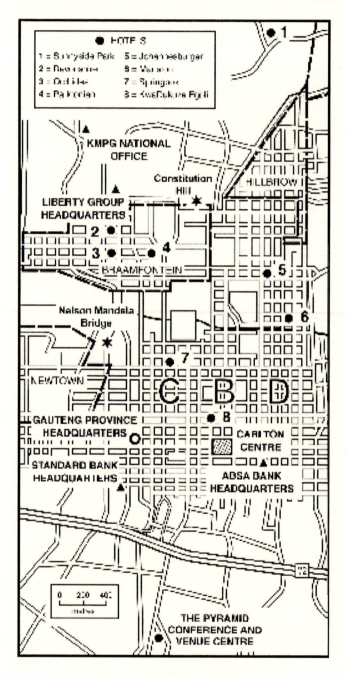

Table 13.3
Inner City Tour Itineraries: In-Bound Operators

Interface Travel and Tours	Inner City included in a longer Anglo-Boer War Battlefields tour: Pick-up from airport, Constitution Hill, Braamfontein Cemetery, Pretoria (to two other forts), the Staatsmodel school, and Melrose House. Overnight in a B&B in Pretoria Other days in Mpumalanga and KwaZulu/Natal
Springbok Atlas	Johannesburg City Tour: pick-up Sandton or Rosebank hotel, Mandela's house in Houghton, Monroe Drive, St Johns, down Louis Botha into Hillbrow, drive past the Fort, past the Civic Centre, top of the Carlton Centre, drive past old buildings on Commissioner Street, Rissik Street, to Diagonal Street, past the big mining houses. If the clients are not going to Gold Reef City, go to the mineshaft at the Standard Bank Head Office. Then, Muti shop under the Rissik Street bridge, past George Harrison Park to Museum Africa Offering a new full-day tour: "Rise to Freedom Tour" (Soweto and Apartheid Museum in a full day) which will include a drive through the inner city and stop-off at Constitution Hill (CH)
Lords Travel and Tours	Johannesburg City Tour ("the mining camp which grew into Africa's dynamic and vibrant city of gold"): City drive, a visit to a traditional African healers' market, a drive through the suburbs of Parktown and then up to the top of the Carlton Centre. Sometimes the guides take people to the Gauteng Legislature or Museum Africa.
Thompsons Tours	Johannesburg City Tour: Pick-up from any hotel in Sandton, drive past the Stock Exchange, the mining houses, George Harrison Park, through Bosmont, past the universities and then back to the hotel. Stop at Museum Africa on request. The tour aims to give an overview of the different living standard in the city
Welcome Tours	Offers a drive-through "orientation" of the CBD on the way to Soweto. No stops included.
Fhulofelo Tours	Present tour of Johannesburg (Museum Africa, World of Beer, Art Gallery, Anglo-Boer war sites, past Gandhi Square).
Gold Reef Guides	Offer a half-day tour of Johannesburg combined with a half day tour of either Soweto Gold Reef City, Rhino Lion Park, the Cradle of Humankind or, the Cheetah Sanctuary. This tour: pickup in Sandton or Rosebank, through the suburbs and then to CH. Drive through CBD (architecture, the Stock Exchange, the mining houses), the Art Gallery, Mai-Mai Village, and Faraday. End at the Carlton or the Westcliff for drinks and snacks. Museum Africa might be included depending on the group

Source: Author Survey

provincial but also national—and large corporations, such as ABSA, Standard, KPMG, and Liberty whose major offices are situated in or around the Johannesburg inner city. One indication of the size of the government-related MICE market is that the 2003 budget for Gauteng Provincial government spending on meetings and conferences was estimated at R70 million (Chetty, 2004).

The regional tourism market for inner city hotels is mainly made up of business tourists (both for MICE and individual business) and, to a lesser extent, cross-border shoppers. Nevertheless, there is some evidence from interviews with stakeholders to suggest that the inner city is losing its appeal for the higher spending group of cross-border shoppers who are gravitating towards certain decentralized shopping nodes, including Woodmead, East Rand Mall and Crown Mines. Nevertheless, for large numbers of individual lower budget cross-border shoppers, the CBD zone of the inner city retains its significance (Liebermann, 2004).

The business of health tourism is weak in the inner city and seemingly is comprised mainly of low budget health tourists from neighboring African states (Melvill, 2004). The more lucrative element of health tourism—involving high value international health visitors seeking elective surgery—takes place outside of the inner city. Currently, it is estimated that there are 300 low-budget international health tourists per month visiting the inner city or approximately 4000 visitors per annum (Melvill, 2004). For impacts upon Johannesburg inner city a potentially more promising element of health tourism is domestic health tourism, which is concentrated upon the hospital node around Milpark, albeit little concrete information exists as to the volume and extent of such domestic health tourism.

Overall, in terms of the supply of MICE tourism products it is evident that while there are sufficient number of small conference venues, accommodating up to 200 people in the inner city, currently there is a recognized shortage of dedicated conference venues that can handle from 200-300 people and upwards. For example, in an interview with a representative of Gauteng Provincial Government, it was made clear that whereas venues at the Pyramid, the Parktonian and Sunnyside could accommodate much of the needs of the Province, at present within Central Johannesburg there exist no large venues that are seen as adequate for meetings of 200 persons or more (Chetty, 2004).

One potential source for a conference venue in the inner city is at the Carlton Hotel. Built in 1973 by a consortium, of local and U.S.-based developers, the Carlton Centre was purchased in 1999 by Transnet, South Africa's largest government-owned transport company. The initial focus of Transnet was upon office development. The office tower is virtually filled with Transnet itself occupying 60 percent of office space. Transnet are now considering options for retail and hotel development. In 2004, (at least) two consortia developed serious proposals for re-opening the Carlton Hotel, which was closed down in the late-1990s before the complex was sold to Transnet. At least one of the serious bidders wants a re-opened Carlton to be a focus for business tourism and especially for MICE tourism. It has been proposed that a re-developed Carlton be linked to the KwaDukuza Egoli Hotel, which re-opened after being mothballed for several years, as the core axis of a proposed inner-city conference precinct. The development of such a precinct would necessitate considerable attention upon upgrading the surrounds in order to provide a coherent precinct (Ochre Communications, 2004).

Another potential inner-city base for conference and events development centers on the Turbine Hall and Transport House redevelopments in Newtown, both of which can enhance the competitive strength of the inner city as a base for MICE tourism. Both of these venues are featured strongly in the Business Plan for the Greater Newtown Cultural Quarter as key projects to attract a daytime visiting public. In addition, both spaces are under investigation as possible venues for large conferences and events and, in the case of Turbine Hall, there is an additional proposal to link it to a new boutique hotel planned for Newtown (Ochre Communications, 2004).

As stressed above, Johannesburg, as the most visited part of Gauteng, is primarily positioned as a business destination. This focus on business tourism to the exclusion of leisure tourism, historically has had more to do with Johannesburg's position as the economic capital of South Africa than on any conscious tourism marketing or branding strategy. It is argued, however, that there is a great deal of potential to follow a dual strategy for tourism development in the inner city, one that recognizes the importance of growing the leisure tourism market in tandem with the business tourism market, more especially in the wake of the actual and planned development of new, and enhancement of existing, cultural and historical visitor attractions in the inner city. The inner city contains several tourism assets in terms of historic and architectural landmarks that are key attractions for anyone wishing to understand Johannesburg history. In addition, there is a high concentration of cultural attractions, particularly in the Newtown area (Dirsuweit, 1999; Rogerson, 2002). According to South African Tourism research, cultural and heritage tourism is the third largest attraction for international tourists visiting South Africa (Monitor, 2004). Culture and history are ranked just behind climate and scenic beauty as motivators for visiting the country, with 22 percent of air travelers and 44 percent of land travelers noting culture and heritage as an important reason for travel. In addition, for domestic tourists, visiting museums, art galleries and visiting Parliament were amongst the ten most popular activities (Rule et al., 2001; Ochre Communications, 2004).

The majority of tour operators operating in Gauteng offer a tour of Johannesburg's inner city as an option for international visitors. This is either packaged as a tour of its own or as an add-on to a Soweto tour. Interviews conducted with a selection of these operators (see table 13.3) indicate that, while the tour of the inner city is popular, it is almost exclusively a driving tour with the majority of operators electing not to stop at any of the various attractions or sites. The three places where operators do sometimes stop include the top of the Carlton, George Harrison Park (now closed) and, less often, Museum Africa in Newtown.

Interviews conducted with several leisure-related product owners in Johannesburg inner city[1] disclose that the majority of current visitors to these facilities are day-trippers from around Gauteng. Of these, the majority of visitors are school groups. It is evident that the museums and galleries in the inner city are not currently attracting significant numbers of international or domestic tourists, nor are they attracting significant numbers of local day-trippers other than school groups. These findings should be looked at in relation to South African Tourism research study which disclosed that while 22 percent of tourists arriving by air and 44 percent arriving by land are "interested" in South Africa's culture, political history and heritage, less than 20 percent of these cultural tourists actually visited an art gallery, museum or cultural site during their stay in Gauteng (Ochre Communications, 2004). This gap between expressed interest and actual visitation can be explained due to both a perceived lack of attractive, exciting, value-for-money cultural and heritage attractions and broader problems such as a lack of transport, a lack of information and the absence of "cultural quarters" or a Central Tourism District that makes Johannesburg's heritage accessible for international tourists.

Overall, the key constraints relating to leisure tourism in the inner city can be summarized under three headings. The first relates to the lack of quality leisure products in the inner city. The second relates to a series of inefficiencies in Johannesburg's operation as a tourism city. The third relates to inefficient marketing and packaging of what exists for leisure tourists. These constraints on leisure tourism in inner city Johannesburg are further elucidated below:

The lack of quality leisure products in terms of heritage and culture is the first major constraint. A comparison between expectations before coming to South Africa and actual experience once in South Africa shows that international visitors are consistently impressed by the scenic beauty of the country whereas their expectations about experiencing culture and the country after political change are either just met or fall short of expectations (Monitor, 2004). This finding is recorded in surveys of satisfaction as undertaken during 2004 with international visitors to South Africa. Surveyed tourists rated "cultural aspects" low as compared to other aspects (such as scenery or wild life) of their visit to South Africa. Moreover, low satisfaction ratings are recorded also for opportunity to interact with local people and to taste local cuisine. Further, amongst European visitors to South Africa, one of their major expressed disappointments surrounds the country's "dull cities" (Monitor, 2004).

Tour operators interviewed as part of this research indicated that, historically, they have not conducted cultural/heritage tours of Johannesburg as they have never felt that the city has enough quality attractions to warrant packaging into a half or full day tour. Nevertheless, the view was expressed that with the establishment of new attractions in Greater Johannesburg such as Constitution

Hill, the apartheid museum and the Hector Peterson Museum in Soweto, they could begin to package heritage-based tours of Johannesburg. Another potential market for heritage tours is day visitors, especially the market offered by local Johannesburg residents. During 2002 a survey was conducted with Johannesburg residents living and working in the inner city and Rosebank areas as to their usage of the city's heritage and cultural infrastructure (Ochre Communications, 2004). The survey disclosed that 86 percent of respondents did not make any use of these attractions for a number of reasons, *viz.* lack of time, alternative leisure pursuits and that the existing museums had little cultural appeal for them or their families.

A second set of constraints upon leisure tourism relate to inefficiencies of Johannesburg as a tourism city. In understanding the reasons for Johannesburg's low levels of leisure tourism it is instructive to look at comments made about the city delegates to the World Summit on Sustainable Development (WSSD) delegates who were surveyed as they departed from Johannesburg International Airport. Their main areas of dissatisfaction with Johannesburg related to poor transport; costs of accommodation, restaurants and transport; low levels of customer service and efficiency; crime; the lack of adequate tourism information, particularly in different languages; and lack of entertainment and sightseeing attractions (Ochre Communications, 2004).

Notwithstanding these problems, the tourism product owners interviewed as part of this research (particularly those located in the Newtown area) all indicated that visitation levels had shown marked improvement as a result of the opening during 2003 of the iconic Nelson Mandela Bridge and the Carr Street off-ramp from the M1 into the inner-city. This welcome development signaling an upturn in the inner-city tourism economy points to the importance of enhanced marketing and for an integrated approach to tourism development in Johannesburg. Without a critical mass of heritage and leisure attractions and facilities, it will be difficult for any individual attraction to succeed in drawing visitors to Johannesburg inner city on a sustainable level. It is argued that the future development of a series of tourism precincts coupled with proper provision of information, targeted marketing, signage and attention to security issues is vital in making the city's leisure attractions more accessible.

Conclusions

During 2004 the prospects for urban regeneration and growing inner city tourism in South Africa's largest city were boosted by two developments. First, was the demarcation during October 2004 by the Minister of Finance of Johannesburg inner city as one of South Africa's first Urban Development Zones (UDZ). The UDZ status provides a tax incentive for the erection, extension or addition of buildings which "is directed at the stimulation of the regeneration of declining urban areas, in targeted inner city areas across South Africa, and the encouragement of economic development" (City of

Johannesburg, 2004b: 1). Second, is the formation of an Inner City Tourism Association that is an organization of tourism product owners "working to refashion Johannesburg as a desirable destination" (O'Reilly, 2004a). This institutional development was launched on September 15, 2004 as one of eight tourism destination marketing organizations encouraged by the Johannesburg Tourism Company as part of its marketing initiatives for the city as a whole (O'Reilly, 2004b).

From our analysis, the challenges of growing this inner city tourism node are several. The current tourism market for Johannesburg inner city can be segmented into two main areas of policy focus. First, is a domestic and regional MICE market based around those organizations situated within the inner city, i.e. provincial and local government, unions, corporations, and NGOs. This market comprising both day and overnight visitors are the key customers for the inner city hotels. Second, is a day-tripper leisure market that does not stay overnight within the inner city. This group consists of two sub-groups: 1) international visitors interested in getting an overview of Johannesburg and its history and visiting either as part of an organized tour or with friends or relatives with whom they are staying; and 2) local Johannesburg residents or domestic tourists visiting for leisure purposes, that is, for a specific event or to visit a specific museum, gallery or restaurant.

The current potential of the inner city for tourism development is, therefore, based around two key short-term thrusts. The first thrust is to capitalize on the existing competitive advantage that the inner city has to attract domestic and regional MICE tourists, particularly those linked to government, unions, NGOs and the large corporations located in the inner city. The second thrust is to build on the wealth of historical and cultural assets within the inner city in order to attract a regular day visitor market.

A number of constraints need to be addressed in achieving the development potential for tourism in this "difficult area," not least the continued poor image of the inner city. The image of the inner city was raised in several stakeholder interviews and clearly continues to be a problem and immediate constraint that must be addressed in order to sustain and enhance the health of the inner-city tourism economy. Despite the acknowledged progress made by the intensive urban management initiatives operating in the inner city in terms of improving the situation of "crime and grime," the inner city retains a poor image among certain segments of the MICE market. Improved marketing of the inner city is essential to enhance perceptions particularly among end users and professional conference organizers. The situation is emerging that the image of parts of the inner city, especially Newtown is undoubtedly improving and this upturn in perceptions needs to be galvanized as a base for spearheading a revival in the wider image of Johannesburg inner city. In addition, the maintenance and upgrading of infrastructure in support of inner city tourism businesses is essential, particularly as regards roads, rubbish removal, greening, and upgrading of pavements.

Lastly, there is a need for economic support that recognizes the importance of domestic and regional MICE tourism to the inner city. The current focus within conference marketing for the city is viewed as biased towards the attraction of international conferences for Johannesburg, primarily into the Sandton area. It is argued that the weakness of support for domestic and regional MICE tourism is a constraint that needs to be addressed in terms of improved information flows. It was observed that the current average size of conference that Johannesburg is "winning" in terms of conference marketing initiatives is approximately 1,000 delegates, a size which is too large to be accommodated in current facilities in the inner city. Overall, there is a need clearly for conference marketing initiatives for Johannesburg to target the domestic and regional MICE markets in which the inner city has a greater competitive strength. Nevertheless, there is also the opportunity offered by marketing the inner city as a conference venue for the "displaced business" that cannot be accommodated in Sandton as a result of successful marketing initiatives that capture the business of large meetings and exhibitions.

In final analysis, it must be concluded that any development strategy for tourism in the inner city needs to be harmonized with the current directions of both:

- Strategic initiatives for inner-city regeneration; and
- Strategic planning for tourism in Johannesburg as a whole.

All of the above strategies are unified by a common approach that must be carried through to a tourism strategy for the inner city. Central to this approach is the focus for the public sector on providing an environment that is conducive to attracting private sector investment and Public Private Partnerships into the inner city. From a tourism point of view this means applying the five strategy pillars of the Inner City Regeneration Strategy, as well as additional tourism-related strategies, to attract private sector investment and partnerships into identified tourism precincts within the inner city.

Acknowledgements

Thanks are due to the City of Johannesburg Tourism and Marketing Company which commissioned the original report upon which this paper is based. In addition, for extended research, Chris Rogerson thanks financial support from the National Research Foundation, Pretoria under Gun Award 2054064.

Note

1. During 2004 interviews were conducted with the following: Museum Africa, 5 April; Gramadoelas, 5 April; African Bank Market Theatre, 5 April; Sci-Bono Discovery Centre, 7 April; SAB World of Beer, 7 April and Kippies Jazz International, 7 April.

References

Beauregard R.A., 1998: Tourism and economic development policy in U.S. urban areas, in D. Ioannides and K.G. Debbage (Eds.), *The Economic Geography of the Tourist Industry: A Supply-Side Analysis.* Routledge, London, 220-234.

Bradley, A., Hall, T. and Harrison, M., 2002: Selling cities: promoting new images for meetings tourism, *Cities*, 19, 61-70.

Buckley, P.J. and Witt, S.F., 1985: Tourism in difficult areas: case studies of Bradford, Bristol, Glasgow and Hamm, *Tourism Management*, 6, 205-214.

Buckley, P.J. and Witt, S.F., 1989: Tourism in difficult areas II: case studies of Calderdale, Leeds, Manchester and Scunthorpe, *Tourism Management*, 10, 138-152.

Chang, T.C., 2000: Singapore's little India: a tourist attraction as a contested landscape, *Urban Studies*, 37, 343-366.

Chang, T.C. and Huang, S., 2004: Urban tourism: between the global and the local, in A.A. Lew, C.M. Hall and A.M. Williams (Eds.), *A Companion to Tourism,* Blackwell, Oxford, 223-234.

Chetty, L., 2004: Interview, Gauteng Shared Services, Johannesburg, 23 March.

City of Johannesburg, 1992: *Johannesburg: the Financial and Commercial Capital of Southern Africa.* A special report on Johannesburg issued as a supplement to Corporate Location Report, Milton Keynes.

City of Johannesburg, 2004a: Johannesburg Inner City Regeneration Strategy Business Plan: Business Plan Financial Years 2004-2007, Unpublished document, City of Johannesburg.

City of Johannesburg, 2004b: Guide to the Urban Development Zone tax incentive for the Johannesburg inner city, available at www.joburg.org.za

Coles, T., 2003: Urban tourism, place promotion and economic restructuring: the case of post-socialist Leipzig, *Tourism Geographies*, 5, 190-219.

Conforti, J.M., 1996: Ghettos as tourism attractions, *Annals of Tourism Research*, 23, 830-842.

Couch, C. and Farr, S-J., 2000: Museums, galleries, tourism and regeneration: some experiences from Liverpool, *Built Environment*, 26 (2), 152-163.

Crewe, L., 1991: Local economic development: new emphases, new images, *East Midlands Geographer*, 14, 1-3.

Dirsuweit, T. 1999: From Fortress City to Creative City: developing culture and the information-based sectors in the regeneration and reconstruction of the Greater Johannesburg Area, *Urban Forum,* 10, 183-213.

Fagence, M., 2004: Book Review on Urban Tourism, *Tourism Management,* 25, 638-640.

Ferreira, S.L.A. and Harmse, A.C., 2000: Crime and tourism in South Africa: international tourists perception and risk, *South African Geographical Journal*, 82, 80-85.

Garcia, B., 2004: Urban regeneration, arts programming and major events—Glasgow 1990, Sydney 2000 and Barcelona 2004, *International Journal of Cultural Policy*, 10, 103-118.

Gauteng Tourism Authority, 2003: *Strategic Plan 2003-2006*, GTA, Johannesburg.

GJMC (Greater Johannesburg Metropolitan Council) 2001: *Tourism Strategy*, available at www.joburg.org.za

GJMC (Greater Johannesburg Metropolitan Council), 2002: *Johannesburg 2030*, Corporate Planning Unit, GJMC, available at www.joburg.org.za.

Haley Sharpe Southern Africa, 2003: A study to undertake baseline research into the volumes of tourists visiting Johannesburg tourism sites, Unpublished report submitted to the City of Johannesburg Department of Marketing and Tourism.

Hall, C.M., 2002: Tourism in capital cities, *Tourism*, 50, 235-248.

Han, Q., Dellaert, B.G.C., van Raaij, W.F. and Timmermans, H.J.P., 2003: Supporting tourism activity planning decisions from an urban tourism management perspective, *Tourism Analysis*, 8, 153-157.

Hayllar, B. and Griffin, T., 2005: The precinct experience: a phenomenological approach, *Tourism Management*, 26, 517-528.

Hoffman, L.M., 2000: Tourism and the revitalization of Harlem, *Research in Urban Sociology*, 5, 207-223.

Hoffman, L.M., 2003: The marketing of diversity in the inner city: tourism and regulation in Harlem, *International Journal of Urban and Regional Research*, 27, 286-299.

Hoffman, L., Fainstein, S.S. and Judd, D.R. (Eds.), 2003: *Cities and Visitors: Regulating People, Markets and City Space*, Blackwell, Oxford.

Hope, C.A. and Klemm, M.S., 2001: Tourism in difficult areas revisited: the case of Bradford, *Tourism Management*, 22, 629-635.

Hoyle, B., 2001: Lamu: waterfront revitalization in an East African port city, *Cities*, 18, 297-313.

Hughes, H.L., 2003: Marketing gay tourism in Manchester: new market for urban tourism or destruction of 'gay space," *Journal of Vacation Marketing*, 9, 152-163.

Hunter, R., Jonker, M., Rogerson, J., Rogerson C. and Tomlinson, R., 1995: Johannesburg Inner-City Strategic Development Framework: Economic Analysis, Unpublished Report for the City Planning Department, Greater Johannesburg Transitional Metropolitan Council.

Ioannides, D., 2003: The economics of tourism in host communities, in S. Singh, D.J. Timothy and R.K. Dowling (Eds.), *Tourism in Destination Communities*, CABI Publishing, Wallingford, 37-54.

Jansen-Verbeke, M., 1985: Inner city leisure resources, *Leisure Studies*, 4, 141-157.

Jansen-Verbeke, M., 1986: Inner-city tourism: resources, tourists and promoters, *Annals of Tourism Research*, 13, 79-100.

Judd D.R. and Fainstein S.S., 1999: *The Tourist City,* Yale University Press, New Haven.

Karski, A., 1990: Urban tourism—a key to urban regeneration, *The Planner*, 76 (13) 15-17.

King, B., 2004: Book Review on "Managing Urban Tourism," *Tourism Management*, 25, 290-291.

KPMG, 2001: Gauteng Tourism Authority: Tourism Marketing Plan for Gauteng 2001-2006, Unpublished report for GTA, Johannesburg.

Law, C.M., 1991: Tourism and urban revitalization, *East Midlands Geographer*, 14, 49-60.

Law, C.M., 1992: Urban tourism and its contribution to economic regeneration, *Urban Studies*, 29, 599-618.

Law, C.M., 1993: *Urban Tourism: Attracting Visitors to Large Cities*, Mansell, London.

Law, C.M., 1996: Introduction, in C.M. Law (Ed.), *Tourism in Major Cities*, International Thomson Business Press, London, 1-22.

Law, C.M., 2000: Regenerating the city center through leisure and tourism, *Built Environment*, 26, 117-129.

Liebermann, T., 2004: Interview, Consultant to City of Johannesburg, 24 March.

McCarthy, J., 2002: Entertainment-led regeneration: the case of Detroit, *Cities*, 19, 105-111.

McKercher, B., Ho, P.S.Y. and du Cros, H., 2005: Relationship between tourism and cultural heritage management: evidence from Hong Kong, *Tourism Management*, 26, 539-548.

Melvill, L., 2004: Interview, Director, Surgeon & Safari, Johannesburg, 24 March.

Mlangeni, B., 1997: Inner-city hotel cuts back on services, *The Star*, 4 June, 6.

Monitor, 2004: *Global Competitiveness Project: Summary of Key Findings of Phase 1,* South African Tourism Johannesburg.

Ochre Communications, 2004: Inner city tourism strategy, Unpublished report submitted to the City of Johannesburg Tourism and Marketing Department.

O'Reilly, T., 2004a: Body set up to boost inner city tourism, available at www.joburg.org.za (22 October)

O'Reilly, T., 2004b: New nodes prove a boon for city tourism, available at www.joburg.org.za (9 November)

Page, S.J., 1995: *Urban Tourism*, Routledge, London.

Pearce, D.G., 1998: Tourist districts in Paris: structure and functions, *Tourism Management*, 19, 49-66.

Pearce, D.G., 2001: An integrative framework for urban tourism research, *Annals of Tourism Research*, 28, 926-946.

Rogerson, C.M., 2002: Urban tourism in the developing world: the case of Johannesburg, *Development Southern Africa*, 19, 169-190.

Rogerson, C.M., 2004a: Towards the world-class African city: planning local economic development planning in Johannesburg, South Africa, *Africa Insight,* 34 (4), 12-21.

Rogerson, C.M., 2004b: Urban tourism and economic regeneration: the example of Johannesburg, in C.M. Rogerson and G. Visser (Eds.), *Tourism and Development Issues in Contemporary South Africa,* Africa Institute of South Africa, Pretoria, 466-487.

Rogerson, C.M., 2004c: Pro-poor local economic development in post-apartheid South Africa: the Johannesburg fashion district, *International Development Planning Review*, 26, 401-429.

Rogerson, C.M., 2004d: Regional tourism in South Africa: a case of "mass tourism of the South," *GeoJournal*, 60, 229-237.

Rogerson, C.M., 2005: Globalization, economic restructuring and local response in Johannesburg—the most isolated "world city," in K. Segbers, S. Raiser and K. Volkmann (Ed.), *Public Problems—Private Solutions?: Globalizing Cities in the South*, Ashgate, Aldershot, 17-34.

Rogerson, J., 1995: The changing face of retailing in the South African city: the case of inner-city Johannesburg, *Africa Insight*, 25, 163-171.

Rule, S., Struwig, J., Langa, Z., Viljoen, J. and Bouare, O., 2001: South African domestic tourism survey: marketing the provinces, Unpublished report for South African Tourism and DEAT, Pretoria.

Rule, S., Viljoen, J., Zama, S., Struwig, J., Langa, Z. and Bouare, O., 2004: Visiting friends and relatives: South Africa's most popular form of domestic tourism, in C.M. Rogerson and G. Visser (Eds.), *Tourism and Development Issues in Contemporary South Africa*, Pretoria, Africa Institute of South Africa, 78-101.

Russo, A.P. and van der Borg, J., 2002: Planning considerations for cultural tourism: a case study of four European cities, *Tourism Management*, 23, 631-637.

Saunders, G, 2004: Interview, Director of Tourism Research, Grant Thornton Kessell Feinstein, Johannesburg, 6 April.

Scott, A.J., 2004: Cultural-products industries and urban economic development: prospects for growth and market contestation in a global context, *Urban Affairs Review*, 39, 461-90.

Shevel, A., 1998: Carlton has shut its last hotel room, *The Star Business Report*, 1 April.

South African Tourism 2002: *Tourism Growth Strategy.* South African Tourism, Johannesburg.

South African Tourism 2004: *Domestic Tourism Growth Strategy 2004 to 2007*, South African Tourism, Johannesburg.

Strom, E., 2002: Converting pork into porcelain: cultural institutions and downtown development, *Urban Affairs Review*, 38, 3-21.

Swarbrooke, J., 1999: Urban areas, in J. Swarbrooke, *Sustainable Tourism Management*, CABI Publishing, Wallingford, 172-182.

Swarbrooke, J., 2000: Tourism, economic development and urban regeneration: a critical evaluation, in M. Robinson, R. Sharpley, N. Evans, P. Long and J. Swarbrooke (Eds.), *Developments in Urban and Rural Tourism*, Centre for Travel and Tourism, Sheffield Hallam University and University of Northumbria, Sunderland, 269-285.

Swarbrooke, J. and Horner, S., 2001: *Business Travel and Tourism*, Butterworth-Heinemann, Oxford.

Van Aaalst, I and Boogaarts, I., 2002: From museum to mass entertainment: the evolution of the role of museums in cities, *European Urban and Regional Studies*, 9, 195-209.

Viljoen, D., 2004: Interview CEO, Johannesburg Tourism Company, Johannesburg, 24 March.

14

Understandings of Urban Regeneration, Heritage and Environmental Justice at Constitution Hill, Johannesburg

Clinton David van der Merwe and Zarina Patel

"Planners would benefit from integrating social theory with environmental thinking and from combining their substantive skills with techniques for community resolution, to confront economic and environmental injustice"—(Campbell, 2001: 251).

The changing landscape of South African cities has been directed by efforts changing the form and function of particular nodes in the city. Whilst these interventions have resulted in spatial changes in the city fabric, they have been underpinned by particular motivations linked to the development and redistribution of human, social, economic and environmental capital. The success of urban regeneration initiatives can therefore not be understood in purely physical terms. Changes in the spatial formation of South African cities need to be understood with respect to the values underpinning change. This chapter assesses the potential relationship between heritage and environmental justice as values informing regeneration at Constitution Hill in Johannesburg by first focusing on the policy process, and secondly understanding the relationship between physical form and visitors' understandings of these approaches. This study therefore focuses on the goal of building cities that are sustainable, by assessing the role of heritage in shaping the spatial changes being experienced.

The need to regenerate and renew South African cities in a post-1994 context has witnessed the introduction of a range of interrelated planning frameworks with a focus on redress, equity and justice (Harrison, 2003a). One such framework is that of sustainable development. Despite its environmental roots, the potential of sustainable development to foster social transformation and democratization has rendered it a crucial element, of post-apartheid planning.

However, early attempts at embracing its potential have met with a number of conflicting outcomes, in a context where market driven economic interventions dominate the decision-making arena. Theorists and practitioners from the fields of planning and development have taken up the question of sustainable development, and the common conclusion is that the theoretical or conceptual frameworks for addressing sustainable development are inadequate (Jacobs, 1997; Adams, 1999; Patel, 2000).

In refocusing sustainable development, McDonald (2002) suggests that environmental justice might provide more theoretical substance to sustainable development within a framework of rights. Despite an emerging literature on environmental justice, its application to questions of policy informing regeneration, and on heritage specifically, remains undocumented. As such, the first aim of this study is to determine the potential links between urban regeneration, heritage, and environmental justice and sustainable development. This is done using a policy and institutional analysis of the development of Constitution Hill.

Rather than examining the market-related forces driving urban renewal, this chapter focuses on the redevelopment of urban space for human and social capital. One of the approaches guiding the implementation of human and social capital is a sustainable cities approach to regeneration, with the specific goal of reducing the human and social consequences of environmental injustice, whilst the focus of heritage is what can be inherited between generations. As both concepts share the same goals and objectives, heritage is assessed for its potential as an indicator of sustainability in regeneration. In determining the success of urban regeneration interventions, Parnell and Pieterse (2002) argue that the social and psychological incorporation of citizens into development plans and processes are as critical as the physical integration of the city.

Although much has been written about urban regeneration in South Africa little is known about the potential of transformed spaces to bring about the social and psychological incorporation of citizens into the changing cityscape. The second aim of the study is to understand the extent to which the users of these spaces buy-into and support the objectives of the regeneration interventions. The study focuses on interviews with tourists and visitors to Constitution Hill, to determine the extent to which visitors' understandings of urban regeneration, heritage and environmental justice are shaped by their interactions with the changes in the physical landscape.

Urban Regeneration and Values: Sustainable Cities, Environmental Justice and Heritage

Recognizing the importance of cities as a key source, as well as solution to global environmental problems, Agenda 21 refocused the environmental debate to the city scale. Since the introduction of Local Agenda 21, numerous local authorities worldwide have been attempting to mainstream environmental issues and sustainable development into local planning (Sowman, 2002). Within debates on sustainable cities, developing world cities have been in the spotlight, as these cities are growing at unprecedented rates, without the requisite delivery of services and infrastructure (Hardoy et al., 2001). However, despite attempts at delivering services and infrastructure in rapidly growing cities, it has become clear that the benefits are not always justly spread throughout society.

Marcuse (1998) warns that programs and policies can be socially just, but unfortunately, they can also be sustainable and unjust. The inverse is also true, where unsustainable programs maybe very just, and so unjust programs may also be unsustainable. Marcuse (1998) shows that sustainability at a macro scale serves to perpetuate environmental and social injustices at the local level (Patel, 2003).

Patel (2003) has argued that the political magnitude of sustainable development as tool for urban regeneration has been underestimated, and largely denied. A consequence of this blind spot has resulted in approaches that can be described as technocratic, mechanical and managerialist (Jacobs, 1997). In the pursuit of sustainable development, new indicators have been developed; new policy instruments have been introduced (like Local Agenda 21); Strategic Environmental Assessments, Environmental Impact Assessments and other tools for environmental management have dominated the environmental policy arena in South Africa. Fischer and Hajer (1999), as well as Beck (1992) argue convincingly that a reliance on the key practices of modernity including the dominance of scientific rationality and expert knowledge serve to accentuate rather than alleviate environmental problems, which are in themselves by-products of systems of modernity.

What is omitted from this approach is a recognition that despite the emergence of joint discourses of environmental politics, are different frames of reference which inspire the way in which behaviors within different cultures are modified to achieve sustainable development. When such cultural differences are ignored or marginalized through the tools used to achieve sustainable development, conflict emerges. In these instances, sustainable development is seen as being imposed by the state on communities, with a large chasm being developed between the goals and aspirations of the various stakeholders. Fischer and Hajer (1999) urge therefore that more attention be paid to the cultural embeddedness of policymaking, and of people's everyday life experiences. It is argued that some of the challenges posed by the need to address the cultural and political nature of the sustainability challenge have the potential to be resolved using an environmental justice framework (Agyeman et al., 2003).

Approaches to environmental justice in South Africa have been largely catalyzed and shaped by the Environmental Justice Networking Forum (EJNF). EJNF define environmental justice as being "about social transformation directed towards meeting basic human needs and enhancing our quality of life—economic quality, health care, housing, human rights, environmental protection, and democracy" (McDonald, 2002: 4). Environmental justice therefore ensures that the distribution of goods (infrastructure and service), does not result in the distribution of bad (environmental impacts) to the poor and marginalized (Harvey, 1999). A recent edited volume on environmental justice in South Africa by McDonald (2002) is an important contribution to understanding this approach, however, little empirical work exists to demonstrate its effectiveness and implications for urban planning.

In assessing the extent to which evolving debates on sustainable development and environmental justice are influencing the discourse and practice of urban regeneration, this chapter focuses on intergenerational justice. Intergenerational justice is interpreted in procedural terms: "doing justice to future generations amounts to acting according to the right principles rather than trying to achieve any particular outcomes" (Holland, as cited in Dobson, 1999: 8). The extent to which these principles are explicitly incorporated into policy, and furthermore understood by visitors who interpret these values through the physical landscape, are important indicators of the effectiveness and usefulness of environmental justice as an underlying value in urban regeneration.

Heritage is a way of tracking how culture and values are preserved between generations and is therefore a good means of testing the intergenerational justice of sustainable development and environmental justice. A useful starting point for understanding the role of heritage in urban regeneration is by referring to the National Heritage Resources Act (no. 25) of 1999, which states: "Our heritage celebrates our achievements and contributes to redressing past inequities. It educates, it deepens our understanding of society and encourages us to empathize with the experience of others. It facilitates healing and material and symbolic restitution and it promotes new and previously neglected research into our rich oral traditions and customs" (NHRA, 1999: 651).

This rights approach often seems like an abstract concept divorced from real life (Enviroteach, 2002: 2). In reality, human rights and their infringement are grounded in the daily experiences of people within their local communities, and influences how people interact with physical spaces. In the context of South Africa, heritage is important as it well reflects the atrocities of apartheid, in many cases being used today as a point of healing and reconciliation. Heritage links us as a group to a shared inheritance and often is central to cultivating an imagined community or idea of nationhood (Johnson, 1999). "Heritage resources" on the other hand, are defined as "any place or object of cultural significance" (NHRA, 1999: 659). Tangible physical resources therefore have the role of fulfilling non-tangible or psychological aspects of regeneration including education, healing and symbolic restitution.

Heritage has been used in a number of ways in urban studies. Some link heritage to tourism (Law, 1992; Chang, 1999; Richards and Hall, 2000) whilst some scholars have focused their research on the commonalities (like inheritance) that heritage and sustainable development share (Fyall and Garrod, 1998). Heritage is seen by many (especially politicians) as a vehicle to nation building (see Cheung, 2003). The premier of Gauteng recently called on residents to "join hands in preserving the country's heritage and advancing social integration to build a new nation, which is non-racial, non-sexist, democratic and prosperous."

Increasingly, heritage is being used as a tool for urban regeneration. Harrison (2003b: 6) notes that, "new interesting cultural patterns, and uses of space, are emerging within an increasingly multi-cultural inner city." Over the last decade Fraser (2003) has done some pioneering work into the use of heritage in urban regeneration strategies in and around Johannesburg. Indeed, Fraser (2004), CEO of Central Johannesburg Partnership (CJP), maintains that heritage is a valuable draw card in any city and can be used as a tool for urban regeneration in that our heritage should be preserved in how we recreate or reuse urban space (Inner City Tourism Strategy, 2004).

In South Africa, 2004 marked ten years of democracy as South Africans celebrated freedom and dignity. Johnson (1999) argues that heritage is primarily a process of tourism expansion and forms part of postmodern patterns of consumption. Detailed attention would make fascinating research of how spaces (and places) of heritage translate complex cultural, political and symbolic processes into popular imagination.

Constitutional Hill–Renewed Urban Space?

The redevelopment of the Constitution Hill precinct is an example of an urban regeneration initiative, driven by the need to redress past oppression and inequities whilst celebrating the ideals of reconciliation, and the prosperity of South Africa's democratic heritage.

Geographically, Constitution Hill is located northeast of the Johannesburg CBD, near Braamfontein, Hillbrow, and Joubert Park/Bertrams (figure 14.1). The Constitution Hill precinct (like many other urban regeneration zones in the cityscape) forms part of the broader Blue IQ development initiative. Blue IQ (the Gauteng provincial government's economic development initiative to create a "smart province") is working in partnership with the Johannesburg Development Agency (JDA) to make Johannesburg an "African World Class City."

Location of Constitution Hill

Constitution Hill has, since 1892, attracted many spatial and temporal attributes: it consists of 95,000 square meters of space that was historically developed to house an Old Fort, the "native gaol," and the women's prison. The area was earmarked in 1994 for architectural and other structural developments—to house the Constitutional Court of South Africa, as well as promote urban tourism, job creation, and the entrenchment of our heritage as the "rainbow nation" (JDA,

Figure 14.1
Location of Constitution Hill

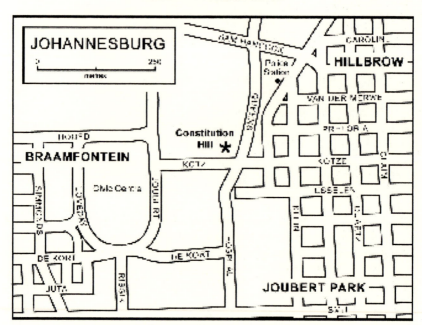

2003). Before the regeneration of the precinct, Constitution Hill was largely an unknown, invisible, and unacknowledged space. The site's history of injustice and brutality remained largely untold.

A key objective of the development has been to redress these past inequities, through a deepening of society's understandings of the past. The key cultural resources that have been included in the regeneration of the area include the Constitutional Court of South Africa. The heritage buildings on the site provide another key focus for the development. Over time, these buildings will be carefully repaired, restored, and renovated, as museum and exhibition spaces:

- The renovation of the Old Fort to accommodate a variety of functions, as well as the allocation of 5500 square meters for exhibition and museum space;
- The refurbishment and adaptation of Section Four and Section Five (the "Native" Prison), to become a museum space and place of reflection and contemplation;
- The renovation of the Old Governor's House to accommodate improved community facilities;
- The rehabilitation of the Old Fort and its ramparts, which will provide a powerful vantage point over the campus and Johannesburg; and

- The adaptation of the Women's Gaol to become a museum space (JDA, 2004c).

The case study of Constitution Hill is used to explore the extent to which this urban regeneration initiative has embraced the concept of sustainable development, a key framework driving the city's planning. At a theoretical level, arguments have been put forward for the need to take a step further, and to incorporate questions of rights and justice in the distribution of the environmental consequences of the delivery of services and infrastructure. Despite the emerging support for an environmental justice approach, little empirical evidence exists from South Africa on how it might work in practice.

Policy Interpretations

The City of Johannesburg has embraced the principles of sustainable development, largely driven through the mayor, who is also the president of the International Council for Local Environmental Initiatives. However, the effectiveness of the incorporation of these sustainable development principles and its links with environmental justice and heritage can only be tested at the micro level of plans and their implementation

Sustainable Development

Broadly speaking, the research has shown that the Blue IQ's ethos and approach have the potential to gear development in a sustainable way. Although the key principles of sustainable development are only covertly present in the policy document informing the development, it is in the architecture and the design of the spaces that sustainable development principles are most obvious. The architecture fuses aesthetics, heritage, nature and energy conserving measures (Lambrecht, 2005). The design embraces the sustainability slogan coined at the World Summit of Sustainable Development (2002)—People, Planet, and Prosperity.

The architects were conscious of the need for visitors to read the function of the building from its design. Consequently, the scale, materials and designs used to create intimacy, and to draw people in. Glass, wood and recycled bricks from historical buildings on the Constitution Hill precinct have been used for their symbolic qualities (Lambrecht, 2005). The geographical location of Constitution Hill speaks of the history and future prosperity of the city. This was where gold was first discovered, and the point from which the city subsequently grew. The need to develop within the carrying capacity of the earth, and hence reflect the planet aspect of sustainable development is reflected in the use of sustainable technologies and green design techniques. These include a passive cooling control system, a "grey" water system, as well as a waste management system, which together help conserve energy (Lambrecht, 2005).

Environmental Justice

The JDA has not specifically made environmental justice a central component of their values, although by implication, many of the development principles enshrined by the JDA have strong links to environmental justice. The JDA's commitments to accountability to all stakeholders, empowerment and responsiveness, have commonalities with the values of environmental justice.

Heritage

The focus on heritage by contrast is a much more obvious driver of the development. "Constitution Hill will be a major national and international heritage site, comprising an integrated and sustainable, multi-purpose and multi-dimensional space with a number of integrated and complimentary physical and institutional components, forming an integrated part of a revitalized City Centre" (JDA, 2004a: 1). This mixed-use development area offers an unique cultural, historical, educational, business, and recreational space. It is a place where visitors can "experience the story of the South African transition, observe the process by which freedom is now protected and learn how South Africa is building the future on the past" (JDA, Media Release, 2 April 2004).

There has been a great deal of emphasis on the heritage of Constitution Hill. Many articles in the media focus on the potential of heritage at the place since it resonates our past so vividly in a spatial (built on the Old Fort and a prison complex) and in a temporal sense (as its existence ties into a decade of democratic rule in a country recovering from the scourge of apartheid) (see Gerber, 2004). Garson (2004:1) describes the Constitutional Court as a "beacon of hope" as it is: "built on the grounds of the City's notorious Old Fort prison where human rights were flouted and oppression flourished, the court will instead be a 'shining beacon of hope' for the protection of human rights and the advancement of human liberty and dignity ... it is symbolic too of the tremendous strides taken in bringing investment, tourism and cultural life back to the city."

The research has shown that despite commitments to sustainable development at the macro-policy level, these directives are watered down, or referred to obliquely when it comes down to precinct planning, only to be reintroduced in the design stages. This, however, has implications for the links between sustainable development and environmental justice, as design interventions are important in reducing environmental impacts, although the translation of these reduced impacts to a rights approach demands a shift in attitudes and values that require more than physical changes.

Visitor Understandings of Urban Regeneration, Heritage and Environmental Justice

One way of testing the success of interventions aimed at regenerating the cityscape is to assess the extent to which the psychological landscape has shifted. This study sought to understand the extent to which visitors were able to reinterpret the physical landscape, and the things they experienced as visitors to Constitution Hill, with respect to the policy intentions.

Urban Regeneration

There is little agreement in the literature as to the meaning of urban regeneration. The American literature often refers to the term urban renewal, including the redevelopment of economic infrastructure. By contrast, the European literature links the redevelopment of derelict residential or industrial areas to the development of human and social capital. Clearly, how one defines the changes in the city landscape will have an effect on the approach taken.

Most respondents recognize that urban regeneration is necessary in Johannesburg, however, interpretations on regeneration varied. One respondent described it as: "incorporating history, culture and heritage with contemporary society that has clear objectives to do with sustainability and the nature of its (the city's) identity" (Anonymous A). Generally, the majority of respondents thought that urban regeneration of Johannesburg was essential: "as there are a number of historical buildings that people do not want to forget about" (Thembi). "The centre of Johannesburg has been reduced to a typical Third World scenario of run down buildings, crime and grime and so forth. It is a shame that so much history is being forgotten" (Craig). Some also identified the benefits of urban regeneration for increased tourism and the investment associated with foreign revenue. More than 70 percent of respondents could identify other 'urban renewal projects' (such as Newtown, the Fashion District, Braamfontein, or the Nelson Mandela Bridge to name a few.

More than half the respondents were aware of and displayed more than a superficial understanding of Johannesburg's economic development strategy, Joburg 2030. In the analysis of Blue IQ and JDA policy documents, a strong emphasis on the need for and importance of urban regeneration emerged, and increasingly this issue is becoming prevalent in the media. Getaway (a travel magazine) describes urban regeneration by saying that "Jozi will never again be a mining camp or the sedate park of colonial-era coronations with street swept white's only by apartheid. There can be no doubt that it is steadily moving towards a vision that will make it one of the great cities of this continent—and the world" (Pinnock, 2004: 114). The media attention and innovative marketing campaign being followed by the City of Johannesburg in partnership with the provincial government, through the Blue IQ, has an important role to play in translating policy intentions into the public consciousness.

Sustainable Development

Understandings of sustainable development were expressed mainly in environmental terms. Many questionnaire respondents have a very "green perspective on what constitutes an environmental issue." Most respondents saw pollution (air, water, and solid) as the main environmental concern in Johannesburg. Most responses tended to locate "environmental" problems as those related to the natural world; apart from these others quoted here, people still rarely see the environment as being about people and the "built" environment—so miss out on important social justice and inter-generational justice issues.

Most respondents did not link issues such as infringements on people's basic human rights; people's right to freedom; safety; choice etc., to the environment. This may be related to South Africa's oppressive past (where too much emphasis was placed on conservation) and natural resources were often made more important than people. Further, approaches to addressing environmental issues in using tools such as impact assessment entrench the biophysical aspects of the environment, with little focus on social, process and governance aspects of sustainability. Most respondents (62 percent) stated that various forms of "spatial inequalities" still exist within the urban fabric of Johannesburg. Understandings of social inequalities were revealed through statements like: "the poor live in slum buildings" to "homelessness, poverty, unemployment—these still manifest in and around Johannesburg."

Very few respondents (less than 20 percent) had heard of the term 'environmental justice' and could not offer a definition for what they thought it meant. When a definition was offered to prompt responses, a fair number of the respondents agreed that Constitution Hill could be seen as a good example of environmental justice (just less than 40 percent); making statements such as: "These buildings speak of the past and tell us how to do things differently in the future" (Anonymous C). "This place is new and clean, we feel safe here, as though this is an area designed for all people, regardless of age, sex, race or religion/culture—to enjoy" (Mr. and Mrs. Rodrigues). Over 40 percent agreed that they thought the government was doing enough in addressing environmental justice in the urban context, saying things like there is a "good balance between preservation of old buildings and (the) upgrading of the area to create a safer and friendlier environment." However, despite attempts to make links with environmental justice, it is clear that this concept has not had an impact on the public's understandings of urban transformation.

Heritage

Heritage is "conceptualized as the meanings attached in the present to the past and is regarded as a knowledge defined within social, political, and cultural contexts" (Graham, 2002: 1003). Based on this rather broad definition, of the ninety-four respondents, various definitions of what they understood by the term heritage emerged. "Heritage refers to your culture. What you have done in your life and how you develop that into your belief system" (Lerato). Some understood heritage as more of a physical phenomenon like "Monuments, buildings and places of interest that have a credible history that could be preserved" (Mrs. Sayman). "Heritage is from the same root as 'inheritance'," it has not always been a facet of the South African past (it may well be in the future). It is the welding of our history and the inheritance of what we have learnt or should have learnt from the past, it encompasses things like your rights ... " (Graham).

Despite people having varying definitions to that of the study's perspective of heritage, more than 80 percent of respondents regarded heritage as an important component of urban regeneration. Sixty-eight percent of respondents identified heritage as an important part of the re-development of Constitution Hill. "(Constitution Hill) is open to the public, it allows everyone to see the past in light of the present (and future). It educates people about those that have suffered" (Ernest). "It blends in our past and our future, ultimately what happened affects all South Africans and needs to become accepted as part of our culture" (Jade-Michelle). "Old buildings of historical importance have been preserved. A very good balance has been struck with the building of the court as well as the commercial components" (Anonymous B). "They have taken the past and juxtaposed it with the present. Our history is used to explain why the Constitutional Court exists today" (Mr. & Mrs. Rodrigues). "Constitution Hill is allowing the future generations to learn about the past...how this has shaped and now protects their human rights" (Mathabe). "How they have used urban space is important, this could make the downtown very viable in the future" (Mrs. Sayman).

The high level of awareness of the integration of heritage with the regeneration of Constitution Hill can be attributed to JDA's marketing of the precinct to both local and international visitors. The Constitutional Court is an enormous drawcard for a range of interested parties, and provides the pivot around which other heritage resources are developed. Most respondents seem to have had a good understanding that heritage is integrally related to urban regeneration—not just from a historical or architecturally significant perspective—but that human rights and people themselves form an important part of heritage.

Conclusion: Implications for Sustainable Cities and Urban Regeneration

Increasingly, the nature of urban spaces and how we use them in the future is under the spotlight. This research shows that the transformation of urban spaces is influenced by shifts in thinking about development and planning, but also has important contextual aspects. When focusing on broad frameworks such as sustainable development, it is shown that the translation of principles from the macro level necessarily requires refocusing at the local level. This chapter shows that level necessarily requires refocusing at the local level. In addition, it shows that although there appears to be an unproblematic link between urban regeneration and sustainable development at the macro policy level, the realities of implementing a sustainable cities approach in a market driven environment mean that interventions often remain at the physical level of design, in the delivery of services and infrastructure. This has serious implications for calls to move towards an environmental justice approach focusing on rights and just access.

Environmental justice is an emerging discourse that increasingly is gaining popularity in much of environmental management. However, despite the theoretical potential for links between environmental justice and heritage to be debated in the context of Constitution Hill, the planning debates have not ventured in this direction, but instead have remained at a physical level. In attempting to assess the extent to which these physical changes have an impact on how visitors' understandings of planning are influenced by the physical spaces, the research has shown that visitors were able to identify better with concepts such as regeneration and heritage as opposed to sustainable development and environmental justice. What is significant here is that visitors' understandings about urban regeneration and heritage reflect the effectiveness of marketing campaigns. South Africa is engaging in the process of redress and reconciliation, environmentally just and sustainable urban regeneration will undoubtedly form part of that process, due to the potential of these concepts to foster regeneration at the psychological level. However, the transition to sustainability and environmental justice will clearly not happen spontaneously, but requires a shift in values and attitudes.

References

Adams, W.M., 1999: Sustainability, in P. Cloke, P. Crang, and M. Goodwin, (Eds.), *Introducing Human Geographies*, Arnold, London, 125-132.

Agyeman, J., Bullard, R. and Evans, B. (Eds.), 2003: *Just Sustainabilities: Development in an Unequal World*, Earthscan, London.

Beck, U., 1992: *Risk Society: Towards a New Modernity*, Sage, London.

Blue IQ, 2004: Blue IQ, Johannesburg: http://blueiq.co.za/what.asp (26/10/2004).

Callewaert, J., 2002: The importance of local history for understanding and addressing environmental injustice, *Local Environment*, 7, 257-267.

Campbell, S., 2001: Planning: green cities, growing cities, just cities? Urban planning and the contradictions of sustainable development, in D. Satterthwaite, (Ed.), *The Earthscan Reader in Sustainable Cities*, Earthscan, London, 251-273.

Chang, T.C., 1999: Local uniqueness in the global village: heritage tourism in Singapore, *Professional Geographer*, 51, 91-103.

Cheung, S.C.H., 2003: Remembering through space: the politics of heritage in Hong Kong, *International Journal of Heritage Studies*, 9(1), 7-26.

Dobson, A. (Ed.), 1999: *Fairness and Futurity: Essays on Environmental Sustainability and Social Justice*, Oxford University Press, Oxford.

Enviroteach, 2004: *Decade of Democracy, A Resource for Educators*, HIS, Johannesburg.

Fischer, F. and Hajer, M.A. (Eds.), 1999: *Living with Nature: Environmental Politics as Cultural Discourse*, Oxford University Press, Oxford.

Fraser, N., 2003: The "Recovery of the CBD" and Heritage—Oil and Water?, in *Citi Chat*, Online Newsletter for The Joburg City Coucil, on the Internet: http://www. joburg.org.za/citichat/menu.stm (8 October 2003).

Fraser, N., 2004: Personal communication, CEO of Central Johannesburg Partnership, Johannesburg, South Africa.

Fyall, A. and Garrod, B., 1998: Heritage tourism: at what price?, *Managing Leisure*, 3, 213-228.

Garson, P., 2004: Constitutional Court: a 'shining beacon of hope', in *Citi Chat*, online Newsletter for The Joburg City Council, available at www.joburg.org.za.

Gerber, C., 2004: Visitors head for Constitution Hill, in *Citi Chat*, online Newsletter for The Joburg City Council, available at www.joburg.org.za.

Graham, B., 2002: Heritage as knowledge: capital or culture?, *Urban Studies*, 39, 1003-1017.

Hardoy, J.E., Mitlin, D., and Satterthwaite, D. (Eds.), 2001: *Environmental Problems in an Urbanising World*, Earthscan, London.

Harrison, P., 2003a: Fragmentation and globalisation as the new meta-narrative, in P. Harrison, M. Huchzermeyer, and M. Mayekiso (Eds.), *Confronting Fragmentation: Housing and Urban Development in a Democratising Society*, University of Cape Town Press, Cape Town, 13-25.

Harrison, P., 2003b: Wits and the changing face of the city, *Arena*, 10 (30), 4–8.

Harvey, D., 1999: The environment of justice, in F. Fischer, and M.A. Hajer, (Eds.), *Living with Nature: Environmental Politics as Cultural Discourse*, Oxford University Press, Oxford, 153-185.

Inner City Tourism Strategy, 2004: Implementation document for the Inner City Tourism Strategy, City of Johannesburg, Tourism and Marketing Department, Johannesburg.

Jacobs, M., 1997: Introduction: the new politics of the environment, in M. Jacobs, (Ed.), *Greening the Millennium? The New Politics of the Environment*, Blackwell, Oxford, pp. 1-17.

JDA, 2003: Johannesburg Development Agency, Introductory document, Johannesburg, available at www.jda.org.za (2 January).

JDA, 2004a: Provisional Report on the Heritage, Education and Tourism Business Plan, Johannesburg.

JDA, 2004b: Constitution Hill: Heritage, Education and Tourism Business Plan, 13 April, Johannesburg.

JDA, 2004c: The Johannesburg Development Agency, Annual Report, Johannesburg, available at www.jda.org.za/annual_report/vision/vision.html. (12 October).

Johnson, N.C., 1999: Memory and heritage, in P. Cloke, P. Crang and M. Goodwin, (Eds.), *Introducing Human Geographies*, Arnold, London, 170-178.

Lambrecht, B., 2005: The rights stuff, *Earthyear*, 1, 71-73.

Law, C., 1992: Urban tourism and its contribution to urban regeneration, *Urban Studies*, 29, 599-618.

Marcuse, P., 1998: Sustainability is not enough, *Environment and Urbanisation*, 10(2), 103-111.

Marcuse, P., 2003: Foreword, in P. Harrison, M. Huchzermeyer, and M. Mayekiso, (Eds.), *Confronting Fragmentation: Housing and Urban Development in a Democratising Society*, University of Cape Town Press, Cape Town, xii-xiv.

McDonald, D.A., 2002: What is environmental justice, in D.A. McDonald, (Ed.), *Environmental Justice in South Africa*, University of Cape Town Press, Cape Town, 1-14.

Patel, Z., 2000: Rethinking sustainable development in the post-apartheid reconstruction of South African Cities, *Local Environment*, 5, 383-399.

Patel, Z., 2003: Environmental values and the building of Sustainable Communities, in E. Pieterse and F. Meintjies (Eds.), *Voices of the Transition: Politics, Poetics and Practices of Social Change in South Africa*, Heinemann, Cape Town, 282-292.

Parnell, S. and Pieterse, E., 2002: Developmental local government, in Parnell, S., Pieterse, E., Swilling, M. and Wooldridge, D. (Eds.), *Democratising Local Government: the South African Experiment*, University of Cape Town Press, Cape Town, 79-91.

Pinnock, D., 2004: Jozi Downtown, *Getaway* (November), 108-114.

Republic of South Africa, 1996: The Constitution of the Republic of South Africa Act 108 of 1996, Government Gazette, Cape Town.

Republic of South Africa, 1999: National Heritage Resources Act 25 of 1999, Government Gazette, Cape Town.

Richards, G. and Hall, D., 2000: The community: a sustainable concept in tourism development?, in G. Richards, and D. Hall (Eds.), *Tourism and Sustainable Community Development*, Routledge, London, 150-169.

Sowman, M., 2002: Integrating environmental sustainability issues into local government planning and decision-making processes, in S. Parnell, E. Pieterse, M. Swilling and D. Wooldridge, (Eds.), *Democratising Local Government: the South African Experiment*, University of Cape Town Press, Cape Town, 181-203.

15

Tourism in Small Town South Africa

Ronnie Donaldson

The South African urban settlement landscape has undergone tremendous socio-spatial, political and economic change since the demise of apartheid in the 1990s. While the metropolitan areas are increasingly positioning themselves to become globally competitive, there are many small towns competing for survival while others have managed to transform themselves into prosperous tourist destinations. Notwithstanding this, when thinking about urban tourism in the South African context, it is the vibrancy, trendiness, and sophisticated infrastructure of the metropolitan regions combined with their impressive skylines that come to mind. From a spatial perspective the post-apartheid tourism boom has, in the main, perpetuated a skewed pattern of urban tourism product provision, where the large metropolitan regions reign supreme. Visser (2004a), refers to a highly uneven tourism space economy that limits the impact of investments in and involvement of previously disadvantaged individuals and communities, and towns outside the core nodes of tourism development. He laments South African Tourism's marketing approach to increase tourist flows and increase the length of stay, by arguing that "what needs to be addressed is how to persuade tourists to go to those parts of the country that are ignored by current visitation trends" (Visser, 2004a: 287). Cornelissen's (2005:163) work also confirms this lopsided picture in her study in the Western Cape showing that "tourism is geographically focused, with tourist activities concentrated in a few locales and sub-regions—most notably Cape Town and other large urban centers."

Although recognition of the impact of urban tourism largely has remained invisible to the scholarly gaze, it is the argument of this chapter that the imprint of urban tourism development is starting to emerge, not only in the metropolitan regions but also in smaller urban settlements in South Africa. Indeed, the briefest of glances through national and region tourism brochures reveal tour itineraries that are replete with references to small-town arts festivals, unique local culinary delights, interesting cultural and social practices, historically significant built environments, and the seemingly ever present "friendly locals" eager to share their pride and interest in their town or village with tourists. Thus, the aim in this chapter is to make visible processes of small-town urban tourism development that have been in operation for some time, as evidenced in tourism marketing material.

To achieve this objective initial attention is drawn to the impact of local economic development planning (LED) which often underpins why small towns pursue urban tourism development, as part, or foundation, of their broader development strategies. The focus then turns to a range of urban tourism initiatives that have developed over the past decade or so. Here, attention focuses on issues such as heritage development and the conservation of the built environment, tourism route development, as well as the hosting of arts and other locally themed festivals and events. Thereafter, the emerging contours of a selection of tourism development-induced impacts are considered. In particular, attention is drawn to the problematic occurrence of second homes development and emerging processes of tourism-led rural gentrification. Finally, against the background of these observations and analyses, the outline of a potential research agenda for urban tourism in small-town South Africa is presented.

Small Towns: Local Development Initiatives

The complexity of settlement types in South Africa is evident from, among other policy documents, the *White Paper of Local Government* (1998) and the *Urban Development Framework* (1997). By the mid-1990s there were estimated to be 500 small towns of less than 50,000 persons in the country (Nel, 2005). Until 2001 urban places were defined by means of administrative function. The census 1996 used an administrative definition as criterion, while Census 2001 applied size and density. Nel (2005: 254) warns that it is important to "recognize a bi-polar categorization" when attempting to conceptualize small towns in South Africa. An analogy between the Australian and South African settlement systems is evident from Murphy's (2002) study, where metropolitan primacy in most states (provinces in South Africa) is the norm. First, peri-metropolitan settings are urban settings that are beyond the edge of suburbs of the metro but within commuting distance. Towns within the zone of influence of metro areas exhibit a significant increase in non-agricultural activities and relatively high incomes fall in this description. Easy access via the national motorways, relatively safer living environments, and a sense of rurality contributed to a population increase in such towns during the 1990s. Second, population turnaround settings are located beyond the daily commuting limit to a metropolitan area. These towns can alternatively be categorized in the tourism context as the pleasure periphery, places to which urbanites migrate over weekends and vacations. Populations are "turning around" because of an increase in permanent residents, especially those in the middle and higher income categories. Inter-provincial transport route settings are a third category that fall beyond the population turnaround settings, but are showing signs of growth and/or revitalization, or the converse. Lastly, idyllic settings showing signs of growth and/or the potential to develop, are outside the perimeter of all above settings. This settlement system directly impacts on tourism development trends in small towns around the country.

Local Economic Development

While most recent case study research on small towns focuses on socio-political and economic aspects, scant attention has been paid to tourism development. Most tourism-related research into small towns in South Africa has centered on local economic development (LED) issues, which have been covered extensively in recent literature (see, for example, Binns and Nel, 2002; Nel and Binns, 2003; Rogerson, 2004; Nel and Rogerson, 2005; Rogerson, 2006). Nel (2001) categorises four variants of LED in South Africa, namely formal local government initiatives, community-based/small-town initiatives (which often develop as a result of NGO facilitation and support), Section 21 Development Corporations,[1] and "top-down" LED in which government, usually at the provincial level, and/or various national organizations are attempting to catalyse and support local initiatives. It is, however, considered that community-based small-town initiatives hold the key for LED-type activities. While some communities want to maintain their own local identity, they have, through renewed investments, property price increases and local economic development, transformed the towns into a commodity. For small towns, one strategy is to "reinvent their past by commodifying the collective memories into activities like tourist ventures" (O'Toole, n.d.).

Communities also have to start accepting that tourism as developmental tool acts as an agent of change. Vital for successful tourism development is the involvement of local communities. One Maputaland case study has shown that, through a co-management model involving the community, NGOs, private sector and public sector, the community received a "cash payment from the conservation authority equivalent to 25 percent of the income generated by tourism" (Ngubane and Diab, 2005: 121). Likewise, a study investigating the opinions of participants in the tourism industry of the Limpopo province identified rural tourism as a viable development tool for the country's most impoverished province (Mafunzwaini and Hugo, 2005).

An earlier observation by Nel (2001: 1015) still relevant today is that "beyond the four metropoles, most cities and large towns are investigating LED options but little concrete progress has been made to date. Quite clearly the lack of resources, the tenuous fiscal position of many smaller centers and the shortage of skilled staff are all serious impediments to the successful pursuits of LED." Most small towns lack the capacity to set up functioning LED units, and where these are operational, they primarily focus on non-tourism-related developments (Nel, 2001). For example, in the tourism strategy of the Khara Hais municipality it is explicitly stated that the community's need for basic infrastructure, like water and roads, is often considered greater than the need for tourism infrastructure. The result is that infrastructure projects that could enhance tourism development are often excluded from current IDPs because of their lower priority. Small towns also do not have standing committees for tourism development. In KwaZulu-Natal province the provincial department of DTLGA encouraged a model of governance based on the principle of a cluster investment strategy, where geographical groups of small towns assist with capacity constraints.

In a case study of the Central Karoo town of Beaufort West, Van Staden and Marais (2005) found, however, that the IDP identified tourism as a key to economic progress. Their survey among visitors examined the tourist potential of the town, a possible tourism product, and an approach to marketing the town as a destination (figure 15.1). The findings suggested that Beaufort West should develop a "destination brand," portraying the town as a "tourism gateway" through which important sectors such as eco-tourism could be marketed. The official Western Cape tourism destination marketing organization, Cape Town Routes Unlimited (CTRU), is currently in the process of finalizing the establishment of a tourism gateway center[2] in the town, where R1.2 million has been secured through the Department of Environmental Affairs and Tourism for the building and the local municipality is in the process of finalizing the transfer of land for the center (Donaldson et al., 2005).

The small coastal town of Stilbaai has, through its hybrid approach in the forming of partnerships, received acclaim for tourism-based development (Binns and Nel, 2002). The formation of a strategic partnership between local business, tourism authorities and the local authority was the key development catalyst for a town in decline. In the mid-1990s a tourism and economic forum was established in which a number of actions resulted in the establishment of a Tourism Bureau, training of a tour guide and women in crafts, establishing a craft center in the township, and promoting an annual Strandloper Festival during the peak summer season (Nel and Binns, 2003).

LED tourism projects contribute to the shaping of civil society. In 2001 BaPhalaborwa received a R1,074,000 grant for a Tourism Centre. Although it is too early to judge the success of the project, De Ridder (2003) observes that "the center has provided a means of unifying the people of the Phalaborwa community, and also provides direct jobs to builders and arts and crafts workers, as well as indirect jobs of people working in the entire tourism industry in the town." She concluded that "many tourism centers were built throughout South Africa with money from the LED Fund, some of them earning more than a million dollars annually due to good management and connections and others standing abandoned as monuments of failure in remote settings."

Figure 15.1
Small Town Tourism in South Africa

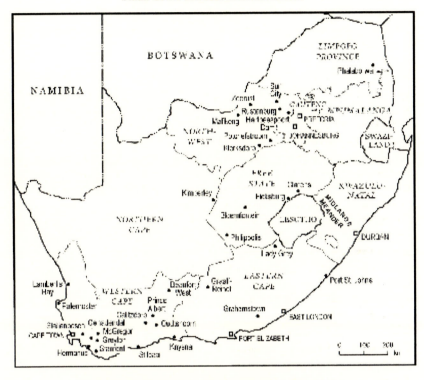

Preserving the Small Town Through Tourism

Heritage tourism "is largely concerned with the cultural legacy of the past, or the 'hard' cultural resources usually contained in old buildings, museums, monuments and landscapes or represented and interpreted in specialized heritage centers" (Richards, 2000: 9). The World Heritage Convention divides heritage tourism into cultural and physical heritage. The built environment thus straddles both as a group of buildings of historical significance and an integral part of the physical aesthetic of a townscape. The geography of urban conservation of the built environment and its importance to tourism development has been a much neglected research theme in South African tourism studies. While some scholars have investigated aspects of small-town heritage (Malcolm, 1998, Kemp, 2000), these studies tend to ignore the link with tourism development. Barnard and Visser (1991) showed how the historic built environment can be showcased within a conservation strategy for the small Western Cape town of Robertson. In a different context, the emphasis on how adaptive re-use of specific historic facilities within the small town of Pilgrims Rest can serve as an example of heritage tourism based on the use of abandoned mine facilities provides a good indication of how to tap into local history (Binns and Nel, 2002).

According to Rogerson and Visser (2005), "the market attractions of political tourism or justice tourism linked to the struggle against apartheid are reflected in developments at Robben Island or the promotion of township tourism in localities such as Soweto, Alexandra, or Inanda among others and present another site for urban tourism expansion." The task of empowering communities to link into heritage conservation is in its infancy. There are many places of struggle history in small towns across South Africa. Testimonies heard at the Truth and Reconciliation Commission in smaller urban centers reminded the world about these. Krog (2004) commented on the wide exposé the apartheid past of small towns received during the TRC hearings and, in essence, this process of healing and reconciliation may have impacted on the way that local residents of previously disadvantaged sections of the towns have become empowered in terms of claiming spaces as theirs. Although the merging of a political process of reconciliation and that of tourism (international and local media) may not have had a permanent imprint, it contributed to "a sense of restoration of dignity and empowerment, if not to oneself in this town, then at least to one's people who are coming from the city" (Krog, 2004). Yet, using the brutal apartheid past as a tourism theme is not viewed as an alternative to tourism development. After all, not every town can have an apartheid museum or memorial. Only the most significant cases, such as those reported on at the TRC hearings, are yet to be explored.

During the 1980s most small towns with a colonial history were surveyed for historically significant buildings. These reports were, at the time, seemingly only of academic merit. Although the legislation changed slightly insofar as the protection of historical buildings is concerned, small-town municipalities today can use these reports as a starting point to list buildings of significance. Some resourceful local authorities have started identifying buildings older than sixty years, albeit the grading process will take some time to complete. Listing proved to be a useful conservation tool for planning and marketing, and "the commercial value lies in its immediate use to the tourism industry" (Naude, 1997: 206). Listing thus enhances the profile of a place and is considered a useful step in a conservation strategy (Australian Heritage Commission, 2000).

Because historical conservation and preservation are considered the Cinderella of urban renewal programs throughout the world, and more especially in South Africa where technocrats are grappling with broader political transformation issues, it is left to communities to struggle to protect their built environment and heritage (Donaldson and Williams, 2005). Conservation is, however, now acknowledged in policy to be a key element of economic tourism regeneration by improving the physical conditions of the historical built environment, increasing residential use and encouraging commercial development in under-used areas. It is argued that, if rejuvenation is viewed from a historical-cultural point of view, the focus should at least be on an integrated environmentally sustainable approach that merges heritage and culture with business and commercial development; and a self-sustaining process of conservation must take cognizance of the broader scope of urban change (Donaldson, 2005). Heritage conservation, town planning and development recently received renewed national interest. For example, the White Paper on Tourism Development and Promotion in the Western Cape (2001: 22) listed as a strength that they should expand and promote provincial cultural assets and experiences such as the "development of historical areas, communities and events ... examples include platteland lifestyles and hospitality." The National Heritage Resources Act (1999: 31) stipulates that any "planning authority must at the time of revision of a town or regional planning scheme, or the compilation or revision of a spatial plan investigate the need for the designation of heritage areas to protect any place of environmental or cultural interest." Of late, the designation of such areas relates to Integrated Development Plans (IDPs). Although it is expected that the resourceful metropolitan areas will take the lead in identifying, demarcating, and protecting heritage conservation areas, some small towns have already done so, such as Graaff Reinet, Stellenbosch, Stanford, and Lady Grey.

An exemplary case study to illustrate the above as an example of partnership (individual home owners and the private sector) to protect and conserve the built environment in South Africa is the small town of Graaff-Reinet. Under the patronage of the late Dr Anton Rupert, the Save Graaff-Reinet Foundation managed to convince over 100 private companies to contribute to the fund. The Historical Homes of South Africa Ltd (a Section 21 Company) provided the administrative support and more than 400 structures have been proclaimed as national monuments since then. Today the town is a major tourist attraction for its architectural merit. However, this town is unfortunately the exception. In general, the involvement of the private sector is restricted to small business firms such as architects, attorneys, medical doctors, and guesthouse and restaurant owners, who usually restore and renovate their buildings without considering historical contexts (Donaldson, 2005).

Festivals and Events

Visser (2005) presents a spatial interpretation of the number, type, and distribution of various festivals in the country. He identified the fact that the majority of the festivals are spatially concentrated in the Western Cape (40 percent). Moreover, he also identifies four festival types: agriculture-related festivals, arts festivals, combination of arts and agriculture-related festivals, and, lastly, festivals dealing with culture and identity.

The natural resource base (using indicators such as availability of developable land, agricultural potential, natural and cultural tourist attractions) can be used to assess the development potential and growth of towns (Ferreira, 2005). It is here where Visser's first category of agriculture-related festivals, has a specific focus on the local attributes and resources. Home-grown fauna or flora products of an area can be marketed as unique to the local context. For example, port has become synonymous with the Calitzdorp Port Festival, cherries with the Ficksburg Cherry Festival, oysters with the Knysna Oyster Festival; also included are the Lamberts Bay Crayfish Festival, Phillipolis Witblits Festival, Prince Albert Olive Festival, and so on. These festivals take place primarily within the major tourism seasons (December-January and April). Whale watching is combined with the annual Hermanus Whale Festival and is said to attract 100,000 visitors annually.

Arts festivals are fewer in number but generate more media attention, funding and revenue; they include the National Arts Festival in Grahamstown, KKNK in Oudtshoorn, and the Aardklop arts festival in Potchefstroom. The target market is cultural tourists of all backgrounds nationally, except the KKNK, which mainly targets white Afrikaans-speaking South Africans. Regional arts festivals mainly attract tourists from nearby major secondary cities; an example is the Gariep Arts Festival, which draws visitors from cities such as Bloemfontein and Kimberley, and caters for the Afrikaans community. The above festivals rely on external sponsorships to make them financially viable.

Festivals have become a major tourism development tool for many small towns. Visser (2005: 155) observed that there is a "current paucity of research" that focuses on festivals. Existing research, however, points to the fact that most investigations have been on small towns. The majority of the events listed on the official South African festivals website are staged in small towns and the impact on local economies is therefore much more significant than it would be in the bigger urban areas. These studies are, however, biased towards the towns that host the national arts festivals, such as Grahamstown, Oudtshoorn, and Potchefstroom (Visser, 2005), and the focus tends to be on the economic and developmental impacts only.

There appears to be little empirical research on corporate investments in festivals and their social investment programs. For example, in 2001 Media24 invested a total of R2.5 million in arts festivals, of which investment in local communities formed an important part. At the KKNK "a community liaison committee was established from the outset to enable local residents, particularly those from previously disadvantaged communities, to benefit from the festival. More than 500 jobs are created annually before and during the event, and people are trained for various positions. Pre-festival shows are aimed specifically at introducing theater to rural school children and farm workers. One of the biggest festival restaurants is run by a school in a previously disadvantaged community, and the taxi service during the event is run by local taxi owners."

Innovative tourism developmental events such as a creative educational experience where tourists are offered the opportunity to become personally involved with local artists and craft persons is a new form of festival taking place along the arts and crafts route of the KwaZulu-Natal Midlands. In the

Midlands Meander Creative Festival (started in 2004) the "common element is creativity involving instruction or demonstration in all that is creative." In practice, courses presented include the visual arts and other creative activities. The event provides tourists with the opportunity to "view the production of and purchase creative products from the area, to be inspired by presenting artists and fine crafters and to meet other creative people" (Anon, 2005: 32-35).

Commemorating the Anglo-Boer War centenary was the first major heritage event to be marked under the ANC government and was launched in the Free State town of Brandfort. At the event a "distinct African flavour was added to the occasion in an unmistakable attempt of symbolic inversion by having young black girls dressed up in white bonnets and Voortrekker dresses to represent Boer women" (Grundlingh, 2003: 6). The ideological ramifications of battlefield tourism has been investigated by Grundlingh (2003). He argues that it is "misleading to regard such tourism as value free, as its narrow focus tends to shut out a fuller understanding of the social and political impact of war and allows stereotypes to go unchecked." Small towns featured prominently in these events and 'each town gave its own imprint to proceedings' (Grundlingh, 2003: 14).

An example of using events to break down stereotypes by hosting them outside their traditional sites are, of late, having a positive social impact on certain small towns. South Africa's premier advertising, communication and design awards which took place at Sun City for the past twenty-seven years moved its event location to the traditional conservative white coastal town of Margate in 2005. Residents were reported to be overwhelmed by the creativity brought to the town, especially through slogans such as "Watergate, Travelgate, Oilgate, Margate" (O'Toole, 2005).

Tourism Routes

Most small towns lost some level of autonomy during the municipal de-marcation process in 2000, when South Africa's post-apartheid government embarked on a policy of rationalisation and re-demarcation of city boundaries. At the time there were 791 local authorities and these were reduced to 231. In many cases local development groups have evolved to fill the void left by the former local government structures. Small towns previously competing with neighbors to attract investments and tourists are now to capitalize on the strong cross-boundary effects—externalities—so as to define whether relations between municipalities turn out to be competitive or cooperative. Developing tourism routes is one way of achieving cooperation.

High unemployment, isolated geographical locations, lack of infrastructure, lack of and/or the inability to exploit cultural and natural resources are but a few factors hindering tourism development initiatives in small towns located outside the weekend-trip zone from the urban nucleus. Not having a unique tourism resource means that a town "enters the realm of generic attractions and the intense competition to draw visitors" and what makes all communities "distinctive is their own geography and history" (Murphy and Murphy, n.d). However, outlying areas can be integrated successfully into tourism regional plans. Success, however, depends largely on outside funding, getting public involvement and marketing existing resources. Route tourism, according to Rogerson (2004: 414), offers "a promising potential vehicle for local economic development in many small towns and rural areas" in South Africa. The rationale behind route development is to group together products—such as arts and crafts, wine, cultural built—environment heritage—to provide a diversity of experience, hence aiming to influence tourist travel patterns. Economically, the success of some routes linked to flora such as the Namaqualand flowers are heavily dependent on rain. Turpie and Joubert (2004:645) estimated that R2.35 million is spent annually in the area, but that the average length of stay in nearby towns would be reduced to 37 percent of its original length "if there were no flowers present."

National and provincial policies are now geared towards tourism route development. In 2001 the Office of the President identified thirteen rural nodes to be targeted through the Integrated Sustainable Rural Development Programme. In one such node, the Central Karoo, tourism has been identified as a key economic challenge. One of the notable successes has been the launching of a tourism route (ISRDP, 2003). The Western Cape government's Integrated Tourism Development Framework (2001) specifically states that "the main purpose of distributor routes is the opening up of the hinterland areas and distribution of tourists into such areas." An increase in tourists to such areas is intended to create products and services such as walking tours of historic villages/towns, accommodation and so on. Route 62 is perhaps the best example to illustrate how the linking of various products across the province provides an overall experience for tourists. Greyton and neighboring Genadendal are among the towns which form part of a cultural historic route in the Western Cape. Greyton is most definitely protecting its own identity and has a strong sense of inclusivity within its own boundary (Donaldson, 2006). Small towns abutting the Gauteng conurbation are also reaping the benefits of the Provincial Blue IQ investment initiative, such as the Dinokoneng Route, which also includes the mining town of Cullinan. This small town has become a favorite stopover for thousands of weekend bikers on breakfast runs.

Specifically designed architecture, history, and small-town tourism routes are developed to link small towns that are located off the main transport national corridors in order to attract tourists. The Horizon Route in the south-western Free State province links five historic towns and many communities into a tourism experience that aims to change tourists' travel patterns between Gauteng and Cape Town. The effectiveness of cultural and heritage routes is, however, questioned in the context of their being viewed as "high culture" tourism resources and they are generally said not to attract large numbers of tourists (Richards, 1994). An example where previously disadvantaged communities are innovatively tied into a route is the example of the Amakuze tourism route in Kwazulu-Natal. The route combines a rail link, nature, and culture, enabling tourists to experience the Amakuze tribal area's history, and its cultural and natural heritage (Gardyne et al., 2005).

As one of the national industries in South Africa outside the metropolitan areas that plays a significant role in regional development (Bruwer, 2003), wine tourism is a way to build a brand and to sell a destination and experience (Elias, 2005). Wine routes in South Africa are geographically concentrated in small towns within a radius of 150 km from Cape Town, attracting in excess of 18,000 visitors per year (Bruwer, 2003). Most routes are private enterprises, resulting in the lack of a cohesive marketing strategy for the region as a whole. Elias (2005: 2) observes that there is a need to partner with other sectors such as accommodation and tour operators.

Another example of a successful tourism route is the Midlands Meander in KwaZulu-Natal. The route evolved as an unplanned local economic development initiative through the collaboration of a group of artists, potters, and weavers. The success of the route is also based on its target niche market, namely high-income daytrippers and groups. The route has been criticized for being exclusive and for not tapping into the cultural experiences of Zulu rural traditionalism, and is now expected to transform into a broad-based LED initiative (Rogerson, 2004). A similar observation was made in the case study of the Highlands Meander in Mpumalanga province, where five towns are collaborating in their LED initiatives in order to promote the area's tourism products, but currently black communities are not benefiting (Rogerson, 2002). This shortcoming in policy implementation is highlighted in the study conducted among tourism administrators, where it was found that the integration of previously disadvantaged communities ranked second after employment creation as the most important tourism policy objective at provincial level (Briedenhann and Butts, 2004).

The contribution of the private sector can be further illustrated in the role played by Open Africa, an NGO with the objective to optimize tourism, to create employment and conserve the continent. This project has been described as "arguably the fastest and most cost effective development project in Africa" (Briedenhann and Wickens, 2004: 77). The African Dream project had thirty-four routes in 2004, of which twelve were developed without and twenty-two with community participation and it involves forty-four towns. A major weakness in this web-based strategy is the fact that Open Africa does not involve itself in any of the internal politics of a specific route, especially if there is no collective will within a community to drive the initiative successfully (Visser, 2004b).

Second Homes and Tourism Gentrification

City dwellers who become despondent about urban living "check out," a move which others refer to as "semigrating" (Hamann, 2000: 18). The dream of many urban dwellers to sell, pack up and move to a stress-free country lifestyle in a small town, leaving behind well-paying jobs and all the luxuries of urban lifestyles, but who cannot let go of these privileges are the semigrators. They choose small towns to settle in that are not too distant from the major urban core area, so that they can drive to the city within an hour or so to pursue their consumption patterns. Urban-rural immigrants are chiefly responsible for the diversification of the rural economies of small towns. These immigrants have significant business skills and, most importantly, capital to invest. The cost of living is also low; they can be self-employed and can achieve a lifestyle change.

Tourism gentrification is commonly described as "the transformation of a middle-class neighborhood [or town] into a relatively affluent and exclusive enclave marked by a proliferation of corporate entertainment and tourism venues" (Gotham, 2005: 1099). A question worth raising is whether the perceived revitalization of selected small towns as propagated in the popular media is evidence that a process of rural gentrification is taking place or not (an assumption more often than not used as a marketing tool). Small towns are endlessly being marketed as a form of "escapism" (permanently or as a second home) from an ever increasingly dangerous urban environment, and propagated as places to retire and probably take on a second occupation. Two other streams of place marketing emphasizes the "other" sub-cultures in society, and establishing a place for tourism and leisure activities. The popular media such as newspapers and living and life style magazines, mainly the *South African Country Life*, romanticize life in small towns. Captions such as "sick of the stress of city life, more and more people are opting for country-style living, not just dreaming about it" (Hamann, 2000: 18) and "cities buzz, but the little town of Greyton in the Overberg just hums. It's a special energy at work" (Richards, 2002: 35) aim to promote small towns and lure potential investors to them. With romanticism comes stigmatization and later commercialization.

Small art towns are now attracting urban-rural migrant artists to start "artist colonies" through arts-related economic revitalization and infrastructure developments. Most small towns in the country that have undergone some form of rejuvenation can attribute the change to artists moving to the towns in the early stages of transformation. Small towns off the beaten track that became artist colonies, such as Clarens, Stanford, and McGregor, eventually developed into fully-fledged tourism towns marked by an increase in restaurants, accommodation establishments and other new developments such as golf courses and retirement and other walled villages.

Hoogendoorn et al. (2005) argue that increased prosperity of the middle and higher income groups, mainly whites, combined with an increase in leisure time explains the demand for second homes in South Africa. They state that there remains a lack of investigation into the impacts associated with second-home developments on factors such as employment creation, environmental degradation and social exclusion as a consequence of rising property prices. It is here where small towns that have undergone a process of small-town tourism gentrification are now being shaped and transformed into spaces of exclusivity. Donaldson's (2006) study showed a direct relationship between higher property prices and property transfers in so-called gentrified towns and those in towns of stagnation or decline. Typically a small town that shows signs of rejuvenation and revitalization does so through the in-movement of urban-rural migrants, or the so-called rural gentrifier, affecting the property prices. There are exceptions, where the motive for in-movement is primarily business related. The case study of Clarens revealed that one businessman saw the opportunity for tourism development in the distant future and decided to buy a large number of properties (Hoogendoorn and Visser, 2004; Marais, 2004).

Donaldson (2006) used empirical data to illustrate how Greyton (located approximately 150 km east of Cape Town) clearly fits the description of a small town that has undergone a process of rural "tourism" gentrification. In using a combination of Zukin's (1990) and Phillips' (2004) frameworks of analysis, table 15.1 summarizes the main observations of the gentrification process in Greyton over time and space. In 2004 the town celebrated its 150th anniversary. Having remained intact for over a century, the town has changed dramatically over the last three decades. Three distinct phases of change are observed. First, the Group Areas Act (the residential separation of different racial groups) forced residents classified as "non-white" to relocate to a township area outside the town, in the process spatially fragmenting the built environment. Second, a largely Afrikaans-speaking agricultural community started selling their properties to city dwellers in the 1980s and early-1990s, either as an investment or as weekend retreat. Improvement in the transport route to Greyton and also the tarring of some streets made the town more accessible for tourists and investors. A third phase currently typifies a town in which property prices have reached "stratospheric levels," where the number of permanent residents has increased and where the town has become a favorite weekend getaway for tourists and second-home owners. Densification altered the country feel through the sub-division of plots in some parts in town, eventually resulting in a mix of land uses. The number of houses increased from 192 in 1938 to 424 in 2000.

It is also commonly argued that, while small towns and rural communities lack finances, they are "rich in an abundance of flair, creativity, warm hospitality, and entrepreneurial skills" (Briedenhann and Wickens, 2004: 77). This is the case even more so in gentrified rural spaces. However, once the original lone gentrifiers are replaced by other gentrified types, then small-town communities tend to become inclusive and anti-outsiders, and the real charm of country folk and lifestyle is replaced with a new exclusive urbanity.

Conclusion

This chapter reflected broadly on six themes on tourism in small town South Africa. These range from policy initiatives that included LED, and a focus on

Table 15.1
Space, time and gentrification process outcomes

Period	Labor/products	Property relations	Demographic	Finance/
1884-1979	Agriculture	19thcentury agricultural village	Afrikaans-speaking white and coloured community	Investments Agricultural products
1979-1984	Agriculture to weekend second home retreats	Distortion of historic aesthetic through development of a township (at main entrance to town). Devalorisation of agricultural properties by lone gentrifiers	Apartheid legislation segregation of community (white and non-white). White depopulation and increased second-home owners	Creation of local real estate market for urbanites
1984-1994	Tourism entrepreneurs, local labour used for renovations.	Architectural restorations, subdivisions	Urban-rural immigration more permanent.	Emerging tourism area
1994-2004	Circulation of ideas (local newspaper), information (tourism centre), committees (historic conservation), recreation of agricultural life style (Saturday market), arts and crafts	Recreations of architectural styles, gated community development, land claims, RDP housing. Investment in restaurants and tourism accommodation	Retirement, second occupation (tourism entrepreneurs), population increase (older than 55)	Property boom (real estate market now exclusively for the rich), exclusive tourist spaces, expanding tourism/hospitality industry

Framework of interpretation after Zukin (1990) and Phillips (2004)

particular attempts made by small towns to encourage tourism through festivals, route developments and heritage conservation of the built environment. In addition, the impact of tourism gentrification and residential property prices on small-town development was also reviewed. Central to all these themes is the economic impact of tourism. However, an apt statement that can be applied universally reads that "tourism is not a panacea, and it may not be an appropriate development strategy for all rural regions or communities. The successful development of a tourism industry is a long-term endeavor; it depends upon planning and the existence of infrastructure, attractions, essential services, management, maintenance, and an accessible market. In the absence of any one of these elements, a rural region may find that tourism is not a cost-effective option, or that other development tools, such as investment in infrastructure and education, must precede the development of tourist attractions and services" (Edgell and Cartwright, 1990: 17). It is also evident that tourism generally positively affects only the towns located in environmentally attractive areas (Nel, 2005).

What is evident from the chapter is that there appears to be a broad array of research themes worth exploring in the context of small town tourism development. First, while LED has been the most significant research theme in small-town tourism development, it is imperative to monitor the outcomes of LED tourism projects. Numerous mechanisms are in place to provide funding, training and skills development, yet investigating the success or failure of these projects in a comparative framework can be considered a necessity. In particular, it is necessary to investigate how previously disadvantaged communities are benefiting from these projects. Second, a multi-sectoral in-depth study on national and provincial non-tourism-specific policies is essential to identify certain linkages in policy attempts. Third, the conservation of the built environment has been a much neglected research area in post-apartheid South Africa. Under-staffed and financially stretched provincial departments should opt for partnerships with community organizations, NGOs, private businesses, and, in some cases, international donors to assist incapacitated local authorities in training and awareness creation. The Integrated Development Planning process is an ideal avenue for the demarcation and conservation of historical areas and, in any case, this is prescribed by legislation. Little, if any, emphasis has been placed on the role that public institutions should play, and the strategies they should devise, to conserve the built heritage environment with the aim to create a tourism-friendly heritage environment.

Fourth, investigation of aspects of quality of life and the cultural and social outcomes of the festivals is another research theme. Internationally there is an extensive tourism literature on festivals as tourist attractions and Quinn (2005) argues that the term "festival tourism" is primarily investigated in terms of its economic potential. She furthermore states that "the tasks of conceptualizing the problems at issue and devising appropriate policies are hampered by the scarcity of empirical research" and where "the literature is replete with passing reference to the social and cultural value of arts festivals, but there is a real shortage of in-depth, empirically grounded analyses of issues involved" (Quinn, 2005: 939).

Tourism routes have been high on the agenda at provincial policy level for a number of years. A fifth research agenda could explore the success of tourism routes in a comparative manner by looking at their nature, extent, and impact (social, economic, and environmental) at an inter- and intra-provincial level.

Lastly, Visser's (2002) gentrification research agenda for South Africa has relevance for small-town tourism studies and still remains largely unexplored. Three rural gentrification aspects are of concern. One is the potential/definite displacement of traditional rural townfolk by in-migrant and upwardly mobile persons from the city. Two is whether these gentrifiers and the economic impact they have on the economies of these towns are contributing towards the livelihood of the disadvantaged communities. Three is the impact the gentrifiers have on the development of tourism in small towns. Finally, on the issue of property aspects and associated tourism developmental impacts, Hoogendoorn et al. (2005) remind us that there is a lack of investigation into the impacts associated with second-home developments on factors such as employment creation, environmental degradation and social exclusion as a consequence of rising property prices.

Notes

1. WESGRO in the Western Cape, a Section 21 company, 'has become the de facto marketing, research and development arm for a range of local centers across the province…[and they] have the potential to actively assist with the facilitation of LED and in doing so, could meaningfully serve as a model for other parts of the country' (Nel, 2001: 1014).
2. Gateway centres are meant to be open for business seven days a week over extended hours. The roles of the Gateway Centre will be to support the marketing strategy generally and, more specifically, to provide information, itinerary planning, accommodation booking, and booking of customized packages (Donaldson et al, 2005).

References

Anon., 2005: Midlands Meander Creative Festival, *South Africa Country Life Magazine*, May, 32-37.

Australian Heritage Commission, 2000: *Protecting Local Heritage Places: A Guide for Communities*, Pirie Printer, Canberra.

Barnard, W.S. and Visser, D. de V.B., 1991: Riglyne vir 'n stedelike bewaringstrategie: die geval van Robertson, Kaapprovinsie, *SA Geograaf*, 18(1), 73-84.

Binns, T. and Nel, E.L., 2002: Tourism as a local development strategy in South Africa, *Geographical Journal*, 168(3), 235-247.

Briedenhann, J. and Butts, S., 2004: Tourism administration and regional integration under transition: policy and practice in South Africa, in D.R. Hall, (ed.), *Tourism and Transition: Governance, Transformation and Development*, CABI Publishing, Wallingford, 201-215.

Briedenhann, J. and Wickens, E., 2004: Tourism routes as a tool for the economic development of rural areas—vibrant hope or impossible dream?, *Tourism Management*, 25, 71-70.

Bruwer, J., 2003: South African wine routes: some perspectives on the wine tourism industry's structural dimensions and wine tourism product, *Tourism Management*, 24, 423-435.

Cornelissen, S., 2005: Tourism impact, distribution and development: the spatial structure of tourism in the Western Cape province of South Africa, *Development Southern Africa*, 22, 163-185.

De Ridder, E., 2003: Addressing globalisation through local economic tourism development: case study in Phalaborwa, Paper presented at the ISoCARP Congress.

Donaldson, R., 2005: Conserving the built environment: international perspectives and South African dilemmas, *Journal of Public Administration,* 40, 796-808.

Donaldson, R., 2006: Tourism development and rural gentrification in a South African small town, Unpublished paper, Department of Geography and Environmental Studies, University of the Western Cape, Bellville.

Donaldson, R. and Williams, A., 2005: A struggle of an inner city community to protect its historical environment. The case of Clydesdale in Pretoria, *New Contree,* 49, 165-180.

Donaldson, R., Boekstein, M., Dyssel, M. and McPherson, E., 2005: A study into the optimal location and service delivery of the gateway tourism information center in the Waterfront, Cape Town, Report prepared by the Department of Geography and Environmental Studies, University of the Western Cape for CTRU, Cape Town.

Edgell, D.L. and Cartwright, M.L., 1990: How one Kansas town used tourism to revitalize its economic base, *Business America,* 5, 14-17.

Elias, M., 2005: Wine tourism can unify the wine industry, *Wine Tourism News,* October, 2.

Ferreira, S. L. A., 2005: Natural resource base as development context for assessing growth and development potential of towns in the Western Cape, Paper presented at the Society of South African Geographers conference held at University of the Western Cape, Bellville, 7-9 September.

Gardyne, S., Hill, T.R. and Nel, E., 2005: Tourism promotion as a local government response to poverty. Ingwe municipality, Kwazulu-Natal, South Africa, *Africa Insight,* 35(4), 121-129.

Gotham, K. F., 2005: Tourism gentrification: the case of New Orleans' vieux carre (French Quarter), *Urban Studies,* 42, 1099-1121.

Grundlingh, A., 2003: Reframing remembrance: the politics of the centenary remembrance of the South African war of 1899 to 1902, available at http://academic.sun. ac.za/history/dokumente/The_state.pdf.

Hamann, H., 2000: Cashing out, *South African Country Life,* May, 16-19.

Hoogendoorn, G. and Visser, G., 2004: Second homes and small-town (re)development: the case of Clarens, *Journal of Family Ecology and Consumer Sciences,* 32, 105-115.

Hoogendoorn, G., Mellett, R. and Visser, G., 2005: Second homes tourism in Africa: reflections on the South African experience, *Urban Forum,* 16 (2), 112-151.

ISRDP, 2003: The progress made towards the implementation within the Central Karoo nodal point, Western Cape Provincial Government, Cape Town.

Krog, A., 2004: Spatiality of the TRC, Unpublished paper presented at the University of the Western Cape, Bellville.

Mafunzwaini, A. and Hugo, L., 2005: Unlocking the rural tourism potential of the Limpopo province of South Africa: some strategic guidelines, *Development Southern Africa,* 22, 251-265.

Malcolm, R., 1998: Townscape reconsidered in School of Architecture, in University of Natal, *Rhodes Re-Assessed: Towards the Conservation of a Unique South African Town,* University of Natal, Durban,39-54.

Marais, L., 2004: From small town to tourism mecca: the Clarens fairy tale, in C.M. Rogerson and G. Visser, (eds.) *Tourism and Development Issues in Contemporary South Africa.* Pretoria Institute of South Africa, 420-435.

Murphy, P., 2002: Sea Change: re-inventing rural and regional Australia, *Transformations* 2 (March), available at http://www.cqu.edu.au/transformations.

Murphy, P. and Murphy, A., n/d: Regional tourism and its economic development links for small communities, available at: http://www.regional.org.au/countrytowns/global/murphy.htm.

Naude, M., 1997: The assessment of buildings and places of significance in urban Settings—the Pietersburg example, *Research by the National Cultural Museum*, 6, 204-244.

Nel, E.L., 2001: Local economic development: a review assessment of its current status in South Africa, *Urban Studies*, 38, 1003-1024.

Nel, E.L., 2005: Local economic development in South African small towns, in E.L. Nel and C.M. Rogerson (Eds), *Local Economic Development in the Developing World: the Experience of Southern Africa*, Transaction Press, New Brunswick, NJ and London, 253-264.

Nel, E.L. and Binns, J.A., 2003: Place Marketing and Local Economic Development in South Africa's "Bay of Sleeping Beauty," *Urban Affairs Review*, 231-245.

Nel, E.L. and Rogerson, C.M. (Eds.), 2005: *Local Economic Development in the Developing World: the Experience of Southern Africa*, Transaction Press, New Brunswick NJ and London.

Ngubane, J.S. and Diab, R., 2005: Engaging the local community in tourism development planning: a case study in Maputaland, *South African Geographical Journal*, 87, 115-122.

O'Toole, K.. n.d.: Competition or collaboration: local economic development, sustainability and small towns, available at http://www.regional.org.au/countrytowns/options/o'toole.htm

O'Toole, S., 2005: Finding a new roost, *Sunday Times Lifestyle*, 30 October, 8-9.

Phillips, M., 2004: Other geographies of gentrification, *Progress in Human Geography*, 28, 5-30.

Quinn, B., 2005: Arts festivals and the city, *Urban Studies*, 42(5), 927-943.

Richards, G., 2000: Tourism and the world of culture and heritage, *Tourism Recreation Research*, 25(1), 9-17.

Richards, G., 1994: Cultural tourism in Europe, in C.P. Cooper, and A. Lockwood, (Eds.), *Progress in Tourism, Recreation and Hospitality Management*, John Wiley and Sons, New York, 97-115.

Richards, N., 2002: The Greyton energy, *South African Country Life*, May, 34-39.

Rogerson, C.M., 2002: Tourism and local economic development: the case of the Highlands Meander, *Development Southern Africa*, 19(1), 143-167.

Rogerson, C.M., 2004: Tourism and uneven local economic development: the experience of route tourism in South Africa, in C.M. Rogerson, and G. Visser (Eds.), *Tourism and Development Issues in Contemporary South Africa*, Africa Institute of South Africa, Pretoria, 399-419.

Rogerson, C.M., 2006: Pro-poor local economic development in South Africa: the role of pro-poor tourism, *Local Environment*, 11, 37-60.

Rogerson C.M. and Visser, G., 2005: Tourism in urban Africa: the South African experience, *Urban Forum*, 16, 63-87.

Turpie, J. and Joubert A., 2004: The value of flower tourism on the Bokkeveld Plateau—a botanical hotspot, *Development Southern Africa*, 21, 645-662.

Van Staden, L. and Marais, L., 2005: The tourism potential of Beaufort West: a study based on visitor demand, *Development Southern Africa*, 22, 233-249.

Visser, G., 2002: Gentrification and South African cities, *Cities*, 19, 419-423.

Visser, G., 2004a: South African tourism and its role in the perpetuation of an uneven tourism space economy, in C.M. Rogerson, and G. Visser (Eds.), *Tourism and Development Issues in Contemporary South Africa*, Africa Institute of south Africa, Pretoria, 268-289.

Visser, G., 2004b: The world wide web and tourism in South Africa: the case of Open Africa, in C.M. Rogerson, and G. Visser, (Eds.), *Tourism and Development Issues in Contemporary South Africa*, Africa Institute of South africa, Pretoria, 335-354.

Visser, G., 2005: Let's be festive: exploratory notes on festival tourism in South Africa, *Urban Forum*, 16, 155-175.

Western Cape Government, 2001: *Tourism Spatial Development Framework*, Provincial government, Cape Town.

Zukin, S., 1990: Socio-spatial prototypes of a new organization of consumption: the role of real cultural capital, *Sociology*, 24, 37-56.

List of Contributors

Ronnie Donaldson is Associate Professor in the Department of Geography and Environmental Studies at the University of the Western Cape, Cape Town.

Gijsbert Hoogendoorn is a Tutor in the Department of Geography at the University of the Free State, Bloemfontein.

Lucy Kaplan is formerly with the School of Geography, Archaeology and Environmental Studies at the University of the Witwatersrand, Johannesburg and now a Consultant with Ochre Communications, Johannesburg.

Zoleka Lisa is formerly with the School of Geography, Archaeology and Environmental Studies at the University of the Witwatersrand, Johannesburg and now a Consultant with Accenture South Africa.

Robyn Mellett is Junior Lecturer in the Department of Geography, University of the Free State, Qwaqwa.

Irene Nemasetoni is formerly with the School of Geography, Archaeology and Environmental Studies at the University of the Witwatersrand, Johannesburg and now a Consultant with ECI Africa, Johannesburg.

Zarina Patel is Senior Lecturer in the School of Geography, Archaeology and Environmental Studies at the University of the Witwatersrand, Johannesburg.

Gordon Pirie is Associate Professor and Departmental Chairperson in the Department of Geography and Environmental Studies at the University of the Western Cape, Cape Town.

Robert Preston-Whyte is Emeritus Professor in the School of Environmental Sciences at the Howard College Campus of the University of KwaZulu-Natal, Durban.

Christian M. Rogerson is Professor of Human Geography in the School of Geography, Archaeology and Environmental Studies at the University of the Witwatersrand, Johannesburg.

Dianne Scott is Associate Professor in the School of Environmental Sciences at the Howard College Campus of the University of KwaZulu-Natal, Durban.

Clinton David Van der Merwe is with the School of Geography, Archaeology and Environmental Studies at the University of the Witwatersrand, Johannesburg.

Gustav Visser is Senior Lecturer in Human Geography, University of the Free State, Bloemfontein.

Index